THE WORLD OF CHILDREN'S BOOKS
A Guide to Choosing the Best

THE WORLD OF CHILDREN'S BOOKS

A Guide to Choosing the Best

Michele Landsberg

With a treasury of more than 400 children's books from around the world

SIMON & SCHUSTER

LONDON • SYDNEY • NEW YORK • TOKYO • TORONTO

For Stephen

First published in Great Britain by Simon & Schuster Limited 1988
This paperback edition first published in Great Britain by
Simon & Schuster Limited 1989

© 1988 Michele Landsberg

This book is copyright under the Berne Convention.
No reproduction without permission. All rights reserved.

**Simon & Schuster Limited, West Garden Place,
Kendal Street, London W2 2AQ**

Simon & Schuster Australia Pty Limited,
Sydney, New South Wales

British Library Cataloguing in Publication Data available
ISBN 0-671-69997-0

Cover illustration by Karen Ludlow
Cover design by Bostock & Pollitt

Phototypeset in 10/11pt Caledonia by
Input Typesetting Limited, London
Printed in the U.K. by
Richard Clay Limited, Bungay, Suffolk

About the Author

MICHELE LANDSBERG is an author and journalist whose columns are widely hailed as witty, incisive, and finely crafted. She has won two National Newspaper Awards for her journalism. Of her first book, *Women and Children First*, Margaret Atwood said: 'This nonfiction . . . reads like fiction – warm, rich in incident and detail, compassionate, funny . . . a delight to read.'

The mother of three children, Landsberg lives with her husband in Toronto, Canada.

Contents

Introduction		1
1	Taking the Plunge	9
2	Books to Encourage the Beginning Reader	31
3	First Novels	47
4	Liberating Laughter	71
5	The Quest for Identity	91
6	Adventure: The Great Game	117
7	Fantasy	141
8	Travelling in Time	165
9	Growing Up	181
10	Girls' Books, Boys' Books, Bad Books, and Bias	205
A Treasury of Recommended Reading		225
Beginning Readers: Ages 4 to 8		228
Young Fluent Readers: Ages 5 to 8		241
Middle Readers: Ages 8 to 12		253
Preteenage Readers: Ages 10 to 12		270
Teenage Readers: Ages 13 and Over		284
Poetry for Children		297
Books about Children's Reading		301
Index		303

Illustration Credits

Page i 'She Asked Me If I Were a Poet,' by Margaret Clayton. From *A Wonder Book of Beasts*, edited by F. J. Harvey Dowton, 1909.
Page 1 'Introduction,' by F. D. Bedford, from *Another Book of Verses For Children*, edited by E. V. Lucas, 1907.
Page 9 Drawing by Catharine O'Neill. Courtesy of the author.
Page 31 'And the Dish Ran Away With the Spoon,' R. Caldecott's second collection of pictures and songs, 1885.
Page 47 'Half Holiday,' from *Child-Land*, published in London by S. W. Partridge & Co., 1873.
Page 71 from *CDB!* by William Steig, copyright © 1968 by William Steig. Reprinted by permission of Simon & Schuster, Inc.
Page 91 Illustration from *The Story of Ferdinand* by Munro Leaf, illustrated by Robert Lawson. Illustration copyright © 1936 by Robert Lawson. Illustration copyright renewed © 1964 John W. Boyd. Reproduced by permission of Viking Penguin Inc. and Hamish Hamilton Ltd.
Page 117 Illustration by Arthur Hughes. Reproduced from *The Victorian Woodblock Illustrators* by Eric de Maré. London: Gordon Fraser, 1980.
Page 141 'The Golden Ball,' by John D. Batten, from *More English Fairy Tales*, edited by Joseph Jacobs, 1894.
Page 165 'Papa Poodle,' by Juliana Horatio Ewing, from *Verses for Children—Songs for Music*, 1895.
Page 181 'Asleep,' from *Child-Land*, published in London by S. W. Partridge & Co., 1873.
Page 205 'Mary's Meadow and Letters From a Little Garden,' by Juliana Horatio Ewing, from *Verses for Children—Songs for Music*, 1895.
Page 225 Illustration from *The Little Bookroom*, copyright © 1955 by the estate of Edward Ardizzone. Permission granted by the Edward Ardizzone Estate.
Page 302 'Duck on Book,' by Andrew Lang, from *The Nursery Rhyme Book*, 1898.

Illustrations on pages i, 1, 31, 47, 141, 165, 181, 205 and 302 are reproduced courtesy of the Osborne Collection of Early Children's Books, Toronto Public Library.

Introduction

The moving accident is not my trade;
To freeze the blood I have no ready arts;
'Tis my delight, alone in summer shade,
To pipe a simple song for simple hearts.

>William Wordsworth,
>'Hart-Leap Well', 1800

INTO THE NARROW, quiet, regular life of a child growing up in Toronto in the 1940s – the overgrown garden, the alleyway where I bounced my ball against the side of the house, the bus trips to piano lessons – suddenly there thundered a caravan of exotic warriors, heroines and horses, swords flashing, animals bellowing, clouds of dust and incense, the blare of horns calling me to adventure. I did not merely stand and gape: sitting on the concrete steps of our porch in the long shady afternoon, or trapped in my wooden prison of a desk at school, I simultaneously leaped astride those sweating horses, swung in a long, stomach-dropping arc on a jungle vine, turned my ship into the teeth of the gale. I was *inside* those children who stepped back through the magic arch into ancient Egypt, shivering their shiver of apprehension and excitement. And nobody knew (except perhaps my librarian) that while I plodded dutifully to school – a new roll-top pencil-box was the thrill of the second form – I was secretly living a hundred other lives.

It began quietly enough with Ping, the Yangtze River duck, waddling across my path. Soon enough the Bobbsey Twins came simpering by; the procession swelled; the Eskimo Twins panted along in the turbulence created by Henty's *Armada*, Blind Pew stumped and stalked beside the girl on the garden swing, Nesbit's *Five Children and It* scampered ahead into an arcadian future, the splendour fell on castle walls and we all galloped from Ghent to Aix, breathless and dazzled.

Books were far more than an amusement in my childhood; they were my other lives, and this visible existence I now lead in the workaday world was touched and transformed by them for ever. The spell was never broken; all through my adult life, children's literature has given me unabated pleasure. It's like those huge gob stoppers we used to buy: the longer you rolled one around inside your cheek, the more splendid and various were the colours revealed. As my own children grew, the books I had loved and the books I discovered through and for them took on ever-new colours and shades of meaning, and confirmed my belief that a child's life without books read for pleasure is a child's life deprived.

My hope is that through this book, many more adults will be persuaded to discover, not only how literature can enhance a child's life, but what surprising delights await the adult who can unbend enough to read along with the child. More, I hope to show, step by step, how any adult can become a skilled and confident chooser of the best books for the particular child he or she has in mind. I do discuss some approaches to learning how to read, particularly in Chapter One, but this is primarily a book on the 'why' and the 'what', not the 'how', of children's reading.

No list, however extensive, can ever do justice to the wealth of children's literature. As Sheila Egoff, Canada's leading writer on the subject, has pointed out, more than 100,000 children's books have been published in Britain and the United States alone since 1957. That's why a list of titles is the merest beginning. I've tried to be more thoroughly *useful* in this book by writing about exemplary books in some detail, showing what strengths and beauties to look for in choosing a book, and by discussing the adult's role in encouraging, stimulating and sustaining the child's interest in reading.

Most adults who pick up a volume about children's books expect or hope for a neat tour guide of the best books for each age group, like restaurants listed by district. But how sound can those age gradings be? I know twelve-year-olds who read *Winnie-the-Pooh* with delight, six-year-olds who zoom through Tolkien, and eight-year-olds who are just cutting their teeth, so to speak, on sophisticated picture books. Reading ability and rigid age groupings do not go hand in hand; furthermore, a child of any age might read widely across the whole range, leap forward, or regress for a while to some simple, comforting book that has just the right balm to soothe a current ache.

For that reason, I've tackled this huge subject matter by theme, rather than age group. If you need a thrilling adventure story for a ten-year-old immediately, you may turn to the chapter on adventure and find a discussion of adventure stories for children in each age group. But remember that themes as well as reading levels overlap, and every child needs a wide variety of books.

Another way to use this book is to consult the Treasury of Recommended Reading at the back of the book. You will find the titles of approximately 400 works of fiction for children from five to fifteen, arranged according to age and reading levels. Picture books have been included, but are chosen specifically for their value in encouraging or enabling the child to read. Many spectacular picture books are not mentioned here only because they didn't fall within this narrow definition.

As far as I know, this is the first comprehensive guide to general children's literature that represents an equal balance of books in which boys and girls play active, central roles. For a discussion of the relative importance of this aspect of childhood reading, please see Chapter Ten.

You may be dismayed to find that some of your own favourite books are not mentioned here. It's chilly comfort, but many of my favourites are missing, too: in choosing boys' and girls' books, a mix of the easy and the demanding, and an ample selection for every age group and interest, I found to my horror that there just wasn't room for a pure distillation of all my most loved books. There are however, representative best works from the whole of the English-speaking world, and almost all the stellar authors are present at least in the bibliography.

A further note about selection: I strove for balance, but the Treasury

INTRODUCTION

is also determinedly personal. I have not included any book that I haven't read and enjoyed myself, no matter what its claim to popularity or glory. What's the point of a guide that lists everything, to cover every taste? You might as well resort to the library's card index. Instead, I've tried to show as clearly as possible my grounds for selection; readers will certainly not share all of my conclusions, but they will at least know how and why I reached them.

Grounds for non-selection are more ambiguous. Since this book was published in Canada, hundreds of people have asked me, in tones plaintive or accusatory, why I omitted one of their cherished favourites. Some books are not on the list because I don't recommend them; some aren't there because, though I loved them, they were hopelessly unavailable (like *The Far-distant Oxus, Escape to Persia*, and *Crowns*, by Katherine Hull and Pamela Whitlock). And some stars in the firmament of children's literature, like *Alice in Wonderland, Winnie-the-Pooh* and *Peter Pan*, are not here because they are so well known that it hardly matters that they glitter rather coldly for me.

In Britain, where these classics are so interwoven in the culture that there can hardly be a town or village where a child has not played Poohsticks or been urged to clap if they believe in fairies, this may seem less forgivable an omission. I can only plead that *Alice in Wonderland* terrified me so much as a child (particularly those sinister, surrealistic Tenniel drawings) that it was the only book I ever defaced; the nightmare of shrinking and stretching held a fevered horror for me. I never read *Winnie-the-Pooh* as a child (perhaps I was too embarrassed by the title?) and, as an adult, I can't read it without writhing at the tone which strikes some North American ears as unbearably twee. Obviously, I would not be capable of adding anything sensible to the already abundant discussion of these books.

That brings me to a special word to British readers, for whom this book has been revised and updated. The disintegration of literate culture is far more advanced in North America than in Britain; my comments on the damages of television addiction and pop-culture mentality should be regarded as a distant early warning. Already, the tides of North American 'know-nothingism' are lapping at British shores. Visiting London, the capital of the richest literary tradition in the world, I discovered whole shelves in otherwise superb children's book stores given over to the lowest-common-denominator works of Judy Blume and Paula Danziger. One argument for propagating such books among children is that they may lure non-readers to the joys of books. But since these works offer no literary pleasures whatsoever – the reading of them is purely mechanical; a way to absorb a kind of recorded television – I wonder how that may be possible. Are children introduced to wholesome food by filling them up with marshmallows? If you debase a child's taste right at the beginning, sate them with the easy and meretricious, is there any hope that they will suddenly stumble with glad cries on works that are far more demanding?

Perhaps these authors have been welcomed by some British critics because, as Aidan Chambers feelingly wrote (in *Horn Book* magazine), some British readers can feel 'more at home' in classless American books than they can in homegrown middle-class literature from which they resentfully feel excluded: cheerfully populist American books, even American trash, have for these alienated readers the glamour of distance, the fresh exhilaration of an open prairie.

I have two arguments with this as a defence for importing Blumeziger. One: brilliant, absorbing children's novels written whole-heartedly from a working-class or rural perspective have blossomed in Britain in recent years. In fact, books with an unconsciously middle-class bias are in a distinct minority now. Two: if North American horizons seem wider, why not reach for popular American works of genuine merit, of which there are so many as yet undiscovered in Britain, instead of the very worst?

I hope this book will serve as an introduction to vigorous, accessible North American authors – like Daniel Pinkwater and Janet Lunn – who are not widely known in Britain, but deserve to be. Several booksellers in the United Kingdom have assured me that they regularly, on customer's request, order books from North America; if I've succeeded in arousing your enthusiasm for a book not published in Britain, I hope you will expend the extra effort and patience to order it.

I hope, too, that adult overprotectiveness about the difficulties of 'foreignness' will not discourage parents and teachers from trying some of these New World gems. Many British books are rejected for the North American market because they contain minor difficulties of idiom, custom and expression. My belief is that when we protect children from the unfamiliar, rinse their books of any linguistic strangeness, and muffle them up in the security blanket of the mundane, we are depriving them of all the globe-girdling liberty that reading stands for.

As a child in Canada, reading British books, I had to struggle to unravel the mysteries of elevenses, prefects, petrol, gymkhanas, lifts, Mars bars, brollies and Wellingtons; I remember piecing together the clues from the context, and savouring the richly exotic feel of such words as though I had just hauled treasures home from an eastern bazaar. Having survived these initiation tests, I discovered with a surge of joy that there was a literary commonwealth out there, to which I belonged. Alienated from my non-reading schoolmates, I had the consolation of citizenship in a republic of imagination that easily spanned the ocean. To purge all foreignness from children's reading matter is to diminish their intellectual skills and narrow their empathy – to make them parochial and limited.

This is a critical guide. I've tried to share my enthusiasm for some wonderful books and to show my reasons for disliking or even detesting others. Criticism, however, is not a popular avocation. Along with the democratization of culture has grown up an almost belligerent attitude that negative comment on *any* book, film or play is a personal attack on those who actually enjoyed it. This seems to be a particular problem in the children's book world. No one would take adult literary critics to task for failing to give serious consideration to Judith Krantz's latest bestseller,

INTRODUCTION

but children's book critics are inevitably accused of elitism, prissiness or bourgeois smugness if they so much as suggest that there is a difference between good and bad children's books. In part, this is a legacy of the counter-culture. An ironic enthusiasm for trash (consider, for example, the zest for cartoons, graffiti and TV imagery in the American art world) is now accepted as the hallmark of a creative and independent individual who defies the norms of bourgeois culture. To encourage children to wallow in popular culture, however, is quite another matter, as I discuss in Chapter Ten.

Still, one must confront one of the main arguments advanced by aggressive populists: they say, and they are right, that adults *do* stand between children and books. Adults choose, buy and convey the books to those too young to act autonomously. Children's advocates often fear that overprotective, narrow or censorious mother figures (librarians, teachers or critics like me) will impose their repressive taste on young people, merely by expressing literary opinions. It is interesting (though maybe not conclusive) that, in my experience, it is often men who take this line, and often in terms so personally rancorous that they would seem still to be struggling against some powerful and suffocating mother. The pop-culture negative image of librarians is, I think, an offshoot of this misplaced misogyny.

Let it be said right here that this book never argues for removing, repressing or censoring any kind of childhood reading. Adult responsibility, as I see it, is not to deny, but to add, enrich, stimulate, amplify. To turn away, with an indifferent shrug, from helping children to choose books, is not good enough. If anything goes, nothing matters. And children's literature does matter, so intensely, that we adults ought to argue ferociously among ourselves about it. We ought to be willing to examine our own tastes and compare them rigorously with the informed opinions of others.

Over the course of forty years of reading children's literature, I've often been grateful to critics for pointing out hidden treasures or overlooked flaws in books with which I was familiar. I hope, with an amateur's ardour, that my readers will approach my judgements in the same open spirit.

One last word on the practical uses of this book. Many of the works I've written about are now, horribly enough, out of print. Some of them, even recent titles, are going out of print as I'm writing . . . so that even if I wanted to write a book recommending only current titles, it would be impossible to do so.

In the last decade, as the market has been flooded with 'commodity' books for children (those based on cartoon, toy or film characters, with sentiments and vocabulary vilely calculated by market survey), publishers have had to hatchet away at their back lists with appalling savagery. They tell us that they can no longer afford the warehouse space to keep classic children's works – or even the award-winning children's novels from the year before last – in print. It's like letting all of Jane Austen vanish from the world because Sidney Sheldon is more profitable.

The obvious answer is to search the local libraries for some of these irreplaceable works that may no longer be available in book shops; lobby the book-shop owner to lobby publishers to reprint vanished works; check the children's shelves at library sales, jumble sales, and second-hand book shops. I have found all the books in the Treasury, even those never published in the United States or Canada, available in American libraries. Some I have found on book-shop shelves, where they had obviously sat, quietly gathering dust, while they went out of print. If your local library or bookseller can't find a title for you, keep your eye open for it in every book shop you visit. The glee of serendipity, when you spot it in the most unlikely place, will reward your perseverance.

Like any commitment, a devotion to excellence in children's literature is going to cost you money. Once you become familiar with superb authors, you will want to buy their most recent book at once, instead of waiting to see when – or if – your impoverished local library will get round to buying it. Indeed, buying books (and frequently they are available in very cheap paperbacks) is the only way to ensure that they stay in print.

A common complaint is that children's books, especially high-quality picture books, cost so much. All I can say is that they always cost less than a dinner out or a new pair of children's jeans. The books I read as a child transformed me, gave meaning and perspective to my experiences, and helped to mould whatever imaginative, intellectual or creative strengths I can lay claim to now. No doll or game had that impact on me; no pair of new jeans ever changed my life.

Chapter 1

TAKING THE PLUNGE

> . . . Jack the Giant-Killer, Robin Hood,
> And Sabra in the forest with St. George!
> The child, whose love is here, at least, doth reap
> One precious gain, that he forgets himself!
>
> William Wordsworth, *The Prelude*

> Those books purified my soul, cleansing it of the superficial layer of impressions produced by that bitter, miserable reality. I came to appreciate what good books really were and realized how much I needed them and they gradually gave me a stoical confidence in myself: I was not alone in this world and I would not perish!
>
> Maxim Gorky, *My Apprenticeship*

> Sometimes when I can't go to sleep at night I see the family of the future. Dressed in three-tone shorts-and-shirt sets of disposable Papersilk, they sit before the television wall of their apartment, only their eyes moving. After I've looked a while I always see – otherwise I'd die – a pigheaded soul over in the corner with a book; only his eyes are moving, but in them there is a different look.
>
> Randall Jarrell, *Kipling, Auden & Co.*, 1955

LIKE ALL MOTHERS, I used to ask my son, when he was six and seven, what he had done in school that day. I misguidedly longed to know what *I* thought was important: the playground adventures, the teacher's comments, the tests and projects. Invariably, he would pause, reflect, and then tell me, with sparkling eyes, whatever story he had heard or read that day. He, at least, knew what had been most important to him.

Imagination is the quality we say we value in children, but in our adult lives we are always in danger of passing it by without a flicker of recognition. To my child, the imaginative life kindled in him by stories was unquestionably the most real and gripping event of his school day, but I would stand metaphorically on one foot, waiting for the *real* stuff of classroom achievement.

'Imagination,' wrote the poet Ted Hughes, 'is the faculty of creating a picture in our heads and holding it there while we think about it.' All human endeavours have to begin with just such an exercise of the imagination, he argued, and yet education completely neglects the task of strengthening this vital human faculty. Perhaps Hughes is wrong in saying 'completely'; after all, there are classrooms, like my son's, where stories are told and read. Dan Yashinksy, a gifted Canadian storyteller, recently wrote:

> *I see it in the eyes of children when I go into schools to tell stories: a deep hunger for the world of wonder, a deep satisfaction with the unadorned spoken word and, most of all, a pride that they too can possess a story to call to their own remembrance.*

Most of us recognize imagination at work, and pause respectfully for it, when a three-year-old stops short on a pavement and contemplates a pebble or an ant for what seems, to the hurrying adult, like an endless moment. Beyond that, however, we flounder.

Paula Fox, an outstanding American author, writes:

> *Goethe wrote that supreme imagining is the effort to grasp truth through imagination. It does not consist in making things different but in trying to discover them as they are. Imagination is random and elusive. We deduce its presence by its effects, just as we deduce that a breeze has sprung up, a breeze we can't see, because we hear and*

see the rustling of leaves in a tree. It is the guardian spirit that we sense in great stories; we feel its rustling. Imagination can be stillborn; it can be stifled. But it can be awakened. When you read to a child, when you put a book in a child's hands, you are bringing that child news of the infinitely varied nature of life. You are an awakener.

To be an 'awakener' now seems to me the supreme challenge of parenthood. Our children are the best nourished, best educated, healthiest and most cherished population of children in history. Yet the single most common cry from the heart I heard from readers when I was a daily newspaper columnist was this: 'Why don't my children seem to have any values?' In the winter of 1985, that dilemma seemed to be crystallized in the news story about an American university student who went to Nicaragua. He took a series of pictures, later to be published internationally, of a Nicaraguan peasant who had been captured by the Contra guerrillas. The pictures showed the peasant digging his own grave at gunpoint, lying down in it, and being stabbed in the throat by the Contras. The young photographer later told interviewers that he didn't really have any reactions while he took his profitable pictures; he was too busy with the speed and aperture settings on his camera.

The incident helped me wonderfully in focusing my own goals in writing this book. It would, of course, be folly to suggest that the student photographer might not have grown into a morally and emotionally numb bystander to cruelty had he only been raised on good children's literature. Still, his icy self-command, apparently born of a bottomless detachment from the human condition, is the spectre that troubles the dreams of civilized parents.

Who can take an honest, dispassionate look at the world in which we raise our children and not be dismayed, not worry that the humane values we cherish will be bludgeoned out of our children by the world's horrors? By now, the mind of every child I know over the age of eight is tinged with nuclear nihilism. No parent can, any longer, protect the child from dangerous and fearful knowledge. Where will the children get the courage, resilience and commitment they will need to cope with the future?

We try to raise our children optimistically, but scientific advances and the relentless push of technology have left our conventional moralities lurching far behind: the sale of body organs for transplant or research, global satellite spying, acid rain, poisoned fish, oil slicks drifting to the silent poles, the march of deserts and starvation across continents, a permanent and growing world population of embittered unemployed youth . . . Everyone knows the litany; no one has answers.

Cocooned in consumerism, we would like to believe we can draw a magic circle of safety around our families. We concentrate our energies on living well – so far beyond the dreams of our parents – and anaesthetize ourselves to the rest. We even have a special term of mock-opprobrium for the rising generation which seems to epitomize this see-no-evil self-centred acquisitiveness: we call them 'yuppies'. But aren't they, with their

Porsches, croissants, health clubs, business degrees and baby aerobics classes, aren't they just the latest wave of threatened villagers, huddling in the castle of consumerism and pulling up the drawbridge to defend themselves and their young from encroaching doom?

They, too, will have to face the task of raising children who may be redundant – or incinerated. They, too, looking into their children's eyes, will wonder what to give them to make them equal to the world's overwhelming challenges. Meanwhile, the children, growing up in a uniquely menacing age, have wired themselves for sound and are doing their best to obliterate thought. They live in a constant din of electronic noise, their eyes glazed with channel-flicking images of fragmentation and visual chaos. Is there any room left for reflection, dream and curiosity?

From the age of nine months, when the typical North American infant watches an hour and a half of television a day, to pre-adolescence, he or she watches 7000 violent deaths during 15,000 hours of TV. That is more time than is spent in play, in school, or in conversation with parents. Our children are being reared by television.

For the past twenty years, the Annenberg School of Communications at the University of Pennsylvania has been studying the impact of television on society. More than ten years ago, I first read their grim conclusion that television is not a *part* of our culture; it *is* our culture. I realized the truth of it as I looked around at cultivated parents with post-literate children whose heroes are Miami Vice cops and He-Man, Master of the Universe. The ages-old natural process by which parents transmitted their culture (ideas, values, ways of speech, heroes, myths) to their offspring has been brutally broken off. Now all our children's values are shaped by the thousands of hours of cops-and-robber shows they watch.

For the most part, those values are shockingly warped. Parents are aware of this; most make valiant efforts to encourage the watching of excellent programmes. But even the most vigilant adults report that their children seem to slip effortlessly past the restrictions. If they don't soak up hours of TV at home, they see it at their friends' houses and listen to inexhaustible verbal replays in the playground.

By now, it is a truism that American commercial television (so popular in Europe) shows a false and crazy world in which the rich are worshipped, violence is the way righteous men solve problems, and only a third of the population is female. Heavy viewers of television are, according to the Annenberg School's studies, more racist, sexist and frightened of the world (hence, more accepting of violent solutions) than non-viewers. Many parents shrug off this danger because they 'don't want to make the children feel different from others' by keeping television out of the house. The result is that the children aren't different; they share a common TV culture with other children, no matter how various are the values of the parents.

The typical TV-watching child is impatient, bored with anything but the most immediate and explosive stimuli, and a worshipper of media fame. Listen to any group of eight-year-old boys in a playground, no matter what their family backgrounds, and you will hear a constant, shrill invocation of machine guns, bombs, tanks, speeding cars and super-heroes. One of the favourite toys of this age group is Go-bots, ingeniously devised small plastic men that can be transformed into weapons. The metaphor is complete.

In the past five years, we've grown accustomed to news reports of hanging, shooting, gang rape and torture committed by children against other children, all in imitation of televised incidents, dramatic or true. We know that there is a correlation between IQ and the amount of violent television watched; we know that heavy viewers of TV have a lower rate of success in school and in reading, and a higher rate of violent behaviour. They are being shaped, controlled, by a medium that has no interest in them except as buyers of merchandise.

Those who rule our destiny are much more aware than we are of how simple it is to seize and maintain power through media control. The history of the Reagan administration in Washington is a study in overwhelmingly successful media manipulation. A few years ago, the president-as-performer was a figment of the satirical imagination; now it's a reality. A genial performer, elected on the strength of his TV presence, rules the western world. A White House public-relations aide explained why the printed word doesn't matter any more: when the president's mistakes are reported in the press, 'Maybe 200 people read it, or 2000, or 200,000,' but when he smiles on TV, in carefully controlled circumstances, eighty million people are watching.

White House public-relations staff have invented a whole encyclopaedia of media-control techniques. TV cameras are allowed to film the president as he boards a helicopter, smiling and waving. The helicopter engines are deliberately revved up ahead of time so that reporters' shouted questions can't be heard. At presidential events, reporters are roped in behind a 'shout line' to protect him from questions. The stationing of cameras at public events is carefully managed to prevent unwanted camera angles or politically revealing shots. The American president is not alone in his awareness that television coverage is crucial. In the 1985 hijacking of a TWA airliner from Athens to Beirut, the terrorists quickly displayed a hand-lettered sign to the waiting media: 'All coverage is pool coverage' (a media-hip phrase indicating that TV journalists from different networks will have to share film taken by one camera).

When the wielders of political power devote such scrupulous care to every TV image, can we any longer doubt that our children who watch are television's mere minions? The effects are profound. The sense of time past, of humanity's continuity, seems to have evaporated. A history teacher in a high-school programme for the gifted remarked, at a parent-teacher night, that he didn't know what to do with these teenagers; they had no sense of the past, of chronology or narrative: 'As far as they're concerned, the Middle Ages and World War I probably happened at the same time.'

We know all that, and yet we continue to allow the TV to flicker away, day and night, in our living rooms. Ted Hughes wrote a brilliant description of the way, in front of a television set

... paralysis overcomes us. What keeps us mesmerized? Why can't we move? Reality has been removed from our participation behind that tough little screen and into another dimension . . . our inner world of natural impulsive response is safely in neutral. Like broiler killers [chickens], we are reduced to a state of pure observation. Everything that passes in front of our eyes is equally important, equally unimportant . . . [we] can only free ourselves from the spell of passivity by a compulsive effort of will . . .

Dorothy and Jerome Singer, leading American researchers into the role of television in children's lives, have added another detail to this pattern: 'Children who spend more time watching television tend to have fathers who are heavy television viewers.' On the other hand, mothers' television viewing, educational level and employment status 'were not significantly related' to the child's success in school or reading attainment. Whether this is because of stereotyped gender roles in our society, or because Freud was right about the father as representative of society's values, this fact implies a heavy cultural responsibility for the father. A father who cares about his child's intellectual and spiritual life cannot afford to spend his leisure hours watching sports on television or to leave the bedtime reading to his wife . . . not unless he is content to let his child grow up imprinted with the values of the commercial mass media.

Only a few years ago, the defenders of TV rationalized that it could do no real harm because even very young children were able to distinguish between fact and fantasy. By the age of five, it was argued, children could tell you that commercials are not always true and that the Roadrunner doesn't really get killed when he is dropped over a cliff.

Strangely enough, however, it seems that this superficial cynicism engendered by television is not so much an ability to distinguish clearly between fact and fiction, as a diffuse blurring of what is real. The producer of *Gilligan's Island* (a silly situation comedy in which a group of adults were stranded on a desert island) once marvelled that faithful fans of the programme had sent indignant telegrams to the US Coast Guard and the Navy, demanding that the castaways be rescued at once. 'Who did these viewers think was filming the castaways on that island?' he wondered. 'There was even a laugh track on the show. Who did they think was laughing . . . ?' He wondered, too, about parents who deny that their children are influenced by TV. Sponsors spend over $2 billion a year on commercials, he wrote, and the more viewers they get, the more money they make. 'How can anyone believe that the viewer is influenced by the commercials on a show, and not influenced by the content of the show itself?' His conclusion, after a lifetime in television: not only do many viewers believe that whatever they see on TV is real, but things aren't real until they see them on TV – 'the most believable news medium' according to countless surveys.

Perhaps television's hypnotic power can best be seen in its positive impact. When a picture book is featured on the excellent American children's programme, *Reading Rainbow*, its sales can leap from a mere 2000 to a steady 25,000 annually, according to the *New York Times*. Alas, *Reading Rainbow* is just one tiny gleam in the wilderness. The entire children's book market amounts to $460 million annually . . . about half of what Americans spend on golf clubs. Just one cartoon show, though – Mattel's *He-Man* – brought in $350 million in toy sales in one year.

I believe that not only are chronic television viewers handicapped in their ability to understand what is real and what is important, but that those who are print literate will become an increasingly rare and privileged elite. They will be the ones with the power to think, analyse, connect and create new meanings. But we are long past the time when traditional schooling alone can teach literacy. Television makes a new kind of child, one who is not easily taught in the methods currently available. And only the parent in the home can control how much the television is allowed to shape the child's life and mind.

The parent who wishes to make the best use of this book will have to come to terms with television, one way or another. Aside from all other considerations, the child who watches five hours a day of television will simply not have time to read widely and deeply. Further, as any contemporary publisher can tell you, the TV-influenced child is likely to be an impatient and reluctant reader, demanding instant action and automatically recognizable stereotyped characters, in his books as in his viewing. Most literature will truly be a closed book to him or her.

Pessimism, however, is not the burden of this book. I began this chapter by quoting Maxim Gorky because he offers one of the most stirring examples in twentieth-century literature of what reading can mean to a child in even the most impoverished and deprived circumstances. In his three-volume autobiography (*My Childhood, My Apprenticeship* and *My Universities*) Gorky powerfully describes his brutal early childhood. Abandoned by his mother, abused, a witness in his grandparents' home to every kind of savagery and depravity, he nevertheless had one glowing advantage: his grandmother was a story-teller of mesmerizing power. Put out of his grandparents' home at the age of ten, the unschooled Gorky had to work at the most gruelling and menial of tasks to keep himself alive. His discovery of books opened the world to him and transformed his life. In his impassioned devouring of books (he had to steal the wax to make crude candles to read in secret, and was more than once beaten into unconsciousness when caught with a book), he gradually pieced together a vision of the possibilities of life that was entirely at odds with his stunted environment.

Gorky's saga is so moving because we see not only the impact of literature on his own genius, but also the lesser pleasures – escapism, refreshment – in the way the illiterate peasants around him responded to the popular and mystic tracts he read aloud to them. 'He took the book from me and carefully examined it, showering the cover with tears. "A good book is just like – a holiday!" '

Wordsworth, the source of the other quotation that opens this chapter, had every advantage, but ironically found the same release in his childhood reading: the discovery of other worlds, the forgetfulness of self. Every poet and critic who writes seriously about literature echoes this idea of transcendence. The difference from television is this: the picture of other worlds served up on the screen is passively received by the watcher; in reading, a far greater imaginative effort must be made. The marks on the paper must be translated into words, the words into meaning, the linked meanings into a mental picture of events that is held in the mind while the narrative goes on. Reading demands an active stretch of the mind, and this greater effort, this deeper involvement, yields a far richer and more complex perception of reality than do the flitting and vanishing pictures on the screen.

Books are portable packages of life and meaning, unimaginably diverse. They can be hugged, chewed, carried to bed or to a secret hideout in a tree, read and re-read, and the reader is always in control – skipping, going back, absorbing deeply or skimming forward. The creative power of reading is as far from the passive watching of TV as exploring a wilderness is from browsing through the supermarket. And because the reader virtually creates in her mind the book in her hands, books offer uniquely appropriate rewards to every age group. The toddler listening to a picture book read aloud may be delighted simply to recognize, in two dimensions, objects from his daily three-dimensional world. This, too, is an important part of learning to decipher print. The middle reader is thrilled to embark on adventures and discover worlds more fantastic than anything on the screen (because the imagination, unlike the special-effects crew, is limitless). Inner exploration, the moral and emotional testing of the child's mettle in folk and fairy tales, is just as exciting at this age. The pre-adolescent, struggling to form some coherent sense of self, is free to try on, in books, the feelings and identities of countless others.

Jacques Barzun said that a work of art, unlike mere escapism, carries the individual back to the real world at last. In my experience, heavy viewers of TV are dazzled by celebrity; they are helplessly envious. But book readers come back to the real world with an inner ferment of ideas, feelings, and the sense of possibilities.

'Identity' is a moot point in our society: in most films and television, it's a matter of physical beauty or fashionable clothes, the outward surface. (Think of teenagers whose 'identity' is a punk costume or the 'look' of the lastest rock star, mimicked faithfully down to the last spangle and bangle.) In good books, identity is character in action, interaction or introspection, the inner self as springingly alive as the outer. The well-read child, like Gorky, knows 'he is not alone'. He is better equipped to interpret his own experience and measure it against that of others; he has an ample frame of intellectual reference for every new encounter or dilemma in his life; his familiarity with many kinds of prose style makes him more receptive, more alert, to all forms of art and communication. Reading fiction allows the child to know himself better, and endows him with an invaluable store of our culture's symbols and archetypes.

The elemental stories, wrote Ted Hughes, are

> . . . *little factories of understanding* . . . *Stories think for themselves, once we know them* . . . *they continue to light up and attract everything relevant in our experience, and continually produce new implications and revelations of meaning.*

The child who comes to school already having experienced the deep satisfaction of listening to stories is, as any teacher can testify, a privileged student, far ahead of the others in literacy skills, attention span, responsiveness to ideas and capacity for abstraction.

As this book will try to show, school achievement is only a small part of what reading can do for a child, but parents, in their anxiety to do the best for their children, often grasp at the sheer mechanics of reading as both the method and the goal. Early reading schemes and flashcard alphabets have become ubiquitous in the last decade. Conscientious parents, especially those who have only one or two children, are understandably eager to enhance their child's prowess.

Extreme caution is advised. If there is one thing on which most reading experts in the English-speaking world agree, it is that early parental teaching of alphabets or words is counterproductive. If you wanted your child to enjoy athletic activity, would you begin by drilling the baby in the crib with pictures of the different parts of a ski harness? Or would you simply take him along in a backpack, and watch the glow come into his cheeks, as you enjoy the exhilaration of skiing on a cross-country trail?

Of course, you would take him along to share your pleasure. And when he was old enough for skis, small ones appropriate for his age, you would encourage him to join you, adjusting your pace to suit his, and laughingly setting him on his feet when he tumbled. The technical knowledge would come to him through the soles of his feet and the seat of his snowsuit; the motivation to learn would arise from his natural desire to imitate his parents, to gain mastery, and to join in the fun.

The reading of books dawns most brightly in just the same atmosphere of mutual delight. How to discover, or rediscover, that delight in reading, and thus to inspire it in your child, makes up a large part of this book. I am aware, for example, that the vast majority of parents have fallen out of the habit of book reading. It's estimated that almost all book reading is done by a mere 10% of the population of North America. A Canadian community-college teacher lamented that, according to an extensive survey, half of all seventeen- and eighteen-year-olds have no interest in reading, one-quarter of first-year students do not open a book outside class, fewer than 15% of students read ten books or more a year and, when they do read, they are likely to choose 'soft romance novels'. In Britain, critic Nicholas Tucker reported in 1981 that a third of all intelligent, middle-class fourteen-year-old boys never read books for pleasure at all; the situation cannot have improved since then.

Despite the frenzied efforts of some libraries in urban centres to lure non-readers with copies of *Popular Mechanics* and *Penthouse* ('I don't care if they use the books to prop open their windows, so long as the books get off our shelves,' one librarian told me), I don't think there is much to be gained in lowering standards and abandoning literary values in order to tempt non-reading adults into the mindless consumption of print for its own sake. In the library with the *Penthouse*-peddling librarian, I was unable to find any Henry Green, Maxim Gorky or Gertrude Stein, to name a few examples. That's serious. The works I sought were out of print; since the library had discarded them in favour of more 'popular materials', a significant element of western culture had virtually disappeared, become inaccessible to the readers in that area. *Penthouse*, on the other hand, could be found on all local magazine racks. At what point in its drive toward 'relevance' and popularity does the library become simply irrelevant?

Making good literature accessible to children is an equally urgent matter. For those of us for whom fiction has fed a vibrant undercurrent in our lives, whose sensibilities have been broadened and emotions deepened by books, it seems senselessly cruel to raise a child without at least trying to instil the love of reading.

Parents who do not try are, I suspect, frustrated by not knowing how to begin. But children's literature offers an almost magical opportunity to non-reading adults to begin again, and to discover the pleasures of reading along with their children. Not only that, but parents who read with or aloud to their children, or at least read some of the books most favoured by their children, gain an enriched intimacy and an enlivened field of conversation, debate and play. The summer my children read the entire *Little House in the Big Woods* series, we all played at pioneers and settlers in the woods around our rented cottage. That imaginative adventure is a more cherished memory, now, in all our lives, than any of the birthday presents given or received that summer.

In my experience, the rote exercises in 'imaginative work' so often seen in schools have limited use because the much-celebrated imagination of children rarely takes the form of inventing new things to order. The deepest current of a child's imagination runs in private places – interpreting the world, making new links among the varied objects and impressions in the child's experience ('Oh, grass!' exclaimed my two-year-old, stroking the soft fringe on my new dress) and giving narrative expression to the fears, hopes and fantasies that compose the inner life.

Through fiction, adults can deepen those capacities in the child in the most spontaneous, unforced way. It's a commonplace to hear a mother doing it as she looks over a picture book with her wide-eyed child. 'Look, that's just like your ball, only this one has a big blue stripe,' she might say, and in the child's mind, newly enriched by words, forms an idea of that ball, its hardness and resilience, its sameness to and difference from the ball in the corner of the playroom. That ball, with its colour and three-dimensional shape, *bounces* in her mind, right through to the end of the book and beyond.

She is practising using her imagination, without being asked to perform an imposed task, and it is all happening without a second thought. If you continue to share the child's world of books, then you are always in a position to stimulate your child's amplifying imagination.

'What would Pa have done *now?*' my children would ask with relish that summer we played *Little House*. Pa had become a rounded, real person in their minds, a permanent archetype of the brave, competent, loving man, and they were generously inviting me to participate in their imagined world. It would not have worked for a moment, however, if I had chimed in with condescending joviality. Some child part of me had joined in falling in love with Pa. That was my ticket of admission.

The intimacy established between my children and me through books continues to this day. Even while writing this book, and discussing with my twenty-year-old daughter some of her memories of loved stories, I found we both gained startling insights into the underlying themes of the narrative we make of our lives. Along the way, I was able to help my children develop their imaginative capacities for recreating the world in their mind's eye, and for seeing new connections and meanings at every turn. I hold this up as one example of the uses of childhood literature, but emphatically not as a tribute to my own virtues: my entrance into this fictional inner world of my children's lives was mostly accidental.

Like many another adult, I became temporarily indifferent to contemporary adult fiction at a point in my life when I most needed reassurance about the purposefulness of life. My babies were young, I was busy and exhausted, and my emotions were unwontedly open and vulnerable. I was as tender and bruisable as a peeled peach. A news flash on television of a distraught mother could reduce me to tears. The violence of most current movies became unbearably painful to me. Contemporary fiction – a surrealistic blur of post-nuclear nihilism, chic despair, fragmentation, incoherence and sexual obsession – left me irritated and sickened. My daily concern was the nurturing of new life; an aesthetically fashionable alienation, or a flippant cynicism about human endeavour, was the last thing I needed or wanted. I tried browsing through the literature that had given me so much enjoyment when I was at university, but, with scarcely ten minutes at a time to myself, I didn't have the sustained intellectual energy necessary for Chaucer, Shakespeare or even most nineteenth-century novels.

It was at that point that I rediscovered Charles Dickens. His tumultuous vitality, his zest for the human comedy, his robust affection and engrossing plots, were just the infusion I needed. And rediscovering that primary pleasure of self-forgetfulness in an author's created world of plot and character led me back one step farther. I found myself skulking off to the local library and returning laden with all my childhood favourites. A stack of Arthur Ransomes stood on my bedside table. Awake at three or four in the morning to nurse the baby. I lay on my side, propped the book on a pillow, and with the small warm bundle nestled in beside me, I read with childlike pleasure.

My two preschoolers were quick to notice how jealously I guarded that changing pile of library books beside the bed. I had no ulterior motives in telling them those books were for *my* pleasure and not to be carried off, but I had stumbled unwittingly on the secret of motivating my children to read fiction. Listening to picture books read aloud by their father (to his and their immense satisfaction) was already one of their favourite pastimes. Now they were itching to discover what it was I enjoyed so much in those long 'chapter books'. Within months, they were reading my library books in my wake and eagerly sharing their discoveries with me.

I don't propose that parents should use negative psychology to stimulate their children's interest in books. The salient fact was that mother was seen to value those stories, and not just for the good they might do the children. I'm convinced that if adults could overcome their prejudice against childlike joys, they could gain a great deal of pleasure from children's novels and open the door for their own children's lifelong reading.

Prejudice there is, however, and it is overwhelming. Many adults who remember only stilted, prissy or moralistic books from their own childhood are unaware that there now exists a vast hoard of children's books of genuine depth, linguistic skill, wit and absorbing drama. Though novels written for children may have a circumscribed subject matter, there are children's authors today (I think of writers like William Mayne, Philippa Pearce, Jill Paton Walsh, Jane Gardam and Janni Howker) who tower above most adult bestsellers in mastery of language and insight. The sheer excellence of many children's books is a breathtaking surprise for anyone who has not read the genre since childhood.

Still, there are barriers of pomposity and conceit to overcome. One winter night, my family left for a concert a full hour ahead of time to make sure of getting there on time. Sure enough, we arrived too early and my son, then fifteen or so, began to read the book he had brought along for just that contingency. An elegant gentleman in the seat next to him leaned over and exclaimed '*Riddley Walker!* Excellent book, just read it myself.' They got into one of those book-swapping conversations. 'Have you read Russell Hoban's other books, like *The Mouse and His Child?*' asked my son enthusiastically. Baffled pause. 'It's a children's book,' he explained. The man recoiled with the surprised expression of a frozen haddock. 'Oh, you'd have to ask my *wife* about that,' he said at last, condescendingly. 'You should really try it,' urged my son. 'No *thanks*, I'll stick to the grown-up stuff.'

Ursula Le Guin has a wonderful passage in *The Fantasists* about 'adult chauvinist piggery', parodying the conversations she has at cocktail parties. 'You're a juvenile writer, aren't you?' Yeth, mummy, she says inwardly. 'I love your books – the real ones, I mean, I haven't read the ones for children, of course!' Of courth, daddy. 'It must be relaxing to write *simple* things for a change.' 'Sure, it's simple, writing for kids,' says Le Guin.

'Just as simple as bringing them up. All you do is take all the sex out and use little short words and little dumb ideas, and don't be too scary and make sure there's a happy ending. Right? . . . if you do all that, you might even write *Jonathan Livingstone Seagull* and make twenty billion dollars and have every adult in America reading your book.'

Le Guin's spoof is pointedly accurate. Of course, the dismissal of children's books as unimportant and mindless is the same kind of egotism that has for so long dismissed child rearing and women's concerns as trivial. And that conceit leads the patronizer right into the fallacy of assuming that even good children's books are somehow less good, less important, than the trash that often turns into adult bestsellers.

Such condescension can be forgiven in adults whose only familiarity with children's literature comes from the supermarket and chain store shelves, laden now with mass market commodities disguised as books. Although they may be packaged in shiny flat boards, such market-adjusted products as *Care Bears* and *Cabbage Patch Kids* are not books. In fact, they are sugar-laden assembly-line products, as detrimental to the intellect as bubble gum is to the teeth.

Countless thousands of parents, misled by their own nostalgia for a mythically perfect childhood, think of children's books as shiny, pretty, cute and cuddly toys. Cuteness, in fact, is the bubonic plague of children's publishing. Every month, while I was writing a newspaper column, I would receive at least one amateur manuscript from a would-be author, almost invariably featuring fluffy little creatures with names like Snowball and Whimsy – darling wee cuddly-wuddlies who would teach children to be nice to each other, brush their teeth and do what mummy told them.

Cuteness is a disease of self-conscious falsity that we inflict on children like unwanted damp kisses. Books do give joy, but joy is not a glucose drip for children any more than for adults. And a tacked-on moral lesson has no more place in children's literature than it has in the fiction that adults enjoy.

Real books are to be found in book shops and in libraries, not in groceries and only rarely in toy shops. Even here, though, there is real danger in the tidal wave of commodity publishing. The bad, the commercial junk and the exploitative 'contemporary' novels, the easy-to-read series and the teenage romances, all heavily advertised, are pushing the more authentic literature right off the shelves. Every time you buy a commercial, television-based book, you are helping to ensure the death of another, better book which simply cannot compete for that shelf space in profitability and quick turn-over.

Another danger is the well-meaning proselytizer. It is one thing to laugh out loud at the humour in a children's novel and to share your enthusiasm with your family; it is quite another to come home laden with good books and press them imploringly into the hands of your reluctant reader or teenage recalcitrant. The frontal approach with older children is almost bound to fail: finding your own good books is, after all, a part of the intoxicating freedom that is gained by fluent reading. In the early years, of course, the children are all yours; the treat of snuggling onto a parent's lap and basking in adult attention is enough to convince a child that books are a reliable source of refreshment and entertainment. If you keep it up, reading aloud from books that you are able to choose with your own child's tastes and inclinations in mind, there is every reason to trust that excellent fiction will hold your child's attention right through primary school.

Today, of course, the child's delight in reading is far more likely to be undermined by an over-ambitious parent than by one who is too prim or restrictive. If I feel alarmed by this turn of events – horrified, in fact, by the thought of an army of determined parents coaching their glaze-eyed toddlers with flashcards – it may be because I remember my own earliest reading with such force. I was allowed to come to it in my own sweet time, at my own will. It was private, and so was the shock of joyful liberty it brought me.

In those days, it was feeding and toileting that were regimented by the experts. Well-meaning mothers, anxious lest their children fall short of accepted standards, held three-month infants over potties and forced their screaming babies to wait the approved four hours between feedings, to their mutual torture. Intellectual ambition had not yet been invented as a fertile field for baby experts. Toddlers were expected to pick dandelions in the back yard, eat nicely with a spoon, build with their blocks, and wait to learn their ABCs when they were old enough for school.

I count myself lucky. That moment when I learned to read, with no adult ego hovering over my accomplishments, is my single clearest memory of being four years old. I was sitting on the floor of the bedroom I shared with my brother Alan, who was nearly two years older than I. His school reader, the ghastly Dick and Jane, a close relative of the British Janet and John, was open on my knees. 'Don't you see,' my brother said, just a little impatiently, 'every one of those letters I taught you makes a sound and the sounds go together to make words. That "a" right there says "aah".'

Even though it made no sense that fat, familiar little 'ay' should suddenly be saying 'aah' on the printed page, I did see, all at once, what he meant. I'll never forget that moment. A shutter opened, light fell on shadowy confusion, pieces sprang magically together to form a whole puzzle. It felt as though my hand had unexpectedly fitted around the great handle that opened all adult mysteries.

That was the second-child syndrome. First-born children are far more likely to prolong the years when their parents have to read aloud to them. They learn to read for themselves, calmly, in the first year of school. None of the bright first-born children I've known raced toward reading with the same ardour I've seen in the second-born, who are always panting at the heels of an older sibling, desperate to catch up. That's important to remember if you are tempted to compare your child's development with that of little Alfred next door. Is Alfred a second-born, spurred on by imitation of an older sibling? Preschoolers are willing to expend reckless energy to become more autonomous. The role model, the hero to be envied and emulated, is the older child, whose pleasures, privileges and accomplishments are so much more recognizable to the younger child, so much more tantalizingly within his reach than the remote and god-like attributes of adults. In our older siblings we can see tangible proof that we too will grow and become powerful.

And could a child today, surrounded by dancing pictures, toys that talk, puzzles that are all but alive, 'interactive' computers and cities bursting with commercial entertainments, feel the same thrill of initiation that I did? I doubt it. Reading has not lost its importance to the child's life, but its glamour has faded and its immediate rewards are not as obvious as they once were. The first task of the concerned parent, then, is not to spoil the child's already tenuous flicker of interest in reading by burdening her with anxieties about early achievement.

The North American early-reading craze of the 1970s – fed by books like Sidney Ledson's *Teach Your Child to Read in 30 Days*, complete with a system of sweet bribes – did a terrible disservice to true literacy, because it shifted the focus from pleasure to performance. It may have been gratifying to parents' egos to have a three-year-old who could belt through Dr Seuss, but most educators are adamant that early reading confers no special advantage. Many a forced sprout of a reader has wilted in motivation by the first day of school.

The goal is to make reading a lifelong source of delight to the growing child. Any competent teacher can train a child in the mechanical decoding of letters. But the *will* to read – the most important thing a child can bring to school on the first day – is nurtured, like the will to live, in the child's early emotional experience.

Reading has its roots in play: the verbal and rhythmic play of nursery rhymes, chants and songs. This old oral culture, alas, has bled almost to death, unnoticed, in the last two generations, mortally wounded by television. Preschoolers chant beer and shampoo commercials now – verbal expressions whose only purpose is to manipulate – while the haunting opacities or breakneck anarchy of nursery rhymes are forgotten. If you dip into a book like Alice Kane's *An Ulster Childhood*, you will be amazed by the verbal richness that bubbled through her childhood and helped to shape one of Canada's best-loved storytellers. And you will perhaps be saddened by the contrast between her times and our own days, when a child may reach five years old without ever hearing a story or rhyme produced from the parent's memory.

To make your child into a reader, forget the flashcards and the alphabet. Concentrate on song, finger play, and the association of loving physical contact with stories told and books read aloud. Create an atmosphere in which verbal jokes are savoured, where language is respected and narrative attended to; a home where parents talk about their childhood and the outside world and dip into stories from the common storehouse of tales. Listen to your child's meandering stories and write them down.

Make sure yours is a home in which books are freely available and enjoyed by adults too, not just prescribed as medicine for children. I would have stacks of picture books around the house, and would read aloud whenever a moment could be squeezed from the daily routine – not just at bedtime. And I would never teach letters or turn reading into a lesson unless the child herself demanded information.

Does it all sound too easy, too mushy and liberal and unproductive? On the contrary. To create a language-loving home takes far more effort than the rote teaching of the alphabet. I know, because, as a true North American, a child of an immigrant generation, just emerging from one culture and not thoroughly blended into the next, I grew up without a large store of fairy tales or nursery games. When my own children were small, I had to learn the finger plays about the two dickie birds on a wall (a guaranteed winner) and the teddy bear going around the garden (tickle under *there!*) from acquaintances and library books. Lullabies came from records. The love of reading was the one secret weapon I could already lay claim to.

All very well, you may say. But what about the child for whom the mechanical skills of reading don't seem to come easily and naturally around the age of six or seven? Ah. That was my hardest lesson of all. My two older children followed the expected pattern. My first daughter learned easily and simply to read when she went to school. My second child, a boy, fell over himself to catch her up and surprised me by teaching himself to read quite fluently at the age of three. My third, going her own stubborn way, was the one who taught me the most.

Jenny was just as verbally bright as her older brother and sister, and a non-stop storyteller from the moment she could talk. But just like a sturdy, bright-eyed pony trotting up to the gate and refusing to jump, she planted her feet and refused to learn to read.

Our first inkling came in nursery school, when the teachers thought Jenny was ripe for a reading-readiness programme. Jenny clearly indicated that she did not agree. By the age of five, in a pleasant, middle-of-the-road school, Jenny was one of the very few in her generation who still didn't (or wouldn't) know her alphabet. Knowing how stubbornly self-determining my daughter was, even at that age, I had asked the teacher not to pressure her into the 'pre-reading' activities she seemed to reject so fiercely. The teacher was bemused. Most of her pupils' parents were pressing for more achievement, not less.

That was the hard part. What if I were making a terrible mistake in not pushing her harder? What if I were sentencing her to a lifetime of academic inferiority? Everything seemed to conspire to increase my fears. At the end of that year, a playmate in the park threw a handful of fine sawdust straight into Jenny's eyes. At the Hospital for Sick Children, a senior ophthalmologist removed the sawdust particles and then insisted on testing Jenny's eyesight by having her read a standard letter chart. 'But doctor, she doesn't know her alphabet.' 'Nonsense! Every five-year-old knows the alphabet.' Jenny blithely read the chart, missing half the letters and identifying only the E's which were backward or upside down.

'This child has such poor eyesight that she needs immediate corrective work!' exclaimed the doctor. 'She didn't even mention that the E's are backward.' I explained again that Jenny hadn't really mastered the alphabet, and normally made her E's upside down or backward. 'Nonsense!' he boomed again. 'I can tell you right now, this child has such deficient eyesight that she will never make it through primary school.'

The next day, we had Jenny tested by an ophthamologist who was willing to accept that a five-year-old might not know her alphabet. It turned out that her eyesight was perfect.

Halfway through her fifth year, I moved Jenny to a small, family-like private school, where each child progressed at his or her own pace. Luckily, the school had an extremely literate programme for the early years: songs, playwriting, artwork combined with narrative and reading aloud were all part of the daily curriculum. Jenny, her receptivity sharpened by her strictly oral personal culture, was brilliant at listening to stories. She had a phenomenal capacity to concentrate and to absorb oral information whenever a story was being told.

Jenny was nearly eight years old when she came into my workroom at home one day, took down a book from the shelves, sat on the floor, and began to read silently. The book was *A Castle of Yew* by Lucy Boston, subtle, beautifully written, and not an obvious choice for a beginner. The first paragraph reads:

> *Joseph and a boy whom he had often seen but did not know by name stood together by the high wire fence peering in at the garden beyond it. Their fingers clung to the wire mesh as they put their eyes against it in order to see through the tangle of roses and honeysuckle that grew over it. There was a path on the other side, narrow and overgrown and overhung, and beyond that, glimpsed between leaves and stalks, the shine of water.*

That book must have been the right choice for Jenny, because she wouldn't stop at suppertime, or at bedtime, or until she had finished. And she hasn't stopped since. An avid reader, she still goes her own way, leaping from the heights (Shakespeare) to the swampy depths (Harlequin romances) when the mood seizes her. We never knew by what mysterious process she had come to a decision to read, but we did learn that you can't force and control a child's reading. You can only enable and enrich it, and prevent it from being ruined by outside interference.

Once your child is past the age of eight or nine, aside from your occasional tactfully expressed excitement about a book you recently enjoyed, you should concentrate on helping the child make his or her own discoveries. Stock your own shelves with children's books you like; talk to your husband or wife about them; offer to read them aloud while the children plough through some purely physical chore. But make sure also to give them the opportunity to choose books for themselves as well as receiving them as gifts; arrange solo book-shop visits for your children now and then – gloriously provided with gift tokens. Books by post are another lure, since every child loves to get post, and the United Kingdom is well provided with children's book clubs through which you can order by post.

Children, as parents know all too well, have a built-in resistance to anything forced on them by authority. Dozens of books I might otherwise have loved were permanently spoiled for me this way by school. I have always hated the memory of *A Tale of Two Cities*, for example, though I love the rest of Dickens; I realized the source of my antipathy recently when I unearthed my school copy of the novel and found that our teacher had required us to look up in the dictionary a dozen words per chapter and write out the definitions. It takes a gifted and unusual teacher to avoid murdering a book's enchantment when it is used as part of the curriculum – all the more reason for parents to instil a love of literature before the children go to school and learn that reading is a task at which you might just fail, rather than one of life's most rewarding pastimes. (There are more and more teachers, I hasten to add, who know the value of silent reading periods in school, when students are free to choose from a wide range of novels and do not have to answer irritating questions on every chapter and plot device.)

Classics are another pitfall for the unwary parent. There was a time when children had access to very few books written especially for them. For want of anything more appropriate, avid readers naturally turned to so-called family classics (*The Adventures of Tom Sawyer, Robinson Crusoe, Gulliver's Travels*), some of them quite beyond the range or interests of childhood, and gleaned what dramatic scraps of adventure they could, skipping the 'boring' descriptions, confused or troubled by the author's ventures into philosophy or satire. Encouraging children to read fondly remembered classics before they are ready for them is a sure way to ruin the book for them, or discourage them from reading altogether.

This book is intended as a guide to the hundreds of genuine classics for children, many of which have been written in the last twenty years and may be unfamiliar to today's parents. There are, of course, grievous omissions in this book; there was, for example, not enough space to write about folk and fairy tales or poetry. The early primary years are the perfect, ripe time for fairy tales. They have become so popular lately, in many single-story picture-book editions, that parents may mistakenly feel that these tales are best suited to preschoolers. There are so many outstanding collections suitable for seven-, eight- and nine-year-olds, however – like the classic Andrew Lang *Colour* series, or the two-volume set of Grimm's called *The Juniper Tree*, brilliantly translated by Lore Segal and illustrated by Maurice Sendak – that any adult could confidently choose among them with the help of a book-shop assistant or a librarian. Beware of garishly illustrated re-releases of fairy tales; there are fine versions and appalling ones, and a knowledgeable sales assistant (as well as your own developing sense of discrimination) is your best ally.

Poetry is a different conundrum. British children, I am told, still study poetry at school, and every British children's book shop I have visited has had healthy stocks of poetry anthologies. But North American children, even the most literate, read very little poetry today and practically none is taught in school. As a Canadian who has watched American popular culture encroach upon and engulf our own more British-oriented tradition, I feel well placed to sound an advance warning. Aliteracy is the wave of the future. Take British literacy for granted at your and your children's peril.

What a strange amnesia has crept over us North Americans! Read aloud from the delicious *Faber Book of Nursery Verse*, for example and observe your children's spontaneous, natural delight in rhythm, rhyme and the spellbinding fascination of unfamiliar words, madcap nonsense and lyrical repetition. Most families, though, don't tread much further than these familiar grounds. It's an extraordinary loss, because 99% of modern children will never come to poetry by themselves. The immediacy, the shock of a new perception leaping into the reader's mind in one perfect image, the music and deep enthralment to words – all the passionate experiences of childhood poetry – are jettisoned.

Poetry, with its reverberating words and images, was one of the most intense discoveries of my childhood; the goblin who howled for the green glass beads, Robert Louis Stevenson's dark brown river, 'the long light shakes across the lakes . . . Blow, bugle, blow, set the wild echoes flying . . . ' from Tennyson – just repeating those phrases sends shivers down to my toes. Poetry was a constant reminder, no matter how dull or disappointing my daily life, that there were other levels of existence, other, more piercing, planes of perception and feeling.

True, it's difficult to know how to bridge the gap between nursery rhyme and more demanding poetry for the middle readers. One of my sadder failures as a parent was my cowardly abandonment of the field with my own children. I tried them on a few poems when they were at primary-school age and then, noting their apathy, abandoned the effort, for fear of turning them against poetry altogether. I assumed they would get around to it on their own, but I was wrong, and not one of my three experienced that keen childhood enthralment to poetry that I had had. I wish now that I had persisted.

Contemporary parents have the task made easier, thanks to many superb anthologies, which I have listed separately in the Treasury.

Difficult books are another category I've not had space to plumb in depth in this volume. William Mayne is particularly difficult to classify; there is no more assured and skilful writer in the whole field of children's literature, and there are few forms he has not tried, all with astonishing success; fantasy, time travel, adventure, preschool stories, adolescent novels, school stories. I've discussed only two (*A Year and a Day* and *Earthfasts*) but parents of talented readers ought to be looking for his books from the time their children are about seven years old. The difficulty lies not in his vocabulary or his plots, but his elusive, oblique manner of expression. It is extremely condensed and evocative, and perfectly honed to catch the flicker of mood and feeling just below the surface of action. Such accomplished writing provides a complex, distinctly literary pleasure for the advanced reader, but may prove too much of a challenge for the less practised. *No More School*, for example, is a brilliantly perceptive story about a group of primary-school children in an isolated village who run their own school – unbeknownst to all the adults – while their teacher is away. It's a moving and vigorous novel of strong characters engaged in an admirable act of independence, and perfect for a good nine-year-old reader. It (and others of Mayne's works) are to be found among the wholeheartedly recommended books in the Treasury at the end of this book.

One of the motives that drove me to write this book was the dismay I felt when I saw literate friends and acquaintances choosing books for their children on pragmatic, nationalist, feminist or didactic grounds. Though I broach this complicated subject in Chapter Ten, 'Girls' Books, Boys' Books, Bad Books, and Bias', I want to emphasize that such narrow selectivity does a severe injustice both to the child reader and to children's literature.

Naturally, adults who care about what children read will want to ensure that their children are given a chance to read about their own culture, that ugly biases will not be overwhelmingly present, and that the overall tone of novels will be neither nihilistic nor tasteless.

Still, there seem to me to be only two essential bases for choice: a sensitive awareness of what a particular child enjoys and needs, and an informed judgement about books based on literary merit. 'Literary': that's a stumbling block. Most parents and teachers quail before the idea of setting themselves up as literary critics.

In the chapters that follow, I try to show in detail what gives each book I discuss its special quality. Before long, anyone who is not yet familiar with children's literature will begin to see what I mean by literary merit and be able to make his or her own informed judgements. Is the language original, fresh and interesting? Are the characters wooden, or do they live and breathe on the page? Do they speak in individual voices, so that you can tell who's talking just by the characteristic speech patterns? If the book in question is a picture book, do the illustrations add to the meaning of the words, or overwhelm them? If it's a fantasy, does the author create a believable world, no matter how strange, and abide by the rules of that world so that your belief in it is never shaken . . . or do you come thudding back to the banal commonplace with maddening regularity? If the story is an adventure, does it convince *you*?

The idea that second-rate, mechanical, mass-produced books are good enough for the kiddies is just another facet of that condescension of which I spoke earlier. And because children's books are usually not as long, complex or intellectually demanding as the finest 'classics' for adults, it is relatively simple to become a competent critic. The point of developing such expertise – an easy and pleasant exercise – is that good books can do so much for children.

At their best, they expand horizons and instil in children a sense of the wonderful complexity of life. Even a book that ends on a mournful note can be encouraging because the child characters do go on, building their lives despite losses or setbacks. Even a book that gives expression to some of children's most haunting fears can be exhilarating, because the reader has had a chance to feel those chills down the spine while sitting safely at home, conqueror of the print she surveys, able to control her imaginative re-creation of the book's horrors to the limits of what is bearable for her personally. The very act of tackling a challenging narrative and winning through to the exciting kernel of the plot reinforces the idea that language and literature can be thrilling. And, of course, by drawing a reader into the inner lives of the characters, good books help her to recognize the all-too-human impulse to cruelty or the radiance of achievement *in herself*. No other pastime available to children is so conducive to empathy and the enlargement of human sympathies. No other pleasure can so richly furnish a child's mind with the symbols, patterns, depths and possibilities of civilization.

But those rewards can't be gleaned from books that are poorly written or thinly imagined. Bad books may have their uses and children will unerringly find them – again, consult Chapter 10 – but, in this cluttered and distracting world, only caring adults can ensure that children will find the immeasurable rewards of good books. That is why I confidently invite you, in the chapters that follow, to become your own literary critic.

Chapter 2

BOOKS TO ENCOURAGE THE BEGINNING READER

I know nothing of myself till I was five or six. I do not know how I learnt to read. I only remember my first books and their effects upon me; it is from my earliest reading that I date the unbroken consciousness of my own existence.

Jean-Jacques Rousseau, *The Confessions*, 1781

At the beginning of the summer holidays, when our city street drowsed under its overhanging maple trees, I would sit on the tiny concrete porch of the ground-floor flat where we lived, with a sense of luxurious pleasure that would not have been out of place in a Venetian palazzo. In summer, we were allowed to take six books at once, not the usual three, from the local children's library. And so, beside me on the porch, was a treasure heap that was sure not to run out too soon. I would open the first page of the first book, smooth down the page (those tough green library bindings always made the covers want to snap shut) and, with a keen sense of anticipatory magic, dive down beneath the summer surface of my world into somewhere else.

Look at a child reading: sprawled immobile, all that restless energy dissipated somehow or gone up into the mind where it is unseen, holding a collection of paper, glue and print in front of her eyes. She is there but not there; she inhabits another world that has mysteriously been created by the words on the page and now lives inside her head, and she is moving invisibly through palaces or shanties that are more real to her at this moment that the living-room rug where she is lying or the dinner waiting to be served. Call to her, and you can watch her self come back, slowly, from far away, into her eyes.

Children's reading should mesmerize, transport; reading ought to be a free-flowing stream of pleasure and consolation that runs beneath their daily lives like an underground spring. But how to begin? How can we ensure that the mechanical process of reading becomes such second nature to our children that it turns transparent like a window? We should consult our own experiences, for a start. Try to remember how and why you learned to read; ask friends who are ardent readers; ask, especially, the ones who never pick up a book.

The experience of my daughter Jenny – her surprising choice of *The Castle of Yew* for her very first book – ought to stand as an epigraph for this chapter. For one thing, any category called 'beginners' books' can be taken only as very arbitrary selection. There really is no predicting what will be the right first book for any given child. He may, in the course of a single day, listen entraptured while *The Hobbit* is read aloud, dip into a classroom encyclopaedia, browse through a Superman comic behind the couch and be ready for a favourite fairy tale at bedtime.

How, then, can you choose the beginner books that will most stimulate the child to want to read for herself? Look for themes that spring from the common emotional experiences of the beginning reader's age group, roughly four to eight years old. The child is growing more independent. She separates from mother to go to school and enjoys the experience (after the first dreadful pangs of cutting loose) and yet she greets with a rush of relief that moment of reunion at the end of the day. At school, the child meets for the first time an impartial and sometimes incomprehensible authority from above. Questions of justice and fairness, therefore, loom large. Friendship, and how to achieve it, is an anxious priority. And since many children will not find a best friend in the first year or two of school, loneliness is an important theme, too. Helplessness (think of those playground bullies) and its delicious opposite, competence, are crucial matters for the beginning reader.

The passionate dependencies of the preschool years are over, but think how close a six-year-old often is to losing control over newly conquered functions: crying, forgetting how to tie shoe laces or wetting one's pants are major humiliations. Humour, therefore (from the raucous guffaw to pointed word play), is a welcome tool to keep the emotional temperature down and enable a child to feel in control. Getting a joke is a splendid way to assert one's knowingness, one's worthiness to belong to the group.

Luckily, this age group is blessed with an abundance of picture books of such splendour of colour and design that the only difficulty is to choose wisely. Illustrations provide both a stimulus and a prop for a reader still struggling to decode printed words. In many less obvious ways, as I hope to show in more detailed descriptions of some particularly apt choices, good picture books encourage reading skills and reinforce rewards that may turn a beginning reader into an eager one.

The colours in *Sally, Where Are You?* by Yvette Mintzberg are so sharp and brilliant that you can almost hear them vibrate; better still, everything about this ingeniously designed book seems perfectly thought through and coherent. The brief story is told entirely in the voice of the mother looking for mischievous little Sally, who is seen in the illustrations only as a pair of round black eyes. 'Sally, where are you?' Sally doesn't answer, but from page to page we see those tell-tale eyes shining out from under a bed, under mother's hat, in a trunk, and so on. The mother's exasperation mounts, she shouts, Sally weeps, and no sooner is she consoled with a kiss than she's up to her mischief again. 'Come, I've made some nice liver for lunch. Sally? SALLY, WHERE ARE YOU?' ends the narrative.

Though the story is about a three- or four-year-old, it seems perfectly pitched to an older sibling who can share mother's crossness with a rambunctious toddler, understand the jokes (that liver for lunch!), and, most important, read it independently. The bold black type, set so sparely on luscious square pages of solid colour, practically begs to be read. The clever spacing on the page is an aid to interpretation: a whole page of colour separates mother's questions to indicate a temporal pause. ('Sally, where are you?' is set at the top left; the question 'Sally?' is repeated at the bottom right corner.) Mother's annoyed shout, in huge black capitals, occupies a solid double-page spread of angry red. The words of consolation cuddle down comfortingly together near the bottom of another page. These witty visual analogues of both the speaking voice and the bell-curve of emotion are adroit examples of illustrations supporting the act of reading. The simple vocabulary, with all its repetitions, has rarely been more deftly deployed to entice and to reward the beginning reader.

Beginner series like the *Happy Family* books by Janet and Allan Ahlberg, with their high-spirited pictorial humour and humane energy, and the spate of *I-Can-Read* books published in America in the last decade, have greatly enriched the available selection. But you would still have to search hard for better beginner books than the now-classic *Little Bear* series by Else Holmelund Minarik, with illustrations by Maurice Sendak. They are just the right grown up book shape and size, with chapters, yet enlivened and made more accessible by pictures on every page. Sendak's early style of rounded, expressive cross-hatching achieves the perfect balance: surely, no ursine family ever had more bear-like claws or convincingly long snouts. Yet how human are their tender looks of amused affection, glances that weave the strands of the story from page to page and knit the family members together in a web of tolerant attachment.

The subject matter is really the way in which Mother Bear tacitly supports the pretend play of Little Bear and his friends. In 'Birthday Soup', the story with the strongest element of suspense, Little Bear fears that his mother has forgotten his birthday. Resourcefully, and not forgetting the duties of hospitality, he makes a vegetable soup to serve to his friends who arrive to help him celebrate. When mother gets home just at the crucial moment, bringing a beautiful cake, Little Bear is no less grateful for the surprise, even though he has coped remarkably well on his own as host and chef. And the story ends with a sentence of resonating maternal reassurance ('I never did forget your birthday and I never will') that is matched in picture books only by the emotional roundedness of Maurice Sendak's last line in the famous *Where the Wild Things Are:* Max journeys back from the land of wild things, after all his adventures, to find that 'supper was still hot'.

Not all beginner books are aesthetic masterpieces. When my husband first brought home to our three preschoolers a book called *Are You My Mother?* by P. D. Eastman, I dismissed it. It looked cartoonish, starring a gawky bird and a gaggle of bulldozers and steamrollers. The story, I thought, seemed trite. How wrong I was!

Torn between terror at the little bird's separation from his mother and superior laughter at his awkward mistakes in interpreting the world, the children sat riveted. They loved the building tension of the search, the repeated question ('Are you my mother?') and the overwhelming relief of the mother and child reunion at the end.

Are You My Mother? is a perfect example of a book that may lack aesthetic appeal to the educated adult eye, and yet has an emotional validity that is immediately irresistible to the child. H. A. Rey's *Curious George* books, the often-repetitious adventures of a too-lively monkey, seem to get the same double response: ho-hum from adults, spontaneous loyalty from children.

Pop-up books have never been more popular, but they're often frowned upon, and with reason, by reading experts. Unless carefully chosen, they offer a play experience, rather than a reading one; their paper engineering is often flimsy and frustratingly perishable in small, impatient hands; their stories rarely provide imaginative stimulus. Still, every child is charmed by the pop-up's element of fun and surprise, so it's worth seeking out the best of them.

See You Later, Alligator, by Tony Bradman and Colin Hawkins, an English example, seems an ideal pop-up book to me. Like the American *Are You My Mother?*, it taps infant emotion in a way that may not be immediately obvious to the adult. A hungry, jaw-snapping alligator pursues a mouse. On each page, a different animal comes to help the fleeing mouse and, as the child pulls the sturdy tab, is swallowed in the alligator's maw, sometimes with spectacular mechanical effects. Across the bottom of the page marches a simple, rhyming text in large black type, and on each page, there are sound effects or brief comments in comic-style speech bubbles. At the end, all the animals are disgorged unharmed.

The wild hilarity and rapt attention that greet this simple story derive, I think, from the universal experiences of oral aggression and the tension of the chase. In fact, it's hard not to be reminded of a roaring father (alligator) and a frantic child (mouse) in this comical pursuit, or, more light-heartedly, the shivery excitement of games when father chases children around the house.

A child of pre-reading age will usually sit still for almost any story that an adult will take time to read aloud; the closeness of sitting on a lap will make up for almost any lack of depth or interest in the book. But a parent who is sensitive to a child's responses will quickly learn to tell when the child has been well and truly engaged by a story and when he is simply listening politely. The story that grips is almost certainly one that will tempt the listener to try to read for himself.

The Bunyip of Berkeley's Creek by Australian Jenny Wagner, with its golden-hazed, mysterious drawings of a dark night, snares the interest at first with its gentle spookiness, its innocent version of the horror movie's opening gambit: 'Late one night, for no particular reason, something stirred in the black mud at the bottom of Berkeley's Creek.' But with the Bunyip's very first waking words – 'What am I?' – the reader is seized by the intrinsic interest of the Bunyip's identity crisis. One great emotional task of the school-age child is to determine 'What am I . . . aside from my parents' child?' No wonder that the Bunyip's plight (unhandsome, unrecognized, unloved) arouses such a sympathetic rush of fellow feeling. With its flat-footed posture and short arms, the Bunyip has the endearingly defenceless look of a child on the first day of school. In the face of an unkind world, he maintains a lugubrious optimism. (If only for its correct use of the adverb *hopefully*, this book justifies its purchase price.) The message is one of acceptance, of self-realization through love – a measure of the large themes that can be tackled unpretentiously and well in a picture book of artistic strength.

Robust, extroverted humour is beloved of preschoolers, and one of the best early readers in the *Cat in the Hat* series from Random House is another P. D. Eastman book, *Go, Dog, Go*. Though there's no plot, only a succession of ridiculous episodes (a greeting on a mountain top, dogs driving cars, a dog party in a tree), the terse captions and energetic pictures sweep you along. It's impossible not to laugh out loud, in fact, at these wiry red and yellow dogs with their expressions of crazed eagerness and wild joy – you can practically hear their yelps of enthusiasm.

At the purely mechanical level of reading, the book is a valuable tool. What non-reading child could fail to recognize the words 'go' and 'dog' after just one or two read-alouds of this madcap endeavour, with its rhythmic repetitions and racy pictures? Like all good illustrations, whether they are as painterly as the *Little Bear* pictures or as Disneyesque as the ones in *Are You My Mother?*, these show more than the words alone indicate. One double-spread picture in *Go, Dog, Go* brings the breakneck action to a sudden halt. All the dogs are asleep in one huge bed, companionably snuggled together. Children love this enormous bed, and never fail to notice that one dog is lying awake, eyes wide open in the dark. Why? No reason given. The unexplained detail gives the young reader something to ponder, to talk about, in the midst of pell-mell activity.

The child beginning to read is just about to embark on the long voyage to self-reliance. It's not surprising that some of the most loved and enduring books for this age group deal with the struggle between autonomy and the rules of group life. As always, and just as we expect in adult literature, the themes are not baldly stated. You can, of course, if you wish to encourage your child in crude and shallow thinking, buy mass-produced kitsch like the *Mr Man* series, sold nearly everywhere, with their simple-minded prescriptions for 'proper' behaviour. These books are worse than useless, since they teach the child a sort of insincere lip service to convention, without respect for the child's inner drive toward growth and mastery over impulse.

To illustrate the difference between the commercial moralistic books and one that looks at a central dilemma of child life through the child's eyes, consider *The Story About Ping*, by Marjorie Flack, which has been in print continuously for more than fifty years. It was, as I've said, the first book I ever read for myself. When I picked it up again, exactly forty years later, I recognized every line in every picture so well that I could actually spot some sloppy changes and colour distortions in a recent Puffin edition (avoid that one and buy the accurate hardback or the earlier Viking paperback, if you can find it).

Ping is a handsome young duck who lives, along with a flock of aunts and cousins, in a 'wise-eyed' boat on the Yangtze River. Every night, as the ducks walk back up the gangplank after a day of diving and feeding on the water, their keeper lightly slaps the hindmost duck with a long switch. It's an offhand, almost benign, ritual, but one so resented by Ping that he runs away. Instead of returning to the boat one evening, he hides on an island of reeds. Few readers will ever forget the wistful back view of Ping as he watches the wise-eyed boat sail into the distance. The duck is so small, and stretches so yearningly for one last look, against that serenely wide river vista. Kurt Wiese's softly greyed blues and yellows, and the sinuous black outline with which he highlights his simple shapes, breathe emotional life into the scene.

Ping does survive alone on the river, but not without hunger and difficulty. One of the most memorable pictures in the book is of Ping's startled encounter with a flock of cormorants: we see him back-paddle furiously in astonishment at the sight of these frightening, hook-beaked birds, with iron rings around their necks to prevent them from eating their catch. I recall my own uneasy mix of fear and compassion when I first saw those menacing, enslaved cormorants diving for their master.

Maybe I loved *The Story About Ping* because it matched my own growing complexity of perception. Family life, I was just beginning to realize, was warm, secure, the only imaginable way to exist in the threatening wide river of life. But along with the safety, one had to endure its small stings and balks. Because the child reader's sense of injustice has been deeply acknowledged through artistic representation, the moment of reconciliation, the acceptance of order at the book's finale, rings true.

The attractiveness of order is part of the appeal of the classic favourite, *Madeline*, and the subsequent Madeline books, by Ludwig Bemelmans. Those twelve little girls live in two such straight lines in the cloistered security of Miss Clavel's school in Paris. On their walks around familiar Paris landmarks, we see them 'smile at the good and frown at the bad'. Perhaps it is this grave decorum that enables them to take part in the life of such an adult city, sparkling with the sophisticated gaiety of Bemelmans's drawings.

Of course, infant insurgency is given its due: Madeline is not only the smallest and bravest of the girls, she is also the cheekiest. In *Madeline and the Bad Hat*, Miss Clavel is taken in by the good manners of the naughty boy next door – Pepito, the son of the Spanish Ambassador. Maybe there's just a hint of social snobbery, too, in Miss Clavel's doting admiration of the elegant boy. But Madeline isn't fooled for a minute. She is severe. She knows what Pepito is doing with that tool kit Miss Clavel gave him: he's building a guillotine for chickens.

Several levels of awareness are working here. The reader knows that Pepito's badness is as skin deep as the manners he puts on for adults. We know it by the cherubic grin under his preposterously villainous black hat, and we know it by the sheer comic gusto of the verse: he ate those chickens '. . . roasted, grilled and frito,/O what a horror was Pepito!' Not to overburden a delicately witty vehicle with too heavy a freight of meaning, part of this story's charm is the ingenious vigour with which the children are working out their own moral order, right under the noses of the adults.

THE BEGINNING READER

Picture books that have strong appeal for a beginning reader are often based on deep-sprung fantasies. *Polar Bear Cat* by the celebrated British picture-book artist Nicola Bayley is a quiet daydream of a distant journey. A black cat, in the embrace of a little girl wearing a yellow sweater emblazoned with a polar bear, looks out of the window at a snowy scene and imagines, in successive pictures, a bracingly arctic adventure: sliding down hills of snow with penguins, leaping from icefloe to icefloe, staring into the blazing polar sunset. 'And if ever I became too cold or wet, I would quickly turn back into a cat again.' The last words accompany a picture of the cat snuggled cosily under the yellow sweater on a chair. The illustrations show us, with fine iconic immediacy, how exhilarating daydreams and literary adventures may begin and end with the most comfortably mundane of materials – that yellow sweater with its polar bear decoration.

The tiny size of the book, the jewel-like decorations on the endpapers, the neat, safe frame around each illustration, all give this small story a dreamy inwardness that is perfect for the quiet, introspective child. Remember that every child in a family has different tastes and needs; my oldest daughter loved gentle books, and doted on the soft, impressionistic illustrations in Brian Wildsmith's *ABC*, while my youngest daughter craved bold excitement in her picture books.

Whose Mouse Are You? by Robert Kraus, with pictures by Jose Aruego, is one of my favourite books about sibling rage, precisely because it takes a sidelong approach to its subject without in the least pulling its punches. A vividly coloured, sparely drawn book, with cartoon-like figures filling up red and orange pages, it leaps straight into the action with the question 'Whose mouse are you?' asked by an unidentified voice-of-authority. 'Nobody's mouse,' answers the sulky little hero. 'Where is your mother?' 'Inside the cat.' And so goes the catechism, with each answer disposing of one more family member. The father is caught in a trap, the sister is far away on a mountain. The brother? 'I have none.'

This is the first clue that the story is about the mouse's rebellious tantrum over an imminent new baby in the family. Then comes the question: 'What will you do?' For answer, there's a completely blank page, a pause while both the mouse and the reader may consider what alternatives there are to getting along with a new sibling, particularly if you decide symbolically to annihilate the whole family and are left alone in the world. Then, with gathering momentum, the little mouse reverses the action. He shakes the mother out of the cat, rescues all his family, wishes for a baby brother, and when at last he is asked again *'Now* whose mouse are you?' he is ready, and happy, to acknowledge his whole family. Restitution has been made.

Whose Mouse Are You? shows the beauty of metaphor, humour and understatement in dealing with direct emotional conflict. With the rage comfortably projected onto the mouse (and eventually diffused, without a new baby ever being mentioned directly), the reader can put his own feelings into perspective. That, indeed, is one of the functions of art. More mechanically conceived preschool books, on the other hand, with their trite, treacly clichés about proper attitudes to new babies in the family, deny the child's true feelings and cannot possibly provide the consolation achieved here. Contrast that preachy condescension with, for example, the wit and tenderness of Jan Ormerod's *101 Things to Do with a Baby*, with its humorous pictorial acknowledgement of all the older sibling's feelings, from aggression to rivalry to love.

Books with strong emotional impact are sometimes all the better for being read aloud by a parent. Though *Whose Mouse Are You?* is ideal, at the mechanical level, for private reading by a beginner, it is emotionally perfect for a shared snuggle and read-aloud, when the participation of the parent is a tacit reassurance that the child's anger about a new sibling is recognized and accepted.

Other picture books are challenging enough for an accomplished reader to tackle alone, and yet are deeply satisfying to a reader at the age of six or seven if mediated by an adult. I'm thinking of the extraordinary series of six Homeric hymns, translated from the Greek poetry of the seventh century BC by Penelope Proddow, and illustrated by the gifted American artist Barbara Cooney, who went to Greece to soak up the light and colours that radiate through these retellings of the ancient hymns sung by wandering bards. I can't imagine a more electrifying introduction to the Greek myths than these six books, all of which, unforgivably, have been allowed to lapse out of print. They are timeless classics, and ought to be hunted down in libraries if they cannot be found in the book store.

The language of the books is strong, rhythmic, incantatory, and filled with Homer's imagery – a revelation for a child who may be more accustomed to the mumbled monosyllables and thin quackings of the television voice. 'Now I will sing of golden-haired Demeter,' begins the poet, in *Demeter and Persephone*, and you can practically see him strumming the first chords on his lyre in some long-vanished banquet hall. 'Demeter the awe-inspiring goddess, and her trim-ankled daughter, Persephone, who was frolicking on a grassy meadow.'

Calm and wise, with the strong profile of the classical period, Demeter in her deep-blue shawl gazes into the heart of a poppy. Behind her, fresh and innocent in diaphanous robes, Persephone plays with a butterfly. On the next page, we see Persephone with the daughters of Ocean, gathering spring flowers in a meadow above the blue Aegean. These opening pictures strike the reader with a thrill of freshness: not just the sunwashed clarity of the pure, lyrical colours; not just the lovely girls in gossamer, their arms full of flowers; not just the delicacy of the irises and violets wound around their tendrils of curls – but the whole vision of spring, and the startling depiction of female beauty without the customary sickly overlay of self-conscious sexiness.

Suddenly Persephone is abducted by the darkly handsome king of the underworld. While in Hades, she eats some of the crimson seeds of the pomegranate he strews around her. Demeter, meanwhile, ravages the earth in her grief-stricken loss. This, of course, is a myth of imperishable power. And this version of the story has great resonance because it includes so much: the many ambiguous names for the mysteriously attractive Hades, for example; provocative details like those ruby-red pomegranate seeds, and the futility of Demeter's attempt to fill up her loss by raising another woman's baby as an immortal.

Demeter and Persephone is almost irreplaceable in any collection for another reason, too: it is one of the very rare depictions in children's literature of strong love between mother and grown daughter. Our popular culture abounds in Edith Bunkers and Playmates and other shaming travesties of womanhood. But womanly dignity like Demeter's is so rare as to be almost shocking in its novelty. Juvenile literature is loud with the exploits of male heroes, and today there is a conscious effort to give equal roles to brave or athletic girls, but you would have to go far to find such a gripping portrait of female power and love as this one. It is an interpretation that is equally important for boys and girls, and is all the more potent for being so visually beautiful and unmarred by propagandist motive. The same series of books offers a parallel affirmation of a boy: *Hermes, Lord of the Robbers* is enchanting in the delicate wit and beauty of its illustrations and in its story of a boy leaping into manhood in a single day.

Before you read any of this series aloud to your child, read it to yourself to note some of the subtleties of the pictures. (See, for instance, how Hermes in his leafy wood-sandals is making the cows walk backward to deceive pursuers.) A book so far off the beaten track needs adult guidance. Your enthusiasm, your willingness to read with greater clarity and cadence than is usually called for, your pointing out details in the story will makes these superb examples of pictorial and verbal art even more memorable. They are worth the effort.

Naturally, most books for this age group won't have the scope or lyricism of Homeric hymns. But even at the most mundane level, picture books can illumine the themes of everyday life. Anyone who has ever watched the excitement of a six-year-old entrusted with an important grown-up task (helping to wash the car or fold laundry) will know how much satisfaction the child gains from making a real contribution to the family. In typical middle-class life, there are few real tasks left for a small child to perform. He may have no role to play other than that of a junior consumer of toys and cereals. With our labour-saving devices, and smaller families than in earlier years, we seem to require less and less from our children. Yet nothing is more undermining of self-worth than to feel useless and unneeded.

A much-loved picture book about a preschooler's push toward autonomy is Shirley Hughes's *Alfie Gets in First*. Alfie, coming home from shopping with his mum and baby sister, races ahead when Mum unlocks the front door and manages to lock himself inside, with the key, while Mum is locked helplessly outside. As the neighbours, the milkman and the window cleaner all rally around to help deal with the emergency, the pictures show us Alfie recovering from his frightened tears, bringing a chair, climbing up and turning the latch by himself. 'He opened the front door as wide as it would go and stood back grandly to let everybody in,' whereupon they all have a companionable cup of tea together. The story and its language are simple and straightforward; the real affirmation of Alfie's triumph comes from the lovingly naturalistic drawings. The houses, shrubs, rambling neighbourhood pets, the shopping basket and all the characters are sketched with the affectionate attention to detail, expressiveness and warm colour which are so characteristic of Hughes's work and which somehow combine to radiate a recognition and acceptance of child nature.

Frederick's Tales, a collection of Italian artist Leo Lionni's best stories, recently reissued in Britain in a handsome treasury, is a longtime favourite of North American preschoolers. Lionni's collages, in a blurred rainbow of colours, may seem fairly low key at first to adult eyes more accustomed to modern hard-edged brilliance and sophistication. But read them carefully, with a small child, and you will perceive how ingeniously these pictures body forth the workings of a child's imagination. In the charming 'Fish Is Fish', a fish tries to imagine the world of the land, and pictures to himself a comic array of people, birds and animals shaped like fish with legs. In 'Swimmy', a tiny black fish invents a way for all the small fry to explore the ocean's beauties and yet avoid being eaten. His happy solution is not only a message of adventure and co-operation, but a superb visual joke. Lionni's stories exert a continual attraction because of their gentle affirmation of children's resilience, growing comprehension and imaginative powers.

Herman the Helper by Robert Kraus, illustrated by Jose Aruego and Ariane Dewey with huge, almost fluorescently bright pictures, is a light-hearted testament to a child's need to be resourceful and self-reliant: Herman, a sprightly little octopus, dashes through the bright blue water, all eight tiny legs streaming neatly behind him as he rushes to the aid of friends and relatives.

Much of the humour lies in Herman's unflagging and kindly ingenuity, always shown in the pictures rather than mentioned in the text: he ties balloons to tired old turtles, for example, to help them swim, and darts into a glass bottle to help his uncle build a miniature ship. Not only does the child 'read' the pictures for much of the action, but he's lured into reading the good-humoured snippets of dialogue that are hand lettered onto the pictures, like the speech bubbles in comic strips.

That, of course, is one of the beauties of books that are most suited for beginning readers: they initiate the child into the art, not merely the mechanics, of reading. The jaunty bits of dialogue from the fishy characters in *Herman the Helper* ('Thanks, Herm!' they exclaim breezily) are written in a distinctly more speech-like tone of voice than the text of the story itself. It is a first experience in catching the feel of naturally written dialogue, and in hearing the shift in the author's tone. The gentle wordplay serves the same purpose: when the baby seahorses spin around on Herman's carousel, and their exclamations ('Whee!') come out upside down, the child is being invited to play with the possibilities and tricks of language. Herman has the very last joke in the book. At dinnertime, Herman's dad offers to help him to some mashed potatoes. 'No thanks,' Herman says, grinning. 'I'll help myself.'

Rosie's Walk by Pat Hutchins is famous for this same quality of a joke shared by author and reader. An adult reader is constantly engaged in the play of the author's mind and several levels of awareness are always at work: what the author knows, what the characters know, and what the reader perceives of both. A child who doesn't learn to read at these different levels simultaneously will miss most of the pleasures and rewards of literacy in adult life. And the process of understanding may begin early and naturally when a five-year-old child can see a whole plot being enacted in the pictures that is not even mentioned in the text. This is what happens in the story of Rosie, the hen. What the words tell us is that Rosie is going for a walk across the yard, around the pond, past the haystack and home in time for dinner. What we see in the pictures is a sly fox chasing Rosie across each double page, and coming to woeful, predictable grief every time he makes an ill-timed pounce. The deadpan slapstick of the action and the stylized bright red and yellow illustrations perfectly enhance the child's crowing delight in being an insider, in getting the joke shared with the author.

Even a wordless book can help the child in the first lessons of reading closely, noticing details, linking them together in sequence and holding them all together in the mind for lightning cross-references as the story progresses. *Moonlight* by Jan Ormerod is justly recognized for the charm of its realistic and touching watercolours depicting an evening in the life of a young, modern, middle-class family. The book begins with a family dinner scene that we 'read' horizontally from left to right: the mother looking informal and capable with her short cropped hair and casually crossed legs beneath the table; the four- or five-year-old daughter, relaxed and loved, glancing perkily up at her mother (and she really is a preschooler, as the litter of crumbs and dropped cutlery beneath her chair tell us); then the father, his curly beard and youthful face letting us know that he is gentle and playful.

The great skill of the narrative in *Moonlight* lies in the way the child reader must make the connections, though all the clues to the story are provided in correct sequence. On pages where four or five separate panels tell the story, they lead from left to right with continuing action, and sometimes the little girl even walks from one frame to another, leading the reader's eye visually and the mind temporally. When the child makes two little boats, from a melon rind and a triangle of orange peel, we are reminded that the food scraps and other makings (toothpicks, a fallen leaf, red paper napkins) have been in the pictures from the beginning. That's an example of the forward and backward cross-referencing I mentioned earlier. Incidentally, the fate of the little boats provides another strand in the continuing story. We see them being sailed in the bath, gradually coming apart, and then being abandoned as the action goes on.

Just as in older fiction, we must read motivation and character from the sequence of events. The father washes the dishes; where is mother? The question is left hanging, like a small subplot in a novel, until it becomes clear, a few pictures later, that she was in the bathroom running the bedtime bath for the little girl. The bathcap and the neatly hung roll of toilet paper become the tags that carry us to the next picture, where the once-tidy bathroom is strewn with the child's clothes, the toilet paper roll is on the floor (a clue to the unstated intervening action which the reader must infer) and the bathcap, just visible above the rim of the bath, tells us where the little girl is.

Action leads to consequence: not only is the child's bathtub play deliciously drawn, but the reader can anticipate what might come next when the bathcap drifts away, and the girl's hair gets more wet and bedraggled by the minute. When the mother comes back, her hands-on-hip stance clearly spells out her exasperation; the last frame of the bath sequence shows mother (whose face wears a 'Well, it's your own fault' expression) combing out the wet tangles, while the child squawks in protest.

The bedtime scene – its rituals, its tenderness, its fears – is just as sensitively narrated. In every frame, the reader is called upon to remember previous details, make connections, deduce causes and consequences and identify emotionally with the characters. Humour, surprise, comfort and family love are all there. All count on the reader's active imaginative involvement to make the story live. Without words, the drama of nuance and character are fully present: the father's amused affection, for example, and the mother's more down-to-earth personality, in which the child greatly resembles her. The beauty of *Moonlight* (and its companion volume, *Sunshine*) is that all this is drawn from the reader without any strain. The reader's work is unconscious, just as it is in an engrossing but complex adult work of fiction.

This is the priceless lesson of beginner books: how to read with an awakened imagination. The ABCs of reading, the mechanical mastery, are mere eye exercises compared to this. As long ago as 1880, Randolph Caldecott, the great illustrator, showed the way. His *Hey Diddle Diddle* is just an old familiar nursery ryhme, but the way Caldecott spun out its meaning is like a blueprint for the reader's inner eye. Nearly every phrase in the rhyme has its own full-page illustration, and these pictures show how the reader's imagination must work to bring the written text into abundant life. The phrase 'Hey diddle diddle', for example, introduces us to a children's party, with a cat as music master leading a dance. 'The cat' shows us a proud papa cat, stuffed into his best jacket before the admiring eyes of his demure wife and kittens. This scene, we realize, takes place just before the first party scene, and shows us the cat getting ready to perform. 'And the fiddle' is also a prior action; we see the fiddle left on a table by a timid music teacher; then we see the cat, having 'liberated' the instrument, fiddling maniacally on a garden wall while animals cavort, the cow nearly transported by the gaiety of the music. When the cow 'leaps over the moon', she is really kicking over the milk bucket, and her flying heels frame the new moon low on the horizon.

Best of all is the conception of the dish who elopes with the spoon. The demonic cat is fiddling so madly that ordinary objects are beside themselves; the vinegar cruet has sprouted breeches-clad legs and even the plates on the shelf kick their heels while a dish steals away with a simpering spoon. And even when the rhyme finishes, Caldecott's wit does not: an endpage shows the dish lying shattered on the ground while the other plates weep, and the errant spoon is marched off between a grimly upright fork and a stern knife.

The parent who reads aloud can help the child to notice these humorous details by taking time to speculate aloud about them. Otherwise, much of the complexity will simply be overlooked, especially by the modern child accustomed to the crude shapes and one-dimensional meanings of Disney books and Saturday cartoons.

I've tried to show, in some detail, how to 'read' the pictures because this is one of the primary goals in sharing a picture book with your child: to encourage the youngster to form detailed and coherent pictures in his own mind, rather than letting the words slip across the surface of his consciousness. Reading on his own, an older child will often be content to 'skip' descriptions and gulp down the plot, but if this habit of active imagining has been instilled early on, he may well go back over the book and gain twice as much from it at a more leisurely pace.

In selecting only a few picture books which have particular reading value for the beginner, I'm doing a conscious injustice to the whole field of picture-book art, which could well command an entire volume of its own. Today, there is such a profuse flowering of this form of children's literature that more and more adults have realized what a sophisticated resource it can be for the older reader, as well. Thousands of picture books have subtle and complex stories, with content geared to a higher level of maturity. Elaine Moss, a British writer who has worked to encourage reading among inner-city children, once described how she put challenging picture books on a top shelf in a library to signal the older children that the books were meant for them, not for the floor-level preschoolers. In the next chapter and in the Treasury, I've mentioned some examples that may prove particularly enticing to a reader who is not yet comfortable with densely printed text.

Picture books are a garden of delight for all age groups. Wisely chosen by parents, they can make an enormous difference in preparing the child to become the best kind of reader, the one who creates whole worlds of images in the mind, who is the author's active collaborator, questioner and fellow explorer.

Chapter 3

First novels

. . . to surrender to a novel is not necessarily weak, any more than falling in love is necessarily weak. That, too, involves not merely surrender but some long-term sinking of one's own consciousness in another person's. One of the symptoms of being in love, which does not mark any other form of love or lust, is that you want to hear everything the other person can or will tell you, not primarily for the information it may give you about life or even about the person concerned, but for the preciousness of seeing the world through his eyes – just as you see a world through the novelist's eyes, and want to hear everything he is prepared to tell you . . . With the novel, you might as well surrender wholly or not at all.

                      Brigid Brophy, The Novel as a Takeover Bid,
                                          Don't Never Forget, 1966

Y OUR CHILD CAN READ – and he can do it without too many agonizing hesitations, without the limping sing-song he used when he could only decipher letters rather than whole sentences full of meaning. Now he pauses only occasionally when he stumbles over a totally unfamiliar word. Most often, he can read right through the print on the page to the meaning beyond, as if he were looking through a clear stream to the coloured pebbles on the sandy bed. That first great barrier has been leaped. Now what?

This is a critical time. If the child has learned to read at four or five, not from internal passion but from parental prodding, the first glamorous glow of achievement may have worn off by the time he is seven or eight. In fact, in the new excitement of independence, reading for pleasure may be rejected along with the bottle and the blanket and other cherished objects of early childhood, particularly if reading has always been a mechanical process of decoding, and has never grown into a thoroughly assimilated skill. And if the child learns to read only when he reaches school age, silent reading may seem a pallid attraction indeed amidst the heady welter of distractions available to his age group. Television – action dramas and sports – may become an important topic of conversation in the peer group, especially among boys; video games, two-wheeled bicycles, active street play, organized sports teams and activities like Scouting all offer the allure of peer group acceptance and new bases of friendship. Ironically, just when a child's decoding skills are good enough for him to begin reading novels, all his motivation to read may evaporate overnight.

Unless there is an active effort by the parent to establish reading as a prime source of pleasure, it is more than likely that, at this age, boys especially will fall by the wayside as readers of books. Most book-world professionals and many classroom teachers acknowledge that boys read for entertainment far less than girls do, and experience more mechanical difficulties in reading. Boys may also develop reading proficiency later than girls because of a difference in brain development. Or it may be that girls read more because, even now, they have less opportunity, and less pressure, to excel in athletics. In any case, girls seem to have more time and more motivation to escape into books, and it is probably at this early primary school age that the patterns are formed which make women the primary readers and buyers of literature.

Pleasure is the word to remember. You may be eager to encourage your child to read, but unless you can find ways to do it through subtle encouragement rather than pressure, it might be better to leave well enough alone. At this age, more than any other, it is useful for you to be familiar with the most interesting books available. But remember, a new reader does not automatically fall with cries of ecstasy on a shiny new stack of books offered by the parent; you can make the difference by your unfeigned enthusiasm for a book or a poem.

Don't give up reading aloud. Just because a youngster can now plough through a school reader (and, by the way, there are few stronger deterrents to reading pleasure than a school reader), it doesn't mean that read-aloud times at home should come to an end. It does take ingenuity to find the right time in your own family's life to share stories. You can take a new book on a family picnic, to the doctor's surgery to while away the time (don't rely on the tattered cast-offs too often found on the waiting-room table) or to the supermarket to beat the checkout-queue doldrums. Don't worry about funny looks from bystanders. They'll just be straining to hear the story themselves.

You will, certainly, be wrestling with the habits of our culture, in which electronic amusement accompanies the child everywhere and effectively closes out all other forms of human discourse. I remember the folk-song marathons our children invented to pass the time on long car trips; the singing was started by their father, longing for some peace while at the wheel, and his animated renditions were eagerly imitated by the back-seat crew. If our car radio had worked more efficiently, the children may never have developed the repertoire that enabled them to sing from the beginning to the end of a two-hundred-mile trip, with no repeats.

Boredom is a great resource. Trap your children at a cottage without television, and watch them rediscover arts and crafts, swimming, games and reading. Refuse their requests for computerized games, and watch them fall back on other wellsprings of invention. The intrinsic fidgety fascination of the machines will easily drive out other interests the way house sparrows drove out the bluebirds. The child who reaches teenage years as a computer whizz kid, but who never had the chance to become a reader in early childhood, probably never will.

What are the right books, then, to lure early readers into the 'falling in love' experience of fiction reading? The child opening her first novel may be as young as six or seven or as old as eight or nine; obviously, first novels will have a wide range of difficulty. They should be long enough to yield the true rewards of the novel: sustained involvement with unfolding characters, and the detailed re-creation of another world in which the reader can live and move. Yet if they bog down in detail at the expense of story, they may daunt the young child.

Simplicity is one attraction of the 'lowest common denominator' books, like Enid Blyton's *Noddy* series or spin-offs from popular films like *Star Wars*. I can remember racing through all of *The Bobbsey Twins*, the impossibly saccharine *Five Little Peppers and How They Grew*, and even the complete *Twin* series, including, most memorably, *The Eskimo Twins* and *The Japanese Twins*. All those series were commercial, badly written, thinly plotted – and devoured by my generation for the exhilaration of being able to read and the easy diversion of their simple, predictable plots and undemanding characters.

Today's less condescending authors (and more sophisticated beginning readers) have created a new genre of first novels. Detective adventures, for example, are intensely appealing to the child who is gaining confidence by deciphering and mastering clues to puzzles about the larger world. *It's Too Frightening for Me!*, by the English writer and artist Shirley Hughes, is a brisk and exciting story (with just the right amount of scariness) about two brothers, Jim and Arthur, who explore a menacing haunted house. The pale 'ghost' they see in a window turns out to be Mary, the lonely granddaughter of the housekeeper.

After some genuinely spooky encounters, the three children become friends, unmask a nasty impostor who lays claim to the house, and help to solve happily the difficulties with which Mary and her impoverished granny are struggling. The true glory of the book for beginning readers is the pen-and-ink drawing by Hughes. The illustrations, circling or interrupting or complementing the text, enlarge the mood of the story, intensify its atmosphere, add energy to its humour and give a warmly personal impression of the characters. The pictures also pique reading interest with brief speech balloons, signs and exclamations – a neat blending of comic-strip and narrative techniques.

Like those earlier, popular easy books of an earlier era, Hughes's book is also, in its way, a family story. And young readers today, whatever their surface sophistication – however much they know from television about alcoholism, divorce or anorexia nervosa – still love and need those stories that breathe an atmosphere of safety, warmth and family solidarity. It is true that older children, ready to confront painful realities, may want to read about the darker undertones of traditional family life. But that comes later. Despair and cynicism are utterly inappropriate for eight-year-olds; no matter what their life circumstances, the earliest readers yearn for stories about the loved and accepted child who moves in a secure world. Though curiosity is at a peak, introspection is not: action, comedy or adventure, in real or imagined worlds, is far more alluring than the tortured problem novels that are considered so attractive for prepubescents.

Simplicity and extroversion, however, are not synonyms for poverty of character and skimpiness of plot. The richer the stories are in truth and feeling, the more satisfying they will be to the reader.

Having said all that, I admit that you may laugh to find here, under the rubric of 'First Novels', the popular *Burglar Bill*, by the prolific British writers Janet and Allan Ahlberg. After all, you may say, it's funny, it's charming, but it's only a slight picture book. The more I looked at it, though, the more it struck me that this enduring, small-sized picture book has all the essential elements of a satisfying novel: adult characters, developing relationships, dramatic irony, suspense, climax and resolution.

Burglar Bill is a relatively affable criminal who 'goes to work, stealing things' each night after a cosy supper of stolen fish and chips and stolen tea. The rosy pictures on each page invite the reader to laugh at Bill's incongruous domesticity: the picture on the wall, for example, is a police mug shot of Bill himself, and his snug surroundings betray themselves (and Bill's ineptitude) with their labels: a useless box of six dozen stolen hair nets, a pitchfork with its price tag still attached, a teddy bear propped beside Bill's slippers.

One night, Bill's haul includes a box with holes in its lid. It turns out to contain a baby (or, as Bill exclaims, 'A orphan!'). Bill good-naturedly sets about interpreting its cries, feeding it beans, changing its nappy and amusing it to the best of his ability. 'Say "Run for it" if you see anybody,' Bill tells the baby, when he takes it for a nocturnal stroll in the park. 'Runfrit,' the baby replies. Then Bill himself is burgled, by none other than Burglar Betty, who turns out to be the mother of the orphan. The two not only marry, but vow to return all the stolen goods to the rightful owners and begin a new and virtuous career in the bakery business.

Underneath the agreeable send-up of criminal life, there's a reassuring decency. I suspect that part of this book's strong attraction for young boys is Bill's clumsy but jovial paternal warmth toward the baby, the comforting theme of transgression and restitution, and the jauntily unsentimental depiction of family solidarity at the finale.

More developed as novels, but equally well suited to the beginning reader, are *Hello, Aurora!* and *Aurora and the Little Blue Car* by Ann-Cath. Vestly. These stories may have seemed gently radical in the 1960s, when they were first written in socially progressive Norway: preschooler Aurora and her newborn brother, Socrates, are being brought up by one of literature's first and most endearing househusbands. Aurora's father, Edward, is a doctoral student in classics and history who cooks, bakes and does laundry while mother works full time as a legal secretary. If *Aurora* sounds like a feminist fable with about as much aesthetic appeal as poached parsnips, then my synopsis does an injustice to the sweetness and individuality of tone in this series.

The story is told from Aurora's viewpoint, no easy feat when the heroine is at most five years old. Yet without condescension, and with an uncanny feeling for the indirect way in which preschoolers often communicate their most intense anxieties, Vestly makes the reader feel the lively affection of a close family and the sensitivity with which the parents respond to each other and to their children. Particularly satisfying to the reader is the way in which the sturdily practical Aurora, with her sharp powers of observation and memory, helps her befuddled father to cope with supermarket protocol, driving lessons or ruined laundry. Father's competence with the baby and his authority as a caring adult are not questioned; the shrewd balance of skill between Aurora and her father is one of this book's strongest assets, along with its tolerant and gentle humour.

It is always a trap to judge a book by its worthy content (that way lies the Sunday-school tract), but when a novel with a 'relevant' theme has ample and well-selected detail, when its characters are drawn with enough depth to seem to have a complex life of their own, and when the density of human experience is felt through prose simple enough for a seven-year-old, we can be fairly sure that the book rises above mere contemporaneity. Aurora and her family have that kind of individuality; Aurora herself is an appealingly brave, vulnerable, natural child, light years away from the smart-aleck, knowingly urbane kid who haunts the sterile prose of many American mass-market books.

The seven-year-old child, reading about Aurora's snide neighbours who disapprove of working mothers, will almost certainly recognize the feeling of those first piercing revelations that outsiders may be critical of one's family values or style. The surprised hurt of this, the first doubts and perplexities about what always seemed inevitable and immutable, are perfectly mirrored in Aurora's stubborn, wounded defensiveness. And the way her parents deal with Aurora's worry is realistic, simple and comforting.

Kit in Boots has all of this – a lively family portrait, perspicacity, humour – and more: brilliantly polished prose by one of Britain's most dazzling writers, Jane Gardam. In this, one of the best 'first novels' I've ever read, a complex, rich and funny story is told with such wit and restraint that the adult reading it aloud (or swiping it from a child's bedside table) will enjoy it every bit as keenly as the seven- or eight-year-old for whom it is meant.

Kit is six when a London artist first arrives unannounced to camp in a pasture on the family's Yorkshire farm. Father, roaring and stubborn as a bull, wants to chase away the 'vagrant' while Kit is filled with curiosity and excitement about his quiet presence, his 'clever-looking' hands and the smell of his oil paints. Somehow, Father is reconciled to the artist camping there. He returns every summer, and begins to teach Kit how to draw. Through her conversations with him, we see her dawning attraction to another way of life. 'My father says only muscle work counts,' she tells him. 'Different sets of muscles,' he answers, 'for different things.'

The family, baffled by his asceticism, dubs him 'Lonesome Jones' and pities his apparent destitution. 'See to it he has eggs and butter and milk,' Kit's father tells Mother. 'There's some terrible poverty in this world. Yet he's a proud man. He keeps himself clean as any of us.' The book is filled with wonderfully self-revelatory dialogue like this; how clearly and completely we understand both father's good-heartedness and his parochial point of view. All the characters, in fact, are immediately alive and themselves in every word they speak. Their relationships to each other, and their deepest private feelings, are palpable in their most casual utterances.

The suspense of the story lies in whether Kit will be able to get to London to be a bridesmaid for 'Lonesome Jones'. The climactic scene, when she and Father do get to the wedding, and, furthermore, see themselves immortalized in the artist's paintings in a London gallery, sparkles with the intensity of a rural child's first impressions of the big city. But Kit is no passive subject; throughout this brief, wholly engaging story, we see this shrewd, outgoing, confident child change and grow – and her father changes, too. His new understanding of an artist's work ends the book on an optimistic, forward-looking note.

Though few other beginner novels glow with an equal literary radiance, some can be just as compelling through the sheer force of the author's conviction. Comfort, highlighted by danger and challenge, is the hallmark of one American family story that deserves to be snatched back from the jaws of television. *The Little House on the Prairie* television series did a disservice to the extremely popular series of books on which it was loosely based. For one thing, Pa – the rosy, robust, blackly bearded giant in the books – was damped down into the smarmy, close-shaven Michael Landon, a psychologizing 1970s dad who was untrue, physically and emotionally, in every detail, to the original story. Landon might have been *nice*, but that's not the point; the viewer of the series gets a transposed, pioneer-costume soap opera that is contemporary in tone and values, and misses the discovery of real frontier life in all its rigour and sensuous immediacy.

Children should be given the chance to read the stories before their mental image of the characters is spoiled for ever by Hollywood's pallid imitation. (Librarians sometimes argue, correctly, I'm sure, that many children are stimulated to read a given book because it has been televised. But I wonder if that works both ways – I know a good many children who can't be bothered to read a book if they've already seen it on TV.)

The Little House in the Big Woods, the first book in the autobiographical ten-volume series by pioneer Laura Ingalls Wilder, is perfect for the beginning novel reader. A large-print paperback with affectionately detailed drawings by Garth Williams, it's a book as deeply engaging to boys as to girls. (In Chapter Ten, you'll find a more detailed discussion of boys' books and girls' books, and the dangers of restricting a child's range of empathy on the basis of gender.)

The family of the Little House books, living in the great woods of Wisconsin, is all action and resourcefulness. From the first page, the reader is caught up in the family's thrilling, challenging isolation. Wolves howl outside, the snow drifts up to the windows, but inside is safety and purpose: Pa makes lead bullets by the fire with his two young daughters to help him, while Ma grates a carrot into the pale winter milk to colour it yellow.

So absorbing are these physical details of pioneer life that two university students recently told me with nostalgic delight how they read the books at ages six and seven, and could still remember the way Pa smoked the deer meat in a hollow log, and the fragrance of the hickory chips with which Laura fuelled the fire.

Pa, not incidentally, is an attractive male figure with whom small boys rejoice to associate. Not only does he play boisterous games with his little girls but he's also a skilled huntsman and protector, a stern but just father and a merry fiddle player. And any child, male or female, can identify with Laura's realistic fears, and the courage she derives from the solid mutual support of the family.

Family stories have petered out in recent years. Modern authors can't seem to help but inject a note of chaos, despair or bleak cynicism into their account of the modern nuclear family. (Perhaps that word 'nuclear' is a tip-off to the source of disenchantment.) But young children are disturbed enough by the intimations of family doom they hear all around them. The enduring popularity of family stories written as far back as the 1930s, like the imperishable *Moffats*, by Eleanor Estes, or the 1950s, like *Henry Huggins* by Beverly Cleary, shows us how much children still want to live, imaginatively, in a world where family love is the unquestioned basis of existence.

'Letters reveal that children want to love and be loved by two parents in a united family,' author Cleary said when accepting the 1984 Newbery Medal (the highest American award for children's literature, given by the American Library Association) for her book *Dear Mr Henshaw*. Cleary is an earthy and pragmatic author who, as a children's librarian in the 1940s, sympathized with the non-readers who wanted books they could understand, 'books in which they do not get lost in the first chapter and can't tell what the author is talking about'.

Henry Huggins, published in 1950, was her response to this need, and teachers tell me that the book is just as popular as ever with beginning novel readers, despite its dated view of small-town life and narrow gender stereotypes. In a kindly universe, Henry struggles with the small dilemmas of childhood: how is he to get home on the bus, on which no pets are allowed, with his starved foundling puppy in a paper bag that threatens to burst open? How might he replace another boy's deliciously new football which Henry has – O horrors! – accidentally thrown into the open window of a passing car?

The familiar settings and the guileless, uncomplicated humour of untoward incident, is very much in the mode of what attracts British children to Michael Bond's *Paddington Bear* series. Henry's scrapes are precipitated by his excesses of thoughtless boyishness; Paddington's, equally innocent, cause merriment because he continually violates British decorum with his impulsivity and sloppiness. Both series are loved for their undemanding, episodic plots and childlike humour.

Even more popular than Henry Huggins is Beverly Cleary's more sharply drawn character, Ramona Quimby. There's more bite, more surprise, in this series of books about another middle-American family, probably because Ramona is a much more original character than Henry. Ramona is a force of nature: a ferociously determined, imaginative, energetic tyke of four when we first meet her, in *Beezus and Ramona*, driving her nine-year-old sister mad by riding round and round the living room on her tricycle, breathing in and out on the same two repeated notes on the harmonica. Clear, unaffected, with a sharp ear for naturalistic dialogue and a shrewd though forgiving eye for children's secret motivation, Cleary manages to be realistic and accepting at the same time. Her descriptions of Ramona's violent temper tantrum in *Ramona and Her Mother* is one of the best I've read – from the inside out – of a child's torrential rage, self-pity, guilt and egotism in the midst of a lie-on-the-bed-and-kick-the-wall outburst. It has just enough distance in it to enable a child to see herself with a rueful eye, even while she revels in the reconciliation with mother at the end of the book.

An even more sensitive and evocative writer for the same age group is Eleanor Estes. Her story, *The Hundred Dresses* (discussed in another context in Chapter Ten), dates from World War II, and, like Henry Huggins and the Ramona books, is set in small-town America, where the two-parent family is rarely questioned and school is strict but kind. It still reads swiftly, delicately and hauntingly. More tautly organized and pointed than the Cleary books, it tells of a troubling incident in the lives of two young schoolgirls.

Maddie, the central character, can't help but join in when her friend Peggy, the prettiest and most popular girl in class, begins to tease the awkward, shabby Wanda Petrowski. (Fredelle Maynard, the Canadian writer, tells of a similar incident of schoolgirl racism in *Raisins and Almonds*, her memoir of a prairie girlhood. In a phrase I've never forgotten, she recalls her troubled conscience as 'a needle of glass that pierced my heart'.)

Maddie is not spared that 'needle of glass'; later, when the damage has been done, when Wanda has moved away, and it is too late for reparations, Maddie wonders 'if she were going to be unhappy about Wanda . . . forever'. The muted, bittersweet ending is not too difficult for child readers to bear; it may arouse in them a recognition that they are not the only ones to have indulged in cruelty, and that an uneasy conscience is both their punishment and their guide to a solution.

Gentle, impressionistic watercolours by Louis Slobodkin decorate the chapter headings and the edges of the page; their effect is so unobtrusive as to be almost subliminal – perfect for this age group, for whom the printed word takes precedence over the picture; and perfect for this story, too, because they evoke the ambiguous quality of happy schooldays – bright autumns, tingling evergreen-scented Christmases, and a melancholy tinge of wronged innocence.

The excellence of *The Hundred Dresses* is reflected in its language. Estes uses imagery that is perfectly suited to the early reader. On the bleak and remorse-haunted autumn day when the two girls trudge in the rain to Wanda's shack to make amends, they find that the family has moved away: 'Wisps of old grass stuck up here and there along the pathway like thin wet kittens.'

Richness of language is always a clue to excellence, for the beginning reader as for any other age group. Of course, 'richness' does not always refer to imagery, and never to mere ornateness.

Fred by British author Posy Simmonds is a funny story in adapted comic-strip form. Sophie and Nick are sad because their family's cat, Fred, has died. 'Fat old Fred. He was the laziest cat in the world,' they remember affectionately. But late that night, awakened by caterwauling in the garden, they discover that Fred was famous in the feline world. He was the lead singer in the rock group 'The Heavy Saucers', and an elaborate funeral is under way.

Simmonds's humour depends in part on linguistic irony. When Sophie and Nick go outside, they find their neighbour's cat Ginger in formal mourning clothes (and a digital watch). They address him in the normal way: 'Pussy wussy! Nice pussy!' Ginger rears back and says: 'I *beg* your pardon! Are you friends of our dear departed?'

Throughout the story, the cats use language and imagery appropriate to their world, while much humour derives from the children's persisting in use of an inappropriately human vocabulary. Nuances like these may seem minor, but learning to catch them is an important step in literacy.

Few authors lavish more expressive, demanding language on their child readers than the American author-illustrator William Steig. In themes and narrative suggestiveness, his picture books really qualify as first novels. The format of *The Amazing Bone*, for example – with its lyrical, impressionistic and colour-drenched paintings – is that of the traditional picture book, but its language is extraordinarily exuberant and varied, and the plot touches on themes of deep interest to the older child.

Pearl is a young pig who loiters in the springtime woods on her way home from school. The world dazzles with its colours:

> *The warm air touched her so tenderly she could almost feel herself changing into a flower. Her light dress felt like petals. 'I love everything,' she heard herself say. 'So do I,' answered a voice.*

A bone (what a strange object for Steig to choose – one whose symbolism, perhaps, doesn't bear too much thought) is lying in the grass and speaking to Pearl. And, as is characteristic of Steig's energetic, overflowing delight in words, the bone speaks several languages, indulges in flights of rhetoric by turns courtly and gleeful, and, in a magical incantation designed to rescue Pearl from a foxy kidnapper, voices some of the most inspired gibberish I've ever read.

On a hidden level, the story seems to be about romantic love and marriage. It disappoints me that one of the only two books the brilliant Steig has written with a female central character (the other is *Brave Irene*) presents her as a passively rescued and enraptured 'princess'. But Pearl's generous soul and poetic sensibility make her something more individual than the standard rescuee.

It's not surprising, either, that a book with such strong appeal to young children elliptically portrays a romantic match, ending with the bone being accepted and loved by Pearl's parents, sharing Pearl's bed every night, and making 'beautiful music'. For though the family story is a tremendous source of affirmation and reassurance to young readers, every child also longs to try out, in fantasy or in fiction, the pleasures of adult autonomy. (See Steig's magnificent *Caleb and Kate* for a fablelike tale of love, anger and reconciliation in marriage.)

For some of the same reasons, as the English author Joan Aiken has wittily said, there is hardly a child alive who doesn't like to fancy himself or herself as an orphan. The orphan, after all, can savour the joys or terrors of independence without feeling guilty toward a hindering parent. This first-novel group includes many rewarding independence fantasies. The time-honoured resource is the fairy tale, and age seven or eight is certainly the right time for these often frightening but also profoundly reassuring tales of children (youngest sons, youngest daughters) struggling to overcome enchantments, evil parents or monsters.

Of modern orphan fables for this age group, *Goldie the Dollmaker* by M. B. Goffstein is one of the most touching, strange and enduring. Goffstein's astonishing line drawings, wiry and spare, yet as distinctly individual as a signature, greatly enhance the fairy-tale feel of the story: they are universal, yet intensely particular.

Goldie lives alone in a forest, in her parents' little house, carrying on the dollmaking work they did when they were alive. In her babushka and wooden clogs, she looks as unassuming as a peasant; in her quiet routines of sleep, carving, painting and carrying the finished dolls to town, we sense the self-contained artist. Note the process by which Goldie paints her dolls' faces. She paints

> *. . . a little gleaming black eye on either side of the doll's nose and finally, holding it firmly around the waist with one hand, Goldie smiled and smiled into the doll's eyes in the friendliest, sweetest way, and she painted a smile right back to herself on the little doll's face . . . They said that if you looked at a Goldie Rosenzweig doll you bought her, even if you weren't going to buy any doll in the first place. Because the truth about that smile was that it was heartbreaking.*

Goldie is crushed when her friend Omus laughs at her dedication. But she is strengthened, in a luminous dream, by the universal fellowship of artists. She has just bought a ravishingly beautiful Chinese lamp, splurging a whole month's wages on it. In her dream, the maker of the lamp comes to her, showing her why she works as she does, and why the lonely life of the artist is finally worthwhile. In an understated, satisfying ending, Goldie looks around the softly lit room where she works, and she knows that it is her house, her tools, her work, that give her life meaning.

The well-loved Tim stories by Edward Ardizzone feature what might be called a 'pseudo-orphan', since Tim's parents stay well in the background and seem to accept his fantastically daring adventures with benign resignation. Ardizzone's illustrations are his glory: quick, sketchy, intimate, they are always gratifyingly detailed when it comes to things nautical, and satisfyingly vague about the faces of the young heroes – a perfect screen, as Ardizzone himself says, for the projections of the daydreaming young readers.

Fairy tales, the original orphan stories (told in 'a tone licked clean over the centuries by mild old tongues, grandam to cub, serene, anonymous,' as the distinguished American poet James Merrill says), still seize the young imagination. They combine a yearning for freedom, the urge to test oneself against adult realities, the terror of being left alone and helpless, and the itch to know who one might become if loosed from family bonds. Since children's literature serves in part to provide dream answers to these unspoken questions, the most popular and esteemed children's books have often placed children in at least a quasi-orphan role, with parents absent, distracted or otherwise rendered harmless. It's something of a cheat, in determinedly contemporary books, to discover that young people no longer enjoy this immunity from the burden of adults. Supposedly in the name of realism, prepubescents in today's novels often have to struggle with malign, inadequate or hurtful parent figures who are the focus for the child's disillusionment or bitterness. The child becomes the victim, preoccupied with oppressors, rather than an adventurer striking out on his or her own, filled with excitement, fear and resolution at the beginning of a new life.

That 'realism' of many modern novels, in any case, is like the realism of televised soap opera: despite the studied banality of the dialogue, the painstakingly reconstructed living rooms of the middle-class, and the surface resemblance to things in the real world, the naturalism of the American soap opera, at least (British soaps are better acted and less rigidly middle-class), is instantly identifiable as fake. The reason, I think, that the speech and plots of soap opera fall so flat on our ears (you could recognize that fake-real speech pattern as soap operatic if you heard it in the middle of a sandstorm in the Gobi desert) is that there is no 'real' in the realism: there is no person under the screen personality, no character under the mannerisms, no tangled junk in the kitchen drawers on the set, no underlayer of perception or resonance of lived lives in the clichés exchanged by the characters.

So it is all the more distressing to read, in a newspaper article about a group of Canadian children at a theatre school, that the eight-year-olds scorn fairy tales, and express an interest in 'more realistic stories'. You just know that when these precocious urban youngsters talk of realism, they mean TV realism, with its clutter of life-mimicking details. A TV drama about child abuse, with its blatant manipulation and control of the viewers' emotions, is more 'realistic' to them (more familiar, perhaps, and undemanding?) than the surrealistic horror of a fairy tale like 'The Juniper Tree'. Yet an important dimension of human feeling, and an artistically valuable literary form, has been abandoned.

Alert parents will want to make sure that every child – particularly the one beginning school and a new life of literacy – will have access to the more invigorating sort of stories, the adventurous and imaginative rather than the reductively realistic: stories in which children go past their parents rather than remaining morbidly preoccupied with them.

The 'wish to be an orphan' is in part a wish for joyful anarchy, and the quintessential orphan of modern fiction is surely Pippi Longstocking, the nine-year-old girl who lives alone, climbs on the furniture and scrubs floors by tying brushes on to her shoes . . . though not always before rolling out her biscuit dough on the linoleum. I have noticed that children's eyes light up when they remember reading Astrid Lindgren's Pippi books: the playful wish fulfilment is so strong that the glee lingers on in memory.

Pippi is the strongest girl in the world; her mother is an angel in heaven (far more liberating, as any Victorian daughter could have testified, than an Angel in the House) and her father is a marooned Cannibal King on a desert island. She lives in her own secluded house with a horse on the porch, a monkey called Mr Nilsson and a suitcase full of gold coins. Pippi's marvellously breezy style ('So long, boys,' she says to the sailors who have brought her home after her father was lost at sea) is a bracing antidote to the sentimentality with which children's vulnerability is so often treated. Leaving the sailors, she strides into her new life without looking back . . . and it's clear that her physical strength is a metaphor for her emotional indomitability.

But Pippi offers more than just a fantasy of omnipotence. Even more wonderful than her physical power is the freeing imagination she brings to play with the rather conventional and stereotyped children who live next door. Pippi is a Namer; she delights in explosively expansive language ('My name is Pippilotta Delicatessa Windowshade Mackrelmint Efraim's Daughter Longstocking, daughter of Captain Efraim Longstocking, formerly the Terror of the Sea, now a cannibal king'), linguistic ridicule ('I have got along without any pluttifikation tables for nine years,' she says in a dreary maths class) and the creation of magic through words. One of her favourite games is finding things: an old rusty can becomes 'a delightful Jar with Cookies' if you put cookies in it, or 'Jar without Cookies' if you don't.

There is an enriching dimension of poignancy to the Pippi story. Headstrong Pippi, in her wilful defiance of convention, does not have it all her way. She may sabotage her neighbour's well-meaning tea party by her unrestrained greed and her *reductio ad absurdum* of adult chit-chat, but there is a price to pay for anarchy. Pippi is left out in the cold, socially and at school.

Not too much is made of Pippi's isolation. The tone of the story, after all, is not emotional realism but liberating tomfoolery. Nevertheless, this slight shading of the book's high spirits tends to deepen its colour and integrity. To see how fresh, how inspiriting a book *Pippi Longstocking* is, compare it to any one of a thousand mass-circulation books for young children in which wayward choo-choo trains or discontented flowers who want to be butterflies finally learn to accept their fate and buckle under to conformity. Pippi never buckles; she may wilt momentarily in the cold draught of society's disapproval, but, more characteristically, she bounces away to a new, ever more outrageously naïve plan of adventure.

For some strange reason, fantasies that feature boys in this age group most often weave themselves around themes, not of power and anarchy, but of deep intimate relationships with the unattainable other. Or perhaps the reason is not so mysterious: fantasies give the child what is most keenly missing in real life. And still, even now, girls miss courage, autonomy, and the chance to be tested on grounds of intelligence and moral strength, rather than mere prettiness. And boys miss intimacy, physical and emotional, which girls can still receive nonchalantly from their mothers and teachers, but which boys seek or accept only at peril of their manly reputations and self-image.

Significantly, the boys in these fantasies long for closeness not with a female figure (though there are rare exceptions, like the boy in *The Midnight Fox*) but with a male, usually an animal, a robot or an imaginary hero. What boys dream of, to judge by their chosen fantasies, is the warmth and acceptance of a loving, all-powerful father without the competitiveness, the authoritarianism and the harsh judging to which so many fathers are prone. In some versions, it is not the real-life father who is rejecting or inadequate, but society, in the guise of school authorities.

Wingman, by Daniel Manus Pinkwater, seems to me to rank among the most beautiful and satisfying of all these fantasies, all the more remarkable because it uses a terse contemporary idiom and comic book conventions to create a story rare in its empathy. 'At school he was Donald Chen, but at home he was Chen Chi-Wing or Ah-Wing,' we are told. Donald is the poorest kid in his class in a run-down New York neighbourhood; he lives with his father and sister in two crowded rooms behind his father's laundry.

Sparely and swiftly, with a few vivid details, Pinkwater evokes for us the whole texture of Donald's life. The illustrations are just as selective and as forcefully modern, thick black magic-marker drawings that resemble a cross between Superman and a Roy Lichtenstein. Each full-page illustration is divided into four comic-like panels, but the pictures themselves use cinematic zoom and close-up techniques. On the first full page, we are offered a series of symbols that give us essential clues to the important things in Donald's life: his father's face, an iron, a stack of comic books (Donald's most precious possession – he has 2000 of them) and a middle-distance view of Donald's father, standing with his arm affectionately around Donald's shoulders while the boy reads a comic.

One of the great pleasures of Pinkwater is the way he can write obliquely, but with complete clarity of meaning. When he tells us that Donald goes to school every day, even in the coldest weather, without a coat but with a fresh white shirt, we know two things without being told: that his father anxiously looks after him in the only ways available to him (the clean white shirt is lovingly washed and ironed, of course, by the exhausted father), and that Donald is impervious to cold because he is numb with misery. Where lesser authors might have hammered home these perceptions in flat declarative sentences, a true writer of fiction like Pinkwater tells us all by telling us practically nothing and letting it reverberate.

Reading about Captain Marvel and Hawkman helps Donald 'not to worry about things, like being thrown out by the landlord'. Rarely has children's escape reading had a more succint or sympathetic defence. When Donald is driven to truancy by an inexcusably obtuse and clumsy teacher, he takes refuge by climbing the giddy heights of New York's George Washington Bridge, where he crouches on a beam and daydreams away the hours surrounded by the rumble of cars overhead, the flurry of seagulls and his stacks of comic books.

The arrival of Wingman, a Chinese superhero, is a masterful blend of fantasy and acute observation: just as pigeons seem to take flight the moment Donald turns his head to look at them boldly, Wingman vanishes when stared at too directly. So Donald learns to discipline his eagerness. He learns that only when he sinks himself into his comics, losing all self-awareness, is he granted a sight of Wingman landing on the beam beside him. With pounding heart, he steals sidelong glimpses of his feather-caped hero.

Later, Donald has another lesson in vision, when a new, more humane teacher takes his class to the Metropolitan Museum of Art on its first field trip. By now, Donald has surged ahead in confidence because of his incredible journeys with Wingman, and his triumphs in teaching the class to read through comic books. When the class sees its first Chinese paintings 'full of mist and space', they fall silent 'not because it was scary like the Egyptian tomb stuff, but because there was something about these pictures that was like a little bird perched on your finger'. Donald, already self-taught in coaxing an elusive bird to reveal itself to him, stays alone with the picture until it comes alive for him. This passage is one of the simplest and most affecting descriptions I've found in children's literature about the self-forgetfulness you must bring to art, and the transcendence with which you may be rewarded.

The Iron Man is better known than *Wingman*, perhaps because of its author, Poet Laureate Ted Hughes, or perhaps because its language is so grippingly intense that teachers have found it a never-fail magnet for the attention of even the most fidgety eight-year-old boy.

The Iron Man came to the top of the cliff.
How far had he walked? Nobody knows. Where had he come
from? Nobody knows. How was he made? Nobody knows.

Hughes's language is as polished, spare and powerful as that of the best poetry; the rhythms, repetition and assonance are enough to assure our rapt attention. Read it aloud and see how the vowel patterns alone force you to speak it at a measured, emphatic pace, full of the immense, ponderous menace of the Iron Man himself. Note the startling simplicity of the images – 'his great iron head, shaped like a dustbin but as big as a bedroom'. Hughes does not forget that his book is 'A Story in Five Nights', a bedtime story, and the images ('a foot as big as a single bed') are arrowed straight at the child sitting bolt upright in bed, listening.

Hughes's verbal pyrotechnics, in fact, are a wonderful introduction to the ways in which a reader must create mental images in order to create the novel. He sets the words out on the page in patterns that force us to pause, to hear silences, echoes and meanings. He sets the scene so carefully that only a spectacularly lazy reader would not be compelled to see the rocky beach, hear the sound of the sea 'chewing away at the edge', 'boiling and booming' while the stars wheel overhead, or see the dawn when the darkness 'grew blue and the shapes of the rocks separated from each other'.

The Iron Man has crashed over the edge of the cliff, flying into dozens of separate pieces: 'Only one of the iron hands, lying beside an old, sand-logged washed-up seaman's boot, waved its fingers for a minute, like a crab on its back. Then it lay still.' The ghoulish scene in which the hand scuttles about, finding the other parts and reassembling them, is brought to a stunning climax when the Iron Man, whole again, red eyes blazing, walks into the sea – deeper, deeper, deeper – until the waves have covered him and 'the gulls circled low over the line of bubbles that went on moving slowly out into the deep sea'.

Of course, it is a young boy, named Hogarth, who becomes the intermediary when the Iron Man returns and terrorizes the neighbourhood. It is Hogarth who dares to ask the Iron Man what he wants – leading to the happy scene in which the monster at last retires to a scrap-metal dump, content to gobble old rusty chains (better than any spaghetti), his 'eyes crackling with joy' as he licks the delicious crumbs of chrome off a greasy black stove. Hughes's dramatic phrasing and cadences sweep the beginning reader along, the many stops and repetitions reinforcing the images but scarcely slowing the pace.

The Iron Man is only occasionally comic, but many books treat this passion for a 'secret sharer' with the lightest of touches. In *Thing*, by Australian Robin Klein, Emily Forbes longs for a pet. Her mother is sympathetic but her landlady is ogrish on the subject. Emily settles for an attractively oval 'pet rock' turned up by bulldozers making a new sports field. When it hatches into an amiable young stegosaurus, Emily and her mother are delighted. The humour of the book derives from the matter-of-fact, though ingenious, accommodations made by both the prehistoric animal and the very contemporary single-parent family. Emily pretends, when the censorious landlady asks, that Thing's startling footprints on the hall stairs are caused by her new swimming flippers, and she wraps the Thing's enthusiastically thumping tail in newspaper so he won't betray his presence.

Thing, in turn, cleverly contrives concealment by disguising himself, at various moments of emergency, as a piece of modern sculpture, a length of pebbled patio, a cactus and a coffee table. His eventual triumph derives in part from his fanatic attachment to television cooking and aerobics shows.

Of course, the archetypal light-hearted story about unusual pets is *Mr Popper's Penguins*, a pre-war favourite that still holds low-key comic charm for young readers. Mr Popper, a house painter and daydreamer who loves to read of polar explorations, strikes us as very much a boy at heart: innocent, impractical, unflaggingly enthusiastic. His devotion to his unusual pets goes to remarkable lengths – in one of the most hilarious scenes, the family obligingly huddles in mittens and overcoats, with the living-room windows open to let in the snow and cold, so the penguins can slide about on the iced floor, 'gorking' happily. This unquestioning care and consideration eventually leads to fame and fortune for all the Poppers.

Even more riotous as a send-up of the boy-loves-pet genre is *Hoboken Chicken Emergency*, by D. Manus Pinkwater (yes, the same one – he shuffles his first names around with each new book). Pinkwater is probably the most sophisticated and surrealistic of American humorists for the young. The deadpan narrative style of *Mr Popper's Penguins* is taken to outrageous lengths here: when Arthur brings home a 260-pound live chicken with a tenor cluck, his parents' most severe reaction is a mild scolding at the dinner table when Arthur sneaks some mashed potato to the gigantically hungry Henrietta. 'I don't want this chicken to get in the habit of begging,' Poppa warns, though he is also pleased about Henrietta because 'Every boy should have a chicken'.

Perhaps the vast sociological shifts of this century account for the gradual disappearance of the anthropomorphic animal story and its replacement by the animal-friend story. Where stifled and well-behaved children once wept sentimentally over the plight of victimized animals like Beautiful Jo, their hearts now beat faster to stories in which lonely children make mystical contact with another species.

In *Stig of the Dump*, by Clive King, eight-year-old Barney meets not an animal, but a shaggy-haired caveman living in a local dump. The two become fast friends. The unreal is made utterly plausible by this talented author because we see the whole story though the eyes of the lively, curious but unsophisticated boy, whose childlike preoccupations are mirrored in the brisk, sturdy prose. Barney completely accepts the existence of his fur-clad prehistoric friend. In fact, much of the humour is derived from the fact that Barney never has to lie to hide Stig's secret life – he simply, calmly, tells the truth and the grown-ups blindly refuse to hear it because it doesn't fit in with their previous version of reality. What child won't recognize that experience?

After Barney's first visit to the dump, for example, he enthusiastically tells his grandmother and his sister Lou about Stig's improvised living arrangements. He's 'a sort of a boy. He just wears rabbit skins and lives in a cave. He gets his water from a vacuum cleaner and puts chalk in his bath. He's my friend.' Lou blandly translates for the grandmother: 'He means he's been playing caveman.'

There are two enduring charms about *Stig of the Dump*. One is the way in which Stig becomes Barney's playmate and protector, always there to engage in some fascinating new project of spear-sharpening or thief-nabbing, and suddenly appearing in all his startling muscularity just when Barney is being bullied by the ruffianish Snargett brothers. Second is the marvellous clarity with which King describes the physical world as Stig and Barney reinvent it together. In fact, Stig's patient, wondering exploration of the junk in the dump (he decides that an umbrella is a turnip spit) exactly parallels the way a young child looks freshly at the world, fascinated by physical manifestations that adults have long since taken for granted and forgotten to notice. A highlight of the book is the midsummer night scene when Barney and his sister Lou are carried back in time to Stig's Stone Age settlement. What is unforgettable is not so much the time-shift fantasy, but the high-spirited description (eeeeyoooTHUMP) of just how and why prehistoric men hauled and levered and chanted those giant stones to their remote sites.

The animal (or primordial man) as friend-protector surfaces again in *Stone Fox*, by John Reynolds Gardiner, a Rocky Mountains legend that is told with a swift intensity usually foreign to this folksy genre. Willy, only ten years old, is left in cruel isolation when his grandfather suddenly 'gives up on life', takes to his bed and refuses to speak. Willy has only his faithful dog, Searchlight, to help harvest the crops and save the farm. The climax of the brief novel is a heartbreaker: Willy and Searchlight take part in a breathlessly exciting sledge race across the snowy countryside, competing with a mysterious giant Indian, Stone Fox, and his magnificient team of Samoyeds, for prize money that may save the farm. Willy wins . . . but Searchlight pays the ultimate price. Only the reticent but moving tribute paid by Stone Fox to the boy and the dog make the ending bearable. Stone Fox – his name and his monumentality place him among the forces of nature – helps Willy to triumph over adversity.

In a completely different tone and style, two gerbils help to draw together a painfully fractured British working-class family. *The Battle of Bubble and Squeak*, by Philippa Pearce, is really the battle of unhappy and resentful Sid with his preoccupied mother Alice and her new husband, the affable Bill. The gerbils are never portrayed as anything but themselves; the author uses the dramatic reactions of the family members to the vicissitudes of gerbil-rearing in order to weave a gentle and perceptive story about Sid's growth to greater responsibility.

Young children of early school age have a well-known affinity for animals, and it's not hard to think of the reasons why. They are at the bottom of their school's hierarchy, uncertain of their ability to cope in the larger world, increasingly private about feelings, and, in today's smaller families, quite likely to be lonely. It is the right age at which to enjoy the feelings of competence and affection earned by caring for a dependent pet. But there is another factor, too. Just as children at puberty may feel a powerful nostalgic tug for the childhood from which they are rapidly departing, the school-age child may be pulled toward the abundant, richly unknowable world of nature and the affinity the preliterate child has with the animal kingdom.

Two powerful stories, *The Sea Egg*, by Lucy Boston, and *The Midnight Fox*, by Betsy Byars, convey a sense of nature rewarding the alert, sensitive child with a precious gift of secret knowledge and communion. In *The Sea Egg*, two English brothers on a seaside holiday with their parents are observant and imaginative enough to notice a particular beauty and egg-like promise about a 'stone' found by a beachcomber. They buy it from him and put it carefully in a tidal pool, isolated from the public beach by chalk cliffs and tunnels.

Boston's style is hypnotically poetic; her precise observation and lyrical description almost envelop the reader in the ocean world of heat, infinite blueness, sand and salt. Seals floating upright in the sea are 'like half-sunk bottles'; seen through the binoculars from a boat, they are like a 'secret vision' that disappears when the boat rocks; they are 'slow balloons' moving on the rocky coast.

From the boat, the boys glimpse something up by their rock pool where they have left the mysterious egg. Stunned, they realize it is a triton – an impish boy with a seal's tail. The next day, despite pelting rain ('The fish-grey waves when they broke sounded heavier for being cold'), they dash along the shore amidst 'an orchestra of sounds' to see this sealboy who, they know, has hatched from their egg.

The boys drench themselves in the life of the sea; they play with the triton, drape themselves in seaweed, learn to swim with the tide through the frightening tunnel, and finally, one moonlit night, answer the triton's horn and swim out through the 'gilded glinting' sea with him, to discover a gathering of seals in an island cave. After their midnight adventure, they must part with the triton, who leads the seals on their annual migration just before a furious storm breaks. The boys have dipped into an enchanted world from which their parents are excluded. They've gained confidence and skill, but most important is their sense of carrying back with them, to the prosaic world of school, a sea memory of magic.

There are some false notes; Boston verges on the mawkish whenever she draws back and comments on the boys from the outside, as when their mother sees them swim through the tunnel: ' "Oh boys!" she said, thinking they looked confident and beautiful and splendid, "you are too provoking . . ." ' or when the narrator makes a few embarrassingly outdated references to the lordly 'young authority' of the triton. Nevertheless, this is an enriching book for a skilful young reader who can cope with the vocabulary.

More contemporary in tone, more realistic, laced with the wry humour of the modern sensibility but no less haunting than *The Sea Egg*, is *The Midnight Fox* by Betsy Byars. The story is narrated by Tommy, thinking back four years to the summer he was eight, when he was sent to Aunt Millie and Uncle Fred's farm while his parents bicycled through France. Tommy hates anything new, and he hates spending the summer apart from his more outgoing best friend, Petie. Comic scenarios run through Tommy's fertile mind, filled with uproarious reversals: when his mother tries to convince him of the charm of watching lambs at play, or collecting eggs in the henhouse, Tommy glumly imagines himself as the first boy in the world to be trampled to death by baby lambs or run down by vengeful chickens.

Any tendency to the maudlin is neatly undercut by Tommy's self-deflating humour. Perhaps he is more imaginative, more self-aware, than we could reasonably expect of any eight-year-old. Yet the tone never falters; few children's books told in the first person manage to achieve such a touching and three-dimensional persona for the narrator. Byars uses an inspired child version of adult narrative irony: it is through Tommy's inner monologue of slapstick comedies, TV dramas, newspaper headlines and parodied interviews that he gains a perspective on himself and his situation, and that we come to know him so much better than the flat, self-conscious 'I' of so many lesser children's novels.

Tommy's fantasies are wonderfully, surprisingly, poetically alive. They make Tommy real in our eyes, and they lend a welcome legitimacy to any child's private world of self-justifying daydreams. He dreams of fulfilment (he will discover a brand-new colour and, for a moment, the whole world will fall silent), of loss (an old hermit arrives at a lonely airfield to announce that he has invented a flying machine; when the young people laugh at him, he quietly presses a button on his knapsack and softly flies away) and of brotherhood (a magical Indian word, when blurted out in emergency, will automatically bring help).

Tommy spends his first few weeks at the farm being wary, uncomfortable and at a loose end. It is only in his private reflections that we see his tender sensibilities. Aunt Millie, fussing kindly over her young guest, offers him a favourite book of her now-grown sons, *The Lamb Who Wanted to Be a Cat*. Tommy greets it with polite enthusiasm, but in truth it only adds to his depression – it makes him feel awful to think about 'someone who was trying to be something he could never, ever be'.

The summer mood, languid and hot, is shocked into vibrancy one day when, across the crest of a hill, a magnificent black fox with pale golden eyes leaps into Tommy's line of vision. The fox becomes his secret sharer, wild and tantalizing with its high clear bark in the distance. Tommy tracks it through the woods, long days at a time. Finally he finds its den and realizes it is the mother of a lone cub, an enchanting, woolly little ball of fur. The tender relationship of the watchful mother and her tiny warrior of a cub is all the more riveting because of Tommy's separation from his parents – and because of his unspoken fears that he can't live up to their expectations of him.

The tenuous bond of trust between Tommy and the fox is threatened when Aunt Millie chivvies Uncle Fred to hunt the marauder who stole her turkey. But because Tommy is too wary for his own good, he can't bring himself to say the word to Uncle Fred that might call off the dreaded hunt.

Wretched and ashamed of his own timidity, he stands by when Uncle Fred finds the den and digs out the baby fox to use as a lure to entrap the mother. At first, Tommy thinks the cub is dead. 'He's just play-acting,' says Uncle Fred. 'His ma taught him to do that.' Tommy thinks that 'if I lived to be a hundred, I would never see anything that would make me feel any worse than the sight of that little fox pretending to be dead when his heart was beating so hard it looked like it was going to burst out of his chest'.

The torpor of the heat wave and Tommy's paralysis both break that night in a tremendous thunderstorm when, in the driving rain, he rescues the little fox. In the moment when he gives up to freedom what he most cherishes, Tommy comforts himself with the consolation of art: some day in an art gallery, he thinks, he'll see a painting called 'Fox with Baby at Midnight', the fox and her baby running beneath the wet ghostly apple trees toward a patch of light in the distance . . . and his heart will stop beating.

At a superficial level, you could say that *The Midnight Fox* is 'about' a young boy's growing self-awareness and confidence. But that would be like saying that *Macbeth* is about troubled family life in Scotland. In truth, the book is as many-layered, as deeply tolerant of human nature, as rich in incident, character and humour, as any excellent novel for adults. And the surprise is that it is not even the best known or most widely admired of its kind.

There are, in other words, so many hundreds of such fine books available that even a splendid example can be overlooked. That argues well, actually, for the abundance and variety we enjoy. Not every child, of course, will be thrilled by *The Midnight Fox* or *The Sea Egg* or *Wingman*. But, with an empathetic adult's help, every youngster can surely find a few captivating novels to love in those early reading years.

Love is not too strong a word. Nearly every literate adult can remember, with an unreasonable surge of emotion and loyalty, one or two books from childhood that had special meaning. They might have been comics; they might have been *Beano* or Blyton; all the better when they were books by authors like E. Nesbit or Philippa Pearce, which led on to other literary discoveries.

The key is that the beloved book spoke with a clear voice to that individual child. Escape was part of the pleasure; so was wish fulfillment, the satisfaction of inarticulate yearnings. But even more there is the deep satisfaction of narrative. From the picture book stage, the reader of early novels has stepped into the temporal world of school bells, timetables and hobbling of freedom, as well as the impending knowledge of evil and decay. But narrative is the orderly pyramiding of a story that builds in time; narrative is the transformation of chaotic and sometimes painful experience into something *made*, something desired and good. Because the reader collaborates actively in imagining that written narrative into an inner landscape, it has a more profound and potentially valuable impact than the electronic entertainments that wash over the passive viewer, twitching the right cry-and-laugh electrodes as they surge past.

The child I've been writing about in this chapter, the child of seven, eight or nine, who experiences the grip of narrative, will likely keep the reading habit alive until the competing claims of other entertainments can be considered from a more mature perspective. But if children are completely lost to television at this vulnerable age, it seems unlikely that they will ever find their way back to the world of books.

Chapter 4

LIBERATING LAUGHTER

'How's that new baby brother of yours?' said Grandpa.
'Willy?' said Louie. *'No fun.'*
'Not cute,' said Mary Ann.
'All he can do is eat and sleep,' said Louie.
'Or cry,' said Mary Ann.
'That bad, eh?' said Grandpa. *'Your parents must feel awful.'*

James Stevenson, *Worse than Willy!*

One morning there was a moose in Mr Breton's yard. It was a blue moose. When Mr Breton went out his back door, the moose was there, looking at him. After a while, Mr Breton went back in, closed the door, and made a pot of coffee while he waited for the moose to go away. It didn't go away; it just stood in Mr Breton's yard, looking at his back door. Mr Breton drank a cup of coffee. The moose stood in the yard. Mr Breton opened the door again. 'Shoo! Go away!'
'Do you mind if I come in and get warm?' the moose said. 'I'm just about frozen.'

Manus Pinkwater, *Blue Moose*

CHILDREN'S BOOKS ARE, of course, drenched in humour. It could hardly be otherwise, since any sane adult tries to raise children in an atmosphere of optimism – and hope, even of the most rueful kind, is the expression on comedy's face. Children, like all the powerless, find their best release and choicest weapon in humour; they are always ready to drop an armload of tension or anger to indulge in a liberating shout of laughter. And, as teachers are well aware, laughter is the reward that lures the most reluctant reader.

Writers for older children, especially mediocre writers, may pick away gloomily at the sores of the pubescent soul the way their adolescent subjects pick at their complexions, but the characteristic mood of the writer for younger children is one of a summoner to glee: hilarity, slyness and the chuckle lie on every hand. But humour, as well as being the richest vein of invention in children's literature, is also the form most open to abuse, exploitation and even, as I shall try to show later, to some rather sinister manipulation.

Though television has nullified most cultural boundaries, subtle national differences still live in humour. In British children's books, one detects a greater willingness to put the adult point of view, even when this is not completely flattering to children; North Americans writing for preschoolers rarely risk a sardonic crack at children's expense. Perhaps North Americans are more determinedly 'child-centred', with publishers erring on the side of the sentimental in their cautious calculations of inoffensiveness; perhaps British children are more attuned to the nuances of language, and therefore less startled by dry or denigrating witticisms. In any case, British authors seem to have more latitude in the varieties of humour they employ in children's books, and the results are often refreshing.

Jill Murphy's delectable *Five Minutes' Peace*, a preschool picture book in which a mother elephant desperately escapes the breakfast bedlam and seeks 'five minutes' peace from you lot' by retreating to the bathtub, is a case in point.

In fact, the pictures of the three little elephants, who pursue mother (Mrs Large) to her sanctum, are so lovably droll that the message is one of tolerant affection . . . despite the maddened gleam of desperation in mother's eye. Surely no artist has ever before orchestrated a trio of elephant trunks to such witty effect. This is a picture book whose wry undercurrent can be savoured by the reading-aloud parent while the children enjoy an uncomplicated delight in the wonderful pictures.

Some of the finest North American humorous writing for children, it is true, is as unsentimental as Murphy – James Stevenson, for example, who is quoted at the beginning of the chapter. The wit is deadpan and droll, but the underlying sensibility is one of tender acceptance of the child's foibles. Stevenson, a celebrated cartoonist for the *New Yorker* magazine, gives his young readers some credit for sophistication: though the unstated theme of *Worse than Willy!* is the children's resentment of a new baby brother, he never stoops to glib reassurances or the usual head-patting condescension. Instead, a poker-faced Grandpa, his straw hat sitting on the table beside his wicker chair on the porch, treats Louie and Mary Ann to a wild story about the antics of his own 'awful' brother Wainey. And, most delicious of all, in the cartoon-like, irresistibly funny panel illustrations of Grandpa and Wainey in their infancy, we see them exactly as the listening children visualize them: junior editions of their grown selves, complete with a brush moustache tucked under the infant Grandpa's button nose.

Where's Julius? by a favourite English picture-book artist, John Burningham, has the same tone of warm acceptance. In fact, Julius's parents could be nominated for a parental nobility prize, so forbearingly do they accept the fact that Julius will absent himself from the table nearly every mealtime. Julius, despite the blandishments of his mother's delicious-sounding menu, is usually too busy riding an imaginary camel to the top of the tomb of Neffatuteum, or cooling the hippos in the Lombo Bombo River. Mildly, Mr Troutbeck, Julius's dad, brings his grilled chops, garden peas and mashed potato on a tray. As always, Burningham's delicately witty pictures sparkle with an affirmation of child life and imagination.

Food, of course, is a great source of merriment and fascination in children's books (and climactic scenes in children's novels are often staged around a dinner table); one of the funniest to use this theme is the British *It's Your Turn, Roger!* by Susanna Gretz. Gretz's evocative colours and wickedly expressive drawings of pigs make this a winner. Roger, a disgruntled pig who resents having to set the table, stomps out to visit the other flats in his building. One family, though elegant, is eating horrible fishmeal soup; another porker family is enjoying a veritable debauch of mud-pie guzzling; yet another is sweetly welcoming, but Roger feels himself an outsider. Home is best, after all. Roger races home, determined to take his turn at helping the next day, and delighted to find worm pie for dessert.

Manus Pinkwater's gourmandizing *Blue Moose* is a more urbane kind of humour, for a slightly older reader; he makes us laugh out loud by the sheer incongruity of his sophistication in the north woods of Maine. Children's humour thrives on role reversal, and here a shy and insecure restaurateur, the good-hearted little Mr Breton, blooms into prosperity after the moose moves in and takes on the job of head waiter, bullying the customers with time-honoured headwaiter hauteur. (The way the townsfolk brag about being on good terms with the moose is a typically sly Pinkwater joke, this time about competitive dining-out.) The style may be terse and jaunty in the best modern manner, but the solid base of the story, what touches and engages us, is the mutual kindness of man and moose and their odd but richly reverberant friendship.

When you stop to analyse why a funny book provokes laughter from many children of very different tastes, you almost always find that there's an unstated theme in the book that is common to the deepest experience of childhood. *Mary Alice, Operator Number Nine*, is the heroine of the popular picture book by Jeffrey Allen and illustrator James Marshall. Mary Alice, a duck with a head cold, has to take a few days off from her job as a local telephone operator who gives the exact time to the public.

'Don't worry,' says Boss Chicken, 'I'll find someone to take your place. It's an easy job.' This, naturally, makes Mary Alice feel even worse. What young child hasn't been made to feel that someone else could set the table, make beds or wash the car faster and better than he? And so we rejoice as Mary Alice's series of substitutes all prove comically inept. That's the obvious message. But there's a subtler one, too. Consider that the five- or six-year-old reader at whom this book is aimed often has a new baby brother or sister at home, and the dread of being superseded becomes sharply relevant. Or think about time and all the anxieties of clock-watching and schedules that drop on the shoulders of the five-year-old, who has lived in a timeless dream world until the first day of school.

Anxiety, as the author Selma Lane has astutely pointed out (in *Down the Rabbit Hole*), is the engine that powers *The Cat in the Hat*, possibly the best-known beginner book in North America. As the mysterious Cat visitor wreaks mayhem and chaos in the children's house, their horror mounts: Mother will soon come back and find 'this big mess'. Uncontrollable mess is a source of panic to more people than just school children; I confess that when I first read *The Cat in the Hat*, I could find very little jollity in the spectacle of an uninvited demon-cat and a house knee-deep in smashed cake, broken lamps and spilled milk. Even the ugly drawings are nervous, edgy and tense: the children are bug-eyed with consternation, walls seem to tilt, tables teeter, and the horizon line wobbles, up-ends itself and disappears in the whirlwind of activity. The laughter that accompanies the end of this book is, I would wager, the laughter of semi-hysterical relief.

There is a place for that, certainly. And since funnybones are as individual as fingerprints, some children will find *Cat in the Hat* humour worth revisiting many times. Others may find a subtler, and funnier, recognition of child realities in a book like *The Judge*, by Harve and Margot Zemach. Every child has had the wormwood-and-gall experience of telling the truth and not being believed. In this book, a boorishly peremptory judge refuses to give a moment's credence to a series of hapless witnesses who are dragged before the bench.

The verse, with its internal assonance and urgency, is perfectly pitched to the mounting suspense and hilarity.

*Please let me go, judge
I didn't know, Judge,
That what I said was against the law
I just said what I saw
A horrible thing is coming this way, creeping closer day by day
Its eyes are scary, its tail is hairy
I tell you, Judge, we all better pray.*

And each defendant . . . beribboned simperer, cringing boy, woebegone cripple . . . adds to the litany of description in a perfect cumulative tale. How delicious, how surprising, how perfectly *deserved* it is when a horrible monster face appears in the window behind the back of the spluttering ('Ninnyhammer! Dimwit! Dunce! To jail at once!') Judge. How just is the fate of the Judge. How mild and deeply satisfying are the smiles of the freed prisoners as they stroll away, vindicated.

Clumsy adults get their comeuppance in scores of humorous children's books. The success of *Jacob Two-Two Meets the Hooded Fang*, Mordecai Richler's bestseller, is testament to the allure of this theme. The book has real liabilities – an overload of belaboured jokes, cliché and sagging plotlines. Worse, it has moments of embarrassing sentimentality and falseness. The villains of Slimers' Island, we are told, shroud the place in fog because they can't stand sunshine. Why? Because 'any big person who cannot stand little ones also fears the sun', not to mention pets, flowers and laughter. The ending is a bit of a cheat, too. After all the hoop-la and the uproariously gothic plot, Jacob awakens on a park bench, and we are left to decide whether the entire story wasn't just a dream.

Still, in addition to occasional flights of inspired verbal tomfoolery, *Jacob Two-Two* has another basic strength, and that is the accurate perception of how it feels to be the youngest in the family, the one who always gets teased, tricked, put-upon, left out and drowned out by ebullient older siblings. If Jacob Two-Two cannot ride a bike or cut a straight slice of bread, he can nevertheless enjoy a comic triumph by seeing clearly through the hypocrisies of adults, judge and jailer alike.

Adults are often reduced to caricatures in children's books; this works best when the characters are sympathetically sent up, as they are in *The Sheep-Pig*, a hilarious animal story for middle readers by the prolific English writer, Dick King-Smith. Mrs Hogget is ludicrously garrulous. Farmer Hogget, her husband, is drastically monosyllabic. Their contrapuntal conversations – in which Mrs Hogget gushes interminably to end up saying nothing, and in which her husband's one-word utterances may contain depths of emotion – are perfectly paced and timed.

When Farmer Hogget, who keeps sheep, wins a piglet at the fair, his sheepdog Fly adopts it . . . and Fly, too, is a caricature of the classic sheepdog, convinced that all sheep are terminally stupid and have to be tyrannized into obedience. Only Babe, the orphan pig, is wide open to the world. Intelligent, eager and loyal, Babe determines to become a sheep-pig. Too tender-hearted to think of bullying the sheep, he addresses them with elaborate courtesy (they speak an appealing Yorkshire dialect) and wins their friendship. The story of his training and his surprising victories is not only irresistibly comic, it is also unexpectedly tense, touching and exciting. Mary Rayner's delightful barnyard drawings add immeasurably to the fun. The comedy of caricature is done with so much affectionate and sharp observation that it turns into a comedy of character.

A very different author, the American Ann Cameron, triumphantly brings off a similar feat of shrewd observation in *The Julian Stories*, six brief stories for seven- to ten-year-olds about a black family which includes two young brothers and an electrifying, funny, sometimes frightening father. The man has such a dynamic presence that, Julian says, 'When he laughs, the sun laughs in the window panes. When he thinks, you can almost see his thoughts sitting on all the tables and chairs.' And when he cooks – as he does in the first story, preparing a special lemon pudding – his language bursts the bounds of the ordinary and makes the world seem larger. ' "A wonderful pudding," my father said. "It will taste like a whole raft of lemons. It will taste like a night on the sea." '

Julian's high-jinks, his imaginative plans and projects, and his naughtiness, get him into difficulties. Sometimes, he's frightened of Father's anger, and sometimes Father (equally imaginative) has surprising reactions. These stories, and the ones in the sequel, *More Stories Julian Tells*, have a startlingly fresh flavour, and the comedy is always suffused with rigorously unsentimental familial warmth.

Linguistic invention is another form of humour that wears equally well. Indeed, the earliest forms of humour in children's literature are nursery rhymes, with their absurd juxtapositions and delight in patterns of rhythm, sound and rhyme.

For young children, folk tales are another good source of strong, repetitive and oddly resonant language. *Tikki Tikki Tembo*, the well-loved Chinese folk tale, retold by Arlene Mosel with subtle Blair Lent illustrations that add a third dimension, is a story of sibling rivalry. The mother has lavished the fanciest possible name, Tikki tikki tembo-no sa rembo-chari bari ruchi-pip peri pembo, on her older son, and bestowed a negligent monosyllable, Chang, on the younger. And just because of this unfairness, the older nearly drowns in the well. But the reason the story has lasted so well is its wonderfully memorable mouthful of nonsense syllables. The comic punch of the story comes at the moment when a breathless, frantic little Chang garbles the message – 'Chari bari rembo tikki tikki pip pip has fallen in the well!'

Vigananee and the Tree Toad, by Verna Aardema, uses onomatopoeia, a familiar device of African folk tales. The effects are almost magical if read boldly aloud: the story leaps into auditory life when the tree toad sits in a deep starry window to sing her friends to sleep (taw-aw-aw-awt) or when the bushy monster comes up the walk (pusu pusu pusu) and rudely gulps the savoury stew (yatua yatua yatua). Rat, who is sweeping (fras fras fras) the walk, hits him with the broom – ZAK!

The purest verbal comedy for older children is *The Phantom Tollbooth*, written in 1961 by Norton Juster and still going strong. You would think that an entire novel based on wordplay would become as tiresome as a birthday party that goes on too long – nothing is more exhausting than forced jollity. But because the story is so elemental (the boy Milo goes on a life-or-death quest through a strange wonderland), the narrative urges us along through showers, fountains and ambushes of verbal play.

Even better than the triumphant climax when Milo rescues the 'fair' princesses, Rhyme and Reason, is the banquet in Dictionopolis when, it turns out, everyone has to eat his words. Since Milo had neglected to bellow out the names of some favourite foods before the meal, King Azaz the Unabridged consoles him with some scraps – rigmarole, somersault, and ragamuffin – while they all wait for their just desserts. Though readers of nine and ten may miss some of the endless, dizzying word play, there are jokes enough, broad and narrow, to keep everyone amused right to the end.

Inspired wordplay, of course, accounts for the spectacular success of *Alligator Pie*, by Dennis Lee, the first Canadian poet to adapt Mother Goose rhymes to a Canadian context, and the enduring popularity of the American *Amelia Bedelia* series by Peggy Parish. Amelia, a neophyte housemaid, interprets all her employer's instructions with strict literalness, and gets into endless difficulties. Told to put the lights out, she hangs the light bulbs on the clothesline; to 'draw the curtains', she gets out a piece of paper and pencil. Seven- and eight-year-olds, embarrassed by their own lapses in comprehension, roar with laughter at Amelia Bedelia's solecisms.

It may surprise adults to know that there is a large body of humorous work for children springing from the idea of literary satire. These books count on a basic literacy among their young readers – not just the ability to decode letters, but an easy familiarity with the enduring literary forms of our culture. Recent years have seen a spate of revisionist fairy tales, in which princesses enjoy the vigorous, central role. *The Paperbag Princess*, by Canadian Robert Munsch, for example, is a running gag that depends on the child recognizing the anachronisms, tricks and discordancies that are slipped into the basic fairy tale. The prince and princess have modern names, Elizabeth and Ronald, and are shown in 1980s preppy style with tennis rackets and 'expensive' clothes – a deliberately jarring word in the fairy tale context, since kings may have ordered costly clothes for their daughters, but nothing was ever expensive for them. The emancipated ending, in which Elizabeth carries the day without Ronald's help, is not only a twist on the familiar pattern, but provides a naughty frisson with its bold use of the word 'bum'. So basic is the fairy-tale structure to our civilization, so ingrained is its accustomed tone and style, that there can hardly be a child in the country who doesn't get the joke.

A more elaborate and sophisticated literary joke is *The Jolly Postman* by Janet and Allan Ahlberg, with the seductive subtitle, 'Other People's

Letters'. And that's just what they are. Every other page is an actual envelope containing a letter to or from a well-known fairy-tale character. There's a misspelled note of apology from Goldilocks to the Bear family, an advertising circular for a witch from Hobgoblin Supplies Ltd (with luscious mockery of advertising lingo) and a solicitor's letter to Mr Wolf, on behalf of clients Miss Riding Hood and Messrs Three Little Pigs. The pictures are choc-a-bloc with amusing and allusive details.

Literary satire exists at all levels. Seven-year-olds recognize and delight in the turned tables of *Clever Polly and the Stupid Wolf*, by Catherine Storr, a witty series of linked stories in which brave and ingenious Polly outwits the babyish wolf at every turn. Even within the book there's a good sprinkling of literary satire: the wolf consciously tries to imitate the tricks that worked for the wolf in *Three Little Pigs*, *The Seven Kids* and *Little Red Riding Hood*, but is always stymied by a combination of modern life (buses and the family car instead of the path through the woods, for example) and Polly's knowingness. The child reader is buoyed by being one step ahead of the wolf all the way, thanks to shared knowledge of the fairy tales.

E. Nesbit used the convention of the heroic narrator to add comedic spice to *The Treasure-Seekers* in 1899, and, curiously enough, the trick still works as well today. We owe our pleasure to her skill in building the character of Oswald, the ostensible narrator of the book. Filled with romantic daydreams, conceit, and a fitful dedication to noble ideals, Oswald is an unwitting comedian and, despite his bossiness, an oddly endearing boy. He has energy, ideas and largeness of soul. 'It is one of us that tells this story – but I shall not tell you which,' writes the narrator. The delicious joke is that by the bottom of page one, Oswald has utterly given himself away, and continues to do so at frequent moments of high excitement during the book. All the way through the high-spirited adventures and amusing scrapes that make up the episodic plots of *The Treasure-Seekers*, the author lets the reader in on the joke. Adult hypocrisy or child preposterousness, we are allowed to see through it all. At the same time, the pleasure and suspense of the stories is not spoiled by Olympian omniscience; it's one of the most successful balancing acts in children's literature, and it works, I think, because Nesbit never fails to treat her characters with affectionate respect. You can see that she loves these imaginative, absurd, brave, squabbling but loyal children as much as we do.

Readers in the middle age-range can be remarkably sophisticated in their capacity to enjoy an adult form, like the thriller or detective story, when it has been tailored to their interests. One example that seems to have universal appeal is the American author Ellen Raskin's *The Mysterious Disappearance of Leon (I Mean Noel)*. While it lay open on my desk for the writing of this chapter, each of my three teenagers – all with widely differing tastes in books – wandered in at different times, noticed the book and lit up with enthusiastic nostalgia: 'Oh, I *loved* that book!'

Raskin has surgically dissected the adult detective novel and used the parts to make up a highly original kit: assemble and solve your own mystery, clues and instructions included. She does it with wit and hectic invention, and somehow keeps the whole concoction both coherent and appealing. The mystery revolves around the obsessive search by Mrs Caroline Carillon, née Little Dumpling Fish, for her missing husband Leon, who vanished after their childhood marriage of convenience. Her two adopted children, Tony and Tina, help solve the puzzle, which requires them to decipher an obscure message delivered by a drowning man: 'Noel glub C blub all . . . I glub new . . .'

What helps to knit together the zany plot, with its clever black and white drawings that serve as clues, is a firm underlying message: all mysteries are solved when the names of things are made clear and true. By the end of the story, everyone comes into his or her own true name, and everyone is freed from the prison of false identity. But the reader need barely be aware of this unstated message to enjoy the comedy of errors and detection.

One English cops-and-robbers story for children that stays closer to the traditional chase pattern, along with some of the 'caper' elements that remind one of *The Lavender Hill Mob*, is *Me and My Million*, by Clive King. It's hard to think of a more engaging hero than Ringo, the undersized Cockney waif, illiterate, naïve and cynical, who is an unwitting participant in a major art theft. Ringo, who has never seen a painting before, is suddenly on the run in London with a 'Pestalotsy' painting of 'a mum and a kid' stuffed in a laundry bag. The fast-paced plot has humour of its own, with Ringo keeping one step ahead of rich but venal art dealers, pretentious art experts, decent cops, hippies, lunatic terrorists who turn out to be animal liberationists, and even his own big stepbrother, Elvis, the original thief of the painting. The subtler humour lies in the way clear-eyed Ringo begins to love and value the painting. He, and a genial art forger who gives him refuge on a canal boat, may be the only true art lovers in the book. I can't think of a children's thriller with a more gripping plot or more sympathetic humour.

Gaiety and high spirits, with no dark undertones or foreshadowings of adult irony, used to be the unique voice of children's humour. That innocence of tone is long gone now. Even Farley Mowat's well-known *Owls in the Family or The Dog Who Wouldn't Be* might not be written with the same carefree openness today, when animal-rights activists are on the alert for every transgression against nature wild and free. But children still enjoy the lovable antics of Wol and Weeps, the two Mowat owls, and the clownish clumsiness of Mutt the dog. These two family stories are still masterpieces of sharp observation and droll, good-hearted comedy.

Examples of that kind of humour are far more common among the picture books; one that springs to mind is *Three Strong Women*, a Japanese folk tale that probably predates women's liberation by a few thousand years. It is a tall tale, an imaginative stretching of reality that has no ulterior motive, no barb in its tail, no moral to press home but the pleasure of laughter.

We catch the mood at once as the story begins, with lovely, delicately funny drawings by Kazue Mizumura. A famous wrestler strolls along toward the capital, where he will wrestle before the Emperor. He is strong, healthy, pleased with himself – just a little too pleased with himself – and we are invited to smile at the way he enjoys the sound of his own voice as he saunters and hums. Then he is distracted by the sight of 'a round little girl with red cheeks and nose like a friendly button. Her eyes looked as though she were thinking of ten thousand funny stories at once.' He longs to tickle her – 'kochokochokocho' – to hear her giggle. But no sooner does he try, than this cheerful girl casually traps him in an armhold.

Maru-me, the girl, takes the wrestler along to Forever Mountain, where her mother and wizened little grandmother turn out to be as chucklingly, self-deprecatingly strong as she is. The lessons he learns from them stand him in good stead in the capital, but in even better stead in his life, which takes a new, more serene and fulfilling path.

Those life-affirming comedies, very much like those well-loved early Hollywood movies that had no quarrel with the world, are rare nowadays. It would be hard to write one without falling into a sickeningly sweet Norman Rockwell tone of voice. Nevertheless, there are a few humanistic gems that veer toward slapstick to avoid sentimentality and succeed with a flourish. *Freaky Friday*, by Mary Rodgers, is a comedy of transformation: thirteen-year-old Annabel Andrews, unhappy possessor of a mouthful of braces, a knobbly figure, a perfect little brother, a messy room and failing exams at school, wakes up one morning in the curvaceous body of her mother.

Annabel is overjoyed to be an adult, with all the supposed pleasures and freedoms of adulthood at her command. Although her exhausting, tense and hilarious day disabuses her of those dreams, it does bring her an almost endless supply of balm for her soul. By the next morning, Annabel has turned into a pretty teenager with her braces off. She has learned that her secret crush, Boris, now thinks she is 'some beautiful chick,' that her teachers believe she is highly gifted ('I admire and love your little girl,' says one teacher somewhat wildly to Annabel-disguised-as-mother) and that even her kid brother, the maligned Ape Face, adores her so much that he hopes one day to have braces just like hers. Blatant teenage wish fulfilment combines delectably with the sardonic Manhattan wisecrack.

The best English writers for children seem to have a matchless verbal brilliance at their command. Joan Aiken, one of the funniest authors alive, dazzles us in *Tales of Arabel's Raven*, a sort of working-class, surrealist *Owls in the Family*. 'Oh my stars, look at that creature's toe-nails, if nails they can be called,' remarks Arabel's mother, when she finds Mortimer, the raven, sitting in her fridge surrounded by the remains of the family's food supply. Aiken is the complete master of throwaway lines: in the midst of Mortimer's squalid mayhem at the dinner table the narrator dryly observes: 'Mortimer enjoyed the baked beans, but his table manners were very lighthearted.'

Physical chaos, of the *Cat in the Hat* variety, is the hallmark of this kind of humour. But Aiken doesn't leave it there. Like a pianist playing riffs, she spoofs the speech patterns of her characters, pushing the dour, the official, the laconic, the crazed and the Cockney to their comic extremes. 'If birds had fingerprints, I wouldn't mind taking the dabs of that shifty-looking fowl,' observes a disgruntled policeman called to the site of one Mortimer-inspired shambles. 'Thoughtless our Mortimer may be,' retorts Mrs Jones at her most haughty, 'untidy at times, but honest as a Bath bun, I'll have you know.' And there are wonderful spoofs of flower-child song lyrics, mad modern technology (viz. the vending machines for olive oil, foot massage or cheerful poems) and even of tough-talking American gangster films. 'You'd better co-operate, Coal-face,' snarls a thug to Mortimer. 'This is a flyjack.' A parent who dares to try a few different voices and accents could enjoy doing a star turn when reading this book aloud.

Another artist in slap-happy chaos, of course, is Helen Cresswell, inventor of the remarkably obnoxious Bagthorpe family, a collection of trendy, upwardly mobile achievers and their offspring, all of whom have more than one string to their bow, except for poor *Ordinary Jack*, the hero of the first Bagthorpe book. When kindly Uncle Parker decides to help Jack win his own little share of immortality by pulling off a ridiculous scam on the rest of the family, the confusion mounts to an almost hysterical climax. Jack's sheepdog, Zero, is second perhaps only to Mowat's Mutt in the sheer, ardent, disastrous clumsiness of his efforts to be loyally helpful.

Slapstick is bearable only because all those dreadfully physical things keep happening pell-mell to people who aren't quite flesh and blood. If we thought for one moment that the characters felt the same shock, pain and humiliation we would feel in similar circumstances, the entire effect would be ruined. The comically horrid adult Bagthorpes, nearly all of whom are as greedy, self-centred, egotistical and stubbornly irrational as very small children, richly deserve their comeuppances. Even so, Cresswell manages to avoid extremes of malice in these portraits. The 'bad guys' are childlike, not evil, and physical harm is not often part of the action. Though there's an edge to the humour all the way through (some competitively ambitious middle-class families may squirm), the mood is upbeat, not grim.

A uniquely Canadian voice in this style of humour is that of Brian Doyle. In *Up to Low*, and more recently, in *Angel Square*, he manages to combine a sort of Celtic plangency with Ottawa Valley tall tale, Canadian colloquialism and working-class deadpan. It's an original mixture that proves particularly rewarding in *Angel Square*, a story of post-war bigotry in Ottawa's Lowertown. Roving packs of 'Dogans', 'Pea Soups' and Jews (Doyle doesn't quite have the courage to name them 'Kikes' in the real slang of those days) beat each other up in the ironically named Angel Square, the junction all must cross on their way to their various parochial schools. Tommy is the young hero who, together with his friend Coco Laframboise, confronts anti-Semitism and tracks down the brutal assailant of Sammy Rosenberg's father. Tommy himself is the epitome of Canadian pragmatic ecumenicism; to earn money for Christmas presents, he waxes floors at the Talmud Torah, sings in the choir at St Albany's, serves as altar boy at St Brigit's and works as stock boy at Woolworth's after school.

The names are wonderful: Toe-Jam Laframboise, Killer Bodnoff, Fleurette Fetherstone Fitchell. So is the evocation of urban winters a generation ago – Flat Fifties (tins of cigarettes) given to Dad for Christmas; the smell of cheap chocolates, perfume and melting snow on woollen mittens in Woolworth's; the muffled approach of trams in thick snowdrifts.

There's plenty of Irish blarney, an unfortunate predilection on Doyle's part for comic drunks, and a touch of romanticism beautifully carried off. Tommy's favourite teacher (and there's a wickedly funny spoof of the bad ones) is Mr Maynard, who stirs Tommy's imagination in a science class one day by talking about the utter eternal lifelessness of the moon. If one leaf falls on earth, he says, it's more change than may occur on the moon in a hundred autumns. The words echo in Tommy's mind as he watches the eclipse of the moon one snowy night, and serve as a guide for individual action on earth, too.

One form of humour that doesn't seem to have survived the Victorian era, luckily, is the ghoulish admonitory tale, like *Struwelpeter*, in which cruel mutilations and other assorted punishments are visited upon naughty children. The only two contemporary examples that come to mind are both transmogrified into something curiously satisfactory.

'Pierre', one of the tiny tales in Maurice Sendak's *Nutshell Library*, is a gem. It is virtuoso in its use of the miniature size; not only do the blue and yellow pictures perfectly exploit the space available in terse expressiveness, but the typography and the use of white space also make a comic statement. Pierre, who doesn't care – not about anything – is taught a sharp lesson at last by a placid lion. Along the way, there are some memorable lines; I'm particularly fond of the father's coaxing blandishment, 'I'll let you fold the folding chair', because it pinpoints so adroitly the kind of excitement small children find in the most ordinary actions.

The other example of admonitory literature in which the children emerge unscathed is the series of books about *Nurse Matilda*, by Christianna Brand, illustrated by her famous artist cousin Edward Ardizzone. To capture the Victorian flavour of the stories, the books are richly produced, small in size, with gold-tooled green leatherette bindings, and even a red ribbon to mark the reader's place. *Nurse Matilda* deserves such attention to detail, because it is a bizarrely original story of a huge, almost numberless and certainly ungovernable Victorian family of children and their unusual nanny, Nurse Matilda, who has eyes like black beads and a nose 'like two potatoes'. Nurse Matilda has unsuspected magical powers. She was apparently not inspired by the earlier Mary Poppins; the author tells us that Nurse Matilda is based on a family story handed down through several generations. I find her a more humane and amusing invention than the egomaniacal and emotionally icy Poppins. The magical adventures she creates are not for herself, as Mary Poppins's almost always are, but for the children, to teach them the seven lessons they must learn before Nurse Matilda moves on.

This book has its cake and eats it, too: the children's inventive cussedness becomes its own punishment, but what wayward fun it can be while it lasts. On Matilda's day off, the children are warned to do *precisely* what they are told. Ordered to put on their hated best clothes for a surprise visit from an aunty (and there is a marvellous description of Victorian children's newly laundered clothes, all starched so the sleeves and legs come apart with a lovely tearing-apart noise) the children obey to the letter. They put them on, all right – on the piano, on the pig, on the donkey, and on the chicken. The chaos that ensues when the dim-sighted great aunt arrives to adopt one of the children is as wild as anything invented by Helen Cresswell, but with an added charm of merriment at a distance of time.

This book, although it would seem on the surface to be stuffily preoccupied with children's naughtiness and how to cure it, actually responds to something rooted in children's nature. A universal experience of childhood is that fevered, itchy desperation of being in a foul mood, being very very bad and *not being able to stop*. Nurse Matilda's 'lessons' evoke that feeling with horrid clarity. Her comforts and consolations, too, have all the soft coolness of Mother's forgiving hand on the throbbing post-tantrum brow.

This is comedy of a fairly demanding kind, despite its occasional slapstick. It asks the young reader to identify both with the naughty children and with their governess, and to picture a world that has long vanished. Does it make children laugh? Not all of them; not all children are sophisticated enough in their literary tastes to enjoy a spoof of Victorian family stories, though Ardizzone's lively drawings do make the story more accessible. Still, it has an eccentrically memorable flavour.

Stories of rebellion in which adults, not children, are naughty, are far more the modern mode. *The Shrinking of Treehorn*, the wittiest and most trenchant book produced so far by the American Florence Parry Heide, is often recommended in Britain for the very youngest readers, perhaps because of its small, picture book format and simple, straightforward text. But deadpan satire and mordant humour at the expense of insensitive, distracted adults is hardly the most rib-tickling fare for four- and five-year-olds. (Revealingly, a British *Treehorn* derivative – *Not Now, Bernard* by David McKee, in which a boy is devoured by a monster while his distracted parents fail to notice, is accepted as a preschool book in Britain; it is possibly considered too ghoulish and negative by North American parents.)

Poor Treehorn. He has begun, inexorably and inexplicably, to shrink. However patiently he deals with his predicament, the adults are relentlessly obtuse. His parents wonder if he is deliberately trying to be difficult;

his head teacher gives him a stunningly banal pep talk; his teacher scolds him in timeworn school clichés. 'We don't shrink in this class.' Even his friend the bus driver doesn't recognize the shrunken Treehorn and doesn't listen to explanations.

> *'Nobody gets smaller,' said the bus driver. 'You must be Treehorn's kid brother. What's your name?'*
> *'Treehorn,' said Treehorn.*
> *'First time I ever heard of a family naming two boys the same name,' said the bus driver. 'Guess they couldn't think of any other name, once they thought of Treehorn.'*

It's a devastatingly funny book, but only for those old enough to recognize, and survive, the inadequacies of adults.

Perhaps this is a good place to look at another, wildly popular school of recent humour which I believe should be approached with some caution. There is no other name for it: 'bum humour' it is and must be called. Most parents are familiar enough with Freudian cliché to recognize, and be tolerant of, that phase in a child's life when a mere shout of 'Poopy!' or 'Bum!' is enough to send a preschooler into fits of wild giggles and hysterical silliness. The shrillness and obsessiveness of the jokes ought to alert us that terrible anxiety – anxiety about losing control – lies just beneath the surface.

Nothing could be easier, for an author with matching obsessions and an eye for commercial gain, than to exploit that vein of bathroom compulsiveness that is universal in early childhood. What surprises me is that adults condone it so eagerly, as though unwilling to be thought prudish or unhip. Raymond Briggs, the fine English artist who wrote *The Snowman* and beautifully illustrated Virginia Haviland's collection of fairy tales, is in my view one of the worst offenders. An extravagant anality and a snidely derogatory portrayal of women are present in many of his books, most disturbingly in the well-received *When the Wind Blows*, a horrific comic-style admonitory book about nuclear war. Crude, music-hall misogyny is also evident in his popular *Fungus the Bogeyman* books, though here it is anality that takes pride (if you can call it that) of place. Unlike its elaborately, even laboriously, witty hardback predecessor, *Fungus the Bogeyman*, the pop-up version, *Fungus the Bogeyman's Plop-Up Book*, has little redeeming satirical merit. In shades of bilious green, puce and magenta, it goes about as far as humanly possible in wallowing in bodily disgust. It revels in slime, stinking feet and reeking underwear, rotten socks, pop-up strings of snot, mouths full of toads, people sniffing at the crotch of dirty trousers . . . and, *pièce de résistance*, the Bogey Umbilical Cord, a weird appendage through which Bogeys 'discharge noxious stomach gasses' into the bedrooms of sleeping people.

Is there any harm in all this? It certainly panders to the child's most primitive instincts. I don't know many parents who would think it helpful to join in, with shrieks of 'poo-poo!' and 'tinkle!' when the toddlers get manic. But giving them this sort of book amounts to the same thing. Far from being supportive or life affirming, as its authors probably think, the adult approval implicit in writing, buying and giving the book strikes me as pure 'acting out', to use a psychoanalytic term. My instinct is to let children discover and enjoy such illicit, rebellious pleasures on their own, with neither encouragement nor censorship.

Toilet humour is supposed to be peculiarly British, but it has its acolytes elsewhere. The celebrated Canadian poet, Dennis Lee, seems to have sensed this dilemma, though perhaps not followed it through, when he told *Books in Canada* (December 1983) that his poem about Georgie, the one with smelly ears, is 'morally corrupt . . . you can be an absolute slob, a real pig, and tell Georgie off while feeling you're on the side of the angels'. Lee admits, in the course of the same interview, 'Sometimes I feel like the Jack the Ripper of poetry, enticing kids to take off their pants. With their parents, well, it's as if the kids and I are looking at dirty pictures together.'

Lee is probably referring to his poems in *Jelly Belly* and *Garbage Delight*, an astounding number of which dwell on bums, ruddy bums, muddy bums, bloody crud, smelly snouts, smelly bellies, nosepicking and various other forms of grottiness. I think Lee is right to feel a little uneasy. These are cheap laughs; he's playing to the pit with a vengeance. Body dirt and anal aggression are legitimate preoccupations of childhood, but simple repetition does not an affirmation make.

While uncontrollable laughter is no great disaster, most parents recognize it as a symptom of uncomfortable tension, rather than literary appreciation or even liberation from repression. Children will discover and celebrate flatulence and excretion all by themselves, among themselves, without any need for adult cheerleaders. While we have their attention with a book in our hands, why strike a Jack the Ripper posture?

It could be argued that humane subversion, in this case the rebellion of the child against adult authority, is a worthy function of literature. Certainly, one of the most enduring themes of children's books is the celebration of the humanity of children, and the dignity of their own concerns, not just 'enticing them to take off their pants'. One laid-back rebel who deserves immortality, especially among the ranks of six- and seven-year-old boys, is Tom, that fooling-around artist and hero of *How Tom Beat Captain Najork and His Hired Sportsmen*, by Russell Hoban.

Quentin Blake, who can't draw a picture that doesn't brim with edgy wit and loopy humour, helps immortalize this slouchy boy with the amiable smile who is somehow unfazed by his bustle-bottomed Aunt Fidget Wonkam-Strong, she with the dreadfully vivid name and the iron hat. When Tom simply won't stop his fooling around and messing around and playing around with bits of string and mud and alley rubbish, Aunt calls in her perennial threat: the moustachioed, debonair Captain Najork, a knee-jerk hearty if ever there was one. Tom's triumph at the games of womble, muck and sneedball, against all the unfair odds stacked against him, is a comic hymn of praise to the ingenuity and resilience of kids.

Part of the fun, of course, is that Tom gets to chug away in his newly won pedal boat to a new town, where he promptly advertises for, and hires, a new aunt, Bundlejoy Cosysweet.

It is no accident that Tom's new aunt sounds something like a cross between a burlesque queen, a flower child and a soft porn star; he even lays down 'his terms' to her in the fine high-handed style of the most old-fashioned chauvinist husband: 'No greasy bloaters, no mutton. . . . And I do lots of fooling around. Those are my conditions.' We are not told what's in it for Bundlejoy, but that hardly matters in this story, which is Tom's. And in Tom's world, there are two kinds of female figures, those in authority, like Aunt Wonkam-Strong who withers nature ('Where she walked the flowers drooped, and when she sang the trees all shivered') and those not in authority, who are as sensually alluring as Bundlejoy.

Tom's story is poetically true; like it or not, this is how young males, at some point and with some parts of their psyche, see the women who bear, raise and teach them. The innate misogyny is well within acceptable limits. Besides, though the aunt is stern and demanding beyond all reason, she is not malicious, and she gets her own happy ending within the story – marriage to Captain Najork, who is smitten by her opaque charms.

The same is generally true of another classic boy's story, the strongly written *Soup* by Robert Newton Peck. The mother, the aunt, the school nurse, and the teacher are all the kind of narrow, sex-hating, repressed, prudish, religion-prating dominatrixes made into a national American stereotype by Philip Wylie in the 1950s. Woman is the implacable Other in Peck's work; though the female reader may find this disturbing, the writing is good enough to convince us that this is an honest account of reality as perceived by at least one small-town boy. 'The wind was as ripe as apples, so full of fall that you could almost bite every breath,' Peck writes, and the atmosphere of tough, small-town boyhood, with its poverty and exhilaration, its cruelties and bigotries, has moments of high farce and moral insight that are relished by generation after generation of school children.

While Oedipal conflict is a main wellspring of humour for male authors, I can't think of a single example that works back in the other direction, with daughters humorously exposing fathers as laughable or despicable characters. Of course, it is mothers who still do most of the intimate, daily work of child rearing and who are therefore still fated, alas, to take the brunt of children's rebellious anger.

Since every child's needs are different, I would hesitate to say that these books have no place on the shelf. But even when – or perhaps especially when – an author is gigantically popular with all kinds and categories of young readers, I believe an adult should be alert to nuance, tone and sybolism that may carry a suprising undercurrent of meaning.

Roald Dahl is overwhelmingly the most popular children's author in Britain; children regularly vote him their favourite author in different age categories and each time he brings out a new book it rockets to the top of the bestseller lists. He holds the same sway over readers' loyalties as

Enid Blyton once commanded, and perhaps it is reckless or even futile to aim one's slingshot at such a Goliath. Nevertheless, I think it is useful for adults involved with children's reading to pause and consider the possible sources of his success, and to weigh his acknowledged strengths against what I think is a disturbing subtext.

Like Blyton, Dahl wins his young readers' affection in part by allying himself with their instinctive drives. She provided patterns of adventurous autonomy in which youngsters triumphed without adult help; he seems to subvert adult strictures by endorsing children's impulses to aggression and vengeance. And, unlike Blyton, Dahl writes with a kind of devilishly zestful energy. His wittily contemporary fantasies have the kind of verbal flair and comic inventiveness that appeal to the most demanding young readers as well as to those merely hungry for swift and violence-ridden plots.

Adults recognize Dahl's powers as a story-teller; still, many parents and librarians have told me that his children's books make them uneasy. In America, where annual Christmas reruns of the television special based on *Charlie and the Chocolate Factory* reinforce the book's continuing popularity, the story's sugar-coating may lull adult apprehensions. Those vats of bubbling chocolate, those cornucopias of sparkling sweets – aren't they tailor-made for children? And Christmas is an indulgent time. (A convincing alternate reading of *Charlie and the Chocolate Factory*, by Hamida Bosmajian, in the critical quarterly *The Lion and the Unicorn*, suggests that it is an extended 'excremental vision' of an inferno, with the factory as a gigantic digestive system.)

Perhaps adult acceptance of Dahl also owes something to the vogue for sadism and black humour, tinged by an unadmitted animosity towards modern children. For though the book seems to sympathize with children as underdogs, it is really a *Struwelpeter* in disguise – one of those gleefully punitive nineteenth-century diatribes intended to frighten little children into better behaviour. Now, as then, children are perfectly capable of savouring the gruesome details while blandly ignoring the moral.

Charlie, the hero and the only worthy child in the book, is, like all of Dahl's heroes, an extraordinarily passive, obedient and compliant little boy. His impoverished family is starving, right in the shadow of Willy Wonka's huge chocolate factory, but Charlie – fading away into a ghostly thin little presence – wearily, uncomplainingly, meekly, the very model of the deserving poor, prepares to starve to death, without protest, without struggle, and without any effort to save himself.

When Charlie's grandfather helps him to win a contest that will admit him to the mysterious chocolate factory, Charlie's life is saved. At the factory, though, he meets four other children who are to be severely, even gruesomely, punished during the course of the factory tour. Veruca Salt, for example ('She needs a good kick in the pants,' says Grandpa Joe) is the spoiled brat daughter of a rich American-sounding capitalist. Her father smokes cigars, tries to buy everything he sees, and her mother is grossly fat. To my ears, this characterization comes uncomfortably close to a common anti-Jewish stereotype.

The humour of the book consists of the ghastly punishments inflicted on the four children by the Oompa-Loompas, the little jungle pygmies who work virtually as slaves in Wonka's factory. In the original edition, these pygmies were fuzzy-headed Africans; Dahl had to change this detail after protest.

Willy Wonka, the factory owner, is presented as a weirdly capering, shrill, hyperactive little leprechaun, a malign dwarf who seems to be the modern opposite of a fairy-tale pixie. At one point, he threatens to make a beard and moustache grow on Veruca – a vengeance on girls that is strangely echoed in a Dennis Lee poem. Finally, Veruca Salt is dropped down a rubbish chute, where she will now, as the Oompa Loompas gloat, have to associate with rubbish like herself, instead of her fancy friends. But where will she go?

'Why, to the furnace,' Mr Wonka says. 'To the incinerator.' The scene in itself is distasteful enough, with its approving images of punishment by fire. But parents may be even more disconcerted when they learn of Roald Dahl's anti-Semitic comments to the *New Statesman:* 'There is a trait in the Jewish character that does provoke animosity . . . I mean Hitler, I mean there's always a reason why anti-anything crops up anywhere; even a stinker like Hitler didn't just pick on them for no reason.' The *New Statesman* had interviewed Dahl after he published an article in a literary magazine in which he speculated that 'the American President and Senate and the Congress [are] utterly dominated by the great Jewish financial institutions . . .'

Holocaust hints and images run through the book, chief among them the sinister factory itself, with its 'huge iron gates . . . and smoke belching from its chimneys', a factory sealed to the townspeople. Willie Wonka's chief competitor, Dahl tells us, is Fickelgruber . . . unmistakably reminiscent of Hitler's birth name, Schickelgruber.

When the Oompa-Loompas watch Veruca's parents follow her down the garbage chute 'to the furnace', they chant victoriously: '. . . we very rightly thought/ That in a case like this we ought/ To see the thing completely through/ We've polished off her parents, too.' The Final Solution, so to speak – though these characters do reappear at the end of the book, not dead but covered in rubbish. Surely we must question the appropriateness of a children's story in which scenes of 'justified' violence have a parallel with the Holocaust.

Misogyny is another distressing motif in Dahl's work. Many of his numerous books rehash the same tired plot: a meek small boy finally turns on his adult female tormentors and kills them. In *James and the Giant Peach*, the noble small boy is treated cruelly by his wicked aunts; he squashes them flat with the giant peach. In *George's Marvellous Medicine*, the noble small boy is tormented by his 'old hag . . . grizzly old grunion . . . miserable old pig' of a grandmother. She is a 'filthy old woman': she had 'a small puckered-up mouth like a dog's bottom'. One of her worst crimes is that she is a castrator: she tells George that it is a crime to grow. 'Daddy says it's fine for a man to be tall,' George bravely defies her. (Fathers are usually wonderful, as self-servingly portrayed by Dahl, and one is reminded that when *Charlie and the Chocolate Factory* was criticized in The *Horn Book* magazine, Dahl angrily defended the book on the grounds that he wrote it for his injured son, to whom he was a devoted father.)

George gets his own back. He mixes a potion of liquids scrounged from kitchen, bathroom and barn (some of the details are explosive with explicit sexual disgust and rage) and detonates his grandmother. Her ghastly physical sufferings, which include an electric shock goosing, go on for a day or two ('There's squigglers in my belly! There's bangers in my bottom!' she shrieks, in a parody of a rape) until she finally is destroyed utterly. 'George . . . felt quite trembly,' the narrator says as the book ends. 'He knew something tremendous had taken place that morning. For a few brief moments he had touched with the very tips of his fingers the edge of a magic world.' This tremulous orgasmic moment of pleasure seems obscene, to say the least, in light of what has gone before.

The depiction of woman as evil is even more explicit in *The Witches*, which is presented as children's humour but which, to an adult reader, seems shot through with a chilling vein of hatred and fear. This time, the kindly adult figure is, for once, a woman, the boy's grandmother. An introductory note starts off the book.

> Listen very carefully. Never forget what is coming next. REAL WITCHES *dress in ordinary clothes and look very much like ordinary women. They live in ordinary houses and work in* ORDINARY JOBS. . . . *a* REAL WITCH *hates children with a red-hot sizzling hatred* . . . (Emphasis is Dahl's.)

Witches, it turns out, hate children and plot to kill them all because, to witchy nostrils, children smell like fresh dog excrement. Dahl creates a very real atmosphere of horror and fear in this book; the witches are genuinely loathsome. At the end of the book, they have managed to transform the hero into a mouse. Still, he has learned the secret of how to destroy them, and we leave the mouse and his grandmother at a peak of excitement: they have just vowed to spend the rest of their lives crisscrossing the globe, seeking and exterminating witches.

Children's literature is so rich in humour of the genuine, humane, affirmative kind. There are so many well-written stories, for every age group, that do not reek of dog excrement or 'red-hot sizzling hatred'. No parent, teacher or librarian needs to be intimidated by the sheer commercial success of an author whose works may trouble them; they need not become advocates and promoters of a comic style, however popular, which they find destructive. Humour can sputter with indignation and rage, and often does, but hatred is not funny.

Chapter 5

THE QUEST FOR IDENTITY

We read books to find out who we are. What other people, real or imaginary, do and think and feel . . . is an essential guide to our understanding of what we ourselves are and may become . . . a person who had never listened to nor read a tale or myth or parable or story, would remain ignorant of his own emotional and spiritual heights and depths, would not know quite fully what it is to be human . . . There have been societies that did not use the wheel, but there have been no societies that did not tell stories.

Ursula K. Le Guin, *The Language of the Night*, 1979

As I READ FOR and mulled over this chapter on the theme of a child's quest for identity, a funny little nursery-rhyme rhythm kept tapping away at the door of my consciousness. 'When the hum was hum-hum, The hum began to hum.'

'What *is* that rhyme?' I finally asked my youngest daughter, hum-humming it out for her.

'When the pie was opened,' she said at once, 'the birds began to sing.' Of course! There is the king, counting his money; the queen busy with her honey; and if we count the little blackbirds tucked up in their pie, we have the whole archetypal nuclear family in its cosy nest. Those blackbirds, bursting forth with such verve, must have pecked at my subconscious because they embody the energy of the emerging child – the child who must break the tight bounds of the family circle and learn to sing a new song.

Books have a special place in this task. Some children, of course, never read, and still manage very nicely to become individuals. In my own childhood, though, books were an essential adjunct: I would walk for blocks unconscious of my surroundings, engrossed by the strangeness, the sheer surprising difference, of the way someone in a book spoke or thought or acted.

The 'otherness' I met in books helped me to define myself; once I was past the quick dazzled gulping of stories for the sheer magic of being transported, I came more and more to value books that let me into some other world that was tangibly real but spiced with strangeness. The one thing I hated was false goodness. When Jo in *Little Women* stopped putting her hands in her pockets, quit whistling, curbed her temper and learned to be demure, I lost all interest. There was nothing to learn from someone who had started out with such promise, only to capitulate to the same stultifying standards that were being imposed on me.

There's nothing in books so likely to make a child mean-tempered and uncivil as a story of saccharine goodness and light; Pollyanna, when I met her, made me savage with cynicism. When she cooed over the crutches in her Christmas barrel (now the barrel interested me; what *was* a Christmas barrel?) I wanted to throw them at her head. I don't know how modern children can tolerate the pap of Holly Hobby and Miss Cheerful, those commercially bland damsels who inhabit cardboard meadows starred with tomato-coloured flowers. The best fantasies, the ones that summoned our delight and commanded our loyalty, were always those that had the solid feel of three dimensions.

Among the charms of Beatrix Potter's *The Tale of Peter Rabbit*, for example, is its delicious frankness: Peter is naughty, Mrs Rabbit is loving but stern, Mr McGregor is emphatically an enemy. He *ate* Father Rabbit. Even small children appreciate the delicate interplay between Peter Rabbit-as-lovable-child (is there any more instantly recognizable childhood gesture of discomfort than that pose of Peter Rabbit's, when he must hold his chin up while mother fastens his top button?) and Peter Rabbit as indelibly rabbit-like, dashing frantically around the garden when he forgets the path to the gate, or hiding in a watering can with his quivering ear-tips betraying his rabbity presence.

In the falsely sentimental toddler books that clog our chain book shops, a rabbit could only be an adorable bunny. In Beatrix Potter's hands, Peter is sometimes silly, definitely greedy, but without question lovable, if only because of the subtle and endearing watercolours in which he appears, and the story's precise, intelligent prose.

The best works always seem to radiate an acknowledgement of children's nature as it really is. Without that deep, sure acceptance by the adult world, no child can be self-accepting. That is why the commercial flatteries of Smurfettes and Care Bears are so irrelevant to children's development: they encourage a simpering niceness that is incongruously imposed on a child's nature, like a crust of caramelized sugar on top of an interesting stew.

Books can be forthright about children's characters, at the same time as they are loving. Both my daughters were devoted to *Don't You Remember?* by Lucille Clifton, the pink and brown picture book about four-year-old Desire Mary Tate, a little girl who 'remembered everything' and suffered, as all children must, from the ardour of her wishes and the maddening carelessness of adults who seem to take for ever to keep their promises. Desire pouts, whines and even takes furiously to her bed with an indignant curse ('Dag double dag!' . . . an expressive oath taken up enthusiastically by my own children). The kindness with which her family helps Desire to overcome her frustration is the strong foundation of this book's appeal.

Tell Me a Mitzi, by Lore Segal, was another favourite. My children loved the homely, rumpled, affectionately portrayed New York family and the wry, observant wit of both author and illustrator. One morning, Mitzi decides to take baby brother Jacob and go to visit her grandparents before her parents wake up. Mitzi patiently wrestles with the physical reality of a baby – climbing into his crib, taking off his pyjamas, changing his nappy, putting on his clothes, filling a bottle, struggling with a pushchair, dealing with a lift, hailing a taxi – only to meet with defeat when the taxi asks her 'Where to?' and she can only reply 'Grandma's house'.

It's one of those shaggy-dog jokes: after Mitzi retraces all her steps, dragging heavy, homely Jacob back upstairs, getting him undressed and putting him back to bed, Mother wakes up, comes in and asks her to be

THE QUEST FOR IDENTITY

a big girl and get out of her pyjamas all by herself this morning. 'You do it,' says Mitzi, 'I'm exhausted.'

Still, she makes sure to ask for Grandma's address. 'Why?' asks Mother. 'Because,' says Mitzi. There's an acceptance here of Mitzi's ongoing private life, her stubborn resolve and the fact that children have capacities far beyond what parents often assume.

One reason, certainly, that my own family doted on the Mitzi stories was that the family is recognizably Jewish; they also loved Desire Mary Tate, who was brown, and Peter Rabbit, who was furry, but it was an added pleasure to see their own identity mirrored, and confirmed, in an engagingly warm and humorous story.

Identity must necessarily be more problematic for immigrant children, or children of mixed racial and cultural background. *Comfort Herself*, by the British writer Geraldine Kaye, is one of the most vigorous and affirmative workings-out of this theme that I've read (always excepting *Kim*, of course), and this optimistic novel for pre-teenage readers avoids the flat characterizations so typical of 'message' novels. Comfort Jones, age eleven, is left stranded in London when her mother, a gentle flower-child-type, is killed in an accident. Her father, a Ghanaian, has long since left them to return to Ghana.

Exceptionally bright, resilient and street-smart, Comfort decides to take charge of her own fate instead of succumbing passively to the child-welfare authorities. Secretly, while outwardly agreeing to go to her ultra-respectable maternal grandparents in a Kent village, she finds her father's address in Ghana and writes to him.

Comfort's attempts at survival hinge on adapting herself to the radically different demands of her different environments. With her Kent grandmother, she speaks in a special soft voice and learns to make pastry; with the fright of the Brixton riots still fresh in her mind, she picks her way alertly around any outbreak of racism among her new playmates in the village; when, at last, she goes to Ghana, she has to learn a new demeanour to please her traditionalist father and his new wife. The most complex new environment proves to be the bush village where Comfort goes to live with her paternal grandmother; sunk deep in tribal ways, fighting to be allowed to go to market (all hope of school forestalled), Comfort completely loses track of time.

Kaye makes Comfort believable partly through her vividly detailed and realistic evocation of all these different settings; the African village, in particular, with its fierce matriarch, its intricate and sometimes strangling family relationships and its physical discomforts, is marvellously present. By her twelfth birthday, Comfort has run away from the bush and arranged to fly back to Britain. Because the reader has intimately shared Comfort's ardent efforts to adapt to and find meaning in each new way of life, her brave new beginning is convincing rather than facile. The book ends as Comfort is welcomed home by Lettie, the Kent village girl who has become her friend and with whom we see her at her most relaxed, confident and forward looking. 'This is where she belongs, isn't it?' says

Lettie. 'Comfort Kwatey-Jones lives in Penfold, Kent, England, the World.'

Friendship is the first bridge a child builds out to the larger world. In a friend's house you first notice how the kitchens of different families smell different; you first sense the different shadings of harshness or jocularity in the way other men and women talk to each other and to their children; in the offhand swapping of stories between friends, you first catch yourself in small betrayals of family secrets, family loyalties; in the first fallings-out, you learn the hurt fury of rejection, and the first stinging recognition that your own values and behaviour are not universal or universally approved.

Stories of friendship can comfort the lonely child, for whom the book friendship is a rewarding substitute, but they can also illuminate the painful shocks and surprises that are inevitable in those first, intense real-life bondings. *The Secret Language*, by Ursula Nordstrom, is particularly sensitive in the way it captures the clinging together of two lonely children at a boarding school. The heroine is the timid and sheltered ten-year-old Victoria; her friend is the tough little school rebel, Martha. Martha is more worldly than Victoria, more imaginative and more troubled. She rescues the tearful Victoria from dreadful homesickness by drawing her into an exclusive comradeship which defies the mores of the rest of the school, a defiance symbolized by their use of a private language ('Ick-en-spik' is Martha's invented phrase of scorn for the goody-goodies).

True to the play of children and the world-opening energies of friendship, the two girls invent fantasy houses for themselves, first with tiny dolls in a drawer, and later in a real hut they build in the woods, with considerable effort and ingenuity. But the little shelter of their friendship is often threatened. At one point, mutual resentments smoulder when Martha scoffs at Victoria for believing in the tooth fairy. And Victoria, who is, after all, the rather prim daughter of a priggish mother, is pained when she realizes that mother disapproves of the outspoken Martha. Vicky, though, is staunchly loyal, and Martha eases the way with a generous gesture, an apology for 'being a dope in front of your mother'.

They may seem like tiny dramas indeed, but these small events trigger, for the girls, significant experiences of loyalty and betrayal, dismay and reconciliation. Nordstrom handles them believably and precisely, always through the children's play and conversation. *The Secret Language* is an emotionally true and sensitive story for girls between the ages of six and ten about how two children can enrich each other's lives, even while in the process of growing past each other.

More sophisticated, witty, glancing and contemporary is *Thunder and Lightnings*, a fine book by Jan Mark about the friendship of two boys in rural Norfolk. Andrew, about ten or eleven years old, is the town boy whose warm, chaotic middle-class family has just moved into the ramshackle Tiler's Cottage. He is befriended by Victor, a working-class boy who lives near by in a harsh, compulsively waxed and polished household. Mark is wickedly funny about the way the boys have to negotiate

THE QUEST FOR IDENTITY

the floors and rugs in Victor's house: they sidle around the linoleum bordering the living room rug 'like ancient Egyptians' and go up the stairs bow-legged, with their feet 'on the wooden bits' on each side of the newly vacuumed stair carpet.

Mark, like the outstanding English author William Mayne, knows how to extract sly humour from everyday sensory perception and incident, and she is superb at evoking physical sensation. Victor and Andrew base their friendship on a fascination with the old-fashioned Lightning jets and World War II Spitfires at a nearby airbase. The crash of sound barriers breaking, the howl and whine of engines, the thrills and thunder of the modern era, are cheerfully present on every page. Behind the excitement of plane watching is a more subtle kind of observation, as the two boys warily sniff out the cultural differences between them, their different ways of defending themselves from hurt, their different ways of being clever or kind. Andrew, who is superficially so much more sophisticated, is actually (as his mother notices) more childishly naïve, and it is only after clumsily bruising Victor's feelings several times that Andrew begins to acquire some of his friend's native tact.

Thunder and Lightnings is so sharply perceptive that it can be read with pleasure on several levels. *Dawn of Fear*, a similar story of comradeship between two English boys, is actually less complex in its writing, and deals with younger boys, but its sheer emotional wallop is so much more intense that it is best suited to a slightly older child, perhaps of eleven or twelve. Susan Cooper is known for her excellent series, *The Dark Is Rising*, but this semi-autobiographical realistic story about the London Blitz is as good as, if not superior to, her better-known fantasies.

As in *The Secret Language*, the children – Derek, the central character, his sunny-tempered friend Peter, and Geoff, who is not quite accepted by the two best friends – are wholeheartedly engaged in building a hut. North American children would call it a 'fort'; Derek calls it a 'camp', but its ritual meaning as the first home away from home, the first tasting of independence and self-reliance, is the same everywhere. While the boys, who are rather middle class and vulnerable, try to defend their camp from their rougher, tougher working-class enemies, the White Road gang, they are also coping with nightly treks to air-raid shelters, fatigue, and a pallid, skimpy rationed diet for which their parents keep apologizing but which is all the children have ever known.

True to the strange intensities of child life, it is the war and the air raids, with their deafening noises and tracer-lit skies, that seem dreamily unreal to the boys, a spectacular sort of game or show, while the planning, building and defence of their camp is desperately real and arouses fierce and even frightening emotions in them.

Dawn of Fear is a scrupulously honest and tautly written book. We watch one week unfold through Derek's eyes; we see him draw new insights from Peter's generous nature; we share his bursting grief on a grim Wednesday morning when Peter's house is gone, all but the front gate.

The misery and fright were growing inside him like a great swelling balloon. Yesterday the world had begun going badly wrong, but it was to have been better again when today came; the bits of nightmare could have been forgotten. But instead today had brought a change that would need more than forgetting. His world had stopped and the world he would live in from now on would be a different world. The old one with Pete in it would never come back again.

The dawn that teaches Derek real fear and pain also heralds a growing up that begins with loss. Yet *Dawn of Fear*, though powerful, is not a depressing book; the constructive strength of friendship carries the reader right past the grief of the last scene.

The same is true of another wartime story, *Alan and Naomi*, by Myron Levoy. The main plot seems rather melodramatic at first: twelve-year-old Alan Silverman, a sensitive only child growing up in Brooklyn during World War II, is asked to befriend a profoundly distressed French Jewish refugee child, Naomi, who saw her father being murdered by the Gestapo. 'Not me,' protests Alan at first. 'She's a girl, she's crazy and I WON'T!' Levoy is particularly skilful at catching the different ways that youngsters talk with different people: the genuinely funny banter and screwball comedy between Alan and his best friend, Shaun Kelly, who has all the toughness and street smartness that Alan lacks; the nervous, defensive and finally tender dialogue between Alan and Naomi; the rough jeering of the ball players at dusk in the streets; the embarrassed formality of Alan talking to a teacher; his fond impatience when he fends off his affectionate, demanding parents; the secret, tentatively sexual voice of Alan, fantasizing about Naomi as his girlfriend.

In the end, though the author clearly intends the relationship with Naomi and her final devastating breakdown to carry the emotional weight of the novel, it is a minor theme that seems fresher, less forced, more genuinely touching. Alan has ruptured his friendship with Shaun because he failed to trust him with the secret of his relationship with Naomi. Alan feared, perhaps pardonably, that rough-tough Shaun might share the macho and xenophobic sentiments of their street pals. It is Alan's suspiciousness (springing, one feels, from his own initial ambivalence about Naomi) that leads, in part, to Naomi's tragedy. At the end, only the reconciliation of Alan and Shaun helps to balance the painful loss of Naomi.

All these stories of friendship carry a sense of risk and strain along with their pleasures; undoubtedly, their authors are remembering accurately the hazards that had to be skirted in those first ventures outside the circle of the family. Another kind of book in which children define themselves seems to hark back to an earlier, more comforting mode of self-definition: the strong identification with place.

There are some books, most loved by girls (and I'll come back to that in a moment), that invite a swooning rapture over landscape. Years afterward, one remembers not so much the characters as the colours of things, the heightened emotionalism that seemed to rise like a dizzying perfume from the grass, the trees, the flowers drowsing in hot sunshine. *Anne of Green Gables, Heidi* and *The Secret Garden* are three that seem curiously linked in this way. As the English psychologist, Nicholas Tucker, points out, all three share a basic plot with heavily Oedipal overtones: a clever, spunky little girl, with more ardour than beauty to recommend her, wins over a gruff, remote older man by the sheer power of her personality. I wonder if the overwhelming seductiveness of the landscape in these novels is the result of an awakening sensuality, unconsciously displaced onto the birds and the bees.

Years later, I remembered the setting of these three novels better than I did their plots. From Johanna Spyri's *Heidi* I remembered the bracing mountain air of Switzerland, the charming simplicity of milk drunk from bowls, meals of fresh cheese and bread, a bed of hay, pastures starred with primroses and snowy peaks flushed with sunset reflections. Re-reading it, I see the charm of that early Swiss pastoral (first published in 1880) which endorsed all the most vigorously progressive views of its day. We first see Heidi at the age of five, struggling up the mountainside in the summer heat, wearing all the clothes she owns to spare her aunt the trouble of carrying them. Sensibly, Heidi rebels, strips down to her underwear and goes capering up the mountainside in splendid barefoot freedom. Furthermore, no one is shocked and no one scolds; indeed, the gruff old 'Alm-Uncle' with whom she is to live merely smiles when he sees the eager little girl clambering up toward him. I can hardly imagine a generation of little girls since 1880, including my own, to whom this would not have represented the most unimaginably heady freedom.

Within hours, Heidi's cleverness, and the ingenuousness of her prattle, have won over the flinty old man who is feared by everyone. The heroine of the Canadian classic, Anne of Green Gables (nearly all of Lucy Maud Montgomery's heroines are named by the houses they inhabit), is another such. Her story, too, begins at the moment when she makes a startlingly unconventional impression on a crusty old man.

In Anne's case, it's her 'imagination' that beguiles the pathologically shy bachelor, Matthew Cuthbert. Anne's imagination is ardently attuned to the landscape: she first tells Matthew that she thought of spending the night in a nearby cherry tree, 'all white with bloom like marble halls': by the time the two of them arrive at Green Gables, Anne has rhapsodized about 'a painted sunset like a great rose window at the end of a cathedral aisle', named an unlikely avenue of apple trees 'the White Way of Delight' and utterly won over the woman-fearing Matthew by 'the rapt light in her eye'.

It's as though the child's heated response to natural beauty has kindled some long-frozen kindred emotion in the cold adult; remote, withdrawn fathers must be all too common, judging by the long-lived popularity of this daydream.

Anne and Heidi share another quality, that of an entirely unnatural artlessness. Both are given to gleeful leaping, singing and sprite-like dancing. But no matter how extreme their response to the landscape, no matter how poetic or exalted, they are never tortured by self-conscious embarrassment. This, of course, is because they are written from outside, seen through the sentimentalizing eyes of an adult. Though Anne and Heidi (and Mary Lennox in her secret garden and Jo of *Little Women*) are loved by girl readers, there is a half-suppressed guilty twinge of envy and alienation that accompanies one's admiration of these idealized heroines.

Was Anne Shirley never ashamed of her outrageous showing off? Did the poison of self-consciousness never cloud Heidi's sunlit days as she lisped to the trees? Nevertheless, the author's sensuous evocation of house and landscape is unforgettable; so is the secret Eden discovered by Mary Lennox, the cross little orphan girl who was healed by nature on those romantic windswept moors so loved by the Brontës.

The Secret Garden, written by the Anglo-American Frances Hodgson Burnett in 1911, still works its magic, even more strongly than *Heidi* or *Anne of Green Gables*, because Mary is not automatically adored. Before she can win over her stubborn old man, she must forge a new character for herself, and she is helped in this difficult task by a wonderful Pan-boy, Dickon. He is as soft spoken, sweet and nurturing as no true adolescent boy who has existed ever before or since, and not only speaks in an enchantingly rustic Yorkshire dialect, but also can charm the birds and the animals with his pan pipes.

Mary brings the long-neglected garden back to life, and in return, the garden bestows on her a serene and giving temperament, a healthy appetite and a new delight in life. It is this possibility of transformation that takes hold of the reader's imagination – a wholesome growth, nurtured and applauded by a whole chorus of earthily wise, rosy-cheeked peasants who know the virtues of hard work and self-sufficiency.

To re-read *The Secret Garden* as an adult is to discover with a nasty shock, however, that though the spell of the garden remains intact, the book goes seriously off the rails toward the end, when Mary sets out to heal her hypochondriac cousin, Colin.

This boy is crippled and bedridden by sheer hysterical dread of death. Helping him, Mary learns new reserves of patience and generosity. Once Colin begins to regain his health, though, Mary disappointingly disappears from the story. The moment of her eclipse is even marked by the author: as Mary's crotchety uncle Archibald returns to his Yorkshire mansion, he is amazed to see his hated, sickly son all healed, racing toward him. 'I can beat Mary in a race,' Colin yells, and, in a fever of omnipotence, 'I'm going to live for ever and ever!' Colin has developed into an arrogant, high-strung little minister of pantheism. He actually leads the forelock-tugging servants (the gardener, Ben Weatherstaff, blinks away tears of admiration) in singing the Doxology in the garden. If Burnett had a weakness for Christlike little boys, she was more realistic, and surer of touch, in depicting Mary, a flawed soul who courageously healed herself. It is for that transformation that the book is remembered and loved.

Blue Willow, by Doris Gates, which won the Newbery Medal in 1940, is another powerful story of rural seeking, aimed at an under-twelve

THE QUEST FOR IDENTITY

audience. Janey Larkin, ten, is the child of migrant workers, Dustbowl refugees from Texas in the years of the Great Depression. Rarely has an author created such a rawboned picture of stark poverty without for one moment reducing her characters to sentimental caricatures. Janey Larkin, too thin, too small, guarded and wary beyond her years, is one of the most believably brave girls in children's fiction, old or new.

Like Anne and like Heidi, Janey triumphs (she gains a home and security for her family) by winning the friendship and admiration of an older, powerful man. And, just like these other stories of Oedipal triumph, *Blue Willow* conveys a sharp impression of place – the heat-dazzled cotton fields of the San Joaquin Valley – along with the heroine's passionate desire to belong, to attach herself permanently to an adopted landscape. But Janey is no sparkler. We know her not through the doting avuncular descriptions (why isn't there a word for auntular?) of the narrator, but from the inside, through her convincingly childlike hopes, fears, hesitations and wellings of excitement.

Perhaps Janey is such a moving character because she has so little. Her only book and her portable school is the New Testament, which her father makes her read daily. She mines it for meaning and for beauty; the moment when she feels love for her stepmother is the moment when that weary, silent, defeated woman suddenly says, about a stand of willows along a swamp: 'Rivers of water in a dry land.'

Janey is deeply attached to the only thing she owns, a blue willow plate, her sole remaining link to an earlier life when she had her natural mother and a real home. For her, living in a dry, harsh and hungry world, the scene on the plate expresses a world of romantic beauty and cool enchantment. Her courage – in defence of the plate against a crude bully, and in grievingly giving it up when money is desperately needed – is what changes the family's luck at last. Though the dusty landscape of *Blue Willow* is not nearly so seductive as the lush beauties of Green Gables, Alpine meadows or Yorkshire Edens, Janey is a more realistic – and more inspiriting – heroine than Anne, Heidi or Mary.

Naturally, a sense of place is a vital element in many novels, but in some it predominates. The Israeli novelist Amos Oz, for example, has written a sparklingly witty and poignant day-in-the-life of an eleven-year-old daydreaming scamp. *Soumchi* (the name of the book and of the scamp) is redolent of a typically mixed, chaotic Jerusalem neighbourhood in the days of the British Mandate. Arched doorways, derelict courtyards, cobbled lanes, evenings scented with pomegranate, all breathe from the page. *Soumchi* is worth reading just for the depth of the boy's reactions as he drinks in the exotically unfamiliar atmosphere in the varying homes of his friends.

Place, as a shaper of identity, is the focus of *Hold Fast*, by Kevin Major, a 1978 novel that marked a breakthrough for the unapologetic use of the Newfoundland dialect in fiction. When both his parents are killed in an accident, Michael, fourteen, is forced to leave the village of Marten and move to a larger town, St Albert, to live with a tyrannical uncle and his cowed wife.

Mike hates to leave what he knows and loves best: running a trapline, riding a skidoo, fixing lobster traps. 'Squiddin is a lot o fun, idn't it?' he wistfully asks his loved grandad before he leaves and the grandfather replies 'Yes b'y, it is so.' The whole story is told in Mike's language and from his limited, belligerent perspective. Angry, grieving and stubborn, he is shipped off, hates town and finds his way back. Mike does not learn much or change during his painful odyssey; in fact, the whole of his accomplishment is to 'Hold fast' to his own rough-and-ready viewpoint, his outport individualism, against the sneers of the townies and the bullying of his uncle.

The problem with this kind of nostalgic stubbornness is that identity doesn't come to a youth as a static inheritance; because Mike modifies nothing of his own behaviour or character (pugnacious, self-justifying, semi-delinquent, hot-tempered) we never see him learn or change. He exploits a town girlfriend who is willing to hold his hand and listen to his endless talk of himself ('I did get a few great kisses out of it, too'), steals a car from an old lady who befriends and feeds him, and finds an excuse for his every action, including knocking another boy unconscious 'by accident' when he punches him.

Major is celebrating Newfoundland dialect and defending Newfoundland working-class values against smug 'brainer' (bookish) townies, and he does forcefully convey the fierce loyalty of an outport boy to his local way of life. What might have strengthened the portrait was a flicker of conflict within Mike himself, any hesitation, doubt or questioning that might have grounded his final choice more solidly. As I'll discuss later, in connection with more powerful works like *The Slave Dancer*, moral ambiguities are a truer and more disturbing truth about the inward life of humans than the brash certainties of a boy like Mike.

Inwardness is the hallmark of these books in which young people are seen sorting through their experiences and trying to forge some sense of who they are, or even find out if they *are* anyone identifiable. Anne of Green Gables voiced a familiar worry when she lamented that there seemed to be so many Annes inside her – if only she knew which one was the real Anne, life would be so much simpler.

The most extreme version of this self-seeking in adolescence is what I think of as the 'lonely vigil' genre: modern Robinson Crusoes who must survive alone in complete isolation. When I first read *Island of the Blue Dolphins* by the American Scott O'Dell, I was astounded by the popularity of such a bleak story. What could be more depressing than the plight of a young Indian girl, left isolated from all her tribe, surviving on a rocky, windswept island for eighteen years with no companion but a wild dog she has tamed?

But of course preadolescents are mesmerized by this account of survival. Aren't they, too, teetering on the perilous brink of adult life, facing challenges that they must meet all alone? Yet these readers are still not far past the age of total dependency on parents, when the fear of being abandoned is the most bone-shaking of terrors.

Survival stories usually involve a lone youth, who is stripped of parents, friends, possessions, shelter, tools and sustenance, and yet who manages through skill and courage to endure. These stories serve as a bracing fantasy reassurance with a comfortingly familiar pattern. The marooned soul is terrified at first, longs for rescue, nearly perishes through ignorant mistakes, and then, because he or she doggedly learns from those mistakes and tries again, begins to adapt to the environment. At the midpoint of the story, we almost always see the survivor reconciled to, even enchanted by, the formerly threatening isolation. At the end, the choice is always to rejoin civilization, a painful compromise made possible because the survivor is strengthened and at peace, having wrested from danger a sure sense of competence, courage and identity.

In *Island of the Blue Dolphins*, Karana begins to thrive when she gives up her numb grieving for her lost people and considers breaking the fearsome tribal taboo against a woman making weapons. Throughout, the narrative is remarkable for showing us, without benefit of human characters with whom Karana could interact and with little inward reverie to break the flow of the action, how she changes and grows.

O'Dell tells the story with a clarity of detail and a restrained, unpoetic narrative style, perfectly reflective of Karana's contained character, which slowly builds a rock-ribbed feeling of reality. So fully imagined is the Island of the Blue Dolphins itself that we feel we know every hummock and ravine. Karana's deepening maturity and her love of her animals are revealed in lively and often touching incidents.

Perhaps because Karana was a real person, and her story is true (the Lost Woman of San Nicolas lived on that island alone from 1835 to 1853), O'Dell was able tell it with complete conviction. The handling of time is noteworthily skilful, too; O'Dell makes us feel the slow rhythmic passage of those eighteen years by keeping track of Karana's repeated seasonal tasks and pleasures, yet he never becomes tediously repetitive. Seamlessly, he balances immediate action and emotion with the lengthy passing of months and years.

Few other stories of lonely vigil can match the power of *Island of the Blue Dolphins*, but *My Side of the Mountain*, by Jean Craighead George comes close in popularity, and even more successful is *Julie of the Wolves*, written eight years later by the same author.

Julie – Miyax, in her native Inuit language – is a thirteen-year-old who has run away from her home in Barrow in Alaska because she has been molested by her slow-witted teenage husband in a marriage of convenience. Lost on the tundra, Julie survives by studying the ways and language of a nearby wolf pack. So well does she imitate wolf-pup behaviour that she is adopted by the pack leader. The wolves feed her (at first regurgitating swallowed meat as they would for their own pups) and take her under their protection; months later, as she treks toward Point Hope on the Alaska coast, the wolf pack is still running near her, protecting her and bringing her food.

The idea is preposterously romantic but George makes it believable, mostly by showing us the workings of Julie's mind as she desperately recalls and uses every trick of survival known to the Inuit peoples. *Julie of the Wolves* works so well, too, because the Arctic is exotically beautiful and strange, a landscape as desolate and challenging, yet as teeming with hidden possibilities of life, as Karana's windswept rocks.

Middle childhood is the season of possibilities, the time when questions arise and roads stretch into the future. After the first books that open doors into new worlds, and before the single-minded narcissism of so much adolescent reading, there are the two quests: the quest for identity and the quest for adventure. The two overlap, of course (there are no simple labels in all of literature) but a book that helps children explore inwardly is a useful one to keep in mind, when so much is available that provides only the relief of escape into action and adventure.

Nor is the search always in deadly earnest. Rightly, there is often a playful, venturesome spirit, a feeling of wonderful rebellious possibilities. *Harry the Dirty Dog* is one of the loved examples among picture books. It deals with identity at the reassuring basic level of the coherence of the individual: even when naughty Harry is unrecognizably covered with dirt, he is still Harry, he is still treated lovingly by the family, and they uncover his real self quickly. Just how important a point this is, though it seems so crashingly obvious, is known to every parent who has seen a three-year-old try on an older child's Halloween mask and then panic when everyone pretends not to recognize him.

Cannonball Simp, by the British artist John Burningham, is more serious, though still in picture-book form. Nobody wants Simp. She is small and fat, a homely little black dog whom we see being cruelly abandoned near a rubbish dump by a raincoated anonymous owner. In one dramatic sweep of a picture, with the menacing black pit of the dump opening beneath the helpless feet of the tossed Simp, Burningham sums up the trembling void of abandonment that is every child's worst nightmare. But Simp does not despair. Hungry and cold, she nevertheless scrabbles for a living. She forges on. And when a yellow path of light lays down its shining ribbon through the woods, leading away through the dark to a shimmering white circus tent, we know Simp is on the road to salvation. Indeed, she saves the hapless clown who befriends her, by inventing a dog-shot-from-cannon stunt. Then we see Simp Resplendent, landing on a drum in the circus ring, star of the show and still her homely self, graceless claws spreading at the end of gangly legs under her tubby little body, tiny eyes gleaming in delight.

The Bee-man of Orn by Frank Stockton, the inventive nineteenth-century American fabulist, is another comical and endearing twist on the search for identity. The Bee-man, as illustrated by Maurice Sendak, is a contented, rumpled, wildly homely eccentric, with a huge bristly chin, a

THE QUEST FOR IDENTITY

foolishly happy smile, a flapping leather coat and hives full of bees who are his best friends.

When a Junior Sorcerer tells the Bee-man that he was surely transformed from something or someone else, the Bee-man is troubled. He feels it is only right to discover his original identity 'even if it's horrid, because no one has a right to keep a form that is not his own'. His adventures are engaging because he plays the role of the fairy-tale innocent, the naïve truthsayer whose honesty shames the pretentious and the phony. At the very end, a sorcerer grants the Bee-man's wish and transforms him into his original self – a marvellously funny baby, with his same ugly mug, grinning with delight in a baby's nightie, snug on his mama's lap and surrounded by doting sorcerers! As though that were not a strong enough reassurance about the continuance of identity, the Bee-man (who now has the option to grow up into anything at all) chooses to grow back into the same happy, sloppy Bee-man, now that he knows he's entitled to that form. The ending is so satisfying because it is the true ending of all transformation tales: we are what we are.

Ninny's Boat, by Clive King, is a sparkling, witty and marvellously well-written quest for a boy's true name and identity. 'They call me Ninny. Yes, they think it's a funny name. But they say it's mine. Anyway, it's the only one I know,' the story begins. The narrator's voice is rueful, humorous, alive with intelligence and spunk. Ninny is a thrall of a savage northern tribe, and, as the story opens, we are swiftly and almost miraculously drawn into the mind of a shaggy boy, sleepily waking in a hayloft to discover that he's been abandoned by the farmer's family to sink or swim in a rising flood. King has never been better than in this adventure, which we experience through the person of a boy with more shrewdness than knowledge.

Ninny is an archetypal survivor, with the survivor's rough-and-ready fellow feeling for other misfits. Spinning helplessly in an old milk tub, Ninny makes jokes with himself, enjoys the craziness of his plight, and sturdily, unquestioningly sets about rescuing the poor dumb creatures left behind, including a dog, a cat, a cow and a witchy old woman marooned in a tree. It's hard, without quoting at length, to convey the quality of merriment and sheer joy-in-being-alive in Ninny's interior monologue. That jokey resignation, the readiness for whatever comes next, never really deserts Ninny in his long search to solve the riddle of his origins.

King makes the most of showing us the world through the eyes of a Dark Ages boy; since we are never allowed to know more than Ninny knows, everything seems fresh, amazing, an age of continual wonders. And, of course, Ninny is a kind of Huck Finn of the north. His innocently faithful recording of events lets even the child reader enjoy the deadpan satire of human foibles.

When the tribe faces a crisis, a wondering Ninny overhears his first council meeting. 'We want nothing but peas . . . we must keep the candles out,' Ninny thinks he hears. 'Sandals? Vandals?' wonders Ninny, and the young reader is delighted to catch on before Ninny does. The spoof of

Dark Ages manners is Monty Pythonesque at times: 'Grrr, Vandals! Myrgings! Gar!' boos a crowd of thick-witted Angles. King is never a dull writer, but in *Ninny's Boat* he seems to take particular pleasure in playing with language. There's a casual reference to the 'bone-fire' when a Viking king is being created – an offhand etymological titbit about the origins of our word 'bonfire.' And familiar nursery rhymes sometimes pop up, in plausibly distorted form, as part of some Dark Ages event, so that we're half convinced we're seeing the true beginnings of a rhyme we met later in time but earlier in our lives.

But this is a quest, and for all the high good humour, Ninny wins through, after daring adventures, to learn at last that he is a long-lost Pictish prince from Britain. By the time he has found his true name (Ninius) he has grown into it, no longer a shaggy, endearing yokel but a weathered and resourceful adventurer who has braved oceans, lived with the 'little people' and seen King Arthur die.

Ninny's quest ends with finding his beginnings, but many a quest novel follows a youngster who is trying to disentangle from family roots. *Josh*, by Australian novelist Ivan Southall, is widely admired for its stream-of-consciousness narrative style. Histrionic, poetry-writing fourteen-year-old Josh visits his Aunt Clara in a back country village and runs smack into a hostile gang of Snopesian local kids. The price the reader must pay for the intensity of Josh's narrative is a certain monotone hysterical quality to his observations, and a muddy confusion of events: not until the end do we begin to realize why the locals are so implacably resentful of Josh. Some readers, of course, relish the puzzle-like quality of this kind of elliptical narrative, and certainly, seeing events from Josh's narrow perspective lets us see directly into his adolescent soul as he moves from self-consciousness, self-pity and fear to a bolder assertiveness at the end.

Family stories are often chronicles of a child's moving away from the family's perception of her character to a greater degree of self-definition. In *Starry Night*, by the British author Catherine Sefton, fourteen-year-old Kathleen is, at first, completely muffled up in the embrace of her ramshackle family in its old farmhouse, just within the Northern Ireland border. With the unquestioning faith of childhood, she accepts their poverty, their prejudices (passionately anti-British, passionately anti-Carmel, the daughter-in-law) and their version of the family's past.

Starry Night is one of those novels where the idiosyncratic intimate life of a family and a neighbourhood is so convincingly alive in the characters' speech and habits that the reader feels drawn into a tangible world, one worth caring about. When Kathleen's summer-vacation friend, Ann from Belfast, starts questioning some of Kathleen's most basic beliefs, Kathleen is angry. But strange disturbances in the unchanging life of the family press themselves on her attention. What is Mammy, the cranky matriarch, hiding? Why is big sister Rose smoking and brooding in the kitchen? Why is Kathleen the only blonde in a family of dark Fays? Soon Kathleen's whole understanding of life – and her place in the family – is toppling in on her like a house of cards. Dramatic revelations, which could have been devastating, instead make it possible for her to see herself, for the first time, as a separate individual, and not just as 'our Kathleen'. At the end, Kathleen is thinking about a future that may take her away from the comfortably soggy dead-end of her family. Fast, poignant, colloquial and funny, *Starry Night* is the kind of coming-of-age novel that is rewarding for readers at every level of ability.

One of the strongest Canadian examples of the family story, and an individual's struggle to define herself within it, is *From Anna*, by Jean Little. Anna is the youngest, and homeliest, of five children in a solid German family in 1933; she is clumsy, awkward and a failure at school. Little is frank about Anna's physical unattractiveness and her frequently sullen demeanour, and yet, because she takes us so sympathetically into Anna's feelings, we are always on Anna's side.

One of Little's finest accomplishments in this book, aimed at the middle reader, is to suggest, clearly but subtly, how a child can feel lonely and angry in the midst of a loving family. Anna's family is stable and affectionate, yet Anna feels isolated; her mother is insensitive, and the older brothers and sisters just a bit heartless in their teasing. Anna knows she isn't stupid, and longs to please her beloved Papa, yet she often manages to do just what will most frustrate him, like refusing to learn English when he decides that the whole family must learn quickly before fleeing to Canada.

'Awkward Anna' her athletic, blonde, extroverted brothers and sisters call her. In Toronto, the reason for her chronic ineptitude is finally discovered: Anna is nearly blind. Fitted with proper glasses, introduced into a kindly and welcoming special class at school, Anna is suspicious and slow to thaw. Her gradual adjustment to Canada is superbly handled; it rings with honesty and close observation, and so does the stubborn, unforgiving way that Anna hugs her new happiness to herself, refusing for months to let her family know how she is beginning to blossom at school.

From Anna is different from the slick contemporary novels in which children suffering from acne, small breasts, premature ejaculation or nasty parents solve their problems strictly within the peer group. Anna's character is as important as her blindness; her family, their patterns of behaviour and belief, are significantly shaped by their own time and place, and not seen in the falsely narrow personal perspective that is so familiar from soap operas and situation comedies. As Anna moves out from her preoccupation with sadness, as she dares to try to belong in her class at school, as she discovers poetry and weaving and friendship, she loses the self-consciousness that spoiled her family relationships in the beginning. At the end, having given herself wholly to making a splendid family Christmas in the new country, Anna is singing carols in her living room and not noticing that she has achieved her goal of being Mama's favourite for tonight – not noticing, in fact, that for once she is special to everyone in the room: 'In her heart it was Christmas, and she was busy singing.'

When children begin to winnow out the true from false in their family's opinion of them, and to find that they are sometimes more truly themselves in contexts outside the family, they are also in the process of testing and sometimes rejecting their family's values. One of the boldest assaults on received values in all of children's literature must be the lonely battle waged by twelve-year-old Patty Bergen, in *Summer of My German Soldier* by Bette Green. Patty, the daughter of a Jewish shopkeeper and his wife in small-town Arkansas in the early 1940s, is a knotted, anxious child. She can't stop herself from telling sly, self-aggrandizing lies, and from compulsive attention-grabbing behaviour with her parents, even though she knows that to draw their attention is to invite put-downs from her lazy, narcissistic mother and vicious abuse from her tense, embittered, neurotic father.

The only one who loves Patty, and who is wholeheartedly loved by her in return, is the family's black maid, Ruth. In fact, Patty sets herself against all the standards of her family and her community: she values the ease and warmth of black life above the status-conscious hypocrisies of the white townsfolk; worse, she finds herself giving shelter to an escaped German prisoner of war, Anton Reiker, in careless defiance of her Jewish family's loathing of the Nazis. More than that, she loves the gentle, literate, decent and caring Anton.

Summer of My German Soldier is a powerful book; it's been continually in print since it was published in 1973 and has surfaced as a television drama. Emotionally, it is devastating; the atmosphere of heat and petty malice in the bigoted little town is stiflingly vivid. Re-reading it ten years after it first appeared, though, I realized that parts of it made me extremely uneasy: there is a sickly taste of masochistic relish in the way Patty, the narrator of her own story, describes in detail how her crazed father beats her with flailing fists and his leather belt.

It rings absolutely true, of course; neurotic families do fall into compulsive patterns, goading each other into the most feared reactions which they then perversely savour. But this is too raw to be illuminating. It almost exploits the sexual edge, the horror of the beatings, to keep the reader fascinated. And then, the gentleness and nobility of Anton beggars belief; not even Green's vigorous prose can really make us believe in a German soldier on the run in the southern United States who would linger for days to cosset a disturbed twelve-year-old and give her lessons in literature.

The true strength of the story is in the side issue of Ruth's love for Patty; in the melodramatically bleak finale to Patty's escapade, when she is sentenced to reform school and her disgraced parents don't bother to visit her, there is an affecting scene in which Ruth arrives on the bus with a sack full of her fried chicken. Ruth has the power to make Patty believe, if only for a moment, that she is a worthwhile person. Patty has defied all her family's and her culture's values, but perhaps her gesture was too coloured by neurotic neediness to signify true independence. At the end, she is only more isolated than ever, and with little more faith in herself, or her future, than at the beginning.

A more understated family novel – and somehow more realistic even

THE QUEST FOR IDENTITY

though it includes a murder, a missing father and a mysterious tombstone – is *The Way to Sattin Shore* by Philippa Pearce, one of the finest novelists writing for children today.

When the story begins, we see ten-year-old Kate Tranter coming home from school alone; she is beginning to be troubled and haunted by the secrets that eddy beneath the calm, working-class patterns of her family's life. It's curiously difficult to summon up the feeling and plot of *The Way to Sattin Shore;* the tone is oblique, matter-of-fact but sensitive to the most glancing of impressions and the most fleeting ripples of disturbance in Kate's consciousness. A 'beam of darkness' lies across her path: it is in fact, her grandmother's malicious overseeing of the family's affairs, her meddling, that has laid this beam, literally and figuratively, in the way.

What is clear at the first is that Kate shies away from intimacy, except with her wonderfully true-to-life ginger cat, Syrup, and that the working out of the family mystery makes life open for her again. When her supposedly dead father is rediscovered and reunited with her mother (through Kate's frantic, last-minute effort) the completed family is like an arch through which Kate is finally free to walk out into the world.

Unlike Patty Bergen, Kate seems on the verge of solving the Oedipal triangle, without ever having been conscious of it to begin with. *The Way to Sattin Shore* is a beautifully rounded, complete story. Though Kate was the agent, she is not the focus of the married couple's reunion; she is content that they should be caught up in one another, and her own concerns have moved from immediate gratifications to expectations of the future.

Yet none of this is stated explicitly; Pearce's control of dialogue and description is so masterful, the meanings so carefully dovetailed into the smallest incidents of plot, that a semicolon can speak volumes, even to an inexperienced reader.

A book like this gives the reader a feeling of quiet satisfaction because the movement of mind and heart go on beneath the surface of the action. We never feel pushed or manipulated by the author. The story is so thoroughly thought out that all actions and consequences seem to flow as naturally and unpremeditatedly as in daily life, yet with a more satisfying coherence.

Most of us are familiar with purely escapist reading in which we know we will be worked on by the author; in fact, we welcome the pumping up of tension or sexual excitement and their mechanical release through predictable plot devices, because that is precisely the stimulating diversion we sought. Less welcome is the sense of let-down and faint disquiet when we have finished the book – like the vague guilt we feel when we come blinking out of a second-rate film on a sunny afternoon, having indulged our taste for trash at the expense of something more wholesome.

Books that work on a subtle, more challenging level, like *The Way to Sattin Shore*, never leave the reader with that restless unease; while they satisfy the taste for excitement with the plot, they are also engaging the whole mind and attention of the reader with unstated moral complexities. The reader is led to notice the ways, however small, in which words, deeds, secrets and intentions affect the lives of everyone in the story.

A story that has seized our attention this way leaves us feeling somehow lightened. Our compassion has been stirred; our sense of empathy stretched; our powers of observation honed. Good novels are wonderful because they give us so much easy emotional reward while at the same time letting us feel the natural pleasure of the workings of the mind.

And, as every parent knows from those searching questions and earnest frowns, children are morally serious beings. At a certain stage of intellectual development, they insist on working out the rights and wrongs of the world for themselves. At that point, the novels that confront moral perplexities are among the most rewarding that a child can read.

The Indian in the Cupboard, by Lynne Reid Banks, is a good example of a story so captivating, so exciting, that the moral choices facing the main character seem to be just a more wrenching part of the action. Omri is the youngest of three brothers in an ordinary London family; we are catapulted into the action from the first line, when Omri's best friend, Patrick, gives him a disappointing birthday present – a used plastic Indian figurine, just like the dozens of plastic figures Omri already owns. His older brother gives him a tin medicine cabinet that he found in an alley. And that night, when Omri puts the Indian in the cupboard and locks it with an old curly-topped key given him by his mother, the Indian comes to life.

Of course, it is an old fantasy – the nursery toys coming alive – but Banks gives it a wonderful fresh immediacy by using a modern toy, and one that turns into a real person, though admittedly stereotyped. The transformation makes your pulse leap:

> *He was crouching in the darkest corner . . . And he was alive . . . though he was trying to keep still, he was breathing heavily. His bare bronze shoulders rose and fell, and were shiny with sweat. The single feather sticking out of the back of his headband quivered, as if the Indian were trembling . . . As Omri peered close, and his breath fell on the tiny huddled figure, he saw it jump to its feet; its minute hand made a sudden, darting movement toward its belt and came to rest clutching the handle of a knife smaller than the shaft of a drawing pin.*

The medicine cupboard is a true Pandora's box. Even before Omri can savour the miracle to its full, he finds himself caught up in the difficulties of having created life. The Indian is imperious, demanding: he asks for a horse, a long-house, a fire, food and tools, and Omri must use all his wits to keep an Iroquois warrior properly equipped from the

THE QUEST FOR IDENTITY

scroungings of a modern suburban house. Almost at once, Omri is made to realize that a live person, no matter how small or powerless, can't be a toy. When he picks up Little Bull against his will ('his body was heavier now, warm and firm and full of life . . . through Omri's thumb, on the Indian's left side, he could feel his heart beating wildly, like a bird's') he sensed Little Bull's humanity – and in the same instant, is struck by the insulting cruelty of handling him.

Life gets more complicated when Patrick insists on being let into the secret. Horses, a cowboy and an old chief are brought to life, sometimes with disastrous consequences. The small creatures weep, fight, wound each other, stab Omri, shoot at Patrick. The pony, a wonderful creation, has to be taken outside for exercise and real grass; Omri desperately warns Little Bull against 'mountain lions big enough to swallow the pony'. He has learned to see the world, and the neighbour's cat, through Little Bull's eyes.

Children, who are the bottom of the pecking order, are naturally fascinated with miniatures; all the more enthralling when the miniatures breathe and ride horses; all the more shocking and sobering when they assume a life of their own and, small as they are, are no longer totally in the child's power. There is humour in *The Indian in the Cupboard*, and excitement to spare, but it has another, more difficult, but enriching dimension that makes Omri a changed person.

Even more high-spirited is *Tuck Everlasting* by Natalie Babbit, an adventure that leads the overprotected ten-year-old Winnie Foster to discover the burgeoning world outside her gate and forces her to make a choice between mortality and eternal life. The narrative has the warm, amused tone of the rural tall tale: the meandering road that led to the village of Treegap, the narrator tells us, 'was trod out long before by a herd of cows who were, to say the least, relaxed'.

But there's a sophistication in the telling that makes us sit up and pay attention. Strong images crop up in every paragraph and the perspectives keep changing. The prim Foster family, for example, owns a forest, with a magic ash tree hidden at its heart. The narrator wonders how deeply one can own any land – does one own a slice that goes down in ever narrowing dimensions to where it meets all the other pieces at the centre of the earth? Or just a thin crust 'under which the friendly worms have never heard of trespassing'?

The most startling perspective occurs to Winnie after she has been kidnapped by the charmingly rustic Tuck family. Winnie meets the handsome seventeen-year-old Tuck son and explores the wood for the first time, discovering the deliciousness of life outside her fenced front garden ('The sweet earth opened out its wide four corners to her like the petals of a flower ready to be picked, and it shimmered with light and possibility until she was dizzy with it'). At this moment of rapture, the Tucks have to explain to her, reluctantly, how awful it is to drink from the magic spring, become immortal, and be excluded from the ripening circle of growth and decay. And just when Winnie realizes with horror that she too will die – 'just go out, like the flame of a candle, and no use protesting' – she must listen to Pa Tuck explaining that the opposite is no good, either: 'Us Tucks are stuck. We ain't part of the wheel no more. Dropped off, Winnie. Left behind.'

Not all books of moral dilemma are as life-affirming and invigorating as *Tuck Everlasting*. Some, written with persuasive force and conviction, are deeply equivocal about the value of human life. A novel of total cynicism is so rare in juvenile literature that it forces one to stop and reconsider. Is there a place for stories of 'grim realism'?

Robert Cormier's *The Chocolate War* won instant critical praise and wide popularity among teenage readers. Its nihilism seems to echo and satisfy the defiant rage of adolescents against the adult world's genteel hypocrisies. It's part of adolescence's task, after all, to repudiate authority, tear down simpering sanctimonies and smash the clay idols. Many responded hungrily to *The Chocolate War*'s emotional extremism, especially satisfying because its target is a classically repressive high school. We live in an increasingly totalitarian and fundamentalist world; massive corruption and official lying go hand in hand with pious rhetoric. For an alert and critical teenager, Cormier's corruption-riddled Catholic high school must seem an apt and courageously chosen symbol of institutional evil.

Still, I am made uneasy by the monotone voice, the patterns of imagery and underlying philosophy in *The Chocolate War*. In another context, Ursula K. Le Guin wrote:

> *Novels of despair are intended, most often, to be admonitory, but I think they are, like pornography, most often escapist, in that they provide a substitute for action, a draining-off of tension. That is why they sell well. They provide an excuse to scream, for writer and reader . . . a mindless response. When you start screaming, you have stopped asking questions.*

In a sense, *The Chocolate War* is one long scream. Jerry Renault is a lonely teenager at a Catholic boys' high school. His mother has recently died, his father is a repressed pharmacist incapable of communication, and the school is run by an unholy alliance of sadistic, manipulative priests and a powerful secret student society, called the Vigil. Jerry is afraid to become a cipher, a nobody, like his father. He wants to 'make a difference in the universe', and that's why he holds out against the annual money-raising chocolate sale and refuses to sell his share. In the end, the sadistic priests and the even more monstrously cruel boys of the Vigil punish him for daring to take a stand; utterly alone and beaten into a pulp ('he collapsed like a hunk of meat cut loose from a butcher's hook'), Jerry is defeated.

The overall effect of the book's language and imagery is a tone of near-hysteria, an unremitting, sickened revulsion. Jerry's own values are no humanistic beacon shining out in the murk. Quite the contrary: 'jacking off' makes him queasy with shame, and the girl he admires from afar ends by disgusting him when she uses the word 'crap'. He despises his father for what seems to the reader, after all, to be a normal human response – the father has taken the telephone off the hook in the middle of the night to stop a persistent obscene caller. Jerry sees this as humiliatingly weak, 'giving in', 'letting them win'. Only one thing gives Jerry pleasure, and that is the 'clean' thrill of playing football. On the field, 'bruised and battered or grimy and dirty', Jerry feels 'part of something'. Only when the coach gives him the supreme accolade of calling him 'a skinny little son-of-a-bitch' does Jerry feel 'absolute bliss, absolute happiness'.

We've met this Hemingway ethos before in modern fiction; it is the predominant tone of many thrillers, and Jerry's macho individualism (standing alone and making himself heard in the universe is his one goal) is an echo of Ayn Rand. Even the depiction of the school as rotted through with evil feels unconvincingly melodramatic; there's more than a touch of the B-movie, with its stock villains, about the satanic priests and the cool, sneering, criminally conscienceless teenage sadists of the Vigil.

No, the energy of the book, the force and conviction of it, spring from something that runs below the surface: a powerful revulsion from the tainted human body and soul. Much of the prose jogs along at the level of overheated cliché; at Mrs Renault's funeral, for example, father and son 'weep without shame, out of a nameless need' and Jerry feels 'anger . . . so deep and sharp in him that it drove out sorrow. He wanted to bellow at the world . . . topple buildings, split the earth open, tear down trees.' The overstatement feels mechanical and emotionally hollow.

But elsewhere, when it comes to bodily functions, Cormier has a piledriver energy. Sweat crawls like bugs on foreheads; cruelty and beatings constantly make boys vomit 'like geysers'; breath always reeks of bacon or pizza; a poor couple's apartment 'smells like pee . . . What the hell were they living for?'; a bully (he 'gets horny' when he beats someone up) likes to leave the toilet unflushed so the next boy will have to look at his mess; an obscene caller hangs up and the dial tone is 'a fart in Jerry's ear'. Physical disgust serves a Swiftian purpose as an expression of spiritual horror.

This intensity of rage with humanity is rare in juvenile fiction, and many reviewers see it as a wholesome antidote to the maudlin manipulations and glib solutions of too much teenage mass-market fiction. Setting aside my own personal dislike of the book, I can see that *The Chocolate War* is provocative, and that it boldly reflects at least one little-discussed truth about adolescence – the wincing revulsion from adult bodily functions. Children and prepubescents are often upset and repelled by adult secretions, bad breath, astonishing amounts of urine . . . harbingers all of the body's uncontrollable growth toward unromantically physical sexuality, and its inexorable march toward death and decay.

What disturbs me about these recognitions in *The Chocolate War* is that there is no authorial distance, no calmer or more accepting voice to lend perspective. (Undoubtedly, this lack of a moderating 'adult perspective' is one of the attractions for some young readers.) As a result, it seems to me that books like *The Chocolate War* masquerade as profound analyses of moral choice; in fact, there is no moral choice to be made, no possibility of meaningful action or redemption. In all of Jerry Renault's lonely heroics, physical violence is seen as his only recourse, and even that is futile; if he achieves any victory over the always exterior evil he tries to confront, it is only in accepting vicious brutality as inevitable.

The question of evil is certainly not taboo for children's literature; as usual, the real issue is not specific content, but the skill, depth and subtlety of its literary treatment. In the hands of a talented author, evil can be legitimately presented with the anguishing immediacy and inwardness it deserves. Paula Fox's *The Slave Dancer* stands as one of the most truthful accounts of evil in children's fiction, and yet the final message is far from the ugly, bleak despair of Cormier. Indeed what makes *The Slave Dancer* so exceptional, so haunting and important, is that there is no final message.

The story tells of thirteen-year-old Jesse Bollier, who is press-ganged from the streets of New Orleans to serve as a fife player on a slave ship, *The Moonlight*. At first, after his brutal introduction to shipboard life, Jesse is comforted by a kindly-seeming steward, Benjamin Stout: 'You'll see some bad things, but if you didn't see them, they'd still be happening, so you might as well,' is Stout's resonantly familiar self-justification for participating in a criminal trade in human beings.

Jesse's new life on board the ship, on its way to the Bight of Benin, is a carefully detailed confusion of the grotesque, the frightening, the uncomfortable and the exhilarating. He learns a strange new vocabulary ('I especially liked the words skysail and moonsail and turned them over in my mouth as though I was licking honey'), and comes to realize that the 'coarse, bawling' Purvis, who kidnapped him, is a friend and that the smooth-tongued Stout is a deadly enemy. And he watches helplessly when Purvis is savagely beaten, in the tender golden light of a radiant sunset, for a crime committed by Stout.

All this moral confusion and anxiety is a fit preparation for the worse that is to come, because when the slaves are brought on board, everything Jesse is told is at war with his immediate perceptions. The crew rationalize that 'blacks ain't like us, and that's the truth', that they're 'mad and bite their own flesh' or 'can will themselves to die'. Jesse must reject the beliefs of his closest friends and protectors on board *The Moonlight*.

Still, the boy's compassionate horror fights with his own revulsion at the stench of the holds, whose excrement buckets he must empty. He once yearned to peep through New Orleans windows at women getting dressed; now that he is free to stare at men, women and children chained naked and helpless, he is appalled at their vulnerability and deeply shaken with shame. The torment, the cries, the music he must pipe while the slaves are forced to exercise their shackled limbs in a ghastly, shuffling dance . . . at first this horror drives him into a rage of hatred against the victims. And this is a more terrible and profound truth than anything in Cormier's good-versus-bad world, and a more important one, too.

Then Jesse throws down his fife and refuses to play; when he is beaten for his small rebellion, his own salt tears bring him back to himself, to a recognition that he is as vulnerable and as captive as the slaves. The mounting horror of the voyage, with disease, death and cruelty vividly evoked for us, is made bearable because we see it through Jesse's eyes as he grows more and more deeply alienated from the ship and its morally corrupt crew.

Fox is courageous enough not to settle for an easy upbeat ending to such an appalling story. Jesse does make his amends in the only way open to him, by saving a slave boy's life when the ship goes down, but there is no absolution of the kind he yearns for, for him or any of his countrymen. A particularly poignant episode is one in which a black runaway slave, living secretly in the bush, rescues the two shipwrecked boys and tenderly cares for the African youth. Jesse yearns to be part of their powerful communion; his whiteness, his participation in the slave trade – however unwillingly – exclude him. He is treated with grave dignity, but cannot be part of their heart-whole intimacy. His sense of grievous, permanent loss strikes me as a true, if often submerged, note in American history.

Jesse takes up his life once more, supports his widowed mother, learns a healing trade (pharmacy) and moves to the North. He is not exempt from his nation's guilt, but neither is the value of life utterly negated. *The Slave Dancer* is an unforgettable book; it is, in a curious way, uplifting, because it takes its young readers seriously enough to make them feel how thoroughly corrupt and corrupting and evil slavery was – without wallowing in the lurid – and does not shirk the moral complexity of the issues.

Paula Fox has a particular genius for depicting the troubled conscience. In a recent novel, *The One-Eyed Cat*, she takes an unlikely and unpromising cast of characters and a plot that sounds positively soporific in summary, and yet makes them not only illuminating but gripping. A sensitive eleven-year-old boy, Ned, whose father is an overbearingly saintly minister in rural upstate New York, commits a tiny crime: he takes a forbidden Daisy air rifle, tries shooting it outside in the dark one night, and hits – perhaps? – a moving shadow. Later, an injured cat with only one eye, and dried blood on its cheek, turns up in the yard of a neighbour.

Add to this scenario a sweet-natured mother who leads a shadowy existence in a wheelchair upstairs, crippled by rheumatoid arthritis; an insinuating horror of a housekeeper, Mrs Scallop, who smugly preens herself ('That's just the way I am, I hate to see anyone hurt') just after she has hooked a poisoned barb into the flesh of her conversational victim; and a lonely, aged neighbour for whom Ned does chores. It all sounds lethally dispiriting.

But the characters are a triumph of roundedness. They constantly develop, turn, change and surprise us, and Ned's prickly conscience is the motor that drives forward a plot that deepens and becomes more absorbing with each page.

Unlike Jesse, Ned does have a way to expiate his crime, and though he, too, comes to hate the victim – the cat whom he so obsessively keeps alive during the long winter after the shooting – he is rewarded, in the slow course of his penitential labours, with several sweet kinds of love. If children can get past the rather drab opening, *The One-Eyed Cat* is a beautifully, subtly elaborated story of a boy's coming to terms with his own losses and gaining believably in depth and strength.

Children do not 'catch' morals, good or bad, from books, and it would be a shame if parents began to pop books down their children's throats like pills. But books can be a thrilling adjunct to that long journey one makes from about the ages of seven to fourteen, the years when 'Who am I? Can I be different? What do other families believe?' are urgent questions. Books let us see how other people grow towards conclusions and solve dilemmas. More than that, they make us *feel* every step of the way; it's as though we could live a dozen lives simultaneously, and draw on the wealth of all of them to help shape our own selves. The literary choices we help our children make are, therefore, important in more ways than one.

I don't mind if my children experience Jerry Renault's nauseated loathing of the world. But I'm glad they have a chance to put that in perspective, that they can confront true evil (slavery was evil; are mean teachers in the same league?) along with Jesse Bonnier and, like him, still taste the freshness of the sea air and know it is good.

Chapter 6

Adventure: The Great Game

Men say he does magic, but that should not touch thee. Go up the hill and ask. Here begins the Great Game.

Rudyard Kipling, Mahbub Ali to Kim, in *Kim*

THE GREAT GAME. What Mahbub Ali meant was Kim's participation in the British spy network in Imperial India, but, as Kipling wrote, Kim would have called it an adventure 'if he had known the word'. Adult life, independent life, 'real' life as seen from the perspective of the child who is waiting for everything to begin, is Great Game and adventure enough.

There were times, when I had grown just old enough to think beyond the cave-cosiness of the family, that my heart skipped and lurched with excitement at the mere thought of the possibilities of life. Adventure stories for the young are surrogate journeys into the wonderful world; a child too young to ride the underground alone can bucket across stormy seas of the imagination, always with those mute questions at the back of the mind: could I be this brave? what would it be like? will I ever . . . ? Adults, too, read adventure stories, but because the realms of possibility have dwindled for them, the adrenalin has to be stimulated with substitute drugs – sex and violence (detective thrillers) or nostalgia (Agatha Christie). And although adult book lovers may savour deeper and more complex literary pleasures, child readers are luckier in this: their adventure stories still have the potent promise of Christopher Columbus's world, when half the map was still blank.

The preschool child's adventures are usually on the small and intimate scale, close to home, where drama is found in familiar small conflicts or mishaps or in the fears of what may be underneath the bed. The popularity of *Little Tim and the Brave Sea Captain* by Edward Ardizzone, however, points to the allure of the Great Game even for a seven- or eight-year-old. It is a fantasy, but a touchingly earnest one, that a small boy should stow away on a great ship, work his passage home, survive a wreck and a lifeboat rescue, and calmly send a telegram to let his parents know he'll be arriving by train.

Unlike the James Bond fantasies of grown boys, these are dreams of competence, hardships endured and sensible heroism: those are real workmanlike knots that Tim learns on the beach from his old friend Captain McFee, and later, when the ship is storm-tossed in a raging sea, the Captain minces no words. 'Come, stop crying and be a brave boy. We are bound for Davey Jones's locker and tears won't help.' And what delicious adult licence and anarchy is earned: there may be seasickness and hard sloppy work in the galley for Tim, but comforting cocoa waits at the end of the day . . . and he gets to sleep in his clothes!

Alas, almost all adventures, for the youngest children as for the oldest, pit boys against hardship, boys against danger, boys against every kind of villainy. It is the rare author, male or female, Victorian or post-modern, who can envision the heroism or grit of a girl. Perhaps for that reason, as well as for its own rousing merits, I cherish a picture book called *The Funny Little Woman*, an old Japanese tale retold by Arlene Mosel and illustrated gleefully – and with delicate, abundant detail – by Blair Lent.

For no better reason, it seems, than her light-hearted character, the funny little woman who loves to laugh chases a rollaway dumpling down into the fearsome underworld, where she is captured by the wicked Oni, a kind of spirit monster. Her silly but endearing laughter as she careers headlong into danger makes her seem childlike but also invincible. Nothing could be more satisfying than the way she makes good her escape at last, carrying with her the magic paddle that enables her to open a dumpling store and become the richest woman in Japan.

As in the very best adventure stories, the narrative is buttressed by rich details – grinning Oni, ghoulish statues, fascinating trivia of Japanese rural life, like the cottage cooking arrangements – inventively conveyed through pictures rather than words. And, both physically and metaphorically, there are several levels of action. While full-page coloured illustrations show the laughing little woman working as a dumpling chef for the Oni, we see a whole year passing above ground in small black and white sketches at the top of the page. An old man comes vainly to look for his friend as autumn leaves fall; then the winter winds blow around her empty little house, and no smoke rises from her hearth. When, finally, spring comes, and flowers sprout from the neglected thatch roof, the old man hopefully returns, and is there to lend her a hand as she climbs up from the hole in the ground. It's a lovely wordless counterplot to her adventures, and lends an extra dimension of emotion to her disappearance and return.

Female heroism in children's literature has clearly been a problem for authors. Fantasy, myth, folk tale and tall tale, with their pliable standards of realism, have been the most favoured forms. Virginia Hamilton blends Afro-American folklore and African legend in her dazzling *The Magic Adventures of Pretty Pearl*, about an overweening female 'god child' who comes down from Mount Kenya to help former slaves; Joan Lowery Nixon turns to hilarious Texas tall tale (in *Fat Chance, Claude* and *Beats Me, Claude*) to immortalize Shirley, the lanky, grinning girl who ropes steers, prospects for gold, and marries sweet-natured Claude only after they've established a fair-and-square friendship.

Most non-mythical heroines appear in stories in which their courage is a question of overcoming fear. In the delicate short novel for beginners, *Storm* by Kevin Crossley-Holland (with beautiful, watery illustrations by Alan Marks), Annie is terrified but rides with a ghostly horseman to get help for her isolated family in a storm. Esther Averill, in her short stories for beginners about a shy little cat in New York, *Jenny and the Cat Club*, hit on an idea that has made her stories popular for half a century: Jenny

ADVENTURE: THE GREAT GAME

Linsky (delightfully portrayed in black and white ink drawings) is a bashful outsider, but conquers her timidity to become a celebrated member of the Cat Club. The club is a wonderful bit of gentle satire – it has its club portraits, its pompous speeches by the president, its own shield and motto ('Loyalty, Fidelity, Truth and Dues'). But Jenny herself is portrayed with such tender affection, and given such implicit support in her small adventures in courage, that young readers identify instantly with her.

Teenage readers are similarly drawn into questions of fear and overcoming in a strikingly energetic novel by the British author Marjorie Darke, *A Question of Courage*. Emily Palmer, a sturdy working-class girl from Birmingham, is enlisted in the suffragettes' bitter crusade for women's votes before World War I. The story is not only extraordinarily vivid in its evocation of working life, class differences and the brutal suppression of the suffragettes, but it sensitively and starkly conveys the terrors that even a staunch teenager like Emily had to overcome in order to face mobs, police violence, prison and force feeding in the name of an ideal.

One of the few contemporary and naturalistic novels to place a girl in a heroic role is *Homecoming*, by the American Cynthia Voight, in which tough thirteen-year-old Dicey leads her younger brothers and sisters on a gruelling odyssey by foot from Cape Cod to Maryland. Unlike the rush of propagandistic second-rate novels in which girls play football or win motorcycle tournaments, Voight's work is grounded in realistic detail and believable character; it won instant and enduring popularity because the suspense of the difficult journey gains extra vitality from the emotional intensity of the heroine.

Emotional depth is rare and has a worth far beyond rubies when it comes to modern adventure stories written for children; typically, they provide an experience more like taking snuff than reading a fine novel. First they create a pleasurable tension and then move right along to a satisfyingly convulsive resolution. The outstanding exception, and the innovative standard by which all others were to be measured, was, of course, the *Swallows and Amazons* series by Arthur Ransome, which made its debut in 1930.

The stories are almost too well known to need description: they concern a family of middle-class children who spend their vacations in the Lake District, where they sail a small dinghy and are allowed to camp out on an island. The Swallows – John, Susan, Titty and Roger Walker name themselves after their boat – join forces with the Amazons, Nancy and Peggy Blackett, in a summer-long adventure of pretend piracy and castaway island life. Eleven other books in the series introduce new characters and locations; there are two notable fantasy adventures (*Missee Lee* and *Peter Duck*) and two that involve some engaging working-class boys in the Norfolk Broads.

It's hard now, when so many other pleasures have blurred the sharp immediacy of the fictional life, to imagine the impact of these stories on those of us who read them for the first time as children in the 1940s.

Passionate involvement is not too strong a phrase for the feelings that still echo when I pick up those sturdy books with their spacious typeface, leisurely chapters, inky and vigorously primitive drawings by Ransome himself, and the indispensable maps on the endpapers.

Here were whole families of children who played the pretend games for which I never could find a partner: no one, on my street, wanted to leave secret code messages under a boulder or understood the thrill of transforming our tiny garden into the pitching deck of a galleon. That was the particular magic of the books. Though Robert Louis Stevenson's *Treasure Island* is richer in scope, drama, language and moral complexity, and stands as an unparalleled voyage of adventure, it was too distanced from me, by time and place and its relentlessly all-male cast, to exert the same spell of possibility. Here were children not so different from me (or the thousands of other devotees) as to be inimitable. Their adventures were all the more heady because they were only one step away from my own daydreams.

We first meet this enviable family as Roger, aged seven and the youngest of the expedition, tacks like a sailing ship up the hill to the farmhouse, where his mother has just received a telegram from their naval captain father in response to their request to go camping on Wild Cat Island. 'BETTER DROWNED THAN DUFFERS IF NOT DUFFERS WON'T DROWN' read that cryptic message, committed to heart by hundreds and thousands of Swallows and Amazons followers. At first I was baffled, then deliciously shocked, and the message has never lost its punch. What a breathtaking mixture of parental insouciance and confidence! I was hooked.

In my own childhood reading experience, only Edith Nesbit's fantasy-adventures rivalled the intense pleasure offered by these sympathetic portraits of child life. How obligingly those kindly or gruff adults stood back at a distance that allowed freedom but guaranteed safety. And yet how forbearingly they entered into the game, content to play the role of friendly natives who would regularly supply the adventurers with pemmican and ginger-beer 'grog'.

Ransome was an outstanding journalist of his day, a prose writer of pellucid technical clarity. He could make you know in your fingers and toes how to sail a dinghy, rig a leading light, invent an electric alarm bell or smelt copper. And he could invest all these vigorous practical pursuits with an intoxicating sense of romance.

Modern critics have sometimes huffed that Ransome's appeal was limited by his middle-class cast of characters. That is a dreadfully mistaken view of fiction. Some of Ransome's most endearing characters were boatmen and working-class Norfolk children, but even that is beside the point: fiction transcends boundaries, and, as a lower middle-class urban Canadian child, who had never seen a sailboat or even been allowed to play outside after dusk, my world was immeasurably enlarged by reading Ransome.

Ardently, I learned to sail and to semaphore from the Swallows and

ADVENTURE: THE GREAT GAME

Amazons. Thirty years later, when I finally had a chance to sit at the tiller of a dinghy, I knew the heft, the feel and the arcane language as though I were a secret inhabitant of a nautical world. As, indeed, I was.

Though Ransome was hailed by his contemporaries, more recent critics have commented slightingly about his powers of characterization. Sheila Egoff, for example, thinks that Ivan Southall's anxious adolescents are more three-dimensional than Ransome's solid citizens. It is true that the Swallows and Amazons were sexually latent far longer than one might have expected. But for ten- and eleven-year-old readers, that seems eminently appropriate. Furthermore, one measure of the successful creation of a character is whether he or she takes on a rounded, independent existence in the reader's mind long after the book is replaced on the shelf. Here I am not a fair judge: perhaps Ransome's people are still so warmly familiar to me because I met them when I was an impressionable child. Still, I would bet that many young readers today, freshly encountering Southall's cast of characters, find as I do that they blur into one another and slip out of memory.

It's worth noting that adventure stories need not fill in every detail of the characters' inner lives in order to attract a strong emotional identification from young readers. A rough sketch, if it is true and pointed enough (think of the success of *Little Tim*) may be even more powerful than psychological verisimilitude. Young readers bring their own generous imagination and willingness to the book.

The Walkers, the Blacketts and the *D*s (and even the little brown-sailed, gaff-rigged *Swallow*, a character in her own right) have staying power, not because Ransome drew them with correctly up-to-date detail, complete with Oedipal complexes and difficult parents, but because they were so real to him, and there was so much of himself in them. John's dogged, conscientious, earnest character was an illumination to me – the youngest and least responsible of my family; his sense of deep obligation to a moral code, part naval and part familial, was expressed so compellingly in his speech and actions that until my mid-teens he was a sort of internalized exemplar for me. I think some adult reviewers may have overlooked the touching quality that John's character holds for children. At an age when self-absorption is the rule, John's thoroughly believable idealism is a weighty counterpoise. The personalities of the others carried equal force: Titty's imagination and courage and Dorothea's authorial passions confirmed my own worth, literary landlubber that I was; Nancy's galumphing hoydenism inspired me to greater liberties and fierce, wayward little Bridget, the youngest, spoke straight to my impatient soul.

The emotional impact is at its most intense in the gripping *We Didn't Mean to Go to Sea*, in which the four Walkers suffer extremes of seasickness, fear and exhaustion when their boat is swept out to sea and they must cross the North Sea in a gale. The climax is Ransome's most moving. Safe in Holland, exhausted, but triumphant, the Walkers meet their father and brace themselves for the worst reprimand of their lives. Captain Walker listens to their story, puts a hand on John's shoulder and says:

'You'll make a seaman yet, my son'. I didn't know until I read Ransome's autobiography that he had a humiliating childhood, the disappointingly clumsy son of a heartily athletic father. He must have put all his childhood yearning into that one moment; its insight and depth of feeling flow straight into the child reader's heart.

Another of Ransome's attractions is the gentle quality of his humour; one of my favourites (then and now) was *Missee Lee*, possibly because she was the first female pirate, not to mention the first pirate who yearned to attend Cambridge, whom I had ever met, and possibly because of the delicious humour and poignancy of her situation. I hope that the pidgin English spoken by the Chinese pirates doesn't ban *Missee Lee* from current book lists; so dogmatic have we become about culturally correct attitudes that even a master storyteller like Kipling has been allowed to drift away to that special oblivion reserved for jingoists. Mild stereotyping is not always malign; Missee Lee, for example, may say 'velly pleased' and 'Camblidge', but her portrait is drawn with so much life and affection that no one could carry away a warped impression, as one might from a racially contemptuous author like Enid Blyton (see Chapter Ten, on bad books).

I would make the same plea, even more strongly, for Kipling's *Kim*. The author was an empire-booster and a chauvinist of the silliest sort in his conscious opinions, but *Kim* breathes out a different air entirely, an air of wide tolerance, made palpable by Kim's devotion to his Indian, Persian, Afghan and Tibetan friends.

Kim is not a book for the halting reader, but for older children unafraid of challenge, it is mesmerizing. This is the quintessence of adventure: a free spirit who defies the prison of identity, a chameleon, master by the age of nine of a dozen disguises and as many dialects, able to vanish in a twinkling through the teeming crowds of the bazaar – the ultimate privileged insider and knower of secrets. He has no parents (he is a gifted survivor by his wits) but is watched over by several admiring mentors, men of special and mysterious skills themselves.

Because Kim is spotted by these men as perfect spy material, he is made an initiate of several worlds – educated in a British-style boarding school, trained by a Persian 'healer of sick pearls' and an Afghan horse dealer, and yet, during school vacations, allowed the freedom of the road to follow his saintly Tibetan holy man.

Only against the background of nineteenth-century India, with its beauty, squalor, spirituality and chaotic variety of people and cultures, could Kipling have made believable such a protean child. Of course, he has language on his side: the rolling, rhythmic, highly artificial but enchantingly coloured speech he creates for his mythical India. There is no lack of excitement – thefts, disguises, secret messages, murders, desperate escapes, slyly comic contretemps – all leading up to the humour of a classic 'sting' that forms the climax and setpiece of the novel. But what makes it all so hypnotic, aside from Kim's cleverness and the exotic language, is atmosphere. We are ready to believe anything once Kipling has drawn us into that world of smoky dusks, lantern-lit bazaars, perfumed brothels, oxcarts, temples and the high thin icy air of the Himalayas.

Against such a dazzling variety of sensual riches, North America is positively underprivileged as a background for adventure; we have nothing to compare with Kim's ability to enter other people's worlds. Typically (and especially in Canada), North American adventure stories, especially from the first half of the century, link two teenage boys, one white and one native, against the challenge of the frontier. Almost always, the native boy, seen through the white boy's eyes, is romanticized as the teacher of lessons: he is wise in the lore of the wilds, patient, stoic, in tune with nature. The white boy, made vulnerable by the threatening wilderness, learns to be less impulsive or greedy, and to absorb some (but never all) of the native wisdom of the earth.

These stories are eagerly read by youngsters seeking a straightforward, energetic plot. All, however, are marred by bad or hasty writing, a crude sense of character development and a flatly exterior view of North American natives. Clichés speed the action along. Heroes are constantly identified by the flattering physical description so familiar from adult thrillers and detective novels: Matthew, in James Houston's *Frozen Fire*, for example, is 'tall . . . with grey watchful eyes . . . sandy hair, slim with narrow hips, a flair to his shoulders that made you know he would be strong. He was the fastest runner in his school . . .'

These descriptions are a lazy shorthand: they tell the reader whom to admire, and absolve him from the imaginative work of learning about the hero's character. For all their literary deficiencies, though, novels like these by Farley Mowat and James Houston do express an honest commitment on the part of their authors, especially when compared to the formula pap now being churned out to exploit the young teenage market.

For true adventure, though, they can't begin to compare to the shocking immediacy of a native-written survival story, *Harpoon of the Hunter*, by Markoosie. The voice of the narrator is so fresh, so startlingly different, that it makes one realize the tragic loss we suffer in not having more native fiction. Here, for the first time, we are inside the Inuit mind. The story reminds me of *Nkwala*, in which Edith Sharp made a valiant effort to show us the inner development of an Indian boy's courage and resilience, but even that cannot equal the vibrant truth of Markoosie, scraped bare of all the sentiment and false glamour with which natives are usually drawn.

Ironically, when authors like Houston or Mowat show us Indian youths through the eyes of white boys, the natives' skills are so unquestioned they are curiously diminished; courage seems less impressive when it is a birthright conferred along with skin colour. Markoosie's hero, sixteen-year-old Kamik, is three-dimensional; we don't need to be told what he looks like – no athletic shoulders or slim hips necessary – because we learn to know him through his speech and his actions.

And we see him fully in context. His mother Ooramik, father Suluk, friends and tribe all have vital roles to play. When a rabid polar bear menaces the storm-bound settlement, Suluk, accompanied by Kamik, leads a hunting party to track and kill the rogue bear. We follow the hunters in their perilous trek, but the narrative leaps back and forth, in rapid vignettes, between the settlement and the hunt. This technique gives us a powerful sense of the fragility of the widely scattered human life in the Arctic wastes, and of the urgent bonds that link these vulnerable humans. Even the usually mushy idea that hunter and the hunted are mystically connected – two forms of hot-blooded life dwarfed by the frozen immensity – has honest immediacy here.

Ooramik, the mother, does not drop out of sight when the hunters leave. She heartens herself with the close friendship of another hunter's wife, and, when the days drag out, she persuades the others to seek help to rescue the now missing hunting party. Ooramik herself volunteers to undertake the crossing of a river on treacherous, swiftly moving ice floes. It is a rare record of native life that gives us so vivid a sense of the conversation of the Inuit, the mutual dependence and dignity of men and women, their ways of argument and courtesy, the pared-to-the-bone directness of lives played out in such harsh surroundings. Factual accounts exist, of course, but here the truth springs to life under the shaping hands of an artist.

Kamik's growth into manliness is seen minute by minute as he anxiously asks his older companions in the hunting party if they think all will survive; 'There is always a chance as long as we are alive,' one replies. 'We have two chances – to make it on foot or to be found by others if they decide to search for us.' When they face the necessity to eat their dogs, and Kamik balks, a hunter tells him that they have all been forced to conquer a similar revulsion.

The reader is made to feel how desperately earned are Inuit expertise and stoicism. Every mistake made by Kamik and his comrades has painful results. It's astonishing how abundant is the sense of life in this slender, eighty-one-page book. Not only do we share Kamik's suffering as he struggles back alone and without food, but we are also given a charming picture of young and lively Putooktee, helping her father lead the perilous river-crossing rescue party, 'jumping expertly from one piece of ice to another' with such verve that she brings a smile to the face of one of the young men.

Swiftly, with the urgency imposed by Arctic life, Putooktee and the rescued Kamik fall in love. Their coming together – the exhausted, emotion-racked Kamik and the confident girl – is as frankly simple as all the rest of the story. 'This is the first time I ever saw a really pretty girl.' 'Thank you,' Putooktee said. 'And I like you, Kamik.' The end of the story is heartbreaking, but as unforgettably honest as all that has gone before.

Heroism of this almost mythic quality has all but vanished from modern children's literature but that, of course, does not mean that it is not missed; note the adoration of small children for cartoon 'superheroes'. It is worth searching the library shelves for heroes just as alluring but less shallow than Mr T. Why not Robin Hood, for example, instead of Rocket Robin Hood or Batman and his version of Robin? Granted, it's hard to find a completely satisfactory retelling of the Robin Hood story; no prose version that I know of has that sweet wild note of Alfred Noyes's poem, 'A Song of Sherwood', with its sun-dappled arcadian longing for the greenwood life.

Antonia Fraser's modern retelling is done in brief episodic fashion, simple enough for young readers, but lacking enchantment and gallantry. Howard Pyle's Victorian version, filled with right good ale and grey goose feathers, has the spirit of the leafy glades intact, but is so awash in forsoothery and inverted sentences that it is all but unreadable today. Between these two extremes is the naïve but exciting first novel by the excellent historical novelist Geoffrey Trease; *Bows Against the Barons* dismisses the struggle between Saxons and Normans as irrelevant (it's the peasants versus the aristocrats instead) and makes Robin Hood's merry band into a sort of mediaeval International Brigade. At least it captures some of the subversive energy that makes Robin Hood so compelling a legend.

The fullest and fairest retelling of them all is by Roger Lancelyn Green, in *The Adventures of Robin Hood*. Green has gone back to the original sources, enriched his tale with scraps of ballad and mediaeval song, and faithfully recorded all the incidents (including the triumphant return of Richard Coeur de Lion) missing from many other versions. His sturdy prose does justice to all the characters, not overlooking Maid Marian as brave archer and venturesome spirit. Some readers may feel he has been too thorough: before the exciting stories begin, the reader must wade through a rather wordy historical scene-setting, and the prose never reaches great emotional or poetic intensity. Perhaps, after all, there can never be a completely perfect version of this elementally important story, one that would draw together all its essential threads of mystery, pastoral, anarchic freedom and the thirst for social justice.

Green at least avoids anachronism splendidly, and anachronism is the great stumbling block of historical novels. Historic settings are ideal for the child's adventure tale, since they offer so many more possibilities for heroic and significant action than prosaic modernity, but how to evoke a period flavour without lapsing into mere 'By our faith!' quaintness? And without the decorative trappings, how to avoid a sterile contemporary tone?

Leon Garfield, one of the most energetically imaginative of modern authors, does it by creating a crowded eighteenth-century London, reeking of smog and skulduggery, and giving his quick-witted characters a Cockney dialect that wryly undercuts any period pomposities. Here is the eponymous hero of *Smith* aged twelve:

> *Smith had a turn of speed that was remarkable, and a neatness in nipping down an alley or vanishing in a court that had to be seen to be believed. Not that it was often seen, for Smith was rather a sooty*

spirit of the violent and ramshackle town, and inhabited the tumble-down mazes about fat St Paul's like the subtle air itself.

Smith, like many of Garfield's characters, is an amoral urchin with grubby face and quick fingers. It is his curiosity and compassion – innate human goodness as opposed to conventional morality – that lead him into his Gothic adventures and that set in motion the breathlessly convoluted plot. Typically of Garfield, Smith is keen on the trail of a hidden treasure, but his warm-heartedness waylays him. He gets his treasure at the end, but only after forsaking the hunt to save his intended victim's life. Garfield's fantastical facility with language, and his ghoulishly gleeful humour (' 'Ere's my 'and, you blind old Justice, you!' Smith offers to a sightless magistrate) lend an extraordinary vivacity to his characters.

Smith, determined to learn to read (for the most mercenary of motives) first approaches the dignitary best known to him: Mr Jones, the Newgate hangman. 'Mind your Ps and Qs,' snarls the gent, chasing him away. 'Bleeding scholars!' thinks Smith. 'Want to keep everything to themselves!'

The treasure is even more illusory in Garfield's *John Diamond*, in which a properly brought-up young country boy runs away to London and falls into that murky 'maze' of back streets that is Garfield's favourite locale. William Jones, the twelve-year-old hero, takes the *Treasure Island* moral one step farther. Not only is the supposed treasure an unending source of grief and violence, but it turns out never to have existed. The real treasure discovered, inadvertently, is the friendship of the ragamuffin Shot-in-the-Head, one of Garfield's most engaging creations. He looks like a large rat in his flapping black coat, with his ragged teeth, sharp little tongue, and tufts of orangeish hair 'as though someone had set out to burn him down, for health reasons, and left him smouldering'.

Shot-in-the-Head is a solemn little roof-dweller, the strangest baby-sitter in the universe, and a true heart. His occupation, as he explains to the baffled William, is 'snick-an-lurk' . . . pick-pocketing. His outlaw perceptions, expressed in terse Cockney, are a marvel of humour. When the terrified William asks if it's true that people are cut to pieces in one fearsome alley, Shot-in-the-Head replies, seriously, 'Yus. But allus very small.'

More strictly historical than Garfield, whose Dickensian London seems to float in some mirthful mist of non-time, is the prolific Rosemary Sutcliff. She is unparalleled in her mastery of the form: in each of her novels, particularly those of Saxon and Roman Britain, she brings alive a complete and spacious world, richly and startlingly detailed, in which the reader can move about, observe, sense and participate in another time and place. Her power lies not only in making us intimate with the daily life of a Bronze Age boy or a Roman centurion, but in letting us see the world through their eyes.

In *Warrior Scarlet*, one of her most emotionally vivid works, the boy Drem must win his place among the warriors of his age group. But he

ADVENTURE: THE GREAT GAME

has a paralysed right arm, which makes it impossible for him to hold simultaneously the traditional weapons of his people, a bronze shield and a dagger.

Sutcliff's prose is lyrical, plangent, almost dangerously romantic, but she certainly make us see and sense the rolling downs and black night forests of primaeval Britain. The landscape is always lit by flaring sunsets or cool grey dawns; when hunters return from the marshes to the huts in the blue summer dusk 'a stain of light came to meet them thick and golden like honey trickling from a tipped jar'; there are the flickering illuminations of mutton-fat lanterns, torches, Beltane fires and shafts of dusty sunlight when the turf roof is rolled back.

It is a complete sensory world, populated by the hard-working shepherds (the Little Dark People who are the more ancient conquered tribe of the place); by wandering Irish bronzesmiths, priests who orchestrate the exotically detailed, hypnotic secret rites of initiation; by chieftains and kings. They command our total belief because we see their grip on Drem. We are never taken outside his knowledge of this world and his acceptance of its ways. All the more dreadful and desolating when Drem fails his ritual wolf slaying and becomes an outcast. Without his rigid role of warrior, without his prescribed place in the tribe, he is nothing. 'A boy who failed in his Wolf Slaying and did not die was dead to the Tribe. It was the custom.' Drem is exiled and must go to live with the despised shepherds on the hill. And his redemption, at last, is also true to the ethos of the tribe; only by stoic endurance and individual heroism does he regain his identity, now enriched by a deeper, gentler resignation learned from his work with the shepherds.

In the portrait of Drem, there is a forcefulness of empathy that is almost unbearable. When my own son, a precocious reader, read *Warrior Scarlet* at the age of five, I found him in anguished tears over the opened book. 'I can't go on,' he explained between gasping sobs. 'Drem has failed his wolf slaying.' I had to hold him on my lap to comfort him and read the next chapter aloud before he could bear to go on by himself. Perhaps he already sensed how different he was and would be from his peers, set aside and 'outcast' not only by his giftedness but also by a lateral lisp which, with his sunny and outgoing character, he seemed outwardly to ignore.

Three years later, when he undertook on his own to work with a speech therapist, he concentrated with such ferocious self-discipline that his speech defect, commonly held to be almost incurable, was totally overcome within three weeks.

I was astonished and moved, both by his dedication and his triumph, achieved so independently. I asked him (as parents so often ask unanswerable questions) how he had found the will and the courage to tackle his problem and to overcome it. 'I remembered Drem,' he said after a soul-searching pause. 'He was handicapped like me.'

No one who knew this intelligent, strong, athletic child, so unfailingly funny and generous, could have guessed that in the secret prison of his heart he felt that he was crippled. Whenever I speak to audiences of teachers and librarians, many of them devoted to the practice of 'bibliotherapy' – prescribing 'problem novels' to children with matching problems – I tell them this story. I ask them if they would have thought of prescribing *Warrior Scarlet* to a five-year-old boy with a lateral lisp.

The whole force and mystery of literature is that it speaks to us privately, one mind reaching to another, its 'therapeutic' power dependent not on mean-spirited calculations of problems and how to solve them, but on the depth of the author's intuition and the strength of her literary imagination and skill. Hundreds of contemporary novelists for children have tackled this theme of the young boy's agonized desperation to prove his virility and to be accepted as worthy by his 'warrior clan'. It is a solitary trial, apparently, as ancient as pre-history. That Sutcliff's Bronze Age version could reach so unpredictably into a boy's life, and profoundly change it, is both a testament to the strength of Sutcliff's writing and a brisk rebuttal to the reductive and presumptuous tinkerings of bibliotherapy.

A defender of teenage mass-market novels once accused me of being 'against pimples and lust'. But a novel's contentious or problematic subject is almost beside the point; what matters is the depth of its treatment, and it is through the author's language that we can most clearly see whether an artist or a mechanic is at work.

In *Warrior Scarlet*, Sutcliff developed a movingly evocative language to create her Bronze Age world. Every image, drawn from the vegetation and animal life surrounding the tribe, deepens the sensory hold the novel exerts on the reader. She makes particularly good use of starkly simple dialogue ('Na, this time there will be no coming back'), as well as a peculiar trick in using the gerund that somehow evokes the primitive mentality: their last hunting, a hard waiting, a long-drawn hushing of wind across open snow.

This elegaic tone is particularly effective in *The Lantern Bearers*, Sutcliff's novel about the departure of the last Roman legions from Britain. The Jutes and Angles raid, pillage and loot in their pouncing forays down from the north; already they have begun to make alliances with British warlords and to settle on conquered farms along the coast. Britain teeters on the edge of the Dark Ages. We see the coming chaos through the eyes of the British-born centurion Aquila, who deserts his departing legion because at the last moment he realizes that Britain, not Rome, is his true home. Here the language is crisper, more Latinate, and the repeated images of beacons and failing lights strongly suggest the struggle to 'hold back the dark'.

Although she never steps outside Aquila's perception that Rome is synonymous with civilization and that the 'sea wolves' are barbarians, Sutcliff allows us to see, out of the corner of our eye, how the Saxons, Picts and Romans have already begun their long, fertile intertwining. She is able to imagine each of these cultures from within, fully and cohesively. Her worldview is capacious enough to contain antagonists but no villains.

One-sidedness is a sore temptation for a novelist, and usually a fatal one. When a novel openly advocates one fixed viewpoint, it robs the young characters of the opportunity to come to these conclusions themselves. Ironically, the drama of that inner struggle can be far more effective in winning over the reader. In *Starry Night*, a contemporary novel about Ireland, author Catherine Sefton allows her confused young heroine to move naturally from passionate, unthinking defence of IRA violence to a more questioning stance, as her personal life changes. The shift is thought-provoking. Nakedly propagandistic motive in fiction, however, seems to lead the writer to heavy-handed prose: when inner conflict is muted or absent, inflated adjectives and engorged verbs must substitute for the tension of psychological drama. The private inward voice that is the soul of the novel – even in action-oriented adventure – is drowned out.

Mystery and detection are favourite forms of adventure for both adults and children; the lesser varieties (like John D. Fitzgerald's *The Great Brain* series) are popular enough – and slight enough – not to need discussion here. Generally, the more important the puzzle factor, the less demanding and the less rewarding the book will be as a work of literature.

John Bellairs is an American writer of Gothic mysteries, with overtones of the supernatural, who is worth noting for the warmth of his characterization. His most popular, and still, I think, his best novel, is *The House with a Clock in Its Walls*, which is enlivened by the humorous, affectionate tone of the relationships between pudgy Lewis Barnavelt, his uncle Jonathan, and Mrs Florence Zimmerman, the uncle's friend and neighbour.

The orphaned Lewis comes to live in Uncle Jonathan's turreted mansion, which, he discovers, is haunted by a mysterious ticking noise. The particularly engaging tone of the book springs from the comical clash between appearances of cosy normality and matter-of-fact revelations of the supernatural: Uncle Jonathan and Mrs Zimmerman, for example, are sympathetic poker-playing buddies – and nonchalant practitioners of witchcraft.

There are some chilly moments of real fearfulness in the book, and one wonderful scene in which Uncle Jonathan casts a moon-eclipsing spell, which fills the garden with sudden magic. Lewis, putting his ear to the ground, can hear the earthworms and sense the slow collapse of 'the delicate ivory skeleton' of a cat. Lewis has coaxed his uncle to this unwonted display of prowess in order to win over a school sports hero as a friend. But the swaggering Tarby sneers at the spell the moment the enchantment is over, and by this token we know he is no true friend. It is indicative of the jaunty humour and offbeat eclecticism of the story that, at the end, Lewis has made a new friend, Rose Rita Pottinger, who knows the names of all the different kinds of cannon: 'Saker, minion, falconet, demi-culverin. . . .' recites Lewis. 'Aah,' screams Uncle Jonathan in exaggerated protest. 'That's all I need! An expert in Elizabethan ordnance!'

Two other styles of adventure story are worth consideration in this chapter. I began by deploring the lack of adventure stories which depict girls acting with skill and courage. The one general exception, aside from

Arthur Ransome, is historical fiction. It's as though the crises of recent historical events give authors the licence to write about girls as agents rather than bystanders. The Second World War is a most fertile source of such stories, perhaps because that terrible convulsion of history involved the female authors themselves in dramatic events.

Wildcat Under Glass by Alki Zei (translated superbly by Edward Fenton) is a favourite of mine because it so richly conveys, through the eyes of its young narrator, the whole life of a Greek family, village and culture under the fascist puppet regime in 1936. Melia and her older, prettier sister Myrto exist, like Sutcliff's characters, in a fully realized world. They have a patriarchal grandpa who feeds them walnuts and honey, tells them Greek legends and teaches them to count in Byzantine; they have their own secret language, as siblings often do, and counting rhymes and games played with the local children; they have a pusillanimous father who wants to toady to the fascists in order to keep his job in the bank; their terse and salty maid, Stamatina, has a tragic history and political convictions of her own; and they idolize their teenage cousin, Niko, because he plays with them and tells them stories.

The looming war introduces sinister new tensions into this already rich constellation of family ties and undercurrents. We see political events entirely through the first small ripples they create in the family, and through the children's own confused perceptions of these disturbances. They know, for example, that they instinctively dislike the bishop who comes to play cards with their royalist aunt, because they must kiss his hand which is 'soft and limp, like a slice of bread'. The pro-fascists of their acquaintance make them uneasy. But then the school principal invites bossy Myrto to become 'a leader' in a new youth corps at school, Myrto succumbs to the flattery, and the girls are headed down diverging paths.

Myrto is drawn further and further into fascism, dazzled by her gold stars, her uniform, and her new importance in the youth group. We see how naturally her political seduction follows from her character: her eagerness for approval from figures of authority, her preadolescent excitement at belonging to a gang that insists on blind allegiance – even beyond the claims of family.

Melia, meanwhile, at once more childlike and more self-directed, is stubbornly loyal to the adored Niko, who becomes a freedom fighter. When Niko is pursued by the police, Melia serves as a courier to take him food and messages. Gradually, the family is painfully wrenched apart by the political forces of the time. It takes a dangerous close call for the fugitive Niko to snap Myrto out of her trance.

Zei has clear convictions about Nazism, but that does not make her story into a political tract. It is a human drama, and shows us how evil forces can subvert good people through their own human vulnerabilities. Children's need for moral clarity has encouraged authors for the young to split the complex human atom; heroes are good, villains are bad, and never the twain shall meet or greet. But the older reader, above the age of ten or eleven, can easily comprehend a deeper level of complexity, especially when the moral struggle is waged and won by a child, against such understandably attractive temptations.

Similarly, the contemporary reader can cope with a story's sadness if the characters are not crushed by evil. One favourite adventure I remember from childhood, and which is still popular enough to remain in print, is Mary Treadgold's *We Couldn't Leave Dinah*. To the impulsive thirteen-year-old Caroline, the Nazi occupation at first means nothing more than the hateful necessity of leaving the family's beloved home on a picturesque Channel Island – and just in the middle of the summer holidays, too, when the pony club is in full swing. The book has some of the dreadful clubbiness of English horse books – 'You couldn't really believe in awful things like Hitler when you were out in sun and wind and sea-spray and with people as marvellous as the pony club' – but it rises above that dated upper-class gush when Caroline and her fourteen-year-old brother Mick are accidentally left behind during the tumultuous night-time evacuation of the island.

Alone with their beloved ponies, some island residents who might just be collaborators, and hordes of comic-book Nazis ('My little Nannerl . . . has long to ride wished') the children are exhausted, frightened, and beginning to realize the seriousness of their situation. When Mick insists on spying on the Germans to help foil their plan to invade England, Caroline protests furiously: 'We're only children. Nobody expects us to help like that . . . we only have to collect money and knit and collect scrap iron and things.' But stay they do, and the pony-club airs and mannerisms fall away as Caroline conquers her fear and joins resolutely in the escapade.

We Couldn't Leave Dinah is a perfect example of the fast-paced, undemanding adventure novel that might appeal to a reader who is not in the mood for complexity – or simply one who is mad for horse stories – and yet is a book that yields rewards well above the average.

A Pocketful of Seeds by Marilyn Sachs is a darker story, shadowed with the horror of the Holocaust but made bearable by the tenacious survival of Nicole Nieman. It is a fictionalized first person account of a true story, told in flashback by fifteen-year-old Nicole, who is waiting out the last days of the war in boarding school at Aix-les-Bains in Vichy France. Our sympathy is immediately caught by Nicole's spiky resistance of the spirit, despite her hunger, the cold, and her desperate fears for her family who were deported the year before. She has just slammed her book shut in the frigid study hall of the school: 'I know how to get warm!' she shouts. 'Everybody up – up – up!' and she gets all the girls doing the jitterbug 'like the American movies'. Headmistress Mlle Legrand bursts into the room where the girls are wildly clapping, laughing and gyrating. 'I cannot understand this display of levity,' she says icily. 'Nicole, the last person in the world who should be dancing is you. What kind of feelings do you have for your parents? For your sister? . . . You must be heartless.'

But Nicole dances to silence the pain and to defy the Nazis the only way she can: by clenching her misery in private rage, refusing to let her

Pétainiste teachers see how she suffers. The book gains its impact from this kind of gritty honesty, and from the picture of Nicole's family life before they are deported. The parents are poor – sellers of sweaters in the local open-air markets – and wilful Nicole constantly clashes with the emotionally expressive Mama whom she loves so much.

It is a touchingly believable portrait of the tensions between the argumentative oldest daughter, her weary but devoted parents, and the cute little sister who gets all the attention. The climax of the story is the moment when Nicole comes home from school to find the tiny flat ransacked and her family gone, taken by the Nazis. She snatches the family picture album and flees on her bicycle, sure of finding refuge with friends and neighbours. But her relatives are gone, too, taken in the roundup; as for the neighbours, some are tearfully regretful as they close their doors against her; at some houses, only the curtains twitch as Nicole pounds frantically at the door. Sachs describes all this without bitterness or judgement. It is a true picture of Vichy France, and the facts of Nicole's abandonment – and the cold refuge offered finally by her school – speak for themselves. What the reader carries away from the book is an unforgettable impression of Nicole's battered but defiant spirit.

An equal dignity suffuses the story of Julilly, a runaway slave and the twelve-year-old heroine of *Runaway to Freedom* (originally titled *Underground to Canada*) by Barbara Smucker. Of all the Canadian historical adventures I have read, this one has the most compellingly simple and vivid story line. We follow Julilly from the moment she is sold away from her mother on a Virginia plantation until the poignant moment when the two are reunited in Canada, thanks to the Quaker abolitionists who organized their escape.

Smucker successfully recreates the steamy heat of the Mississippi plantation to which Julilly is sold – the mosquitoes, the bone-cracking labour, the filthy shacks where the slaves collapse in numb exhaustion at night, and the vileness of their treatment by overseers: at 'feeding time', a man ladles corn-meal mush into a trough in the yard and the slave children 'push and shove on their hands and knees, dipping and sucking with their hands' to get their meagre food. Through all this degradation, the tall, strong Julilly holds on to the secret dream of the northern star, which her mother whispered to her before they parted. When she escapes, she takes with her the thirteen-year-old Liza, hunched and crippled from brutal beatings, embittered but determined to be free.

The story of their desperate journey is remarkable. It hardly seems possible that such an epic – and such an honourable chapter in Canada's history – has not been dealt with in children's literature before. So stark are the facts that Smucker nowhere has to belabour a moral; so convincing is Julilly's strength and longing to be free that the story is a joyful one, rather than a horror.

The ultimate adventure for children who are not caught up in the great events of history is not one of overcoming hardship, but of learning how to 'read' the world. The mystery, that is, is not whodunnit, but whom to believe, whom to trust, and how to know. This is the subtext, of course, of *Treasure Island*, as Jim Hawkins learns that even his enemies can be kind, and even his friends can be tainted.

Two British books tower above most others in tackling this problem of 'how to know' – which is, after all, one of the central tasks of any novel. The first, *No Way of Telling* by Emma Smith, is a thriller that poses the question: how is a child to know about strangers who might be dangerous? What resources can a defenceless child marshal against an armed and sinister adult?

No Way of Telling is a minor work of art, a tense heart-thumper written with precision, intensity and a sensibility so tuned to the inner workings of the child's mind that it quivers on target as truly as the needle of a compass.

Amy Bowen, who seems to be about ten or eleven years old, gets off the school bus in a whirling, blinding blizzard. Climbing the hill to the isolated Welsh hill cottage where she lives alone with her grandmother, Amy is caught up in the mysterious excitement of a snowstorm:

> *Snow was a marvel . . . it was like nothing else; it changed the world, the whole of life, in a matter of moments. Not only the shapes of trees and grasses were changed but daily habits – even laws lost their power and had no meaning when snow fell.*

Everyone has felt the delight tinged with fear of this kind of transformation, and Smith uses it to marvellous effect to wipe out the Bowens's normal daily ties to the outside and to muffle them in a strange, isolated and transformed world.

That night, as Amy and her grandmother enjoy the enhanced cosiness of their usual quiet tasks by the fire, a monstrous figure suddenly crashes open their door: 'In an instant the storm had rushed inside, filling the room, destroying its peaceful inviolability . . . a turmoil of Mick barking and barking, the lamp guttering, the tablecloth lifting, and snow blowing across the floor . . .'

The intruder is a giant of a man, wild and silent, covered with snow, who lurches across the room, grabs some of their food, stuffs it into a sack and vanishes back into the blizzard. After an anxious night, Amy goes out to the woodpile in the lean-to and notices, after a while, that there are signs that the man sheltered there for the night. And their 'hacker' (hatchet) is gone. One of the keenest pleasures of the book is the precision with which Smith captures the way people notice things – obliquely, confusedly at first, merely a sensory impression that slowly clicks into place in the mind with, finally, a sudden shock of understanding. Later, for example, Amy sees that a man to whom she has been talking has something black in his hand. At first, her mind unconsciously seeks the nearest explanation, that it is a torch. Only seconds later does it dawn on her that it is a gun. Very few suspense stories, whether for adults or children, take the trouble to track the movements of perception so exactly. Very few, therefore, carry the same emotional punch.

Amy and her grandmother are ensnared in a mystery. Soon, hot on the trail of the first man, come two graceful skiers, assumed by the Bowens to be police in pursuit of the huge intruder. By hunch, intuition, minute but telling clues and the exchange of silent signals between the old woman and the girl, a frightening truth is patched together: the two elegant skiers are murderous.

The story works up to a breathtakingly suspenseful climax and a deeply satisfying conclusion. Amy has been worried about not having enough courage to deal with their crisis. 'I'd say brave isn't mostly what people are, Amy, it's what they decide to be,' says her grandmother, a prime exemplar of her own words. 'Don't fret. . . . you'll find yourself brave enough whenever the time comes that you've got to be.' And she is, and believably so, since Smith has taken such care to fill in all the living details and the rounded characterization that make cause and effect seem so inexorable in a well-crafted story.

Furthermore, Amy, who at first felt helplessly that there was 'no way of telling' which man to trust and which to fear, learns by the end that there is indeed no certainty, but that complete perception is a mesh of compassion, swift intuition, experience, shared knowledge and alert intelligence. The important things can be known.

A complex and impressive variation on this theme is found in *The Emperor's Winding Sheet*, a story about the mediaeval fall of Byzantium by the distinguished British author Jill Paton Walsh. Piers Barber, wrecked on an English merchant ship and a fugitive from Turkish pirates who rescued and then brutalized him, tumbles from an orange tree into the garden of the Emperor Constantine. At first, he assumes he has fallen in with another lot of incomprehensible barbarians.

The Emperor has just heard a prophecy that he will be safe from the gathering storm so long as he keeps a little bird of good omen with him. Piers is dubbed 'Vrethiki', the lucky find, and is promptly washed, clothed and made the ceremonial companion of the Emperor.

Walsh is a masterful writer, and Byzantium with its shimmering domes, marble walls and fragrant gardens arises like a mirage before the dazzled eyes of Vrethiki – and the reader. At first, rebellious and mystified, he submits resentfully to the buckets of water in the courtyard of the bathhouse: 'Grey shining snakes and slopping goblets of water struck him and glazed his goosey skin. The cold seized and bit him and cut off his breath in gasps.'

Walsh's vibrant prose brings the ceremonies and war councils of the Empire into racing immediacy; she can move us, and Vrethiki, with the Emperor's gentle, grave, spartan demeanour amidst the pomp of his court and the gilded splendour of banquets. She can make us sympathize with Vrethiki while exposing to us his narrow condescension toward his Byzantine captors. At first, he hates the idea of Byzantium ('There's no accounting for barbarians,' says the emperor's cupbearer with a shrug) and boasts of his crusader ancestors to a horrified court eunuch who promptly tells him ('You barbarian whelp . . . is there *nothing* you know?') what savage despoilers the crusaders really were.

At length, as the Turks besiege the city and the reek of death lies over them all, Vrethiki knows what is most to be loved and admired. 'Effendi Mou, my true lord,' he cries, kneeling to pledge allegiance to the doomed Constantine. Walsh has solved the problem of historic language; all the characters speak believable English, with the colloquialisms or formality appropriate to their nationality or class. The sense of a distant time is conveyed delicately by a slight strangeness of cadence or diction. This barely noticeable tilt into a foreign voice serves to deepen our empathy for Vrethiki's sense of dislocation; as it begins to fall more familiarly on our ear, it draws us into Vrethiki's own slow growth into wisdom. Unwillingly free at last, wretched at leaving behind the dead Constantine and the ruined Byzantium, he sails home. 'In the very house I was born in I shall carry an exile's heart, thinking of that immortal City, and how it passed away. And nothing will be simple for me, ever again.'

Worlds and centuries apart, another journey of the innocent heart toward true understanding is *Huckleberry Finn*. To anyone old enough to cope with the spiralling satirical layers of meaning, Huck's raft ride down the Mississippi River with the runaway slave, Jim, is pure deliciousness.

I remember first reading *Huckleberry Finn* as a fairly naïve twelve-year-old; earnestness and emotion were more natural to me than irony. Still, the book filled me with a swelling, almost painful mix of elation, bafflement and wonder. I can still taste that disturbing flavour, the intoxicating strangeness, of Twain's humour. All the way through, I stepped as cautiously as a walker in a quicksand bog, not knowing at any moment whom to take seriously, whom to believe.

As a literary perception, that was somewhat crude but still of the essence: the book is an amazing lexicon, an encyclopaedia of religious, social and racial hypocrisy. There is the gross, in the person of Huck's drunken, reprobate father: 'Look at it, gentlemen, and ladies all; take ahold of it; shake it. There's a hand that was the hand of a hog; but it ain't so no more . . .' he swears. It is the very voice of the television evangelist, transported in a vulgar excess of fake piety. There is the riotously sanctimonious, in the person of the salivatingly morbid Emmeline Graingerford, who paints portraits of the dear departed with titles like 'I Shall Never Hear Thy Sweet Chirrup More Alas' and 'Art Thou Gone Yes Gone Alas'. He knew he ought to like such splendid art, Huck confesses, but 'I somehow didn't seem to take to them because if I was ever down a little, they always give me the fan-tods'.

Then there is the undertaker in his black gloves, mutely ushering in latecomers to a funeral, squeezing people into place and 'getting them all shipshape and comfortable' says Huck, admiring his 'softly soothering ways. . . . he was the softest, glidingest, stealthiest man I ever see; and there warn't no more smile to him than there is to a ham'.

Huck's pre-Civil War south is a rogue's gallery, a feast of every form of bombast and fakery, the sentimental, the rapacious, the high-toned and the ludicrous. Through it all runs the earnest voice of Huck, spouting the revolting conventional morality he has been taught by the Widow Douglas and Miss Watson, even while acting according to the instincts of his anarchic heart. When he sees the ruthless charlatans, the Royal Nonesuch con men, tarred and feathered, he can't help but feel sorry for them. 'It don't make no difference whether you do right or wrong,' he concludes ruefully, 'a person's conscience ain't got no sense, and just goes for him anyway. If I had a yaller dog that didn't know no more than a person's conscience does, I would pison him.'

But it is precisely Huck's real conscience, his inner promptings, that lead him right, and it is the imposed voice of received morality that is so shockingly wrong. When the loyal, tender Jim confides to Huck that he dreams of buying back – or even stealing – his own children out of slavery, Huck reacts 'properly' according to the morally stunted teachings of the slave-owning south. 'It most froze me to hear such talk,' says Huck. 'Here was this nigger which I had as good as helped to run away, coming right out flat-footed and saying he would steal his children – children that belonged to a man I didn't even know, a man that hadn't ever done me no harm . . . I was sorry to hear Jim say that, it was such a lowering of him.'

Minutes later, Jim and Huck are nearly caught by a pair of armed strangers in a small boat; instantly, Huck is spinning one of his fantastically cunning and elaborate lies (always tailored with uncanny psychological shrewdness to trap his listeners) to save Jim's life. His spontaneous actions constantly betray what he takes to be his 'conscience'. In fact, Huck finally gives up the dictates of morality completely and resigns himself to being damned to hell for remaining loyal to Jim. 'I knowed very well I had done wrong, and I see it warn't no use for me to try to learn to do right; a body that don't get started right when he's little ain't got no show.'

At the beginning of *Huckleberry Finn* Twain mockingly posted a 'Notice' of threatened prosecution against anyone attempting to find a moral in the story; of course, the book is a deeply moral comedy of human error and a devastating satire of hypocrisy. It's interesting that, nevertheless, groups as divergent as black parents and right-wing fundamentalists repeatedly try to have the book banished from public schools and libraries; blacks because their children are wounded by Twain's use of the demotic 'nigger' and by what they feel is the demeaning stereotype of the slave Jim; southern fundamentalists because they are infuriated by Twain's mockery of conventional morality.

In Chapter Ten, I argue for increased sensitivity in the books chosen for school curricula. Minority youngsters, already on the defensive in school settings in which they feel themselves outsiders, cannot possibly open themselves to Twain's humane message. Members of the white majority may argue, with literary and lofty purpose, that Twain shows us one of the most loving portraits of black-white friendship in all of literature, and they would be right . . . at least from a white point of view. But they can't know how it feels to be black, to sit in class and to hear the word 'nigger' over and over again.

To force the classroom study of *Huckleberry Finn* in cases in which black parents and students resist is to admit inadvertently (no matter how disinterested the stated educational goal) that one is unmoved by black suffering and indifferent to how little the student really can learn in such circumstances.

Huckleberry Finn is not the only classic work of literature to misfire in the classroom. In one small Canadian city, where the school board insisted on teaching *The Merchant of Venice* to eleven-year-olds, the few Jewish students were later pelted with coins by sneering classmates.

Perhaps these painful incidents are the best possible argument for reading literature at home as an education in true knowing. Books, all by themselves, can't banish bigotry. But any youngster who is well read in adventure stories of high merit would be less likely to misinterpret the meanings of great works of literature, and better able to translate humour, irony and metaphor into generosity of spirit.

Chapter 7

FANTASY

A genuine work of art must mean many things; the truer its art, the more things it will mean . . . It is not there so much to convey a meaning as to wake a meaning . . . The best thing you can do for your fellow is . . . not to give him things to think about, but to wake things up that are in him . . .

George MacDonald, 'The Fantastic Imagination', 1893

[The task of poetry is to create] imaginary gardens with real toads in them.

Marianne Moore, 1921

As A CHILD I had what I thought was a fixed dislike of fantasy. It was a long trek, once or twice a week, to the library, and we were limited in those dim days to only three borrowed library books per visit. I would spend hours making sure that not one of my precious three choices would turn out to be 'fantasy'.

Now I realize with amusement that most of what I read and loved best was, indeed, fantasy; it's just that I didn't call it that because, to me, it was grippingly alive and real. I didn't, in fact, hate magic, but its opposite: that sneaky cheat of a writer who would compel my whole quivering attention and make my heart pound faster, only to sneer on the last page, with insufferable adult condescension, that 'it was all a dream' or 'who knows whether it really happened?' A child who gives herself to a story, who lets herself be seduced by the author into believing in another world, who goes to the effort of imaginatively submitting to its rules and customs, is rightly enraged when the author turns out to have been mocking her naïveté all along.

The other kind of fantasy I loathed was the 'talking bunny' type (not, I hasten to add, *Peter Rabbit*), which trotted the young reader through an allegorical zoo of right-thinking animals who existed only to chirp – false lisping little beasts – the author's moral message. Allegory, I resentfully intuited, was trying to get at me with underhand purposes of its own, and I wanted none of it.

The best fantasies, even if they resound with high humour, are morally serious. The author believes in his imaginary garden, has taken pains to make sure that roses do not bloom there at the same time as trilliums – that there is inner coherence and a natural order in the garden – and he leads us by the hand there not to lose ourselves but to find something true. Ursula K. Le Guin, probably the finest fantasist writing in North America today, puts it better than I could when she compares Elfland, the world of fantasy, to a vast and beautiful national park where a person goes, alone, to get 'in touch with reality in a special, private, profound fashion. But what happens when it is considered merely as a "place to get away to"? Well, you know what has happened to Yosemite [a national wilderness park]. Everybody comes, not with an axe and a box of matches, but in a trailer with a motorbike on the back and a motorboat on top and a butane stove, five aluminium folding chairs, and transistor radio . . . They arrive totally encapsulated in a secondhand reality.' To accommodate the tourists, says Le Guin, some fantasy writers are building 'six-lane highways and trailer parks with drive-in movies, so that the tourists can feel at home just as if they were back in Poughkeepsie. But the point about Elfland is that you are not at home there. It's not Poughkeepsie. It's different.'

This chapter assumes that you do not want your children (or the children you teach or hope to inspire) to travel through literature in a bubble-pack of portable Poughkeepsie. Even without the mushrooming popularity of fantasy-as-teenage-escapism – sword-and-sorcery sagas with flinty-eyed heroes, a liberated woman or two and a brace of laser guns to give the whole enterprise a gloss of modernity – even without this whole new category of fakery, the reach of the fantasy form in children's literature is immense. Half the books in earlier chapters about humour, beginning readers, quest or adventure could just as easily slip in under the fantasy label, since children's authors have traditionally enjoyed a greater freedom to stretch the borders of reality.

Faced with this unmanageable torrent, I decided to narrow the field drastically. I began my reading surrounded by a mountain of currently popular fantasy: dragon epics, space epics, trilogies and quadrilogies and quintologies of popular paperbacks. Some authors are more competent than others, but almost all the recent crop are leadenly derivative of J. R. R. Tolkien's *Lord of the Rings* trilogy. Worse, they are no more magical than guided tours in which travellers eat hamburgers on the Champs-Elysées; the plot ingredients, in other words, are the familiar modern heroes and villains of television, tricked out in mediaeval finery. Their dragons, not to mention their unicorns, are all too often no more than disguised horses, noble steeds sentimentally loved by teenage girls. Their plots are typically escapist, and whether the enemy is a leathery-skinned monster toad or a beautiful witch, it is always an exterior enemy. Escapist reading, be it the adult thriller or the detective story, depends on the basic good-guy-beats-bad-guy mechanism. Moral ambiguity, in which the good guys (and, by implication, the readers) must painfully recognize the evil as a part of their human selves, both asks more of the reader and gives more.

It is this deeper dimension of complexity which distinguishes the fantasy written for older children from that aimed at the prepubescent. At eight or nine, children may be distressed by a story in which villains are attractive and heroes flawed; in *The Hounds of the Morrigan*, by Pat O'Shea, a recent and popular fantasy for middle readers, the young boy Pidge and his five-year-old sister Brigit are like fairy-tale babes in the woods, pursuing a long quest, attended by a changing cast of good fairies (animals and elfin varieties) and pursued by irrationally bad ones. Though the forces of evil may try to trick the children with ruses and blandishments, they have only to read the clues rightly to escape unharmed; their innocent optimism is almost never stained by the temptations of evil.

By the age of eleven or so, youngsters are less satisfied with this simple opposition of purity and foulness. Good readers especially are ready for the more discriminating task of literature, ready to grapple with the central dilemma of human life, the struggle in our own souls to distinguish and control our most destructive impulses.

So it's sad to see that the new teenage thirst for fantasy (and what could be more natural, and potentially useful, in this traumatic and threatening era?) should be slaked by so much bilge. Beware, then, of the meretricious 'fantasies' that are no more fantastical than transposed video games, where cynical and violent heroes defeat 'evil' with a magic ring, and 'heroines' are borrowed from the television series *Charlie's Angels*. It takes more than burlap costumes, papier-mâché monsters, and pseudo-mediaevalisms ('I'faith, my lord') to disguise the accents of Poughkeepsie . . . or to make them worth listening to.

All this dross, therefore, I whittled away from my stack of books. They offer no genuine shocks or surprises, no twists of sharp new perception which are the essence of the literary experience. There are no real toads in those gardens.

Tolkien, too, I've omitted from this chapter. His *The Hobbit* and the Middle Earth trilogy are so well-known, deservedly, that I scarcely need remind readers of their existence. But perhaps my selected short list of fantasy may serve as an inoculation against Tolkien fever, that unpleasantly pseudo-religious fanaticism that I first encountered when I was at university in the 1960s and that made me shun Tolkien until my own children read him years later. Tolkien cultists of university age, in full retreat from adult realities, named their cars Gandalf, claimed to have furry feet like Hobbits and swapped Elvish runes and Shire genealogies like kids swapping sweets and transfers. I think this fey frenzy mostly afflicted those who had never read fantasy before; they were like dazzled tourists to Elfland bringing back native hats and a self-conscious smattering of foreign phrases to impress the suburban neighbours.

Children who are better-travelled in the realms of fairy tale and fantasy are not so likely to bring back cheap souvenirs. Anyone who has, for example, read *The Wind in the Willows* in childhood knows that that is a charmed country, a world you keep whole in your mind and revisit at will. *Wind in the Willows*, in fact, is a good place to begin in discussing fantasy; it has all the most satisfying ingredients, though the recipe has been passed around among subsequent authors until it is tattered and grubby. There is rural bliss, the glint and ripple of the river, the summertime freedom of messing about in boats or spanking new caravans 'with all the little fitments', the comfort of firelit sitting rooms or wicker picnic baskets bulging with good food. It is a reverie of home, a childhood home where snugness is all 'clear of the clash of sex', as Grahame himself wrote.

But half the charm of those kitchen feasts and expansive fireside evenings lies in their contrast with the tingling excitement of adventure: glorious, wild, irresponsible adventure, reckless speed and mad self-indulgence, all embodied in the lovable person of Toad. Toad is, as the English critic Nicholas Tucker has astutely observed, the children's Falstaff. Unrepentant to the end, grandiose, boastful, sly, rich enough to gratify every impulse, Toad is still generous enough of soul to keep the undying loyalty of Ratty, Mole and Badger (those kindly Edwardian gents) and of child readers everywhere. Their prudence, their cosy bustle, their sturdy and sometimes stern affection are the anchor against which Toad's balloon irrepressibly tugs. Who can forget, or resist, the allure of that first motor car: 'a small cloud of dust, with a dark centre of energy, advancing on them at incredible speed, while from out the dust a faint "Poop-poop!" wailed like an uneasy animal in pain.'

Grahame's prose is so spacious and rich that it begs to be read aloud; remember the descriptions of the river 'as sleek, sinuous and full-bodied as an animal' or the moment when a tingling scent reaches Mole's nose – 'a fine filament, the telegraphic current . . . home!' An adult reading aloud might judiciously choose to omit the central chapter with its vision of Pan, a passage whose religious effulgence tips the book's delicate balance of ironic humour and calm affections; I remember skipping past those intensely embarrassing pages when I was a child.

The pull between home and adventure, the cosy burrow and the Wild Wood, is a natural theme of younger children's fantasy. One of the most brilliant workings of that idea is in *The Borrowers* by Mary Norton, a book that, as I discovered to my surprise on re-reading it, is perfect. The writing is lucid, precise, and lithe enough to stretch effortlessly from the minute observation of the under-the-floorboards miniature world of the Borrowers to the sudden shift to gargantuan scale. By the time Arietty, the Borrower child, has her first glimpse of the human world, we are so steeped in her perspective that we are as shocked as she is to look across the 'immense plain' of the gleaming hall floor to the monster stairs, rising into the distance to 'worlds upon worlds' that shimmer just out of sight.

Arietty is thirteen years old, one of the little people who live secretly by 'borrowing' tiny objects (all those lost safety pins and crochet hooks) from the inhabitants of a well-regulated home. 'Even their names were borrowed and not quite right' and it is a mark of Norton's skill that those names echo in our minds, chimingly perfect for their characters and just a little hallucinatory, a little bent from the norm, like a spoon in a glass: Pod and Homily Clock and their child Arietty, the snooty Overmantles, Uncle Hendreary, the gardener Crampfurl, the harridan cook Mrs Driver, and, in the sequel, the marvellous wild boy Spiller.

The home of the Borrowers has all the charm of a doll's house, but is more real. Homily grumbles ('Really, Arietty! Not on your clean jersey') when Arietty, helping to prepare dinner, lightly slings an onion ring round her shoulders. Arietty nods off to sleep in a cigar box bedroom, where lovely ladies in wispy chiffon bedeck the ceiling. And Pod comes back from a foraging expedition with his hatpin (used for climbing) looking queer: 'I been seen.' Fateful words in this secretive civilization; being seen by humans is supremely dangerous. When three laconic words can carry such foreboding, we know we are not in a doll's house.

Indeed, it is a complete world, wholly imagined, with its customs, family history, livelihood, greeds and envies, even a demonology (cats) of its own, and all of it revealed swiftly and with the utmost vivacity through conversation. Sword-and-sorcery fantasies, by contrast, pile on details in the strained effort to create credibility, but they read as excitingly as a hardware catalogue, and dialogue is typically sparse and wooden.

The plot of *The Borrowers* builds to the climactic moment when a visiting human-size boy, in his clumsy efforts to befriend the Clock family, prises up a floorboard to lower doll's-house furniture into their bedroom. The jolt to the reader is tremendous: so thoroughly have we entered the Borrowers' world that the crashing invasion via the ceiling is as terrifying as though monsters stepped casually through our own roofs. Mrs Clock, houseproud and acquisitive, is indignant at the violation and yet greedy for more of the useless but sumptuous doll's-house furnishings. Norton captures her ambivalence in a characteristically economical and revealing snatch of dialogue: the looming boy offers to nail back the floorboards if the Clock family doesn't want any more doll's-house treasures. 'Tell him to nail us down lightly,' Homily whispers to Pod.

It is Arietty, the impulsive and daring adolescent, who has brought this havoc into the family by secretly breaking a first rule of Borrowers: she made friends with the boy. This friendship, and the dreaded exposure to the adult world of authority to which it inexorably leads, causes the final expulsion of the Clock family from their tight, dark, secure – and claustrophobic – underground home. They are forced to 'emigrate' into the great outdoor world.

But even before this ultimate upheaval, Arietty's world and the boy's have clashed, to their mutual delight and dismay. One of the finest comic scenes in the book is their meeting under a blossoming cherry tree, during Arietty's first ecstatic venture into the outdoors. Boldly, Arietty confronts the speaking giant who casts a cold flick of shadow over her when he moves; she is scornfully certain that the world was made for Borrowers and that there can be very few of these giants alive: 'Surely you don't think there are many people in the world your size? . . . Honestly . . . I mean, whatever sort of world would it be? Those great chairs . . . Fancy if you had to make chairs that size for everyone? And the stuff for their clothes . . . miles and miles of it . . . tents of it . . . and the sewing! . . . their great beds . . . the *food* they eat . . . great smoking mountains of it, huge bogs of stew . . .'

The boy is younger and more timid; when he first sees Arietty, he can only perceive her as some kind of rodent: 'Don't move! Or I'll hit you with my ash stick,' he threatens, trembling, 'in case you came and scrabbled at me with your nasty little hands.' It is a perfect paradigm of the way children make friends, warily, with initial hostility and shaky bravado. But he, too, like Arietty, learns to abandon his smugly egocentric view of the world and take other human realities into account.

This, despite the book's constant bubble of wit and humour, and the author's consummately skilful play of perspectives between the two worlds, is moral seriousness. (*Charlotte's Web* by E. B. White, an American classic for a slightly younger age group, is another example of a superbly written fantasy with deep moral overtones.) Not all fantasy has this serious purpose, nor need it have – I'll discuss the humorist Joan Aiken later in this chapter, for one example – but clarity of intention, coherence of tone, and a respect for the child reader are essential. When E. Nesbit satirizes Victorian society, she speaks directly to the intelligent child, not over her shoulder to some imaginary and smirking adult eavesdroppers.

A book I heartily loathed as a child, and loathe even more now that I've re-read it as an adult, is *Mary Poppins* by P. L. Travers, whose heroine was recently beatified by an American critic as 'a combination fairy godmother, guardian angel, shamaness, priestess, witch and guru . . . like Mary Magdalene, she speaks as a woman who knows the All.' There speaks a man who in all likelihood did not read the book when he was young.

P. L. Travers is constantly playing to the adult audience, with an air of coy whimsy that can only be described as bloodcurdling. She digresses from her story to pretend that Mr Banks 'makes money' by snipping coins out of gold paper to bring home in a little black bag; she toys with the servant problem, indulges in a little byplay, utterly meaningless to a child, about Royal Academy art, and throws in two or three episodes of stardust and star fairies that seem to have derived from J. M. Barrie via the treacle vats.

Worst of all is the persona of Mary Poppins, the nanny with magical powers. Beady-eyed, peremptory, hardhearted, her most characteristic (and repulsive) utterance is a contemptuous sniff. She keeps the children in perpetual agonies of suspense about whether she will abandon them or not. In fact, she is extraordinarily vindictive, with the disconcerting megalomania of a baby. Her magic is inconsistent and perverse: she takes them to see an amusing uncle for a jaunty airborne tea party, and then righteously denies that the whole episode has taken place. Prim, conceited and greedy, she self-satisfiedly flaunts all the petty sins for which she reproves the children, teases the children with promises of magic and snaps at them when they respond with excitement, jeers at their most natural emotions and saves the best adventures for herself.

The most unpleasant event in the book is the celebration of Mary Poppins's birthday, in honour of which the animals at the zoo brutally humiliate elderly women and pin-striped gents. Mary preens herself over this display like a veritable Nero at the circus. The second most unpleasant episode is the magical circumnavigation of the globe, when the children are introduced to black natives at the South Pole (the geography is as inconsistent as the magic) who welcome them obsequiously – 'Youse mighty welcome. You bring dem chillun dere into ma l'il house' – and offer them watermelon; then there are the Indians in the West who offer hospitality: 'My wigwam awaits you; we are just frying a reindeer for supper.' Even this silly and racist journey is coherent compared to a bizarre episode in a bakery, where a malignant old crone snaps off the babies' fingers and makes them into gingerbread, breaks into menacing and berserk cackles of laughter and is then deemed by the children to be 'very nice after all'. Mary Poppins, as usual, fails to explain things to the children or to protect them. Some fairy godmother, some guru.

Travers's writing is shallow and self-indulgent; her helter-skelter plot, with its utter lack of inner logic or character development, is casually and mistakenly accepted by adults as 'magic' appropriate for children just because it involves some hocus-pocus. I can't help but think that many children, lured to the book by its Walt Disney film version, are rattled and privately puzzled by this meaningless and even sinister concoction.

In all fairness, though, I must say that I have met many adults who did read *Mary Poppins* in their childhood and who tell me they revelled in her infantile character. Here we run smack into one of those difficulties of assessing children's literature: because children have so little intellectual distance from the books they read, their reactions can be a tangle of the personal and extra-literary. Two of my own most anxious concerns in childhood were fear of abandonment, and adults who didn't believe me when I told the truth. Perhaps other children could accept Mary Poppins's quixotic and hostile behaviour with equanimity, or enjoy it as a sort of vengeful satire on their own less-than-perfect guardians, whereas I felt angered and threatened beyond endurance.

Even allowing for such individual responses, though, I still feel that the Poppins fantasy is too sloppy and unworked-out. As Le Guin says, 'fantasy is a journey. It is a journey into the subconscious mind, just as psychoanalysis is. Like psychoanalysis, it can be dangerous; and *it will change you.*' E. Nesbit's fantasies, written at the turn of the century, changed *my* life, so I know firsthand that Le Guin is right. You can't, of course, prescribe or dictate which book will change a child's life; one of the profound powers of literature is, as MacDonald intimates in the passage I quoted at the head of this chapter, that each reader plumbs a different depth and carries away a uniquely private treasure. The most you can do is make available, and accessible, the books that you believe to be rich enough to afford this kind of serendipity, and let the child's mind do the rest.

I had librarians who were knowledgeable and tactful enough to recommend Nesbit's books to me at precisely the right moment of my life. On the surface, they are comedies of Victorian family life. In *Five Children and It*, the five children (Robert, Anthea, Jane, Cyril and the baby, called the Lamb because its first word was 'Baa') discover a crotchety sandfairy, the Psammead, who can grant wishes. Their adventures are classic variations on the old 'foolish wish' theme of fairy tales, amusingly modernized to include the pony carts, snobbish aristocrats, gypsies, servants and townspeople who normally populate the worlds of Victorian children's stories. Nesbit's genius was to give these adventures to a realistically grubby, quarrelsome and thoroughly decent family of youngsters whose conversation reads as freshly today as it did when it was written.

The same children appear in *The Phoenix and the Carpet* and finally in *The Story of the Amulet*, both of them inspired works of humour and adventure. It was *The Story of the Amulet* in particular that sent a shiver of wild surmise into my nine-year-old soul. I can still recall the moment when the five children, now travelling in time thanks to the powers of an ancient Egyptian amulet, go forward into the London of the future. Nesbit, a Fabian socialist, draws a vision of a green world, a world without poverty or cruelty, through which the Thames runs sparkling clear and school is so fascinating that children cry when they are expelled for a day. There the children meet a boy named Wells (after H. G. Wells, 'the Great Reformer') and his mother, a gentle woman who tells them stories of the horrid Dark Ages when coal smoke darkened the London sky and says 'the suffering of the people hardly bears thinking of'.

It was this contrast of two societies – one cruelly workaday, and one a green utopia influenced by William Morris's *News from Nowhere* – that changed me by giving me my first, astounding intimation that *the world could be different, and that people could change it;* it was a primitive perception, perhaps, but an earth-shaking one for a child utterly, unthinkingly wrapped in the cocoon of unchanging family life in the Toronto of the late 1940s. From that moment on, a gleam of rebellion glowed in me; I knew that my life mustn't pass without my trying to make some difference in the world. (From the point of view of a conservative, of course, this proves Le Guin's point that fantasy can be dangerous.) It's a sidelight on the power of childhood reading that when, at university, I read *News from Nowhere*, it went straight to my heart . . . even though I didn't realize then that I had visited that land before, in *The Story of the Amulet*.

With Grahame, Norton, White and Nesbit we are still in the world of the middle reader, where home and parents are a loved and loving counterpoise to the tug of adventure. In *A Year and a Day*, a haunting book for the middle age group by the prolific and lavishly gifted author William Mayne, the pull is all toward home and hearth. Two little girls, Rebecca and Sara, living in a working-class cottage in a nineteenth-century Cornish village, draw the eeriness and strangeness into their own family when they find a 'wild boy' and bring him home.

It is worth quoting the opening passage as a sample of Mayne's prose:

> *Rebecca sat with her feet in the water and her head in the ground. That was what she thought she was doing. Her feet were in the sea, feeling a soft mud. The top of the water came up and down slowly on her legs, warm as it came up, and cold as it went down. The rest of her was lying on some grass, and she was looking with her head upside-down towards the church behind her. The tower went up very steeply into the blue sky.*
>
> *Something seemed to walk across her face. She put her hand to her eyes to push it away, and sat up. She kicked the sea, getting up so fast. The sea kissed the back of her knee, very wet. The thing that had crossed her face was only a horse and a cart and a man, not touching her at all, but dropping a shadow on her, and coming between her and the church . . .*

Mayne conveys minute physical sensation with such intense clarity and precision, in the same order as it is felt and then understood by his characters, that it draws us almost physically into the character's mind and sensory world. As Rebecca goes up the pasture lane in search of her sister, on the brink of that strange moment when they find the naked and speechless boy, the sand on her legs dries to sparkling pottery, and then to dust, in the baking heat of the day. We feel not only the sea's kiss and then the heat, but Rebecca's quick reflex of fear and then her flicker of annoyance when she calls her sister in the silent woods, and a cow replies with a 'long bellowing message that sounded rather stupid. Some cows will shout senseless messages.'

Sara crashes out of the woods (Becca, the more sensitive and imaginative of the two, likes to stay at the edge and imagine herself in it): 'See what I have found.' Sitting in a grassy tangle like a nest, it is a little boy with dark hair and dark eyes and skin pale as milk. He looks at them. He has no clothes on. Their conversation, as always in Mayne, is teasingly tangential and totally revealing. 'No clothes. Sacred,' says Becca. 'Naked,' says Sara. 'That's the word. Like Adam and Eve.' Becca replies – and here we are left to imagine her surprise and earthy realism – 'Like but only Adam.'

Janey Tregose, a local 'wise woman' and midwife, comes to see the strange foundling, and insists that it's a fairy child: 'And since you kept him across a candleteening, why, he's here a year and a day, and then he'll be here no more, one way and another. A year and a day. You remember that.' This enigmatic speech, the longest so far in the book, gains all the more force from that one strange word 'candleteening'. All the dialogue in the book, in fact, is rich in overtone, colour and humour; the girls' parents don't have to be described because, through their tersely affectionate and colloquial speech, almost poetic in its evocation of country beliefs and ways, a kind of elemental solid goodness shines through.

Mayne has an uncanny feel for childhood perceptions, thoughts and emotions, and the artistic genius to express them in the most movingly oblique moments of gesture and speech. Through the simple events of a country year – the arrival of the laden fishing boats and the salting of the winter's fish, the winter fox hunt, the ripening of the blackcurrants – he shows us also the tender ripening of the children's awareness. The story is beautifully rounded out, with poignant loss balanced by the birth of mother's new baby.

A Year and a Day has little to do with conventional ideas of magic or fantasy, but it is so densely packed with a complete social structure (all this in ninety-six pages), and so vibrant with character, drama, sensory vividness and sly humour, that it is as haunting as any story ever written. Yet all the nuance and depth of emotion are accessible to a careful reader of ten or eleven, for whom the passionate family drama is still at the magical centre of being.

Joan Aiken, the ebullient English humorist, aims at the same age group with her linked stories of *Black Hearts in Battersea, Night Birds on*

Nantucket and *The Cuckoo Tree*, but she takes her readers a jaunty leap sideways: home is where the rogues are. All the adults are eccentric, hapless dreamers or villainous schemers, and her exuberant young heroes do very nicely on their own. They live in a mythical England where King James the Third is on the throne and the dastardly Twite family, abetted later by the Slighcarps, are involved in a series of lunatic Hanoverian conspiracies to overthrow him.

Aiken is closest to Leon Garfield in her virtuoso use of language. Dido Twite in *Black Hearts in Battersea*, who nearly runs away with the story by sheer brash scrawny vitality, speaks a cheerfully invented version of Cockney: 'Brush on, cullies,' she urges her comrades in derring-do on a listing ship, 'The ship's betwaddled. . . . you *are* a loblolly.' Dido, with her rowdy appreciation of 'ripsmasher' and 'slumdigger' moments of excitement, is softened by the friendship offered by fifteen-year-old Simon, the sturdy, sensible good-hearted sort of hero who is most at home in a fairy tale.

And these are fairy tales, breathlessly exaggerated and sent up, to be sure; complete with lost princes, switched identities, silver bracelets and frantic plot reversals. Though there are villains and wolves and pirates and gunpowder plots, there is no true horror. It is the spunk, natural goodness and high spirits of the heroes which are in the foreground, overcoming even the most daunting difficulties. In *Night Birds on Nantucket*, perhaps the most tightly and sparklingly written of the three Simon and Dido books, Aiken goes so far as to spoof *Moby-Dick* – but friendship, not slaughter, is the finale of Captain Casket's lifelong pursuit of the pink whale, Rosie. Dido is at her best as she rescues the captain's daughter, Dutiful Penitence Casket, from a life of pious repression ('Oh, *scrape* ladylike behaviour!').

Scattering colourful oaths around her like confetti ('Croopus!' and 'Cor, love a lily-white duck!' and 'Great Snakes! I'm crabbish hungry') the resourceful Dido is sharp as a tack in puncturing yet another Hanoverian plot. This time, the plot involves a lovable dupe, Professor Breadno, who is constructing a giant cannon (in his weird Scando-German dialect, the professor dotingly calls it a 'monstershoot grosseboom') to fire all the way from Nantucket to St James's Palace. ('Is cleverness, not? Will be magnifibang!')

Through all the slapdash merriment, Aiken keeps tight control of her plot, makes the improbable characters come alive through their language, and weaves in some bright threads of convincing friendship and kindness. It is sentimentality, not emotion, that is briskly undercut by Dido's salty practicality. And, almost imperceptibly, we have seen friendship change Dido from an impetuously self-centred urchin to a self-assured and compassionate girl.

Most fantasies, in fact, beyond those for the earliest age groups, are journeys of self-discovery and coming of age. While the so-called 'problem novelists' have battened joyously onto the growth market for adolescent novels, they seem to have mistaken the symptoms for the disease: relentlessly, they write about acne, masturbation, divorce, abortion, stupid teachers, witless parents. The best fantasy writers, though, know better than to trample all over the fragile terrain of puberty like cattle at a watering hole. There are agonies worse than acne, most of them too deeply felt and complex for easy expression or solutions, and good fantasy writers approach these mysteries at a tangent.

Grinny, by Nicholas Fisk, is a genuinely horrifying science-fiction tale suitable for children of eleven and up. Fast-moving, colloquial and utterly accessible, it is exactly the sort of book that can be offered as an alternative to the badly-written, shallow, 'realistic' stories which teachers often insist are the only thing that slower readers will read. True, a story as quiet and strange as *A Year and a Day* might be savoured only by a literate, perceptive reader, but it's hard to imagine any child who wouldn't be riveted by *Grinny*. It's told in lively, almost slangy first-person style as the diary of eleven-year-old Tim. Though we are immediately unsettled by the arrival of the sinister Great Aunt Emma, who somehow mesmerizes the adults into thinking they remember her, the tension and mounting spookiness are leavened by Tim's sarcasm and boyish humour – usually at the expense of his maddeningly adorable little sister, Beth, aged seven. 'Beth was ever the Outstanding Social Success,' writes the disgruntled Tim. He takes consolation in banter with his father about the soppy emotionalism of women and the unfair advantages they enjoy.

Great Aunt Emma swiftly turns out not to be quite what she seems, and it is the despised Beth who twigs first. 'Pooh,' she says, after being forced to kiss GAE goodnight. 'She doesn't smell. It's all wrong.' And then Beth swears that when GAE slipped and fell in the backyard, her hand was dangling from a wrist that was all too genuinely broken: the skin was open in a gash, the bones were showing – and there was no blood. 'The bones were made of shiny steel, like little collections of umbrella ribs.'

Once Tim is convinced by Beth that 'Grinny' (as Beth spitefully calls her) is not a real person, but a visitor from a spaceship, the children are plunged into the real dilemma: the adults are hypnotized. No matter how many inadvertent clues Grinny lets slip that she is a highly sophisticated and malevolent robot, the adults refuse to believe the evidence of their senses.

One of the most disillusioning passages of prepuberty is just this realization that adults are not infallible. And the first and most frustrating revelation of adult frailty, to many children, is the experience of standing by, helplessly, while adults are duped (viz. *Madeline and the Bad Hat*) by a fraud transparent to children.

As Tim begins to realize that the three children – Tim, Beth and their friend Mac – are utterly alone against this powerful invader, he must gradually shift ground. Only on second reading do you notice how deftly Fisk has planted the hints at Tim's transformation into the developing story. Once the adults have proven impervious to the truth, Tim begins to distance himself from that manly English reticence of which he boasted earlier. Derision for his parents' 'hear-no-evil' stance creeps into his tone;

he begins to imagine a ghastly scene in which the adults line up, chatting about tea and the price of beef 'and being marched off to the slaughter, absently swiping away the screaming, begging children' who know the truth.

In the end, it is precisely by the concentrated power of intuition and emotion – Beth's despised emotionalism has finally roused not only Tim's awareness but also his compassion – that the children conquer Grinny. The last triumphant scene, when the children turn her mysterious electric torch on her (it bites her apart, tears and nibbles with 'humped-up scurryings and lunges and tugs like a rat', until Grinny is nothing but a pile of metallic rubbish) is absolutely revolting and superbly satisfying. Fear and horror are familiar emotions to a child; the conquest over nightmare is a legitimate literary experience, particularly when it is so well controlled by the author and so thoroughly exorcized by the young protagonists themselves.

The flip side of horror is, of course, comedy, the celebration of hopefulness in human life, and an apt medium for tales of youthful growing pains. Two excellent examples of comic fantasy spring to mind: Helen Cresswell's *The Bongleweed* and *Alan Mendelsohn, the Boy from Mars* by Manus Pinkwater.

In *The Bongleweed*, we first see Becky in the potting sheds at Pew Gardens with her father, Finch, the head gardener, and in three quick lines of dialogue, their characters and their companionable relationship are established. ' "Oh Dad," said Becky. "Polishing spades again!" "A good workman," he began, not even lifting his head. "Oh I know," she said quickly, "Don't tell me again. I believe you." '

Becky loves the garden, perhaps more fiercely than her father does, but she is restlessly poised on the hinge of adolescence: Finch reproaches her for not having enough respect 'for the things that really matter'. True enough, Becky distrusts the scientific botanical mania shared by Finch and his boss Dr Harper. Impatient, scornful, but curious, she spies on the adult world through a peephole into the dining room of the Harpers' grand house, separated from the Finches' own little house by one thin wall.

In a moment of petulance – annoyed, too, because she is expected to entertain twelve-year-old Jason, a brainy but sickly boy who has come to visit the Harpers – Becky plants a mysterious seed, prized by Dr Harper, in her mother's kitchen garden. That night, she hears a strange whispering noise under her window – 'a hissing like wind in poplars, a conspiracy of leaves . . . bless, bless, bless . . . or was it wish, wish . . . or again us, us . . .'

It is the bongleweed growing, growing phenomenally, magically, and soon the giant plants are rioting in growth, springing to fifteen feet tall overnight, smothering the cemetery next door in a twining, leaping jungle of greenery. While Finch and his sturdy wife Else are badly rattled by the bongleweed (and their working-class pragmatism, touched with endearing eccentricity, makes them a marvellous creation), Becky and Jason are drawn into the conspiracy of uncontrollable life.

> *She wanted to laugh at the sheer nerve of it, the life, the cheek of the thing, with its careless lack of consideration for walls, boundaries, rules – even for all the laws of nature. . . . With a sudden rush of affection, she realized that she loved it, found it bold and splendid beyond anything she had ever known.*

Becky and Jason are like a prelapsarian Adam and Eve, sitting under the apple tree lost in wonder at the lush beauty of the bongleweed: when it flowers, the blossoms are apricot-coloured, of extraordinary sheen and delicacy, like silk umbrellas. This is, however, no passive flower; it has the strength and wiliness of a panther, a lion; its rush to growth is unstoppable, like Becky's own. And Becky learns that she has power over the weed. She created it, she named it and, at last, she can command it to draw back and make a passage for her through its densest thickets.

The whole of this adventure is written with the most engaging poetic exuberance, always balanced by the gruff realism of Finch and the believably acerbic sparring of Becky and Jason. The bongleweed must die, of course, and it dies not by the hand of the scheming undergardener, but by 'nature taking its course' – a spring frost. But Becky has changed. She has experienced not only the exultation of adolescence, with its sudden burst of joy when it realizes its own surging power, but also 'a complicated sadness' at the opening of a subtle gap between her and her parents. But she is most definitely not sorry for having planted that seed. And when the bongleweed dies ('wish . . . loss . . . miss . . . ' are the last evocative whispers Becky hears from it) she consoles the grieving Jason. She knows that now there has been one bongleweed, anything – anything desperate, beautiful and reckless – is possible.

Not one youngster in a thousand may explicitly recognize the images of puberty, the echoes of the Garden of Eden, in this lovely and funny story, but many will respond to its energy without knowing why.

Alan Mendelsohn, the Boy from Mars is a comedy in an entirely different tone. This is the wry, sophisticated, satirical voice of the North American city boy, woefully exiled with his parents to a new home in the suburbs. Portly Leonard Neeble is too short and rumpled to be acceptable at his new school, Bat Masterson Junior High, where all the gleaming tanned youths match each other in their permapress clothes and conspire together to ostracize anyone who doesn't conform.

Pinkwater, as usual, is the tender-hearted champion of every harmless eccentric and hapless outsider in America. But that doesn't stop him from spoofing their nuttiness, either: Leonard's grandmother, a health-food maniac, who likes to be called the Old One, lives 'basically on what grandfather's parrot eats': sunflower seeds and nut cutlets. And Leonard's father, when he is not compulsively barbecuing, is complacently showing off his new electric remote-control garage-door opener.

Leonard is more than usually lonely now that the family has moved far from his grandparents and his inner-city buddies who don't care what people look like. But he is saved by a new friend at school, the tough and self-sufficient Alan Mendelsohn, a boy who refuses to submerge his individuality.

Together, the two boys stumble on Samuel Klugarsh's shop where they buy his patented mind-control system and learn to achieve 'mental state 26'. Until they run into the biker and folk singer Clarence Yojimbo, a Venusian, all they can do with their 'mind control' is to make strangers take off their hats and rub their bellies . . . But no synopsis can do justice to the galloping hallucinatory quality of the boys' adventures, spiked all the way through with satirical swipes at contemporary life. It is part of Pinkwater's comedic skill that he can captivate readers with precisely the foibles he's trying to send up. Of course, a deepened consciousness of life's complexities is what the boys arrive at, but their journey through the mumbo-jumbo of the occult is rich in lunatic pleasures, like the Bermuda Triangle Chili Parlour (three strengths of chili: regular, H-Bomb and Green Death), throwback genius chickens, and Nafsulian linguistics (the ancient Nafsulian words, Haya and Doon, survive today in a common American greeting).

Leonard's loyalty to his friend, Alan, and his bravery in following through the demands of 'interplanar existential communications', have their reward. After all the science-fictional escapades, Leonard has figured out how to survive in high school, how to co-operate with the system without surrendering. Disguised in antic colours like a court jester, Pinkwater is nevertheless steadily, subversively on the side of human life and sanity.

Science fiction has an innate fascination for boys, compounding electronic gadgetry with cowboy characters. The phallic speed and thrust of missiles and spaceships notwithstanding, there are other forms of fantasy that might prove just as appealing and offer deeper pleasures. Diana Wynne Jones is a British fantasist of astonishing originality and power. She is equally adept at those mind-opening reversals of perception (*The Power of Three*) that make *The Borrowers* outstanding, and at wittily elaborate magical farces (*Witch Week* and *The Magicians of Caprona*). Like Joan Aiken, she happily borrows from myth, legend and folk tale for her basic plot ingredients. But so accomplished is she at sleight-of-hand and bewildering complications that they exist just out of sight, submerged like the concrete underpinnings of a fantastically ornate bridge.

The Homeward Bounders, in fact, is based on the craze for fantasy and war gaming, and is a bracing antidote to the excesses of both. Not till halfway through *The Homeward Bounders* does it become clear that the first-person hero, thirteen-year-old Jamie Hamilton, has been permanently exiled from his nineteenth-century English working-class home by a shadowy group of futuristic gamers who play 'the Real and Ancient Game' with real people and overlapping worlds.

Struggling through endless worlds, some more tormented than others,

Jamie begins to discover other Homeward Bounders, who, like him, are doomed to walk the boundaries of the worlds for ever. Among them are legendary or mythological figures like Prometheus, the Flying Dutchman, the Wandering Jew . . . all of them plausibly entangled in the complex plot, and all of them springing into a curious new life in Wynne Jones's hands.

Just as *The Homeward Bounders* is tailor-made for the youth who can't be coaxed to read anything but Dungeons and Dragons handbooks or sci-fi, *Dogsbody* may entice a girl who's stuck on animal stories to reach a little farther. The story begins when Sirius, the dog star, a hothead among the stellar beings, is exiled by a heavenly court of judgment for an alleged murder and for the accidental loss of a 'zoi', an object of supreme magical power. Sirius is cast down to earth in the form of a newborn puppy, an unwanted byblow who turns up (red ears and all) in a pedigree setter's litter.

Sirius grows to dog's estate, and his growing strength and understanding are brilliantly delineated from the dog's-eye point of view – albeit a supernatural dog who just happens to be cared for by a lonely orphan girl, Kathleen, living with her unlovable aunt, uncle and cousins.

Sirius's dawning realization that he is a fallen star on a mysterious earthly mission is perfectly integrated with his clumsy, enthusiastic growth from puppyhood. Somehow, Wynne Jones conveys a doggy nature of wagging optimism that perfectly accords with the boundless energy of an astral lord. Sirius's growth, not coincidentally, parallels a child's development into maturity and skill, and also the progress of the meek, almost Cinderella-like Kathleen toward self-assertion and independence. As in all Wynne Jones's books, the narrative suspense is muscular enough to carry the reader right through mazes of bewildering plot twists. *Dogsbody* is, however, one of her more coherent and accessible fantasies, a sometimes rueful, sometimes lyrical journey toward self-knowledge.

This transformation is as its most explicit in a new flowering of fantasy. Both Wynne Jones and the brilliant New Zealand writer Margaret Mahy have begun to use fantasy as a way to speak of a young girl's transition into womanhood. This is an exciting departure that should gratify every adult who has yearned to lure teenage girls away from the masochistic formula eroticism of traditional romances. In the hands of these two gifted novelists, witchery and magic are metaphors for the sexual dawning that liberates the young girl from half-formed notions of herself. In *The Changeover*, young Laura embraces her own embryonic powers of witchcraft in order to save her little brother's life. In accepting an offer to 'change over' ('We will marry you to some sleeping aspect of yourself and you must wake it. Your journey is inward but it will seem outward,' says an older witch), Laura steps into potent womanhood – she chooses to become more powerful and sexual; the young male witch to whom she is drawn is at the same time struggling (ironically, through reading cheap romances) to move beyond eroticism and discover what love feels like.

Sophie, the timid and self-deprecating oldest sister in one of Wynne

Jones's most deliciously funny and deft fantasies, *Howl's Moving Castle*, is cast under a spell which turns her into a rheumatic old crone. In that guise, she becomes a servant to the dreaded young wizard, Howl – and in her crusty nature as an octogenarian, discovers at last her own powers. Incidentally, she discovers along the way that the wizard, who is said to 'suck the souls from young girls', is as vulnerable and good-hearted as she is. Both these stories of adolescent love are exhilarating romances in which the sinister potency of the male wizard is unmasked as a mere charade, and the weakness of the female is abandoned as untrue to her real nature. The eroticism, at last, crackles as the electricity between two equally attractive and powerful forces.

At the pinnacle of all such fantasies stand two trilogies: *Earthsea* by Ursula Le Guin and *The Ice Is Coming* by Australian author Patricia Wrightson. There are remarkable points of similarity in the structure of the two trilogies, and it is this underlying pattern that makes them both so vividly appropriate for adolescent reading. In the first books, a boy goes through trials and crises to emerge in manhood as a powerful magic user. (Magic as a metaphor for adult potency and knowledge is particularly apt for young readers; these two books are unusual in that it is the boy who attains that power, not a wizardly father figure who has it already.) In the second books, the youth helps an enchanted (in the sense of 'sung into a spell') girl-woman free herself to become fully sensually alive and self-determining. In the third books of each trilogy, the man accomplishes his lifework – a struggle against evil that lies partly within himself – grapples with death, and passes beyond the active, heroic stage of his life.

The publication of *A Wizard of Earthsea* in 1968 immediately established Ursula Le Guin as the leading writer of fantasy in North America; her invention of a 'secondary world' is second only to Tolkien's (if that) in richness, detail, consistency and fascination. Le Guin's 'archipelago' is complete with island nations and tribes, each with its own commerce, language, culture and religion, and into this lucidly imagined world, on the island of Gont in the storm-racked Northern Sea, is born an impetuous, neglected, dark-skinned boy whose birthname is Duny.

Duny (later he takes the name of Sparrowhawk, with the secret true name of Ged) is reared harshly by an aunt who dabbles in cottage witchcraft. The boy soon shows frightening depths of magic power, and a frightening arrogance in using them carelessly. By the age of twelve he has mastered all the local lore of 'finding, binding, mending, unsealing and revealing, various tricks and pleasantries and spells of illusion', and is taken on as an apprentice by the mild and wise Ogion the Mage.

A fantasy writer, in creating a wholly fabricated world, spins a web of imagination that is easily torn. A clumsy word, an anachronism, an accent of 'Poughkeepsie', and our eager belief is fatally torn. Le Guin, however, never puts a word wrong. Her prose is vigorous, precise, clear and sturdy enough to sustain a whole archipelago; even at her most incantatory ('. . . this was the way he was to follow all his life, the way of magery, the way that led him at last to hunt a shadow over land and sea to the lightless coasts of death's kingdom . . . ') she does not embarrass her readers with a falsely exalted tone. Her mages speak with the kind of runic simplicity that delights young readers while it illuminates her mode of thought: when Sparrowhawk, impatient for more dazzling feats of magical power, asks Ogion, 'When will my apprenticeship begin, sir?' Ogion answers, 'It has begun.' 'But I haven't learned anything yet!' 'Because you haven't found out what I am teaching.'

What Ogion is teaching is restraint and moderation, the search for the innate Balance and Pattern in all creation. But Sparrowhawk wants more, and rashly uses a spell to raise the dead. 'Looking over his shoulder, he saw that something was crouching beside the closed door, a shapeless clot of shadow darker than darkness.' Ogion rescues him from the nameless nightmare that Sparrowhawk has summoned, but deeply reproves him: danger surrounds power as shadow does light, Ogion tells him, and he sends his headstrong pupil at last to the school of wizardry at Roke to learn the High Art.

A school of wizardry offers almost unlimited scope to a gifted writer, and Le Guin makes the most of it; we are shown in fascinating detail what Sparrowhawk learns, and it is the densely realized detail that is enchanting: the lessons in shape changing, the spells over wind and weather taught by Master Windkey, the long hours in the Isolate Tower under the stern tutelage of the Master Namer, who teaches them the thousands of true and hidden names of things, in which real magic inheres.

Unlike most fantasy writers, however, Le Guin does not equip her hero with nifty weapons and send him out to defeat evil in one great clanging battle. Sparrowhawk-Ged's true battle is with himself. Time and again, arrogance and ego lead him to rash acts of excess. His enemy is the dark thing, 'the shadow,' the Archmage tells him, 'of your ignorance, the shadow that you cast'.

Scarred and humbled, Sparrowhawk leaves the school at the age of nineteen, in a blue cloak and clutching a yew staff, to work as an unassuming neighbourhood wizard on the remote sea-washed island of Low Torning, where housewives row across canals to take a cup of rushwash tea with a neighbour. From there he begins the series of voyages and crises – battles with dragons, journeys to far seas with his rough-hewn friend Vetch – to 'finish what he began', to find, face and name the shadow he unloosed.

One reason the fantasy never loses its grip on our attention is Le Guin's power to create intensely attractive male heroes. Ged's potency is admirable rather than bellicose and repellent. His maturity is not that of a warrior or conqueror, but that of a man who recognizes and leashes his aggression. His tenderness is the movingly gentle gesture of a man of great power and self-knowledge.

The second story in the trilogy is equally compelling and even more tautly written. In *The Tombs of Atuan*, the scene shifts to a distant, dusty island of the archipelago where an order of priestesses presides over ancient rituals in the place of ancient tombs. Images of ruin, dryness and emptiness predominate in Le Guin's evocation of this grim place. As usual, details of food, work, materials and crops, herbs and songs appear naturally, unforcedly, in the narrative. And this is a convincingly three-dimensional world, in which all these details accord. You always know, with Le Guin, that if the local people eat corn porridge, there will be cornfields, workers who must draw water for the fields, a ritual and a pattern for the watering and harvesting, and a sharp feel for the taste of the thing.

Tenar, the peasant girl chosen in infancy to be Arha, the Eaten One, the high priestess of the Tombs with their dark gods, is the heroine of the story. By the time she reaches the age of fifteen, we know her fierceness, her sombre resolution and the deeply buried gleam of defiance in her character that will lead her, with Ged's help, to shatter the ancient maze of underground tombs and find her freedom. The clutch of a fearful religion on a young soul is shown this powerfully in only one other children's book that I know of: *The Blue Hawk*, by Peter Dickinson, in which a boy, Tron, is doomed to priesthood in an equally baleful ancient order. Like Tenar, he too is freed at last with the help of his own questioning mind and of a young man on a quest of his own.

But as a story of young womanhood bursting the bonds of repression, *The Tombs of Atuan* is unique, reverberating with archetypal echoes that Le Guin herself recognized as Jungian only some years after writing the book. And though Ged is at his prime in this book – gentle, knowing, profoundly resigned – it is friendship, not sexual love, which he offers the struggling Tenar. All his magic is placed at the service of her emergence from the suffocating, impersonal dark. 'You told me to show you something worth seeing,' says Ged, imprisoned in the tombs by the priestesses, and ordered by a hostile Tenar to create a magical illusion. 'I show you yourself.' Later, when the two have escaped, Tenar wakes outside the temple compound on a hillside, filled with sweetness and pleasure. 'Living, being in the world, was a much greater and stranger thing than she had ever dreamed.' Though Tenar naturally is drawn romantically to her rescuer, Ged, the impulse is unexpressed except for one sentence ('What was in her heart as she looked at him in the firelight she could never say'). This reserve deepens the impact of the story, mirroring a truth in the lives of young girls and leaving Tenar as the centre of energy and action in a story that is open-ended.

The last book in the trilogy, *The Farthest Shore*, is the most complex and least satisfying; perhaps that is inevitable, since its subject is the confrontation of the ageing Ged, now Archmage, with death itself. The sense of confusion in the philosophical underpinnings of the story is reflected in the first falterings of Le Guin's pristine language: there are more 'Aye, lad' slips into strained dialogue, and the overwhelming aura of moral disorder and decay is disheartening. But the book is distinguished by the most original and magnificent dragons in literature, ancient and thunderously immense creatures whose eyes glitter with a remote and ironic amusement at the doings of men.

FANTASY

Like Le Guin, Patricia Wrightson places a dark-skinned hero at the centre of a magic-drenched land, but this is not a mythical world – it is Australia. In a flowing, open voice, the rolling rhythms of the tale-teller rather than the flat choppy edginess of most contemporary prose, the narrator begins by showing us the vast landscape set in a tumbling, beating sea. White people are marginal here. Wrightson, in a clever distancing trick, calls them the Happy Folk, and shows us a frantic, cavorting society of consumers scattered along the fringes of the 'great open hand' of the continent. We see them rushing about in pursuit of pleasure on beaches and in shopping malls, but we see them as though through the wrong end of a telescope, tiny as puppets and somehow irrelevant to the massive ancient unknown land slumbering behind them.

We see them also through the old eyes of young Wirrun, an aborigine who lives among but not of them, quietly working in petrol stations and taverns but keeping his own counsel and listening uneasily to voices from elsewhere. A teenager, he notices first some small newspaper accounts of ice being found – in midsummer – in isolated rock hollows and gullies. Quietly, he begins to collect evidence, unnoticed or dismissed by the Happy Folk, that something is going wrong in the land.

Wrightson draws on aboriginal folklore to create a secret population of earth spirits who have always lived in the land. There is the Mimi, thin and frail rock spirit from the far north, with round frightened eyes like a possum, carried away accidentally to the south by an errant wind to the desert where 'the sun beats down like a gong'. There are the Ninya, men of ice in caverns of ice, whose voices creak and grate as they plot to take over the land . . . the sinister summer frost is their first sly attempt to repossess the country. And there is the Nargun, most ancient and powerful rock spirit of all, whom Wirrun must find in order to stop the ice.

It is Wrightson's extraordinary accomplishment to have found a vigorous, startlingly fresh language for all these ancient spirits. Amidst the spate of children's fantasy novels that work and rework the Arthur legend and Celtic history, this is the most original and surprising creation of them all. The whole face of Australia leaps into majestic and secret life.

Wrightson's earth spirits are vibrant, varied and individual: the sullen Bagini has clawed fingers and sly hard eyes; the faces of the prankster Pot-Kuroks are clownishly woeful; the fierce, angry-buzzing little Wa-tha-gun-darl growl, 'Very long time not see that Nargun'; and every species has its characteristic speech. One almost believes it possible to buy an airline ticket to Australia and be greeted by a spring-kneed, cantankerous, twiggy-fingered Mimi.

The Mimi accompanies the reluctant hero, Wirrun, on his journey to the country's far corners; it is she who gives him courage, and who watches with old spirit eyes as he engages finally in the battle to save the land: 'This, [she] knew, was the curious thing that men were made for: to care.' Between these two, there is a beautiful ripening of respect, trust and friendship, as Wirrun grows in understanding and tolerance.

In *The Dark Bright Water*, another female spirit is lost from her rightful place. This time it is a Yunggamurra, a wild, heartless water-spirit of uncanny beauty, one of a tribe of sisters whose sport it is to lure men to their deaths. Wirrun is again called on by his people to save the country, this time from a drought. But already he has been troubled by a mysterious, disembodied song – the enchantment song of the lost Yunggamurra. If Wirrun is 'called' by her, his friend Ularra is obsessed. In the town where they both work, Wirrun is disturbed by his friend's dissolute ways; Ularra drinks too much, boasts and likes to spend evenings in the pub staring at waitresses – 'eyeing off a chick,' he calls it. Ularra joins Wirrun on the quest to find the cause of the drought and is destroyed, finally, by his sexual drives; Wirrun, also driven but more complex and aware, struggles to conquer his lust and grows finally into love.

The love story of Wirrun and the Yunggamurra who chooses mortality to be with him is tense, funny, lyrical and unabashedly sensuous without ever becoming crudely explicit. It's a splendid accomplishment, given the 'Blue Lagoon' perils of writing about teenage eroticism played out against a backdrop of wild nature. And though the passages between the two are written in the highly charged language that Wrightson uses for the spirit world, the aesthetic effect is neatly balanced and anchored by the laconic, earthy and knowing exchanges between Wirrun and the other aboriginal people.

The relationship of Wirrun and Murra, as he calls her, is elaborated in *Behind the Wind*, third book of the trilogy. Their marriage ('he taught her tenderness and she taught him laughter') is an arcadian romance. Unable to contemplate bringing his lovely wild wife into the Happy Folk cities of flats and jobs, he has chosen instead to lead the old tribal life with her, nomadic and free. But Wirrun has transgressed in mating with magic, and his intense happiness is short-lived. First he loses Murra, who is lured away from individual freedom and back to immortality by the songs, 'sharp and sweet as wild honey', of her sisters. Then he must embark on a long, bitter pursuit of the mysterious enemy, an evil spirit, a thing of death. At the end, when he has lost the battle with the Wulgaru but won a triumph of will and spirit, he dies physically and joins Murra in an immortal spirit life.

Like Le Guin, Wrightson boldly tackles the huge perplexities of adolescence: how to live by guiding principles, to reconcile liberty and responsibility, to know what is truly of value, to learn the nature of love and to accept the fact of death. Like Le Guin, she is most abstract and least comforting in the final volume – but then, the very nature of the question of mortality means that it is most remote to young readers, and that no ultimate answer can be given.

Both create heroes of touching nobility; both carry off persuasive portraits of potent men who are also emotionally vulnerable; both have the courage to depict love and friendship as rigorously challenging as physical courage. Both have dealt with difficult, rewarding themes that could have fallen as flat as a political tract, without the depth and range of their imaginative power to create new worlds, so richly and strangely peopled. It is their lasting achievement to have pushed the fantasy form to its farthest reaches without once straining credulity; their triumph is to have written books that, long after they are closed, go on 'waking meanings' in the minds of young readers.

Chapter 8

TRAVELLING IN TIME

Sherwood in the twilight, is Robin Hood awake?
Grey and ghostly shadows are gliding through the brake;
Shadows of the dappled deer, dreaming of the morn,
Dreaming of a shadowy man that winds a shadowy horn . . .

Oberon, Oberon, rake away the gold,
Rake away the red leaves, roll away the mould,
Rake away the gold leaves, roll away the red,
And wake Will Scarlett from his leafy forest bed . . .

Friar Tuck and Little John are riding down together
With quarter-staff and drinking-can and grey goose feather;
The dead are coming back again, the years are rolled away
In Sherwood, in Sherwood, about the break of day.

Alfred Noyes, 'A Song of Sherwood'

TIME IS THE ELEMENT in which we live, like fish in water, and yet the realization that time flows on and on and never flows backward is one of the most stunning of childhood discoveries. Perhaps the shock of that revelation derives from the way time stands still, like a deep dreaming pond, in our earliest years. Those endless summers, lapped in maternal safety that we never dreamed would end, flecked with sunshine and leaf shadows that we always forgot would turn to decay and frost, gave us the blessing of boredom, a time standing still in the heat of noon.

Tranquil, serious, we could lose ourselves in reverie as we contemplated a shadow, a leaf, a minnow's transparent flicker in the bars of sunlight beneath the dock, the precise parallelogram of cool shade behind the house.

I wonder if modern children, rushed from school to summer camp, with Flintstone reruns to use up any moments in between, have time for that contented, sad and solitary boredom in which one's being is lost in, or rather, merged with, the fragrance and colours of the perceived world. Do modern children have long afternoons to lie on the Persian carpet, staring at the march and swirl of deep red geometric patterns until they blur, sharpen, blur and become part of one's inner universe?

If timelessness is the taste of early childhood, the rush and spin of time is the dizzying revelation of later years. It does not surprise me that time-slip fantasies, in which the heroes travel backward and forward in time, are among the most enthralling of all children's books. They arouse, and sometimes satisfy, that intense longing of middle childhood years when a lost golden age seems tantalizingly close and yet for ever beyond reach.

Is that golden age the Eden of lost childhood, whose memories lie just too deep for recall? Or is it the confused impression of a child who, born into the ongoing lives of others, begins to piece together the fragments of talk and family reminiscence and to reconstruct in imagination a past time that was fuller, more precious and perfect?

The charm of time travel has less mysterious origins, too. What child has not tried to bring the past to life, or wished desperately that some talisman – an ancient stone, an arrowhead – would unlock the door to vanished worlds? And, of course, once you realize that you are indeed a traveller in time, a traveller to a certain end, time has ceased to be a reflecting pool and takes on a momentum that is half dreadful, half exhilarating.

On the edge of adolescence, with the future unimaginable and the present a formless flux, the past is burnished by nostalgia. An adolescent's nostalgia is not the doting over quaint objects or the trivia game it fades into for some adults, but the precise original meaning of the word: nostalgia is 'the ache for home'. It is the backward step we take on the brink of adulthood. We are about to reject our parents and the safety they offered us; we are about to set our lives in motion, and our first exciting step into the future is shadowed with regret that it will take us farther and farther from that stillness of stopped time in childhood's garden.

'The dead are coming back again, the years are rolled away' – I memorized these lines when I was twelve or so, and they never failed to wake that pleasurable pang of longing. Part of it, of course, is simply that insatiable childhood curiosity to *know*, to spy like Becky of *The Bongleweed* on the grown-up world of the past, partly as a reassurance about the future. But not all time-slip fantasies take the reader back to a golden age. In fact, had it not been for my oldest daughter's love of *Charlotte Sometimes*, by Penelope Farmer, I might have entirely missed another aspect of time travel, which is the chance to find consolation for present sadness, to escape temporarily from the prison of our days and to return with the solace that we, too, will change, that sadness or loneliness will pass.

Charlotte Sometimes, on the face of it, is a book steeped in melancholy, frustrated affections, missed chances at emotional connection. The motherless Charlotte Mary Makepeace, age twelve or thirteen, is the new girl at boarding school: sober, withdrawn, a girl who worries too much to be able to fit in easily with a crowd of boisterous schoolmates. Arriving at school, she is met by a tall older girl, Sarah Reynolds, who inexplicably helps her to find her room and choose the best bed, the one by the window, before the other girls arrive. 'My mother,' Sarah later explains, cryptically, 'told me that if a girl called Charlotte Makepeace came to school I was to be kind to her.'

Charlotte's first day at school is so confusing (looking for her name on dozens of lists, finding her initials here, her surname there) that she feels herself to be many different people . . . and half of them she doesn't recognize. When she wakes next morning in a room mysteriously transformed, and is addressed as 'Clare' by a little girl in the next bed, her confusion deepens. She looks at her hands, touches her face, wonders if you can recognize your own face just by feel.

Charlotte, in fact, has slipped back into the school as it was in 1918 and switched places in time with the bed's earlier occupant, a devout and straight-laced thirteen-year-old called Clare Moby. Day by day, Clare and Charlotte switch about. Much of the story has a desperately bleak uneasiness to it as Charlotte struggles to cope with unfamiliar schoolwork, and the scrambled perceptions of her by teachers and schoolmates when she reappears in her own present world after Clare has been in her place. Worse, when she is Clare in 1918 she must cope with Clare's ten-year-old sister Emily, a quick-witted and mercurial child who reminds her of her own little sister Emma at home. (The similarity in names of the two sets of sisters is, I confess, somewhat harassing to the reader.) Most of all, Charlotte is worried by her own wobbly identity – 'not by how Emily knew she wasn't Clare, but why and how she seemed so much like Clare that Emily mistook her for several days'.

Though the world of 1918 is comfortless, with its horrid wartime food, its air raids and slippery linoleum and difficult deceptions to avoid detection, Charlotte is stabbed with regret whenever she leaves it. It's as though there is something hidden in that past world that she has to find . . . or something in the present world she wants to avoid.

What she has to find is a surer sense of her own identity. That confusing process begins when Charlotte finally gets stuck in the past; she and Emily are moved out of the school, with its magic bed, and into grim lodgings at Flintlock Lodge. There, stuck with Clare's identity for months, Charlotte begins to lose all sense of her Charlotte self.

Caught up in the drab lives of the Chisel Brown family at Flintlock Lodge, Charlotte begins to brood about the bull-necked Chisel Brown son who has been killed in the war. Playing with his toys, looking at a picture of him as a youth, she is frightened by the awfulness of how people grow up.

This dread of one's grown-up self is a small submerged theme in children's literature. E. Nesbit uses it to great comic effect, and has one character take comfort from the thought that you grow up so gradually that you have time to get used to it. In Charlotte's case, the worries over her identity have no such easy comic release. One of the book's most hallucinatory and upsetting scenes is the celebration of the armistice, when Emily and Charlotte get separated in a wildly buffeting, hooting, surging crowd. The moment of losing her own self is radically dislocating, surrealistically horrible.

All this seems a long way from the time-slip fantasies of a vanished Eden. Farmer is a powerful enough writer to make the smothering little world of school and Flintlock Lodge almost unbearably uncomfortable; re-reading it, I wondered what makes this book so popular that it has run through a dozen printings since its appearance in 1969. Only the ache is there. One night, when Emily puts some marbles in a glass of water, Charlotte muses on their transformed beauty, and how they shrink back to their normal size and plainness when taken out of the glass:

> It was like the difference between what you long for and what you find . . . It was like other times, her own proper childhood time, that seem so near to her memory and yet so far away. It was like everything that made you ache because in one sense it was close and in another unobtainable.

Charlotte never meets Clare, the girl with whom she has been switching places, whom she has imagined as a friend; when Charlotte gets back into her present time, Clare is, of course, gone. But now Charlotte finds a new, tentative alliance with another marginal student, the prickly but bright Elizabeth, who has guessed about the time switch. Elizabeth recognizes Charlotte the minute she reappears . . . even though Clare has been successfully taking Charlotte's place in present time, undetected by most, all this while. Identity, it seems, is for ever elusive, but absolutely unmistakable. This, too, seems chilly comfort.

The last shock is the discovery that Sarah Reynolds's mother (the woman who told Sarah to be kind to a girl called Charlotte if she ever turned up at school) is not a grown-up Clare, as Charlotte had wistfully begun to hope, but Emily, the little sister from 1918, old enough now to be a grandmother, plump and grey, but having 'lived a happy life after all'. Clare, it seemed, died in the 1918 flu epidemic right after she returned to her own time. And Emily, writing to Charlotte about all this, sends Charlotte the toys they had played with together at Flintlock Lodge. Charlotte puts the marbles in a jar of water on her dresser, and now that she has some small personal ornament, her dresser looks as though she, too, 'belongs' at school.

These are the book's rather wan consolations: Emily has told her it is possible to grow up and have a happy life; Charlotte now realizes that though Clare is gone, her own memory of being Clare will go on mattering in her life just as the war goes on mattering. Charlotte, in our last glimpse of her, is riding on the bus from school and joining in a rowdy song 'No more beetles in my tea / Making googly eyes at me, No more spiders in my bath / Trying hard to make me laugh.' But that is not quite the last word. 'She had never seen spiders in a bath, in either time, thought Charlotte seriously . . . '

Charlotte, with her stubbornly serious mind, will never be wholeheartedly part of the extroverted crowd. But she is more sure of herself now, less fearful of the future, and so able to enjoy friendship in the present. In the grey and anxious light of the novel's mood, this small illumination has the special radiance of hard-won optimism. For a time-slip fantasy, *Charlotte Sometimes* is a rare displacement: the glimmer of a golden time is not in the fantasy past, but in the real world of the child's barely glimpsed future. No glory, no sunlit gardens, but hope. I believe, partly on the evidence of my own daughter's undimmed memories of the impact the book had on her life, that this unconventional approach to time travel is intuitively inspired, and speaks straight to the heart of an introverted child hovering uneasily on the brink of adolescence.

Much more common is the heroic or pastoral past, the 'Sherwood' of the poem and my daydreams, in which a child derives new strength and wisdom from a magical foray into history. *A Traveller in Time* by Alison Uttley is one of the most lyrical of these. A young girl of Edwardian England, Penelope Taberner Cameron, visits Thatchers, the Derbyshire ancestral farm of her mother's family. There, in a manor house that predates Elizabethan times, she has an almost double experience of the past: the old country ways of her affectionate Aunt Tissie and Uncle Barnabas surround the child with warmth, love and the nostalgic fragrances and tastes of the rural past. But Penelope goes even further back; a quiet, daydreaming, fanciful child, she opens a door in the ancient farmhouse and there are ladies in long brocaded gowns, who look up at her, startled, from their game with ivory counters beside the firelit hearth.

Penelope goes back more and more often into that Elizabethan era, when the house sheltered a warm and lively family who tried to help Mary Stewart, Queen of Scots, escape from imprisonment. She slips back and forth like a ghost from the future, materializing as a niece of the housekeeper in the Thatchers of 1582, an eager participant in the exciting escape plot, though helpless to change history. The time transference is beautifully and naturally handled:

The fivefold hills were lavender, indigo, violet in the soft light, one behind another, concealing the small villages in their shadowed troughs. Life went on unseen in those misty shallows, and another life moved in the folded layers of time.

The most satisfying aspect of this book is its loving idealization of Elizabethan times; the bustling, kindly aunts (Dame Cecily in the past is an ancestor of present-day Aunt Tissie), their hands always in a basin of plump dough or floured to the elbow from pastry making, the busy domestic hum of the cool dairies, pantries and kitchen, the scented herb gardens, all are as rosy and appealing as a ripe apple.

Perhaps the wittiest of all time-slip fantasies is *The Ghost of Thomas Kempe* by Penelope Lively, in which the spirit of a seventeenth-century sorcerer and alchemist, the maddeningly high-handed Thomas Kempe, haunts and bedevils eleven-year-old James Harrison, whose family has just moved into the old village cottage where Kempe once practised his arts. The invisible Kempe, released from a bottle where he was imprisoned like an errant genie by an earlier inhabitant, takes James for his apprentice and issues peremptory orders, in writing, on papers, mirrors, school notebooks and even blackboards.

The humour, which is sometimes tart, sometimes hilarious to the point of slapstick, comes from Kempe's meddlesome interventions in the busy, modern, quarrelsome life of the Harrison family. 'I am glad to see thee at thy studies, though I lyke not thy bookes,' Kempe harrumphs when James does his homework. 'Where is thy Latin?' Kempe's busybody invisible spirit breaks pots when the family watches weather forecasts on television ('Thy familie shall knowe what the weather will be from me and not from that eville machine or I will breake more pots . . . '), yanks a chair out from under the bottom of a visiting clergyman and scrawls furious curses on the walls of an old woman next door ('Widdow Verity is a wytche'). Of course, James or his dog Tim usually gets the blame for this mayhem, and James frantically tries to lay the unquiet ghost to rest.

Before he succeeds, though, he is brought into contact with all the townspeople who are, in one way or another, trying to delve into the past – and mostly getting it all wrong. The archaeologists busily digging on the town outskirts are oblivious to the real ghost of the past that accompanies

James; the teacher, self-satisfiedly lecturing the class on the gullibility of their forebears who invented witchcraft as an explanation for the inexplicable, falls smack into the opposite fallacy right in the middle of his lecture: 'Pick up those papers, would you, Simon, they keep blowing off the desk,' he says distractedly, as the invisible Kempe surges around the classroom.

Others are more tuned in: Mrs Verity next door, who had seemed like just a nosey old lady to James, tells him an impish anecdote about her youth that makes James realize that people are many-layered, with the past still alive in them somewhere. Bert, a local workman, matter-of-factly helps to exorcise Thomas Kempe. The local library turns out to be 'inexhaustibly surprising', another place where the past is still alive and acknowledged, like 'opening a grocery box and finding it full of Christmas presents'.

Most of all, James is aided by a diary he finds buried deep in the rubbish heap of old belongings cleared out from the cottage during the Harrisons' renovations. The diary belonged to a good-hearted Fanny Spence, owner of the cottage in 1856, who entertained her visiting nephew Arnold with boating on the river, a new puppy named Palmerston and sumptuous feasts of homemade desserts. Arnold, too, it turns out, was plagued by Thomas Kempe. But Arnold, unlike the harassed James, was helped by his sympathetic Aunt Fanny to trap and bottle the alchemist.

To James, Arnold and his dog become even more real than his own doubting friends; he spends long hours in their imaginary company. His daydream of playing with Arnold comforts him for the 'odd, lonely, deprived feeling' he had when he had finished reading the diary and grieved because 'he would never know about the further adventures of Arnold and Palmerston the puppy'. But that's not so; the past is still alive in a hundred different ways, and James learns that the school's portrait of a whiskered benefactor is, after all, a picture of the grown-up Arnold – grateful, apparently, for all his happy holidays in the village.

Penelope Lively is fascinated by the theme of time; another of her skilful and amusing novels on the subject is *A Stitch in Time*, about a shy, introspective little girl on a seaside holiday who makes the same discoveries as James about the complex ways in which past history doesn't vanish but becomes part of the web of human existence. Both novels are deeply reassuring about the continuity of time (a moot point in our nuclear era), and about the role of the sensitive, alert child whose own developing maturity parallels and enhances the evolution of humanity's history on earth.

As in *The Ghost of Thomas Kempe*, the past unsettlingly invades the present in *Earthfasts* by William Mayne, this time in the person of Nellie Jack John, an eighteenth-century drummer boy who comes marching – rumpatatump rumpatatump – right out of a crack in the earth before the horrified eyes of two boys in a Cumbrian village. *Earthfasts* is more uncanny, confused and frightening than *The Ghost of Thomas Kempe*, and the plot less controlled, but it is a gripping and sometimes very funny story. It is also typical of many English novels in its powerful sense of places suffused with past life that threatens to break into the present (not always benignly) at any moment. Again, as in Penelope Lively's work, this is a brisk antidote to the prevailing romantic view of history as a tranquil retreat from present perplexities.

Two recent ventures into time-slip by Canadian authors take their characters back to a time of war and struggle, in which important truths are to be discovered.

The Druid's Tune is the first novel by a young Canadian writer, O. R. Melling, who sends her two heroes – Rosemary, seventeen, and her fifteen-year-old brother Jimmy – on a holiday to relatives on an Irish farm. Their father hopes that the trip will shape them up, since Rosemary has become romantically involved with a law-breaking hippie: he wants them to have a summer of 'clean air, hard work and a good simple way of life . . . maybe you'll come back a little wiser'.

If that sounds simplistically reactionary, so is the plot of the book. The teenagers are carried back into Celtic prehistory where Jimmy learns to be a charioteer and then a warrior at the side of the legendary hero Cuculann. Rosemary, in the war party of Queen Maeve, falls in love with a flirtatious princeling called Maine. The agent of their time change is a wandering Druid, a brooding and tormented soul drifting through the centuries, who calls himself, in the present time, Peter Murphy.

There are thumping echoes of C. S. Lewis's Narnia cycle in the way the two youngsters go through a baptism of blood, steeling themselves for righteous war as part of their character building, and there are borrowings from John Masefield (*The Midnight Folk*) and T. H. White (*The Sword in the Stone*) in some of their shape-changing adventures.

Worse than the derivativeness, though, is the flat, North American tone in which all characters, both ancient and modern, speak. 'Fetch me a Druid. I have enough problems without this infernal delay,' snaps Queen Maeve, in the very voice of an impatient matron who summons a tardy plumber. The Druid, fetched, is equally up-to-date: 'What is it you want, Maeve?' And Finnabar, a Bronze Age princess, languidly drawls to Rosemary, 'Don't mind my mother – she thrives on all this war and slaughter and glory.'

Nevertheless, the book has proven remarkably popular, thanks to its strong story line. What it lacks in finesse, it makes up in swiftness, urgency and contemporaneity. It has romance, melodrama, the eeriness of the occult ('I see it! Blood pours from the knotted trunk of the sacred tree of fire!') and thoroughly modern ideas about gender roles: Jimmy learns to cook and to be more emotionally responsive, and Rosemary, when not revelling in romance and beautiful gowns, develops muscles and aggression through her training for war.

O. R. Melling's second novel, *The Singing Stone*, is a more complex and rewarding story, and her narrative style has shed most of its earlier clumsiness. Still, it's worth reading *The Druid's Tune* in tandem with another recent Canadian novel, Janet Lunn's *The Root Cellar*, for the sake of contrast, and to see how satisfying the time-shift theme can be in the hands of an author with depth, subtlety and a real feel for history – not just for historically correct language and customs, but also for the way earlier generations perceived and thought in a different way from ours.

Like so many heroes of time-slip novels, Lunn's twelve-year-old Rose Larkin is an isolated, precociously prim youngster who has had an unusually solitary childhood. She has been brought up by a cold, wealthy grandmother and now finds herself on threatening new terrain. We meet her as she arrives from New York, wary and resentful, at the dishevelled rural Ontario home of her aunt, uncle and rowdy boy cousins. As an orphan, Rose is more than usually rootless; she has no memory of her father, and all she has from her mother is a silver rose on a chain, a copy of *The Secret Garden* and a music box. Part of her task in the novel is to learn to accept her new family on their own terms, and to accept herself through discovering, as the title hints, her own roots.

In fact, she begins by making 'a secret garden' of her own, in a beautiful glade near the old house, a place of soft autumn colours which she first explores by moonlight. It is in this garden that Rose stumbles, literally, on the way into the welcoming past. Under the leaf mould, she finds a trap door that leads into an abandoned root cellar; she has just pushed her way through the rotting door and is examining the rows of jars on the shelves when somebody – a girl of her own age in a long brown dress, boots and apron, with one long braid and bright black eyes – stands on the steps behind her and blocks her light. 'You'd best get out of the root cellar,' says the girl, Susan. 'Missus will be terrible cross.'

It's an interesting phenomenon that, while boys in time-slip novels are often preoccupied with laying the past to rest, girls often rush into the past to be nurtured by a transforming and empowering mother love. Susan, for example, is one of Lunn's best creations, a practical, affectionate, hard-working hired girl, whose friendship with Rose is an education of the heart.

When Rose emerges from the root cellar to find herself outside the same house, but back in 1862, she also shifts seasons, from a damp autumn to a sunlit, basking June. And this, too, is typical of time-shift stories, when children magically find themselves in that longed-for summer of rapt memory.

This 'secret garden' is a vision of colonial prosperity, where the sun glitters on Lake Ontario and where the house, neglected and run down in Rose's own time, is surrounded by bright flower beds and apple orchards in full bloom. The boy of the house, fifteen-year-old Will Morrissay, feels as restless and rootless as Rose; just across the bay, the American Civil War is raging, and, because his mother came from the American shore, he is itching to be off to fight on the Union side.

The Root Cellar is particularly fine in making the reader feel Rose's real joy and sensuous delight in the rural past, and her grieving sense of loss when she is accidentally whisked back to the uncomfortable, messy, unresolved present. But it goes much farther than this. Eventually, Rose takes part in a great adventure which has the welcome effect of making the complicated American-Canadian mingling of history and culture on the shores of eastern Lake Ontario seem resonant, intimate, a significant shaping force in the development of both countries.

Will has run off to join the Union army, and, when the war is over and he fails to return, Rose (who has learned how to use the root cellar to travel in time) urges Susan to join her in a search. In a long, picaresque and lively episode, the two girls disguise themselves as boys, cross the lake, and search for Will across the eastern United States, working at odd jobs and finally ending up in Washington, tracking Will from one military hospital to the next.

In this section of the book, the past loses its enchantment and becomes menacingly realistic. It's a time of harsh, postwar dislocation and hardship, and a world of dust, heat, ravaged fields and reeking hospitals crammed with the war wounded. And when they finally find a battle-shocked Will, his stories of war are more like Stephen Crane's *Red Badge of Courage* than the glorified gory exploits of C. S. Lewis or O. R. Melling.

Like the characters in Penelope Lively's books, Rose must eventually leave the past behind her and engage herself with present realities. The story of her reconciliation with her family is believably tentative, touching and optimistic. Particularly robust and joyful is her grand gesture of appeasement at the end. She cooks (disastrously) a whole Christmas dinner; the shambles is turned into a gloriously savoury Christmas feast, evergreen boughs, candles and all, with the invisible aid of 'old Mrs Morrissay' . . . the ghost of grown-up Susan, come back into the future to help Rose. Like James in *The Ghost of Thomas Kempe*, Rose has also found contemporary allies whose memories and fidelity to the past are an important source of continuity. In keeping faith with Susan by vowing to help restore the Morrissay house to its former beauty, Rose gives herself a new sense of rooted identity and purpose.

A dream landscape or a house, suffused with emotion, is a central feature of time-slip fantasies. When shy, withdrawn Anna, the heroine of *When Marnie Was There* by the English writer Joan Robinson, is sent by her anxious foster mother to a Norfolk village to recover from asthma, Anna feels instantly drawn to a lovely old house on the edge of a creek. Anna, who has long bottled up her bitter anger at the mother who died and the grandmother who she thinks abandoned her, has been cut off from the easy flow of relationships with other children. But here, tracking through the sand dunes, listening to the marsh birds, dreaming over sunset-lit water, her wariness and isolation become something less taut. Then she meets Marnie, an exciting, strangely different girl, who appears mysteriously in the window of the empty house, or in a rowing boat at night.

The intensity of their secret friendship melts Anna's frozen unhappiness. Later, after Marnie has disappeared, and when a lively, affectionate family moves into the Marsh House, Anna is ready to be drawn into the warmth of their family circle. The tone of the narrative modulates beautifully from the rapturous, tense and baffling encounters with Marnie to the sunny, easily flowing play with the Lindsays.

The idyll with Marnie is more of a ghost story than a time-travel fantasy, but it has the dreamy quality of stopped time, when emotions are so heightened that minutes expand to hours. The themes of abandonment, grief and forgiveness are delicately paralleled in Anna's past life and in her relationship with Marnie. At the last possible moment, all these threads are believably drawn together, and the mystery of Marnie's identity and Anna's link with the Marsh House are both resolved. It is one of the most touching and gratifying denouements in children's literature.

One of this book's finest qualities is the way Anna's memories of Marnie begin to blur and fade as she becomes involved with the Lindsay family, even while the meaning of her relationship with Marnie is still agonizingly unresolved. It is as tantalizing and maddening as the way our wisps of early childhood memories drift in and out of our awareness, as though some perfect primal bliss were always slipping out of reach of our fingers. The reader holds her breath. Will the author, like so many lesser ones, make Anna 'forget' all the magic . . . a convenient ending for adult writers, and a bitterly disappointing, almost despicable one for every reading child? The suspense is not relieved until the very end, when we know that Anna has recaptured that profoundly precious knowledge of maternal love in early childhood, and that she will remember always.

An author who dips into that still pond of timelessness must, it seems to me, provide some balm for the anguish of its loss. Two memories of my childhood still carry that sharp edge of loss for me. The first was my conviction, when I was five or six years old, that the towering maple tree on our tiny front lawn had blossomed the previous spring. All of one winter, I waited for that lavish, scented, pink and white flowering foam to reappear. My mother told me that I must have dreamed it: maple trees don't blossom. I stubbornly believed that she was wrong. I knew I had sat under those blossoms and been filled with their sweetness. Every year, I waited. No matter how keen my disappointment, I was never able to feel, in my heart of hearts, that I had been mistaken. Almost to adulthood, some primitive insistence on the realness of that flowering tree persisted underneath my rational understanding that maple trees don't blossom, and I never quite lost the feeling that somehow I had been cheated.

The second memory is even more explicitly arcadian. When I was eight or nine, my mother took me to see the film version of *A Midsummer Night's Dream*. That enchanted forest, with its imps and fairies who made an airy but palpable link between nature and humans, absolutely haunted me. For several years, I dreamed of myself blissfully roaming in those woods. To wake was to be bitterly exiled; I would shut my eyes as quickly as I'd opened them, hoping to dream my way back into Eden. Unless a time-slip story evokes that moment of longed-for paradise fading away right before our tantalized eyes, I know it has not hit the mark.

What makes it possible to accept the loss of paradise in children's books is the promise of future happiness, after the waiting of late childhood and adolescence has ended. In *Playing Beatie Bow*, Ruth Park achieves that optimistic finale with tremendous vigour, properly linking that future happiness to tasks accomplished by the child during her sojourn in the past.

Instead of a rural idyll, her hero, fourteen-year-old Abigail Kirk, stumbles into a squalid, dangerous slum of nineteenth-century Sydney, stinking of 'horse manure, tidal flats, wood smoke, human sweat and an all-pervading smell of sewage'. But it is, nevertheless, a kind of emotional paradise for the discontented Abigail. Unlike most such fantasies, where the charm of slipping back and forth through time is an intense element in the story, both worlds in *Playing Beatie Bow* are vividly realistic in detail. Once Abigail has slipped backward, she stays in the world of 1873 for almost a year, always desperate to return to her own time despite her growing attachment to the Bow family: old Trooper Bow, a sweet-maker who is half-mad from an old head wound; saintly Dovey; scrappy and ferociously intelligent little Beatie; Granny Tallisker from the Orkney Islands with her deep sureness of right and wrong and her gift of second sight; hateful nine-year-old Gibbie, a self-pitying, morbidly pious invalid; and, above all, the young man Judah, with his 'ruddy and snubbed country kind of face'.

Abbie has come from the contemporary world where she is a loner, a self-preoccupied teenager who lives with her mother in a modern highrise, prickly, resentful and unforgiving of her father's desertion of the family four years earlier. Her only gesture of involvement with the outside world is her kindness to four-year-old Natalie, a neighbour in the apartment building. Sometimes she takes Natalie outside to play, and it is Natalie who shows her 'the little furry girl' – the woebegone Beatie, head shaven from a bout with fever, visiting from the past to watch modern children playing an eerie, frightening game of ghosts called 'Beatie Bow'. Abbie follows the mysterious 'furry girl' one day and is led down a narrow alleyway straight into the past.

Nothing is fudged: the dreariness of housework, the smells, the hideously uncomfortable clothes, the unpleasant sanitary arrangements, the degradation of the poor, including prostitution. In one ghastly scene, Abbie is actually kidnapped to a sleazy gin house and makes her escape from the grotesque inhabitants just in time.

Yet, remarkably, the mutual kindness of the small tradesmen, the warmth and strength of family ties, and the uncomplaining willingness of family members to work hard and help each other, convincingly offset all the hardships with an enduring impression of vitality and purpose.

Abbie's purpose in being there, it turns out, is to fulfil an ancient Tallisker family prophecy about 'a Stranger' who will save the family from extinction. At first, Abbie is surly and resentful at being kept in the past. Then she schools herself determinedly to recover from her rage and to fit herself into the family's life, hoping to earn her return, one day, to her own time. The many small shocks of Victorian slum life, as well as its unexpected pleasures, begin to do their work on Abbie. She becomes less self-centred, braver, more tolerant.

In all this, Park is at her best, showing us Abbie's changing character through dramatic action and dialogue. Most affecting is the moment when Abbie falls hopelessly in love with Judah. The first delicious, painful infatuation of a fourteen-year-old girl with a much older boy – and Judah is already betrothed to his distant cousin Dovey – could have been embarrassingly banal. But Park makes it both poignant and true. Even better, this infatuation is seen as an invigorating force in Abbie's life. It leads her to an act of bravery and altruism that will, much later, end the book with seventeen-year-old Abbie's unexpected, startling and completely satisfying romantic fulfilment.

Strong as *Playing Beatie Bow* is, it is still outranked in my mind by the most subtle, moving and beautifully written time-slip fantasy of them all, *Tom's Midnight Garden* by the consummate English writer Philippa Pearce. Perhaps I am biased by my predilection for enchanted gardens, or perhaps it is the sheer unfaltering authority of Pearce's burnished prose, but this novel, even on second and third reading, never loses its force for me.

Tom Long has been packed off, weeping and angry, to spend his summer holidays with his Aunt Gwen and Uncle Alan in their 'stuffy flat' in an old converted house – all because his younger brother has measles. Pearce has a sympathetic genius for portraying young boys, their worries and rebellions and their stubborn mental processes, in a manner so understated it is almost translucent. Tom seems like a perfectly ordinary boy, neither more aggressive nor more introverted than others; perhaps just because there is nothing pronounced about his character to set him apart, readers are easily drawn into the magnetic field of his emotions.

Feeling caged up, longing for outdoor play, sleeping badly because of all Aunt Gwen's good cooking, Tom lies awake at night listening with irritated anticipation for the chronically mis-striking grandfather clock in the entrance hall of the building. And at last it strikes . . . and goes on striking to thirteen. Uneasily, Tom feels 'that this had made some difference to him. The stillness had become an expectant one; the house seemed to hold its breath; the darkness pressed up to him, pressing him with a question . . .'

Tom has been forbidden by his rigid Uncle Alan to get out of bed on these sleepless nights; now he cleverly argues with his conscience that the clock has struck an extra hour, and so he can spend time out of bed and still have his mandatory ten hours' rest. Throughout the book, we see Tom's mind work in this dogged way, patiently worrying away at puzzles or dilemmas until he arrives at a comforting rationalization or a sensible explanation. It's one of the novel's underpinnings that gives it such lucid plausibility.

Eventually, Tom discovers that the rear door in the downstairs hallway – rusted shut during the days, and giving onto a strip of pavement cluttered with garbage cans – mysteriously opens onto an immense, beautifully intricate garden when the clock strikes midnight. Gradually, he becomes almost obsessed with his stolen hours of play in the garden. He works out a cunning system of adult evasion to escape into the garden undetected; he whiles away the days in dutiful boredom, impatient for the magical nights. In the garden, however, it is not always night. Almost always it is full summer, and though Tom is uncannily invisible there, one of the garden's inhabitants (a family of three boys, with one small girl cousin tagging pitifully after them) is watching him.

The girl, Hatty, is a poor relation, despised by the cold aunt who has been forced to take her in. It is she, after all, who can see Tom, and who becomes his constant playmate. She loves the garden as passionately as he; it is her refuge from a bitterly lonely and unhappy life.

Pearce's powers of description make the garden and all its delights shimmer with almost surrealist intensity: the geese in the meadow beyond the hedge, the stone walls, the trees, the feathery green tunnels between the asparagus rows, the steamy greenhouse. The garden's strange loveliness is so seductive that we are as impatient as Tom to get back to it, but the forward movement of the plot is delicately restrained by passages in which Tom spends his days worrying away at the garden's mysteries. Why do the seasons switch around so abruptly there? Why does he see the tallest fir tree crash to the ground in a lightning storm one night . . . and see it standing there, tall and rooted, the next? Why does Abel, the gardener, mutter prayers whenever Tom stands invisibly (or so he thinks) in front of him?

At first, Tom is as impulsive and unobservant as any active, ordinary boy. But his friendship with Hatty changes that. Bit by bit, through excitements, griefs and crises, he becomes more sensitive. A lovely pattern of imagery throughout the book underlines that almost imperceptible growth in Tom, and the more startling leaps to maturity of Hatty, who begins to grow older than Tom. It is a series of images of climbing: first they climb the trees, higher and higher, so they can see the meadow beyond; then they scale the towering orchard wall, over which Tom can see the village and the whole countryside. Finally, at the book's intense climax, just when Tom tingles with excitement at the plan he has worked out to elude time altogether and live in both worlds, the grown-up Hatty and still-young Tom skate down the frozen Ouse river and climb the tower of Ely Cathedral, to look out over the whole landscape, with its frosted river going down to the sea. (The description of the skating is breathtaking in its icy exhilaration, speed and dazzling impression of freedom.) At that dizzying summit, Tom looks away from the view and turns to Hatty – and realizes at last that her own time, moving onward, has defeated his plan to foil the passage of time. She has grown up and grown past him.

It is a haunting and heartwrenching moment. It is the moment of loss and the beginning point of growing up, the moment that lies at the core of all time fantasies and that gives rise to them in the first place, the moment when the passage of time, and the certainty of death, become real.

There are few climaxes in children's literature more affecting than Tom's despair when he knows that the garden and Hatty are lost to him for ever. But, like Farmer, Lively, Lunn and Park, Pearce ends her book on a note of healing optimism, and the conclusion is genuinely thrilling. Tom finds the answer to all the torturing bewilderments of time passing and time past – the mystery of the legend on the clock (TIME NO MORE) and of the strange sequence of events in the garden. And he is consoled, in a surprising and deeply touching new friendship, by the knowledge that though time sweeps on, it does not sweep away everything that we love. The dead do come back again in the lives they have touched, in the gardens they have made and in their children's children; the years are rolled away in stories and poems, and in the Edens we remember.

Chapter 9

GROWING UP

This is then the real meaning of not being any longer a young one in living, the complete realizing that not any one really can believe what any other one is believing . . .

                Gertrude Stein, *The Making of Americans*

The first demand any work of art makes upon us is to surrender. Look. Listen. Receive. Get yourself out of the way.

                C. S. Lewis, *An Experiment in Criticism*

Though I think it is possible to learn from works of fiction, I don't think it possible to teach from them . . . One does not rush to give Anna Karenina to friends who are committing adultery. Such impertinence is limited to dealings with children.

                Jill Paton Walsh, in *Celebrating Children's Books*

Anyone who writes about books for adolescents must do battle with a paradox. The urgent message of literature's most thoughtful critics (and the message, I hope, of this book) is that the reading of good books can work in a mysterious, compelling way to enlarge the reader's life. Vast numbers of books for beginning and middle readers, both the most praised and the most popular, seem to have exactly that effect. On the other hand, a tidal wave of books with an obsessively narrow focus on contemporary teenage preoccupations has inundated the market in the last decade, triumphantly carrying with it the majority of readers in this age group. At precisely the moment when a youngster hesitates on the brink of the larger world, the popular literature for him or her is totally given over to navel gazing and trendy 'problems'. In this chapter, I'll try to grapple with the questions posed by the lucrative market in teenage fiction, and to propose some alternatives to what is currently most popular.

The special quality of self-forgetfulness that we cherish in reading the best fiction has been lovingly and painstakingly described by many critics over the years. T. S. Eliot called it the 'radical innocence' of the person who is amused and entertained, and thus wonderfully distracted from self-concern. Gertrude Stein wrote about the shocking discovery of immutable otherness which yanks us permanently, disillusioningly but liberatingly, out of our egocentricity. Helen Gardner drew our attention to the mother reading to her child: both mother and child, she said, have 'thrown open the doors of the prison of the present' and the child is temporarily distracted from 'the clamant needs and desires of childhood'.

Mere distraction is not the goal; rather it's that while the claims of the ego are temporarily stilled, the mind and the imagination can fearlessly explore other ways of being. The unique gift of literature, its priceless contribution to our children's lives, as C. S. Lewis said, is to make us see with other eyes, imagine with other imaginations, feel with other hearts *as well as our own*. Even children can distinguish, if they are pressed to analyse it, the different qualities of reading experiences. The best books demand a depth of involvement that is clearly missing from purely escapist literature, and, in return, they reward us with something that is added to our essential selves; we come back into the real world with a more tantalizing sense of its complexity than we had imagined before. Our sensibilities are stretched and enhanced; our intellect provoked; our apprehension of the world around us changed in some way.

This is the unique purpose and profit in reading good fiction. I'm hard pressed to find any other. For passive escapism and whiling away time, television wins hands down. For instruction, our society brims over with pamphlets, videocassettes, discussion groups, films, hotlines, night courses and public agencies. For practice in the mere mechanics of reading itself, the backs of cereal boxes are omnipresent. 'Bulk reading' has its uses, which I discuss in the next chapter, but most of us hope our children will not stop there.

Why, then, the unparalleled rush, on the part of many parents, teachers and librarians, to press second-rate mass-market books into the hands of preadolescents and teenagers? Perhaps it's a roundabout acknowledgement of the merits of reading good fiction. Adults in our swiftly changing society are made uneasy by the electronic culture of the young. When youth shows an interest in reading something, anything, adults are eager to foster that interest.

This, I think, goes a long way to explaining the Judy Blume phenomenon. Blume is such an overwhelming presence in modern prepubescent reading that any book which aspires to serve as a guide for parents must take account of her. David Rees, a critic, author and teacher at the University of Essex, in an essay entitled 'Not Even for a One-Night Stand', wonders whether 'perhaps the best thing to do with Ms Blume would be to ignore her altogether; she is so amazingly trivial and second-rate in every department . . .'

But though Rees complains that reading Blume feels like 'a bashing on the head with a blunt instrument', neither he nor I can afford to ignore such a singular success story. Blume's paperbacks have sold more than thirty million copies, a number equivalent to more than half the number of children between the ages of five and seventeen in the United States. No other author even comes close to having such universal access into the minds of North American youth . . . and British ones, too. Yet I would assume that most adults have not actually read her works. For that reason, I feel compelled to devote part of this chapter to a discussion of her style, techniques and substance, and then to offer a range of valuable alternatives for preteen and teenage reading.

It is revealing, I think, that Judy Blume and S. E. Hinton, another popular American writer for young teenagers, have both explained their motivation thus in interviews: 'When I was young, I could never find any books about kids like me, and that's what I wanted to read about.' Their almost identical statements lay bare an almost identical narcissism, as well as an astonishingly limited knowledge of available children's literature.

'Kids like me.' Of course children want to be able to 'identify' with the characters in books, in the sense of recognizing similarities in emotional experience, if not in precise situation; the finest authors have always been able to show us the universal in the unique. Mary Norton's Arietty and Ursula Le Guin's Ged are quintessentially themselves – they are never described physically but we know them intimately, would recognize their characters at once in a crowd – and yet they share the boldness, impatience, the dreams and fears of all young people.

Hinton and Blume cater to quite a different level of self-knowledge. Without question, puberty brings with it a consuming absorption in the self as a social and sexual being. Normally, however, this is only one aspect of the adolescent's self-awareness. The difficulty arises from the single-mindedness of Blume's focus. For her, it seems, books are only 'about kids like me' if they mirror the lives of young North Americans with a constant repetition of brand names, fashionable problems and current 'lifestyles'. This facsimile realism, like television soap opera, has the ultimate effect of shrinking the world to a small, square frame, leaching it of complexity and depth and draining it, finally, of all that is most elusive, pungent and vital. It is as though we invited youngsters into an art gallery where every frame held only a mirror.

I don't mean to imply that youngsters should be prevented from reading these books (please see Chapter Ten for a discussion of this conundrum). However, concerned adults have a duty to consider whether badly written 'problem novels' are in fact a distortion of reality and whether they may reinforce some of the more questionable values of our culture.

Judy Blume, Paula Danziger, Paul Zindel and, in Canada, Kevin Major are among the leading exponents of the modern problem novel in which contemporary children, from the ages of eleven to about sixteen (or seventeen, the acceptable problem-novel age for sexual activity), usually tell their stories in the first person in a loosely chronological diary of events. Though the social class of the protagonists ranges from middle-class suburban (Blume) to Newfoundland working-class (Major), all these youngsters see themselves as ill-done-by. They suffer from incomprehensibly repressive teachers, obtuse adults, social dislocation not of their own making (death, divorce, rape, acne, scoliosis, sexual frustration, infuriating siblings or disgusting classmates) and a vague, discontented sense of meaninglessness in life. (British contemporary novels for teenagers, as I shall discuss a little further on, diverge significantly from this pattern . . . so far.)

From all that I have been able to observe, Blume and Danziger are read almost obsessively by youngsters from about the age of nine to twelve. At an age when social acceptance by the peer group is the longed-for panacea, when prepubescent anxiety and narcissism are at their peak and when a restless curiosity about sex is linked with personal inadequacy, fear and excitement, these books become classroom bibles, passed from hand to hand and giggled over at break. They become almost a talisman of belonging, like the latest style of trainers or gimmick pencils. Sheila Egoff, in a memorable phrase, called these books 'a social glue'; reading them assures one a place in the in-group.

Some of their glamour comes from their naughtiness. Here, in the flat and stumbling language of the prepubescent, mirrored by Blume with uncanny accuracy, are all the 'gross' preoccupations – pimples, smells, breast size, wet dreams – given the imprimatur of authority by their sheer presence in print. And the books make no demands: there will be no surprises, no unusual words or feelings, no plots to speak of, no shocking 'enlargements of the self' or imaginatively taxing viewpoints of a world seen through other eyes.

Judy Blume is overwhelmingly the most popular, and overwhelmingly, in my opinion, the poorest writer of all the problem novelists. I am continually amazed when parent groups rise up in protest against Judy Blume because of her *sexually explicit content;* her sexual forthrightness is the least offensive of all her qualities, particularly given that her readers grow up in a society saturated with sexual symbolism and rampant exploitation.

What may indeed corrupt the children (again, see Chapter Ten) is not Blume's frankness, but her bland and unquestioning acceptance of majority values, of conformity, consumerism, materialism, unbounded narcissism and flat, sloppy, ungrammatical, inexpressive speech. Her success with youngsters, paradoxically, springs from these very qualities: unlike more probing authors, who raise uncomfortable questions in the readers' minds, Blume seems to endorse trivial self-centredness by embodying it in her books. Blume once told an interviewer that she had herself founded a club, at the age of eleven, called the Pre-Teen Kittens, and says that long after she began writing she was 'a little girl with little-girl dreams'. I believe her.

In *Then Again, Maybe I Won't,* Blume tries to give us – in the person of eleven-year-old Tony – a contemporary, working-class version of Holden Caulfield, the sensitive and disillusioned hero of J. D. Salinger's *Catcher in the Rye*. We catch the authentic Blume tone – monosyllabic, surly, cliché-ridden – in the first paragraph: 'Who says March is supposed to come in like a lion and go out like a lamb? That's a lot of bull. All it's done this March is rain. I'm sick of it.'

Tony belongs to a struggling Italian working-class family which strikes it rich, suddenly and improbably, thanks to the father's invention of 'electrical cartridges'. As usual, in Blume, we are given a rough sketch of Tony's character, not through action or interaction, but by his interior monologue. He is concerned about being short ('Basketball is my favourite sport. I just wish I was taller. My brother Ralph says I'll probably sprout up at fourteen like he did. I hope I don't have to wait that long. It's important to be tall when you're playing basketball. You're that much closer to the basket'); he is hostile (he daydreams about shooting Mrs Gorsky, who wants him to put the newspaper under the mat when it rains) and he is sexually avid ('I wonder what it's like watching ladies try on underwear all day? I'd really like to get a look at that!').

Because the book is narrated by Tony, and because the author uses no ironic or distancing techniques, his character emerges as flat, uninflected and diffuse as his nearly moronic style of speech. Complexity or inner conflict is shown by two limp devices: physical distress whenever Tony is confronted by a problem ('I get real bad stomach aches. My mother says it's gas') and the repeated use of the single phrase that gives the book its title: 'Maybe some day I'll marry a girl like Angie. Then again, maybe I won't.'

When Tony's family becomes instantly rich and moves to a wealthy suburb, Blume tries to show us how disgusted he is, *à la* Caulfield, by his family's burgeoning materialism. She fails in this attempt to give Tony a moral dimension, however, because he is just as much a prey to his family's consumerism as they are. Dotingly, Tony describes the floor plan of the new house, complete with five bathrooms. This is a frequent feature of Blume's books, in which room-by-room descriptions of layout and furniture often substitute for the vivacity of daily life.

Tony is ostensibly disapproving when his grandmother is ruthlessly edged out of her central position in the family because she upsets the new maid by insisting on cooking as she has always done. (As Rees points out, the ostracizing of the grandmother seems far-fetched in what is supposed to be a close Italian family.) But Tony is as emotionally passive as the rest of the family, and makes no attempt to mitigate his grandmother's lonely imprisonment.

He despises a girl at school who admires him ('I hate skinny girls'), loathes his baby niece ('Maybe she'll get better looking. Then again, maybe she won't'). He gets stomach aches when his new friend Joel steals apples from the school cafeteria. But what are we to make of this supposed moral scrupulousness when Tony himself participates in the malicious ragging of a waitress, and asks for binoculars for Christmas so he can spy on Joel's sixteen-year-old sister Lisa every night while she undresses? Tony's self-righteous contempt for his parents always seems unfounded. He objects to his piano teacher because she has bad breath, badgers his parents to let him stop, and when they agree, telling him they are only concerned for his happiness, he thinks, 'Sometimes they're so full of bull they make me sick.'

The secret of the book's success is not that Tony is morally superior to those around him, but that Blume gives an earnestly liberal *carte blanche* to all his own peccadilloes. We are told in painstaking detail how Tony hides his sheets to conceal his nocturnal emissions from his parents; how he carries a raincoat to conceal involuntary erections; how, when he is sent to a psychiatrist because of his stomach aches, the psychiatrist does not disapprove of Tony's voyeurism – and even how, when he is hospitalized, 'curvy' Lisa, the unwitting object of his peeping Tom activities, brings him 'dirty books' to read.

It is certainly true that Blume has tried to graft some twigs of sprouting conscience onto the main trunk of the story. The harassed waitress Bernice, for example, finally turns on the boorish boys and indignantly tells them she needs their insolent penny tips (usually drowned in the milk shakes) to buy herself bread. The boys' sheepish but limited reaction: they never sit in her section of the restaurant again. But such incidents fall far short of moral revelation; the focus of the book is relentlessly on Tony's self-preoccupation. The author's 'non-judgemental' reportorial style reassures preadolescent boys that peeping, wet dreams and emotional numbness (Tony can never feel anything about the neighbourhood friends he left behind or his brother killed in Vietnam) are normal and okay.

Blume's books, in other words, are intended to offer a therapeutic, not a literary experience. From a literary point of view, her work is a disaster. All her characters, of any social class, speak in the same lowest-common-denominator voice: 'Bundle up good,' says a middle-class mother, and 'I do pretty good in school,' says a surburban youngster. Style, it must be emphasized, is not a detachable frill that 'fancier' writers tack on like a ruffle on a dress. Style *is* the writer; it is not possible to differentiate the manner of expression from what the author notices, what she values, how she reacts to it, what she thinks it important to mention, the emotional weight and colour of her own experiences. Since all Blume's characters speak without subtlety, indirection, metaphor, vitality, originality or even basic grammatical precision, the very least one can say about the effect of such indifference is that a youngster who reads only Blume will remain unaware of the possibilities of fictional language to create new realities.

In Blume books, there is rarely any natural world outside shopping malls; there is not even a vestigial political or social awareness; no consciousness of injustice; no soul-searching beyond petulance and spite ('I was making Debbie feel bad and I was glad. Sometimes I am a mean and rotten person' is the farthest reach of self-awareness attained by her characters) and the potential for human action is, to put it mildly, circumscribed: the painfully simple plots are wrapped up neatly at the end of an hour's reading, just like television drama.

Even as therapy, however, Blume's books are often wide of the mark. She flatters her young readers by mimicking all their most superficial concerns, and proposes to deal with difficult dilemmas, insofar as they are recognized at all, with a spate of practical instruction. In one of her most flat-footed books, *Deenie*, the reader is offered an encyclopaedia definition of scoliosis, detailed descriptions of visits to the doctor and medical procedures and some unbelievably naïve ruminations on masturbation from the thirteen-year-old protagonist: 'As soon as I got into bed I started touching myself. I have this special place and when I rub it I get a very nice feeling. I don't know what it's called or if anyone else has it . . .'

Undoubtedly Blume conceives of her books as liberating and helpful. My own impression is that her values break through at every turn – values that many alert parents will find questionable. Girls come in three varieties: pretty and popular and boy-obsessed (these are always the heroines); smart and ugly (big or little sisters), and the truly loathsome (always fat). Blume's anorexic writing is a true measure of her anorexic obsessions with personal appearance; not only are her female characters narcissistically obsessed with clothes and appearance, but they are always justified by the author in hating anyone who doesn't measure up to their standards of physical beauty.

Mothers never go out to work in Blume books except in dire emergency, and then they are resented by their children. Fathers are usually more caring than mothers, though equally characterless. No one in Blume ever reads a novel, thinks about any sphere of human congress beyond the classroom or bedroom, or rises above a materialistic self-absorption.

Even physical love rarely transcends mere self-infatuation in Blume's books; girls love and pursue boys as they pursue the desirable position of cheerleader, in order to see themselves reflected admiringly in the eyes of others.

This emotional impoverishment is most embarrassingly on view in Blume's controversial book *Forever*, in which seventeen-year-old Katherine and Michael consummate a love affair. Joyce Maynard once reported in *The New York Times Magazine* on the horror expressed by a group of middle-class New Jersey mothers who felt that their thirteen-year-old daughters, all of whom were wild to read the book, should be kept from such explicit sexual knowledge.

Their concern smacks of self-deception: no ten-year-old in our sex-drenched society can be unaware of adult sexuality, and every eleven-year-old I've ever known has secretly riffled through parental copies of *Playboy* or *Lace* to learn what adults do together. Innocence, if it ever existed in the sense of sexual ignorance and/or purity, is a vanished quality. Perhaps it is adult innocence that is threatened here: if statistics can be believed, the vast majority of North American parents prefer not to know that their children masturbate from infancy on and are naturally possessed by ardent sexual curiosity, sharpening in intensity and secrecy at the age of ten or eleven.

Forever follows the patented Blume method of giving the young reader a great deal of mechanical information. There is, for example, instruction on how to masturbate a boy; the highlight of the book for giggling eleven-year-olds is the moment when Michael undoes his trousers and tells Katherine 'I'd like to introduce you to Ralph', his penis, which, she discovers, 'feels like ordinary skin'. Blume teaches readers how to wipe up semen with Kleenex; how to make an appointment at a Planned Parenthood clinic ('You wish to make an appointment?' 'I guess so'), what it's like to have a gynaecological examination ('This is a vaginal speculum . . . Would you like to see your cervix?'), what it's like to put aftershave lotion on a boy's 'balls' ('Ralph was small and soft and just hung there' and then 'Ralph stuck straight out as if he was watching too' – I don't know which is worse, the lack of grammar or the lack of humour) and how laborious effort is rewarded by mutual orgasm.

The thrill of this for the very young reader is in receiving first-hand sexual information without the unease of listening to a parental lecture or ploughing through a boring technical book. Bearing in mind, though, that seventeen-year-olds do not read Judy Blume's books, one must ask if the depressing banality and crassness of these sexual interactions are a rewarding depiction of teenage erotic life for the prepubescents who do read them. How is it possible to devote an entire novel to teenage love without conveying one tremor of rapture, joy, delight, intensity, sadness, dread, anxiety or tenderness? Blume's 'love' is all fumbling and bra hooks, semen and birth-control pamphlets, and the featureless Katherine (all we really know about her is that she weighs 105 pounds and is conscious that cold air gives her becomingly rosy cheeks) moves on from Michael, her 'forever' love, to Theo, a green-eyed, twenty-one-year-old tennis instructor.

Children are, perhaps, the best unconscious critics of Blume. They skip over all the mind-numbing conversations that fill the pages between the explicit passages: 'Do you by any chance like spinach?' 'Ugh, no . . . why, do you?' 'It's only my favourite food.' 'Like Popeye?' 'Like Popeye.' 'In that case, maybe I'll try to develop a taste for it . . . but I can't promise.' 'Hey, you know tomorrow's Friday?' 'I know.' 'How's 7:30?' 'Fine.' 'Well, see you then.' 'See you then. Oh Michael . . . ' 'Yeah?' 'I'll be ready.'

Blume introduces a few scrawny side-plots. Michael has had VD but that's all right; the repulsively fat Sybil who has a high IQ 'just by luck' (nothing to be jealous of) has an illegitimate baby; a tense boy tries to commit suicide; a grandfather dies . . . it all reads like a laundry list of 'okay' adolescent concerns, with no more emotional depth than Katherine displays on achieving orgasm – 'I came right before Michael and as I did I made noises, just like my mother.'

The indictment against Blume is not that she is too frank, but that her depiction of human beings is so shallow, flat and limited, so preoccupied with clumsily perceived surfaces, that she reflects back to children, and seems complacently to validate by her unquestioning journalistic style, a repugnant image of the ideal teen: mindless, sullen, ruthlessly self-centred, emotionally stunted.

Preadolescents are desperate to know what teenagers do and how they feel about it; they are preparing themselves for the next exciting stage of life. Adolescents, on the other hand, from the age of thirteen on, rarely read about other teenagers; if they read at all, they most often devour adult mass-market paperbacks like Steven King's and Judith Krantz's in an attempt to understand, not just the mechanics of adult sex, but how adults feel about their relationships, and what adult life will be like. Their escapist reading leans to romances, westerns, mysteries and thrillers.

Young Adult books, then, as they are called in the trade, cater to an ambiguous market, much younger than their stated target audience. What purpose is served by *Thirty-Six Exposures*, Kevin Major's Newfoundland novel about a seventeen-year-old boy's coming of age? As a slice of life, it displays the same limited verisimilitude as Blume's efforts: we're shown how Lorne masturbates while reading magazines and listening to taped music, squeezes pimples, watches pornographic movies at a stag party ('He felt as if he had just joined in on a great secret') and, in a repulsively mechanistic scene with his girlfriend, tries to arouse her sexually ('His hand curved to enclose her bare breast. His heartbeat quickened. He stroked it, his fingers brushing against the hardness of the nipple. He began to massage it with quick pulsations of his palm and fingers').

Major tries his best to make us see Lorne and his friends as multi-dimensional. But his hard-nosed 'realism' about working-class Newfoundland speech patterns ('Jesus, I got a good mind to slip my dick into that one of these nights,' says Lorne's friend Trevor, leering at a local bad girl) undercuts the supposed humanity of his characters. If, as seems likely, the book is read mostly by thirteen- or fourteen-year-olds, it will cater to their prurience, but give them little else to take back into their lives.

The whole idea of realism in 'young adult' novels is problematic anyway. Does an individual child struggling with grief, unpopularity or parents' divorce really gain fresh insight or consolation from reading about these dilemmas in a novel? When you think back to your childhood reading, what was it that stirred, excited, thrilled you with the unfolding potential drama of life, moved you by hitherto undreamed-of riches of possible experience, touched you to tears of compassion, relief or sorrow? Was it Black Beauty, Mowgli at the ceremony of fire, Tarzan discovering his nobility, Alice pertly talking back to the Queen? Or was it 'a kid just like you', worrying about indigestion, tomorrow's maths test and mum's pap smear?

Richard Peck, one of the most skilful contemporary authors for adolescents, who has written some excellent books, nevertheless exemplifies the difficulties of this genre in his book 'about' rape, *Are You in the House Alone?* Peck is his usual accomplished self in evoking the terror experienced by sixteen-year-old Gail Osburne as she is followed, harassed and menaced by an unknown telephone caller. In fact, he has it both ways, like the makers of teenage-mayhem movies: he rivets the reader's attention by playing on the fears of all young girls who babysit alone in other people's houses or answer the telephone to hear hoarse breathing.

But the limits of the 'realistic' novels are severe. From the moment of the rape, Peck dare not use his novelistic powers to the full in letting young readers know how Gail must feel; the rage, the sense of violation, the helpless horror would be too devastating. Instead, he retreats to a benumbed clinical documentation of the aftermath: brutish and blaming policemen, detached lawyers, the doctors ('I'm going to check your cervical lumen for traces of sperm . . . Now I'm looking at your posterior fornix'). And the cumulative message of the last half of the book is almost worse than more imaginative probing would be: the psychotic rapist escapes without even a reprimand because he is the son of the town's most prominent citizen. Neither in law nor in person does Gail ever attain the cathartic relief of confronting the rapist. She is emotionally abandoned by her repressed parents, betrayed by girlfriend and boyfriend, shrugged off by authorities. The last words in the book go to Gail's ineffectual mother: 'What could we do?'

The pitfall of the realistic novel, when it is based on a one-dimensional contemporary reality, is that it is by definition too specific to be of much use. In 1976, when Peck wrote the book, the rape victim faced almost insurmountably hostile and sceptical authorities. Today, that is rarely true. Peck's careful realism is already dated, because he did not explore in any depth the wellsprings of prejudice encountered by a sexual victim.

In fact, the liveliest spark in the book comes from Peck's only truly fictional device, the fading and eccentric film artiste, Madame Malevich, who teaches at Gail's high school and understands what has happened. Fiction, when it reassures, does so not by a factual rendition of problems, but by luring the reader into discovering the possibilities of the imaginative life. Some of the best writers for young people deal in fantasy (Ursula Le Guin, Susan Cooper, Patricia Wrightson) precisely because the power of young sexuality, the urgency of life and death questions, are diminished and shrivelled into lifelessness by too direct a representation. Distancing, obliqueness, texture, subtlety, layers of meaning and complexity of human response are essential elements of good fiction; there are no 'problem novelists' writing today who have these qualities in full measure. What they produce is utilitarian at best, squalidly trivial at worst.

Another popular mass-market writer for teens is S. E. Hinton. Both *Tex* and *Rumble Fish* have been made into widely admired films, and the books are read and re-read avidly by young teenage boys . . . perhaps the only books which can claim such a ready audience among this least reading-motivated group.

The characters in S. E. Hinton's books have an undeniably forceful presence, preposterous though they may be; the ardent, almost sexually adoring descriptions of her teenage delinquent heroes lend a feverish animation to the fan-magazine prose. The fourteen-year-old first-person narrator of *The Outsiders*, Ponyboy, introduces himself proudly as a 'greaser', a wrong-side-of-the-tracks tough kid and orphan who glories in his class warfare with the privileged middle-class kids in town. Two pages into the first chapter, Ponyboy has already boasted about his lovely hair and greenish-grey eyes, his good build, his 'high IQ and everything', and his unique abilities to 'dig movies and books'. Then Ponyboy describes his sixteen-year-old brother Sodapop in these words:

He's movie-star kind of handsome, with a finely-drawn, sensitive face that somehow manages to be reckless and thoughtful at the same time. He's got dark-gold hair that he combs back – long and silky and straight – and in the summer the sun bleaches it to a shining wheat-gold. His eyes are dark brown, lively, dancing, recklessly laughing eyes that can be gentle and sympathetic one moment and blazing with anger the next . . .

As the monologue of a tough street kid, and a male one, at that, this is simply absurd. So is the weary repetition of stock phrases meant to show the humane decency of the older members of the gang towards the younger ones: on every other page, one of these paragons, affectionate and amused, will 'cock an eyebrow and ruffle the hair' of a younger one.

It's easy to see why this burble is swallowed whole, and eagerly, and repeatedly, by young boys. For one thing, the unbridled impulsivity of the delinquent is inherently fascinating to teenagers. I remember the wave of popularity enjoyed by an adult mass-market paperback in the 1950s, *The Amboy Dukes*. I read it myself, at age eleven, for its shock value and for the heady sense it gave of teenagers living in complete defiance of adults. Hinton's work, furthermore, flatters the egos of young male readers with its barely subliminal sexual praise, and lets them escape into the fantasized glory of attention and approval from an older teenage tough. Adult criticism is neatly fended off by the fact that the delinquent heroes (Tex, Ponyboy) are clever at school, talented readers, disapproving of drugs, good athletes and invariably develop worthy crushes on middle-class girls with clean hair.

What are the alternatives, then, to all this undernourishing popular material? When I was approaching adolescence, there were no Young Adult novels. Once I passed beyond children's fiction, I read whatever novels I happened to stumble across that seemed to illumine adult life. I remember *How Green Was My Valley, Cry, the Beloved Country, A Tree Grows in Brooklyn, Gulliver's Travels, For Whom the Bell Tolls, Tender is the Night*, and *All Quiet on the Western Front*, a book I had to start again immediately because I couldn't quite believe I was reading about *German* soldiers as real human beings. It was the shock of that moment that remains with me, the feeling of a full and empathetic portrayal of a human reality – without manipulation, without propaganda – but with the power not just to change my opinions but to shift and rearrange my basic assumptions about the world and the way I was in the habit of perceiving it. It led me to question, not to conclude.

British writers for the young have a much richer literary tradition to fall back upon. Even when they reject the middle-class conventions of prewar books, even when they briskly undertake to depict a contemporary 'reality' of industrial suburbs, unemployment and technical colleges and teenage disgruntlement, they rarely lapse into the narcotized adolescent solipsism of the 'Blumziger' school.

This saving grace, I think, is at least partly due to the very class-consciousness against which these authors rebel. Americans perceive themselves as classless; political consciousness or commitment is minimal. When the sullen young heroes and heroines of 'problem' novels wish to express their disaffection, they can only lash out at the nearest embodiment of authority – teachers or parents – and console themselves with sex, clothes and peer-group popularity. Typically, they exist in a political and social void, cut off from any concern with, or even awareness of, the larger world. By contrast, British writers for the young, like the Angry Young Men of an earlier era, have a tailor-made framework and focus for adolescent angst. Their characters are aware of their parents as oppressed and exhausted by the class structure; school may be a galling burden, but presents itself as a way out of an economic dead end. These characters, in other words, exist in a less claustrophobic novelistic world than that of their American counterparts. They have contacts with, and care about, other adults, and no matter how slang-ridden their speech, it is almost always more individual and expressive than the teevee-speak of Blumeland.

Robert Leeson's Jan in *It's My Life* is overburdened with housework when her mother abandons the family and her father struggles with night school, in addition to his job, in order to better himself. Jan has a love affair with the self-centred Kevin. In Blume's hands, this would be an apotheosis, a confirmation of Jan's worth. For Leeson, it is only one more step on the way to Jan's recognition that she must resist and escape, by her own efforts, the trap which crushed her mother. For Jean Ure's Marianne, in *See You Thursday*, withdrawn, hostile and out of her element at the 'snob school' her mother insists on, a love affair with a musician leads her out of her self-preoccupation and helps her to discover strengths and talents she hadn't suspected.

In *The Coal House* by Andrew Taylor, a rather strained attempt to combine contemporary realism with eeriness, a romantic mystery from the past and a sense of place, thirteen-year-old Alison goes to live with her widowed father in the Coal House, the old pit owner's Victorian mansion in a northern mining town. Passionately, she identifies with the local coal miners on strike, solves the lingering mystery left by a shattered Victorian love affair and stands by while her father muddles through an affair with a coldly ambitious professor. *The Coal House* is not an entirely successful novel (we learn rather too much of the smug father's inner life, and rather too little of Alison's, and there's a streak of second-hand D. H. Lawrence that runs right through), but it differs from its American equivalent in its sense of balance between the private and the communal life. Alison does not drown in a trough of self-pity because she has too many connections to the continuing life of the place where she lives.

Anne Fine, a writer of contemporary novels with a sharper focus, wit and ear, presents a common dilemma in *The Granny Project*. An urban family with four children is groaning under the stress of caring for an ageing and demanding grandmother. The tempestuous Russian mother, Natasha, wants to put Granny in a home. The children, including two bright adolescents, Sophie and Ivan, are in angry opposition. In an American problem novel, the impasse would be worked out sentimentally in moments of 'communication' and personal reconciliation. In Fine's novel, an all-out family battle rages, and the granny problem, while amply detailed in itself, is also the ground of a running debate between bloody-minded revolutionist Ivan and the more humane gradualist, Sophie. The terms of their arguments are political, and when they lose their tempers, they hurl hilarious epithets ('Stalinist thug!' 'Cringing revisionist!') which, funny as they are, would simply be unthinkable in an analogous American novel.

While not all British problem novels are works of genius, most seem to exercise a tactful reticence on the subject of teenage sex, rarely confusing it for the ultimate meaning of life, and most place their characters in a competently realized social and geographic setting.

In other words, no adult searching for 'relevance' in an adolescent novel is forced to turn to the lowest-common-denominator books which have so captured the market. Aside from the fantasists (who are the most popular among literate teenagers, while the 'problem novelists', as Sheila Egoff notes, are the preference of less accomplished readers), there are a number of first-rate authors who write perceptively and refreshingly about adolescent experience.

Unlike Blume, Danziger *et al.*, they reach more deeply into their characters to transform raw experience into something coherent, shapely and complex. Or they may have a broader reach, setting young heroes in an historic or geographic context that allows them to be seen as members of a wider world and invites the reader to 'get the self out of the way', at least temporarily.

In the hands of a talented writer, even the most unpromising material can sink taproots into the unconscious and bloom gloriously. Virginia Hamilton, in *A Little Love*, presents us with a sweet-faced, overweight black girl, Sheema, who lives with her ageing grandparents in Dayton, Ohio. Sheema is a slow learner, a student in 'food services' at the local vocational school; her boyfriend Forrest, who works as a movie usher at night, is a classmate on the same course.

On the surface, it sounds like the dreary stuff of a sociologically correct novel, as appealing as orthopaedic shoes. But Hamilton is a gifted writer; the slow, lilting black dialect of Sheema's speech, the drift of her daydreams and fears and yearnings, draw us deeper into a reality we could never have known or loved without Hamilton's art. This is the opposite of a Blume experience: no smug conceit is reflected back on a complacent reader. Instead, she is stretched to comprehend someone else's life, to taste the difference and waken to the common underlying humanity.

Sheema is alive and complex as Hinton's narcissistic braggarts never are. Her horrified hypnotic daydreams are haunted by mushroom clouds, by her grandparents' gradual decline, by the menace of the erratically hostile heavy-metal dudes at high school. Sheema may be 'slow' academically but she is alertly confident, absorbed, delighted by her own skill in the food-preparation classes; it is one of the more moving experiences in teenage literature to see through Sheema's eyes as slowly, seriously, she cooks, cleans and launders in her grandparents' house, staving off their death with her responsibility.

Forrest, too, is an endearing and believable teenager. He is the lean and quick one, tense with the weight of his plans and ambitions for both of them; he knows how to value Sheema and how to keep her anchored. Nearly every night, Sheema tiptoes out of her grandparents' house to drive with Forrest to hidden country lanes where they make love in the car: their 'serene and silky pleasure . . . softening the time around them . . . holding them strongly together' tells a curious teenage reader everything that Blume doesn't. So does their squabbling, when Sheema strains against Forrest's possessiveness, or pressures him to wake up to the dangers that surround black youths in their society.

When Forrest and Sheema finally set out in search of her long-lost father (a glittering fantasy figure of charm and talent to Sheema), their journey is a classic 'on the road in America' odyssey, sharply realized in contemporary detail and felt urgency. Sheema and Forrest, who have none of the affluent privileges of Blume's Katherine, and who resist the slick alienation of Hinton's delinquents, exist in a real world of hopes, loves and responsibilities, not a hermetically sealed bubble of teenage self-obsession. One of the book's strengths is the largely unspoken tenderness of Sheema's relationship with her grandmother: 'I know, baby,' Grandma whispers when Sheema returns broken-hearted from her search for her father, 'I know all about it. Like fallin' weather. Life have its hard edges.'

A foreign or minority culture can be a freeing framework for both writer and reader; the sense of a shared humanity pierces us most sharply when we have intuited it in a strange setting, or through the experiences of quirkily individualistic characters.

Black American culture has provided us with some exhilarating examples. *Philip Hall Likes Me, I Reckon Maybe* by Bette Greene, a delightful book for prepubescent Blume-readers who need to be weaned to a richer diet, shows us a strong-willed, bright, impetuous eleven-year-old in rural Arkansas. Beth is smitten by 'sweet, cute' Philip Hall who lives on the neighbouring farm. Philip, who sneers at her whenever he's in a group of boys, doesn't hesitate to exploit her crush ('I'll let you clean my dairy barn') but likes her only so long as she tacitly agrees to come second to him in every school subject. Eventually, without relinquishing her admiration for Philip, Beth fights back. While the story is never didactic, it certainly dramatizes a central dilemma for junior school girls: how a young girl can like a boy, and get him to acknowledge their friendship, without sacrificing her own self-definition.

A similar rivalry sparks off the conflict in *Words by Heart* by Ouida Sebestyen, in which twelve-year-old Lena, a black girl in the rural Midwest, competes in a Bible-quoting contest at the local white church. The beauty of the fierce verse-swapping ('I am black but I am comely,' quotes a defiant Lena, who knows that the crowd is rooting for white Winslow Starnes) springs from the aptness and poetic lucidity of the biblical quotations, but the freshness of the rest of the novel is Sebestyen's own. This is a novel for more mature readers, movingly depicting a girl's inner struggle with hatred and racism and illuminated by the elemental wisdom of Lena's loving father, Ben.

Teenagers, problem novelists to the contrary, are not insensitive to bigotry, irrationality or conflict in the wider community. *Across the Barricades* by Joan Lingard, written in bare-bones, utilitarian prose, nevertheless gains authenticity from its setting: sixteen-year-old Sadie is a Protestant and seventeen-year-old Kevin is Catholic, and they dare to love each other in a strife-torn Belfast seething with religious hatred. The scrimping narrowness and harshness of the lives of both their working-class families is identical, and provides a believable background for the teenagers' growing critical awareness of their parents' limitations, as well as their longing for escape.

One More River by Lynne Reid Banks is not nearly so accomplished as her later *Indian in the Cupboard*, but it is a curiously convincing coming-of-age story about a spoiled Canadian Jewish fourteen-year-old girl who finds herself transplanted to an Israeli kibbutz. The most poignant aspect of Leslie Shelby's 'enlargement of self' is her tenuous, fragile, wounded friendship with a Palestinian boy who lives on the other side of the Jordan River. The wound of disillusionment – 'the complete realizing that not any one can believe' just what you believe – is delicately probed in this book; it touches not only on Leslie and the Arab boy, but on Leslie's difficulties with the Israeli teenagers and on the many inevitable rifts within her family. The adult task of re-making wounded relationships after the ruptures of disillusionment is one of the book's encouraging themes.

The Village by the Sea offers a distant world made brilliantly alive in the hands of a wonderful writer: Anita Desai uses all the physical senses to make us realize the stark and desperate poverty of a brother and sister, twelve-year-old Hari and his thirteen-year-old sister Lila, who live in an Indian village. The setting is far from bleak, however. Desai, a distinguished novelist for adults, evokes the lush and haunting beauty of the sea and the countryside, ironically as exhausted in nourishment as it is fertile in loveliness. The plot is rich with satirical portraits of local derelicts and tycoons, with the mingled menace and promise of encroaching industrialization, with crippling superstitions and profound faith – and, most of all, with Hari's vivid trials and adventures when he runs away to Bombay to find work to feed the family. Befriended by kindly Mr Panwallah of the Ding-Dong Watchworks, Hari stoically survives gruelling hardships and learns a trade.

For a privileged western child, there must be something bracing – even enviable – about the struggles of Hari and Lila, freed of middle-class self-consciousness and self-pity by their determined battle to survive. There is vigour, hope and reconciliation in this fine story, with no sacrifice of honesty about India's overwhelming difficulties.

Fireweed, by Jill Paton Walsh, has some of that same force. Bill, a working-class fifteen-year-old, finds himself on the run and on his own during the worst year of the blitz in wartime London. He meets up with another runaway, the obviously upper-class Julie, and they pool resources and wits to survive – creating, by the end, their own little family – in the midst of one of the most sulphurously luminous and grippingly fearsome descriptions of the blitz that I have ever read.

The friendship is drawn from Bill's point of view, obliquely and delicately. We become aware of his growing love for Julie without its ever being belaboured; their one physical encounter, when they huddle together under a shared blanket for warmth, is left ambiguous.

Fireweed has been criticized for its squeamishness about sex, though I think it is both sensitive and accurate for those youngsters in that time and place. But the criticism raises a larger question: can sexuality between teenagers be written about more frankly without sacrificing literary values or emotional depth?

The evidence is scanty. *Snow Apples*, an unevenly written first novel by Canadian Mary Razell, is nevertheless overwhelming in its sense of a particular time and place – a British Columbia outpost in the 1940s. As in *A Tree Grows in Brooklyn*, one feels the presence of a passionate, sometimes angry, adult sensibility, reliving the bitter injustices as well as the intense yearnings of young womanhood. Razell recreates what Richard Peck could not: the frightening, queasy aura of male sexuality that closes in on an attractive young girl who is not protected by her family. Those who grew up in the 1940s and 1950s, and can remember the code of puritanical silence which left girls to fend off molesters and aggressive boyfriends without information or support, will find this a disturbingly accurate portrait. But the book is meant for teenagers and it does achieve what more clinical authors have failed to: Razell forcefully conveys the driving urgency of teenage eroticism and the need for love.

These same themes are present, just as openly, in *The First of Midnight*, a historical novel by Marjorie Darke which is particularly satisfying for teenage girls with a taste for romance but the intelligence to yearn for something more substantial. Jess is a sparky, defiant poorhouse waif in eighteenth-century Bristol, a port that prospered on the illicit slave trade. Escaping from a brutish employer, the ignorant, filthy Jess dresses in boy's clothes and takes refuge on a ship anchored in Bristol harbour. There her fate becomes entwined with that of Midnight, an improbably noble black slave who has been made literate, even well-educated, by a former owner.

There are overtones of both Joan Aiken and Leon Garfield in the colourful language and pell-mell adventures into which Jess and Midnight are propelled, but there is a serious love story here, too, and a deepening of Jess's understanding as she comes to realize the meanings of slavery and freedom. The scene of their lovemaking does not flinch from 'the pressure of thigh on thigh, the honey-mouth taste, the smell of cloves and salt . . . the abandoned animal joy'. This may not be the pinnacle of erotic literature, but it is an honest and successful attempt, suffused also with a very real tenderness, to convey the experience of sex from both the male and female point of view. And Jess and Midnight do not live in a vacuum; despite their mutual love, the cultural chasm between them is too deep, eventually, for them to bridge. Midnight longs to leave his free but brutish life as a sideshow prizefighter; Jess is too limited by her past to be able to visualize a life with him back in Africa. Judy Blume wrote that in *Forever* she wanted to show that teenage sexual love can be transient even if sincere; her effort is one-dimensional and trite, but Darke makes us feel its brief happiness, confusion, loss and ultimate gain.

Bilgewater, by the superbly witty and deft Jane Gardam, is a more lighthearted, satirical story. Marigold Daisy Green, who describes herself as 'frog-like – squat and ugly' with bad eyesight and orange frizzy hair – grows up in sheltered and bizarre circumstances in a boy's school where her gentle, eccentric father is headmaster. Indeed, the characters are a gallery of endearing and sometimes buffoonish eccentrics, and all of them, young and old, reticent or extravagant, act out the various and resplendent follies to which they are driven by love.

'Bilgewater', as she is unkindly nicknamed by the oafish boys in their girl-hating prepubescence, leaps into her own adolescent madnesses. First she lets herself be duped by her adored Jack Rose, the school's 'silver spoon boy'; sadder but wiser after a comically ghastly visit with him to his parents' house-cum-dental office, she flees to the romantic arms of the mysterious Terrapin, who had looked 'like a small albino ape' to her in his childhood.

As the first-person narrator, Bilgewater escapes all the dreary, slovenly mannerisms of her American counterparts. She is a funny, shy, clumsy girl, a whizz at maths, a mordantly sharp observer of the adult life around and a brooder over books. Her narrative sparkles with self-mockery; keen, though often naïve perceptions of others; and wonderfully fresh and genuine literary references. We see how stories have fed her daydreams, and how the symbolism of various books is absorbed into her consciousness. Before our eyes, Bilgewater metamorphoses into a bright, engagingly idiosyncratic adolescent who is no more misguided in love than all the adults around her astonishingly reveal themselves to be.

Bilgewater's eventual triumph is tinged with a certain sadness: at the peak of her distinguished career, she looks back briefly on this chronicle and hints that she knows what she gave up when she chose a safe, good man over a treacherous but erotically electrifying scoundrel. Although the novel deals with Bilgewater's childhood and adolescence, the education of her heart and mind – and though the sexual encounters stop short of explicitness – this novel makes few concessions to inexperienced readers. It is written with adult sharpness of insight and hilarity, and yet remains perfectly accessible to a good reader over the age of twelve.

Bilgewater's choice is one that every adolescent must make; the 'fool's gold' of misplaced teenage affections is a frequent motif in books for this age group. When the theme is handled well (as it is also in Gardam's *A Long Way from Verona*, in K. M. Peyton's *Pennington* books, and in *Up a Road Slowly* by Irene Hunt), it is an idea of enduring human interest. When, as in *Bilgewater*, it is illuminated at so many levels, and with so much understanding and gentle irony, it provides far more valuable insights than a mere description of sexual intercourse.

The erotic life in all its dimensions has its rightful place in adolescent literature. The adult writer who is aiming at more than mass sales will take the matter seriously enough to write about sex without crudity, without banality, and will not offend any but the most prudish. The prerequisites seem to be tact, emotional depth and a sense of the power of the unspoken word. Shakespeare did not have to show us Juliet mopping up semen to make us feel the force of her passion. Such well-intentioned literalness is the kiss of death for the imaginative apprehension of what love might mean.

Wit – polished, ironic, deflating or heartening – is the special quality of some of the most appealing adolescent literature. Anyone who has heard thirteen-year-old girls lampooning with deadly precision the genteel sadomasochism of Mills and Boon romances knows that teenagers can hear several tunes at one time: they can be enthralled by romantic daydreams while their intelligence simultaneously plays a sardonic counterpoint. The humorous handling of adolescent tensions is not necessarily belittling. On the contrary; wit can signal the reassuring news that you will live to laugh at your traumas, that adulthood will bring a calming perspective. And laughter is the best defence against that most limiting of all adolescent tendencies, self-pity. To laugh means that you have gained some distance from your self.

In *Goodnight, Prof, Love* (*Goodnight, Prof, Dear* in the United States – another misguided concession to linguistic parochialism) by John Rowe Townsend, it is sixteen-year-old Graham Hollis's wry self-awareness that gives life to a potentially hackneyed story. Graham is a gangly, shy teenager who fantasizes romantically about rescuing pale-faced maidens from cliffs. When his parents leave on a week's vacation, though, it is a very different kind of girl he meets and tries to rescue: a hard-luck, chipper, working-class girl of eighteen, Lynn, who works in a local greasy spoon and is at the mercy of her domineering employer. She calls Graham 'Prof' because of his bespectacled schoolboy innocence; teases him fondly ('I've took quite a fancy to you . . . ') and gets him a temporary job washing dishes in the restaurant.

Graham, of course, eventually falls madly in love with Lynn and persuades her to elope with him. Half-tempted by his boyish ardour, she agrees, takes him on the road, initiates him sexually with earthy kindness and sends him home at last. The sex scenes are notable for their discretion. The focus is on the emotional transaction between the characters – his shamefaced failure at first, her cheery tolerance, his eventual exhilaration. The novel gains from the play of Graham's sardonic self-awareness and his innocence; it is swift, funny, colloquial and decent, a slender but believable story.

Richard Peck, too, uses wit to convince us of the credibility of his unalienated teenagers; they may have problems, but they are not embittered or cynical. Two of his best are *Representing Superdoll* and *Father Figure*, both of which are distinguished by their sympathetic humour and their splendidly fresh settings. *Superdoll* is a satire of the beauty contest mentality, as seen in the rise of Darlene Hoffmeister from Miss Hybrid Seed Corn to Central United States Teen Super Doll. The narrator is the temporarily mousy Verna, farm girl; her style is easily conversational and as polished as a freshly husked cob of corn. Verna has native intelligence on her side, along with the natural grace to be tolerant, though mildly envious, of her beautiful classmate. When she accompanies Darlene on the Superdoll promotional trip to New York, though, Verna comes splendidly into her own. The reader, and Verna, can see that a tantalizing future – uncomplicated by self-conscious beauty – lies just over the horizon for her.

Father Figure lacks the sunniness of *Representing Superdoll;* the seventeen-year-old narrator, Jim Atwater, is a more tormented, more sophisticated and introverted hero whose story of reconciliation with a long-lost father, down on his luck in Florida, is peppered with dry New

York witticisms. Jim is a private-school boy, a well-behaved and tightly controlled upper-class kid who worries too much about his self-contained little brother Byron. He's given to knowing observations about his grandmother and her wealthy, stiffly respectable Republican friends, whom he calls the 'Gray Panthers'. When one of them pulls strings to arrange a summer job for Jim, Jim remarks to himself, 'The elderly can't deal with you, but they sure as hell can deal you in'.

The novel is at its richest in its depiction of the summer the boys spend – Jim resentfully and Byron expansively – with their estranged father. Their mother has commited suicide after a lengthy struggle with cancer. Jim is besieged by complicated feelings: he's jealous of his father's growing closeness with Byron, sexually competitive with him for the favours of yet another waitress-with-a-heart-of-gold and unforgivingly enraged by his father's long neglect of the family. Peck, however, is utterly unlike problem novelists in that he never allows his adult characters to become cardboard villains in order to indulge teenage readers in a pleasant wallow of self-righteousness. Jim's dad, Howard, knows he is a failure, more pathetic than evil. By the end of the summer, Jim has painfully learned to accept both his father and the warm-hearted Marietta as people in their own right, not players in his private drama.

It's a touching and brave novel, with rounded characters who are capable of surprising you, and with Peck's special gift: a devastatingly accurate eye for class distinctions, social styles and affectations of dress and speech.

Peck, like Townsend and Le Guin, has a talent for drawing male characters who are clearly masculine without being crass, super-athletic or conceited. If you read enough adolescent novels, you will know this for the rarity it is. Contemporary novelists, like many of their subjects, seem to think they must choose between only two kinds of male characters: brutes and wimps. Because the male hero is rarely admirable in modern teenage novels, I think it worth a special discussion of two books that are wonderful exceptions.

Johnny Tremain by Esther Forbes is as fresh and compelling now as when it won the Newbery Medal in 1943. It follows the fortunes of Johnny from the time he is a fourteen-year-old silversmith's apprentice in Boston to the emotionally patriotic ending two years later when he plays a part in the American Revolution. This is a vigorously written historical novel, busily populated with rich merchants, tradesmen's daughters, eloquent revolutionaries, dreamers, affable British enlisted men, arrogant officers. But as much as it is a dramatic and lively account of a busy seaport, and the conflicts that gave rise to the Revolution, it is also the story of Johnny's coming of age.

When we first meet him, he is as headstrong and domineering as many another precociously gifted boy. A quick-witted orphan who must make his own way, he has grandiose dreams for himself and little patience with the less fortunate. Just as his star is rising (he has been noticed favourably by the famous silversmith, Paul Revere), Johnny suffers a ghastly accident which costs him the use of his right hand. Soon, he knows the bitterness and despair of being without work, a home or a future. His arrogant assumptions crumble.

It is an old-fashioned plot, the proud brought low, but youngsters read it as ardently now as they ever did. Whatever the current fashions in teenage cynicism, the elemental challenges of youth – to make something of yourself, to learn the art of friendship, to make sense of the adult world, to discard false idols – remain unchanged. Johnny's transformations take place through dramatic action. He rebuilds his life, wins friends, abandons false pride, discovers love. It's a sturdy, extroverted story, with a wide enough slice of life (Johnny becomes a courier for the rebels and practises one-handed axe wielding so he can take part in the Boston Tea Party) to make the reader experience history as a series of human actions.

If the amplitude of *Johnny Tremain* is daunting to a less motivated reader, then there is, last but never least, Pennington, rebellious hero of K. M. Peyton's *Pennington's Seventeenth Summer*, a delinquent whose surging energies make Hinton's self-conscious male models seem like a parcel of poseurs.

Pennington is an overgrown schoolboy from the north of England, a working-class hulk, whose antics are the despair of his teachers. 'May God forgive this boy for abusing so unusual a talent,' rages Mr Crocker, Penn's maddened music teacher, on the report card. For Pennington is not just massive and physically gifted, the pride of his school's soccer team; he also has huge hands that stretch easily across the octaves. And his mother, an argumentative, erratic shrew who works in a trousers factory and gambles away her earnings, has nagged him since he was three to stick to his piano lessons.

Pennington is sublimely indifferent to his musical talent; what he likes to do is to noodle on the harmonica whenever his buddy Bates, the cowman's son, gets drunk enough to sing plaintive ballads in a sweet tenor voice. Pennington is the kind of teenager who makes respectable adults yell, 'Hooligan!' after him in the street. Irreverent, laconic, a thoughtless prankster, he is nevertheless enormously sympathetic. He may provoke fistfights with his arch enemy, Smeeton; he may have nicked some Easter eggs and ten cigarettes from a local store, but Pennington is not a bully and not mean-spirited. All he really wants is to be left alone.

But Pennington's life is a series of pratfalls and choking injustices; his own thoughtlessness leads him into a tumultuous series of scrapes in which he is constantly running foul of adult authority, usually through some utterly plausible misunderstanding. Rueful, harassed, saved from mournfulness by his own animal high spirits, Pennington cannot fail to endear himself to the reader. It's the sheer dash, humour and energy of the writing that serve to enlist our sympathies on Pennington's side; somehow, Peyton makes us believe wholeheartedly in the way the hapless Pennington constantly trips over the rules.

The dialogue helps: Peyton has a perfect ear for Penn's surliness as well as shaggy-dog amiability with friends, and for the characteristic speech of all the adults, too – the mother who makes the house reverberate as though it's 'wired up for canned invective'; the father who alternately thumps Penn and slyly incites him to rebellion; the avuncular local constable, always chastising Penn more in sorrow than in anger; the frustrated but decent Crocker, who believes in Penn; and Penn's spiteful and sadistic nemesis, the teacher Mr Marsh, appropriately nicknamed 'Soggy' by the boys.

What transforms Pennington's chaotic life is that Mr Crocker has entered him for a piano competition, and arranges for an enforced three hours of practice at school every day. Despite himself, Pennington begins to be drawn into the music he had despised. Part of music's new appeal for him is that he has been inarticulately, helplessly smitten by a silvery apparition of a girl, a folksinger seen at a distance. ('All the girls he knew were busty and thrusty and strong, all private giggles and shrieks, nudging and daring and passing notes.') From the moment when he slumps resentfully on the piano bench, 'resistance setting in like arthritis', as Crocker sets him to work, until the suspenseful climax at the music competition, Pennington is unwillingly discovering the rewards of hard work.

The plot is dazzling for its physical impetuosity, its inventiveness, and the inevitability with which all the incidents are drawn together in a comic chain of overlapping cause-and-effect. Peyton triumphs at graphically clear descriptions of physical feats, whether it's Pennington taking a reckless fifteen-foot dive into shallow water, or his friend Bates, drunkenly and hilariously uncoordinated, turning pages for him at a stuffy school concert. The pace during the last few chapters is absolutely breathless. So relentless are the complications, so frantic is Pennington as he tries both to elude the police and to accommodate a dozen conflicting adult demands on him, that the reader is almost as exhausted by tension as the hero.

But Peyton is not just a whizz at physical action, slapstick and offhanded satire of the way adults are always getting things wrong. In this, her best book, she can also make you feel the plangent sweetness of Bates's voice coming across the water from a wrecked old fishing-boat (followed, of course, by muffled curses and the splash of a can being hurled into the water); she can make you *hear* the way Pennington plays Mendelssohn, hands raw from a school strapping, but doggedly thinking of 'Mendelssohn's flaming fairies'.

Best of all, I think, is the way Peyton keeps Pennington's character true to itself. He simply never thinks about his effect on others; he doesn't give a damn for adult opinion, not even when it might be approving for once: after he risks his life and the piano competition to save old Crocker's life out at sea, and then the town wrong-headedly gives the credit to Bates who was a mere bystander, Pennington just shrugs. He cares about Crocker, but never does anything about expressing it verbally. He accepts a piano scholarship to London from a distinguished teacher – whom he mistakes for a bothersome vicar – because he fancies having a room of his own.

The modulations in Pennington's attitudes towards the end are beautifully underplayed. Music has begun to mean something to him, he has begun – perhaps through sheer force of exhaustion – to stop and *think* before he acts recklessly, but Peyton never spoils her portrait of Pennington by sentimentality. Never once does she dilute or fudge the impact of Pennington's character by descending into the kind of maudlin self-dramatization that makes Hinton's characters glow with a sickly phosphorescence, like 'a bad lobster in a dark cellar', to use Dickens's phrase.

Two sequels, *The Beethoven Medal* and *Pennington's Heir*, are told sympathetically from the point of view of Ruth, the girl who loves Pennington helplessly and whom he eventually marries. Both are notably competent portraits of the pains and pleasures of young love and a musician's life. Peyton seems always to be warmly on the side of her young protagonists, inarticulate though they may be, wrongheaded as they often seem to be to the adults around them. She can empathize with their energies and their wilful passions without condescending, and without ever being, like Blume, a mere conduit for their egocentricity and banality.

It would be a shame to leave this chapter on alternatives in teenage reading without mentioning two fictional works with strong elements of autobiography, a genre that is particularly attractive to adolescents. Both *A Bird in the House* by Margaret Laurence, and *Lives of Girls and Women* by Alice Munro, are series of linked stories that share a precision and sharpness of insight, a luminous imagery and a scrupulous honesty about girlhood that goes several layers deeper than almost any other fictional work that comes to mind. This is the kind of writing that helps a young person to 'set the self aside' for a moment, only to regain it more profoundly when the story has been absorbed. That – and not problem solving, not sexual instruction – is what teenage fiction is most deeply concerned with.

Chapter 10

GIRLS' BOOKS, BOYS' BOOKS, BAD BOOKS, AND BIAS

Whatever my children read, I have faith – indeed, I would say that I know – that they are resting for a while in the recesses of their souls, in places where I will never know them, can never know them, am not supposed to know them.

       Julius Lester, *Horn Book* magazine, April 1984

It is sad that childhood is only one seventh of one's life, and only five years of one's reading life.

       Gillian Avery, in *Writers, Critics and Children*, 1976

Junk books can dull the hunger of a child's mind, stuff it with unearned certainties . . .

       Paula Fox, in *Celebrating Children's Books*, 1981

I RESPOND with visceral and instant agreement to all three of the above statements; I suspect that most parents would find themselves on the horns of the same dilemma. If we care what our children read, if we know what a wealth of literature is available to them for those too-short years of reading intensity – what shall we do about the junk?

The first thing, I suppose, is to know about it. Recently I met a friend with her two children at the theatre. She is energetic, independent and talented, a university professor and published author. Her son and daughter, about eleven and nine years old, are sensitive and highly intelligent. The little girl was carrying a paperback copy of a Judy Blume novel. 'Oh, horrible!' burst out my own fourteen-year-old daughter. And there I was, embarrassingly stuck with explaining our aversion while trying not to seem overbearingly critical.

As it happens, my friend was interested rather than defensive. She had thought (being a feminist) that these modern novels might as least be contemporary in tone and without the sexism of older children's works. She wanted to hear more.

It is for her and other adults like her, who have not had the time or perhaps the inclination to read children's books for themselves, that I have taken pains to point out what I feel is shoddy and meretricious in authors like Blume. I know that I risk flaming indignation from her loyalists, who are legion: when I wrote about Blume in my newspaper column, I was attacked by some teachers and librarians for my supposed 'elitism'. Children found freshness and insight into their own current problems in these books, I was told, and I had no right to try to suppress them.

But I do not want to suppress them. If my own children had loved Blume's books (or Hinton's or any of the legion of their imitators) I would have respected their choices while tactfully offering others – or at least keeping the door open to other rooms, other voices. As the English reading expert Margaret Meek has stressed, children do seem to need 'bulk reading' which, by its very nature, is undemanding and often of very low literary quality. My own observation is that at crucial moments of change and growth, children often need to fall back temporarily, as though to test the firmness of their former ground before stepping forward into the unknown.

At the age of seven or eight, when reading skills have recently been integrated, a bright child will gobble endless junk books, like Enid Blyton's, or recycled pap from films like *Star Wars*. Comics are another familiar form of transitional reading, still using some of the easy picture-book format while introducing more sophisticated vocabulary and either slapstick humour or exaggerated violence. Speed, comfort, familiarity, a reassuring simplicity, devotion to surface actions and conventional behaviour, a complete absence of introspection – these are the ingredients of bulk reading. The 'bulk' is not a total loss; as Meek and others point out, the child is learning the shape of stories – episode, climax, resolution, even rough outlines of such archetypes as heroes and villains – in privacy and independence. No teachers correct mistakes; no parents hover over the page to reprove. The freedom to chose one's own books is in some ways the most bracing and dramatic taste of liberty a child can know: at five or six or seven, browsing in the library or book shop and then reading at home, the child is suddenly free to enter other worlds, spy from within on a thousand lives, leap oceans with a single bound.

Safely and with the undiluted pleasure of pure pastime, the child unwittingly practises the recently acquired skills of reading until they become smoothly unconscious. There may also be the spice of naughtiness in 'bulk reading'; intelligent children know very well that they are skimming along with the merest surface involvement, and they even know that this is a tiny betrayal of that more complex demand made by real books. I distinctly remember the headiness of this reading libertinism when I was six years old and reading *The Bobbsey Twins*. Series books, of course, offer the most simple enjoyment: you don't even have to bother becoming acquainted with the characters. You can go on and on, like skating up a frozen creek, the characters and incidents blurring past you.

Good books, though, can spoil the sheer mindlessness of bulk reading for you. By the time I was ten or eleven, and a friend begged me to read her complete set of Nancy Drew, I was bored stiff by the stilted writing and cartoonish characters. Without realizing it, I had already become addicted to the more intricate rewards of good prose; from then on, when I wanted bulk reading, I had to resort to magazines. A book that didn't give me the total absorption I craved was not a distraction but an irritation and a fraud.

Though every age group has its cherished forms of private reading indulgence, it is especially at puberty that junk books reassert their claim. Rapid change is frightening. A twelve-year-old's development may be drastically slower or faster than that of her friends; the known safety of the primary school has been exchanged for the threatening gauntlet of senior school; the future rushes in and the past drops away. Romances, mysteries, thrillers and westerns provide a haven of completely reliable escape structures. The tough-jawed cowboy will never break down and grovel before the bully; the heroine of the romance will never be rejected by all the men in her life; if change or death has a role in the drama, it will never stab the reader with real anguish. Furthermore, the youngster who relies on these predictable stories is at least gaining pleasure and distraction from the reading of fiction, and this may be a base to build on for more satisfying reading in the future.

That said, bear in mind that bad books, the mindless-but-benign as well as the insidious, have their own distribution system. The child who needs them finds them as though by magic; they are pervasive, unnoticed and disposable as Kleenex. My local libraries – and that includes the libraries in primary and secondary schools – have shelves full of mass-produced, assembly-line junk reading. Since librarians have become, often unwillingly, cogs in the consumer machine (boost those circulation figures! get a book, any book, into the hands of that video-loving non-reader!) instead of the custodians of literary civilization, we don't have to worry about young people getting their fill of junk reading.

We do have to worry, however, if those five or six years of childhood reading time speed past, crammed with television, sports and Care Bears, and presto – a young adult emerges who has never been deeply moved by a book, who has never had experience transfigured into art through reading, and who, consequently, may never again think of books as a serious adjunct to life. A priceless opportunity will have been lost for ever, and one of the most humanizing and profound resources available to us as parents and teachers will have been abandoned without a second thought.

As long ago as 1958, when the American critic and poet Randall Jarrell surveyed the immense proliferation of American commercial publishing, he wrote, 'And yet, the more words there are, the simpler the words get. The professional users of words process their product as if it were baby food and we babies: all we have to do is open our mouths and swallow. Most of our mental and moral food is quick-frozen, pre-digested, spoonfed. E. M. Forster has said: "The only thing we learn from spoon-feeding is the shape of the spoon." Not only is this true – pretty soon, if anything doesn't have the shape of that spoon we won't swallow it, we can't swallow it. Our century has produced some great and much good literature, but the habitual readers of Instant Literature cannot read it; nor can they read the great and good literature of the past.'

Instant Literature, he said, anticipating Blumeziger by twenty years, is a wish reinforced by a cliché – it tells us always that life is not only what we wish it, but also what we think it. The writers of Instant Literature 'humour us, flatter our prejudices, pull our strings'.

Yet it is so easy to take the other route. The child may read Instant Literature on the living-room rug, but hear Joan Aiken, Ted Hughes, Clive King or E. L. Konigsburg read aloud at bedtime. (And if the child insists on hearing Care Bears stories read aloud, read them, but follow up with something as vibrant as William Steig.) It is as easy, and nutritionally more sound, to take a five-year-old child to the library every week as it is to make an outing to McDonald's part of the family routine.

The problem of preadolescent reading is admittedly more difficult. No eleven-year-old wants to have Mummy or Daddy peering over her shoulder at the library and recommending books, and the most heartfelt urgings from a parent or teacher may have a stubbornly contrary effect.

Still, with children's book shops in every major town and city, it is as easy to buy a paperback version of *A Bridge to Terabithia* or *Carrie's War* as it is to head for the shelves of teen romances. Book tokens may yield surprising results; a young shopper on his own may be astonishingly receptive to guidance from knowledgeable sales staff. It's the same principle by which your churlish young heel-dragger, who cannot be persuaded to pick up his socks from the middle of the living room, will gladly, gallantly mow the lawn and wash the windows at his friend's house. The sheer independent generosity of the act, free of all compulsion, has a propulsive glamour of its own.

I've had concerned, literate parents beg me to tell them how to wean their children from trash reading. Alas, there is no easy answer, although a parent who reads and enthusiastically enjoys a sprinkling of the most highly recommended children's books is a vital example for any youngster. Though I would never attack a young person's choice of a book, good or bad, I would never pretend to a false approval, either, any more than I would feign a rapt delight in those boring recitals of television plots to which some children are so given. The 'mm-hmmm' response is one I have polished to a high gloss. It signifies an interest in the child and his feelings, while withholding an ecstatic approval of the subject matter: it might be of keen significance to me that a child is wildly excited by a police shoot-out on television, for example, while the programme itself is interesting only as an example of cultural aberration. And the child gets the message: he is left with an uneasy question in his mind about what exactly the adult *thinks* of all this. Our reticence can provoke a wholesome uncertainty; all understanding begins in questions.

Reading aloud is a more offbeat tactic at this age, but perfectly plausible: consult Jim Trelease's *Read-Aloud Handbook* for a down-to-earth description of his practice of reading aloud while his teenaged son washed dishes.

'Problem' novels, as I argued in the previous chapter, present a particular challenge. North American utilitarianism predisposes us to think of books as medicine; one whole school of reading experts wholeheartedly endorses something called 'bibliotherapy'. For anyone who has experienced reading as one of life's most intense aesthetic pleasures, the very word 'bibliotherapy' must sound thumpingly perverse. The thinking behind it seems inexpressibly crude: child is in pain from parents' divorce, give child a cheerful novel about divorce, child will feel better. The child is not a questioning mind and seeking heart, but a patient. The book is a commodity, like a patent drug.

My entire life as a reader rebels against this prescription. As a sheltered little girl in tranquil Toronto – far more sheltered than my brothers – I read, with palpitating excitement, stories of adventures in which brothers and sisters shared alike. I would have loathed books about sheltered little girls who lived in rented houses in Toronto and argued with their parents for permission to play outside after dark.

As a twelve-year-old, I read Japanese haiku with chills of discovery chasing down my spine: they had all the compression, coherence, delicacy and purity of design and intention that my life did not. Furthermore, they had an artistic existence of their own, quite apart from my immediate personal needs. On and on through my life, they would still be there, offering new facets of themselves, new depths, with each re-reading. They meant many things – remember George MacDonald's observation on the multiple meanings yielded by each work of art – and every time I came back to a poem, I brought new worlds of experience to it, enriched by my history of conversation with each particular poem. No one can have that ongoing intimacy with a 'problem novel'; it is by definition static, chained to particularity, a throwaway designed to handle one problem and then be discarded.

Even more to the point, perhaps, was my experience of agony in adult life. When I was broken-hearted after my mother died in a horrible accident, I went, after a few days, blindly and instinctively, to a book shop to buy some Swedish detective stories. I did not want to read – could not have borne to read – about middle-aged women in mourning. Neither realistic contemporary novels about common problems, nor the consolations of high art, could offer me anything in that state of crisis. (Critic Lissa Paul has pointed out to me, too, that murder mysteries deal at a comfortably cool remove with the ultimate puzzle of death.) At first it was hard even to focus my swollen eyes on the detective stories. After a while, though, they served to blot out the world, and blot out myself, so I could fall asleep at night. Five months later, on holiday where I could hear the sea and the wind at night, I found myself rereading *To the Lighthouse*, with an almost unbearable sharpness of response. After that, my life began to go on again.

I think those two poles of experience illustrate what anyone – child or adult, the pain is the same – may seek in books: obliteration or transcendence from the bottom of one's soul. I would have been enraged, insulted or baffled by anyone who had tried to press into my hands a trite little novel about overcoming the pain of loss of one's mother.

Art 'works' by tangents and imaginative leaps, and it is both arrogant and tactless to assume that we can supply machine-made books to heal a child's wounds. It is far more likely that the child well-supplied with good books that range widely in style and substance will find the needed consolation on his or her own, in the most unforeseeable ways, out of the richness and multiplicity of art.

The greater danger in junk books is the 'mind-stuffing' referred to by Paula Fox. A Canadian study a few years ago revealed that one of the prime sources of advice and moral guidance for teenagers is the television soap opera. Soap operas are a kind of open-ended story-telling, in familiar settings and with stereotyped roles, in which problems of family, sex, morality and relationships are taken seriously by all the characters. Talk is their main ingredient. Who has ever heard a male character on a police drama stop to discuss his emotional life in leisurely intimacy? Where in our society are adult men as openly, loquaciously, obsessed by gossip and love relationships as they are on the daily soaps? I can imagine that this openness is of absorbing interest to young people yearning to plumb the secrets of adult life. There may be more frank conversation on one episode of a soap opera than they would hear in a month of dinnertimes at home.

The shortcoming of this form of public continuous storytelling, as I need not stress, is that it is so shallow. It shares the penchant of prime-time dramas for glib transformations of character, swift and unequivocal justice, cheap moral certainties. Devotees of soap operas are often given to a watery version of Freudian insight; for each wayward or harmful action, there is an 'explanation' which excuses all.

Very well, but is there any harm in it? Can 'unearned certainties' gleaned from sociological teenage novels really hurt anyone? The answer is complex. There is lasting harm, certainly, if a young person becomes accustomed to lazy, self-indulgent reading and never learns what more may be gained from books. Literature, however, works at a different level from films and television, and, unlike graphic, violent pornography, it is rare for a book to stimulate imitative action. Because they appeal to the imaginative life, good books in particular may provide children with patterns of play – but usually children are well aware that this is the realm of fantasy. I may have sailed the South China Sea with Arthur Ransome's Missee Lee, but I knew better than to save my allowance to buy a junk.

Confusion arises when a book pretends to offer a mechanical representation of 'real life', implicitly justifying all the destructive impulses of childhood but raising no questions of moral perplexity. I apologize to my forbearing readers for returning once more to this particular bogeyperson, but I'm constrained to say that Judy Blume's *Blubber* is the one children's book I know of that, to my personal knowledge, has provoked many incidents of classroom viciousness. I think it is worth dwelling for a moment on the kind of writing that has this unfortunate potential.

Blubber has one main plot and one subplot; both deal with incidents of group spite against isolated individuals who are perceived as being different. Both victims are disagreeable in appearance: the grumpy neighbour has 'eyes that turn down at the corners', and the victimized classmate is fat. The heroine, Jill, participates in both campaigns and is justified, both in her own mind and in the tone of the story, in her actions.

The main plot shows the permanently aggrieved narrator, Jill, ganging up with the classroom leaders, Wendy and Caroline, to bully a girl named Linda Fischer. Her crimes are that she is fat, has a grey tooth, and 'lets people walk all over her'. In a mounting campaign of excited cruelty, the girls not only call her 'Blubber' but force her to say 'My name will always be Blubber'; they tease her for bringing cupcakes in her lunch, and taunt her all the more cruelly when she tries to go on a diet.

Jill participates willingly in all the most disturbing sequences: the girls accost Blubber in the girls' bathroom, rip the buttons off her blouse while threatening to strip her, force her to curtsy to 'Queen Wendy' and even to kneel and kiss Wendy's shoe. They hold her arms behind her back while lifting her skirt to expose her to the boys, and finally bully her into eating what she supposes to be a chocolate-covered ant. Linda vomits the chocolate all over her desk, but even then the girls are unrepentant and unpunished: the teacher and the headmaster are easily duped by Wendy's smooth lies, which manage to humiliate and turn the blame back on Linda for the whole expisode.

Though there is no introspection in Blume's books, we are meant to understand, from one brief dialogue, that Jill is bothered by the Blubber campaign – bothered not by the cruelty, but by Linda's acquiescence. She talks to her mother about a girl 'who lets other people walk all over her'. The best strategy, says mother, is to laugh off any teasing. Then people will respect you. Anyway, says Jill defiantly, 'I could never be in her place!'

Jill does become a victim, though. Predictably enough, Wendy turns on her, incites the class to call her names, isolates her and seeks to humiliate her. Jill fights back. She laughs off the jokes at first, then defies the bullies. At home, she weeps tears of self-pity. But her abasement is short-lived. She quickly makes friends with a new girl in school, and as we leave her at the end of the book, we see her wholehearted again, merrily joining in the group teasing of yet another victim on the school bus.

Contrast this story with *The Hundred Dresses* by Eleanor Estes, discussed earlier in this book. *The Hundred Dresses* also shows the prettiest and most popular girl in class bullying a girl who is different – Wanda Petronski with her ragged clothes and funny name. The main character, like Jill, is a sidekick to the leader of the girls. There is the same feverish impetus to the teasing: the children are caught up in the daring game of aggression against a victim who can't fight back. But there is a world of difference in the tone of the two books; Maddie, the heroine, is vividly observant. Through her eyes, we not only follow the classroom events, but share the delights of friendship, activity, the changing seasons and the excitements of holidays. Jill, Blume's modern heroine, is too neurotically self-obsessed to take such natural pleasure in life. She sees everything in her world through lemon-coloured glasses. Her voice is one of perpetual sour disgruntlement with everyone and everything; adults, except for a few idolized men, earn nothing but contempt; holidays, like Halloween, yield pleasure only in the opportunities they present to torment victims or win contests. Nothing is good and rewarding in itself.

From the beginning of the persecution of Wanda in *The Hundred Dresses*, the reader's pleasure is clouded by the tiny shadow of Maddie's uneasiness. Through her dialogue and actions, we see that she is torn: she furtively identifies with Wanda's poverty, yet is loyal to her friend Peggy, the ringleader, and afraid of her scorn.

Because Maddie's response is so much more complex than Jill's, it is more true to life; it draws the reader into the heart of the conflict. Even an adult reader is smitten by sheepish memories of the price paid for membership in the gang; Estes evokes this inward dismay with needle-sharp delicacy. In the end, even though victim Wanda is seen to be triumphing in a new school, though she has made a lovely gesture which would seem to pardon them all, though ringleader Peggy has leaped at the reconciliation without a pang, Maddie's relief – and ours – is tinged with sadness. Not even forgiveness and good resolutions can totally absolve you from the consciousness of the wrong you have done. This is infinitely more thought-provoking, rounded, vivid and touching than Blume's morally lobotomized Jill, and its effect is profoundly different too. The reader emerges from the book a changed person: she has not been *taught* about cruelty and guilt, but has experienced it, in bearable doses, through the flow of feelings of a child very like herself.

Blubber's amorality leaves the reader confused. I have known of three classrooms, and heard about others, where readers of *Blubber* have been so keyed up by the book's apparent acceptance of viciousness that they have actually instigated a 'Blubber' crusade against the nearest fat classmate. There is something more that is troubling. No child is free of vengefulness and spite, and a kind of blithe, wilful unconsciousness of the sufferings of others. But the torment of Blubber has sado-masochistic overtones that seem to go beyond the normal hit-and-run meanness of children. Would ten- and eleven-year-olds really revel in the systematic debasement of another? Would they think of making a classmate grovel publicly and kiss the feet of the tormentor?

My friend who thought that Blume was 'at least modern' was worried about sexist stereotypes in children's fiction. It seems to me that although Blume avoids overtly sexist remarks, her fixed loathing of physical ugliness, usually directed at females, is even more insinuatingly deprecating. Not all Blume's readers, after all, are as naturally skinny or pretty as her heroines always are. A bright-eyed, attractive but plump nine-year-old slapped down a copy of *Blubber* on her desk and said, choking with emotion, 'I can't see why anyone who isn't fat would even be interested in this nasty book, and a fat kid reading it would just feel terrible!'

Sexist and racist stereotypes are an immensely difficult question. My friend was right, in one way, to be wary of the literature of an earlier time; much of it is riddled with casual contempt for the feminine, and with offhand slurs on different racial groups. So, however, is some of the most modern writing for youth. It's no use simply dismissing anything that smacks of bias, because, provokingly enough, some of the best-written books carry traces of thoughtless stereotyping – and some of the worst-written stuff available is conscientiously liberated and free from every trace of prejudice against women, blacks, homosexuals, the aged, the disabled . . . the list goes on to include every worthy cause known to the aroused conscience. Some of this determinedly progressive fiction for youth has an eerily Victorian ring to it: didacticism clangs on every page like an iron bell, heavy, clumsy, reverberant with good intentions.

We can't always have it both ways. Art springs from the anarchic spirit of the artist, and, if we are lucky, if the artist is possessed of a humane and capacious spirit, the work of art will transcend pettiness and narrow prejudice. Worthy motives and a raised consciousness do not an artist make, and novels which are calculated to exalt our levels of tolerance rarely emerge as more than earnest tracts. All ulterior motives tend to undermine a work of art: C. S. Lewis's *Narnia* cycle, which he said he wrote to make children aware of 'the suffering of Christ', has been called forced and unconvincing by more than one critic.

By their sheer abundance of perception, the most gifted writers for children can endow both male and female characters with fully realized humanity. When Eleanor Estes wrote *The Hundred Dresses* in 1942, she certainly depicted boys and girls in the narrow gender roles of the time (the class art contest: boys draw motorboats and girls draw dresses), and yet this book is indispensable and humanly liberating. Both Edith Nesbit and Arthur Ransome cast some of their girls in anxiously mothering roles; both also created girls of spirit, daring, imagination and resource.

And what of the most rebelliously modern authors, those pioneers of new forms and subjects of fiction for youth? The works of Ivan Southall, Robert Westall and Robert Cormier all smack of misogyny. They have a single-mindedly male outlook in which girls are referred to by their breast size, sex appeal or relative sexual repulsiveness; Southall is at his worst in a recent book, *A City out of Sight*, in which he strives to depict a girl finding liberation from her sex-object style when she is stranded on a desert island. The strain shows: he reverts, time and again, to the crudest male dismissal of girls as either rapaciously boy-crazed, or dreaded potential wives who are homely, shrill nags.

Come to Mecca by Farrukh Dhondy was rightly praised for its startling energy; these short stories about Caribbean and Bengali youth in London's ghettos catch the jagged, vibrant rhythms of different speech patterns; the quick, colloquial prose perfectly embodies the underlying tensions of racism, baffled poverty and the painful, often humiliating, collision of cultures. But Dhondy's young men derive their fragile peacock pride from women-denigrating cultures. Their favourite taunt to another man is 'son of a sow', 'girl', or to imply that the other's sister is a whore. Dhondy's crabbed Cockneys are even more repellently chauvinist, with their constant talk about 'tits'. Because the stories are so sharply and honestly observed, we know that this really is the way these characters speak and think. Can we fault the author for recording reality? Perhaps we could accept this version of the male half of reality more easily if the other half were shown with the same vibrant immediacy. But there are only two central female characters in *Come to Mecca:* one is a tough, smart Jamaican girl with hard-bitten pride and theatrical ambitions. She ends as a humiliated topless dancer, and then as a cheap whore. In another story, about the Caribbean Carnival, we see fourteen-year-old Esther tentatively blossom into womanhood . . . but it's all sexual. She reveres and feels competitive with a beauty queen; she's stirred when JoJo, a Carnival costumer, flirts with her. On the great Carnival day itself, when she spreads her butterfly wings, the police spoil the atmosphere. At the end, timid Esther finds the courage to attack a policeman who is forcing JoJo to the ground.

The portrait of Esther is delicate and touching and has the same ring of truth as the evocations of young men in Dhondy's stories. Still, it's troubling that we see Esther's femininity solely in terms of her 'awakening' by an older man, and her consciousness of budding physical beauty. One wishes for the same inward complexity and struggle for self-definition that Dhondy accords his male subjects.

Robert Westall, a powerful writer with an urgent, compelling style, is even more disturbing, since his females are almost always portrayed with what feels like a compulsive undercurrent of contempt. *The Machine-Gunners* is an extraordinarily tough book about a group of boys in wartime England who steal a machine-gun from a downed Nazi plane and create their own foxhole on the edge of town. Their ingenious, stubborn physical effort; their mounting war hysteria; their unconscious parodying of fascist behaviour as they set up their own military unit; and their final, strange bonding with an escaped German flier whom they take prisoner and who becomes their ally against their own parents – all make for a gripping and brilliantly told story. Yet there is no denying that Chas, the fifteen-year-old central character, is a sexual bigot: girls, to him, are 'silly cows', 'bossy females'. He flies into a rage of disgust with a woman neighbour who comes into his family's air-raid shelter one night; he hates her because she sits with her knees apart. His own mother 'nags and whines'; Nicky's mother is hated for being upper crust and sleeping with sailors billeted in her mansion. She gets her just deserts in an air raid one concupiscent night, but all the boys see her promiscuity as having been unforgivably damaging to her son.

Audrey, the one girl who is allowed to join the group, automatically takes a submissive role as 'quartermaster' in the dugout and does the cooking and cleaning for the boys. Chas hates her voice and her 'bulging hockey muscles', and takes sadistic pleasure in reducing her to 'all eyes and a woman for once' by showing her a rotting corpse.

I assume that Westall meant us to see that this panicky revulsion against female sexuality is part of Chas's pathology. Nevertheless, I remember too well what it was like to read this constant male harping on female loathsomeness when I was a child. It hit me like a physical blow in the stomach; I fought it, but it deeply shook my sense of self. The authority of print carried great weight with me and I certainly internalized and accepted, however protestingly, however unhappily, the relentless stereotyping of girls as sweet, pretty, passive and inferior – and sly, bitchy, envious schemers too – at least until the age of twelve when I became a conscious feminist. Even female authors, and even contemporary ones – especially the British – frequently make casual reference to girls as barely tolerated inferiors to boys. 'She was all right for a girl' is a commonplace of children's fiction; worse is the accepted convention that normal, lovable boys in fiction will naturally prefer the company of other boys and will usually harbour real spite against girls.

Soup, by the American Robert Newton Peck, for example, is a high-spirited and perennially popular story of boyhood, written in 1974. The prose is crisp and vivid, the humour racy, unsentimental. It is, in other words, a superior book. Yet it is laced with vignettes depicting women as repressive, prudish, religion-prating authoritarians. Should we quietly remove this unpleasant distortion of reality from the shelves? What about the splendidly written, moving coming-of-age novel, *And Now Miguel* by Joseph Krumgold? One would want every boy to read this unusually vivid novel for intermediate readers, and yet there's no gainsaying the fact that the women in Miguel's family are little better than slaves – no doubt the reality of that time and place – and that Miguel exults once or twice too often in his superiority as a male.

The answer, I believe, is to make sure that we express our non-sexist and anti-racist values to children in every area of their lives, and to ensure that *both* boys and girls have a balanced exposure to books which feature both sexes in leading, admirable roles. In choosing books for children, we should select those works that offer a depth in characterization that will compensate for any lapses into gender bias. There is no reason to endorse (though we can't prevent) the reading of teenage romances, such as the *Sweet Dreams* series, or detective thrillers, which deliberately trade in extremes of gender stereotypes: tough macho heroes and love-sodden girls. Well-read youngsters, who are sensitive in their family lives to questions of fairness and equality, will soon be alerted to biases in books, and perhaps there is something salutary in having to come to grips with recognizable prejudice in the writings of those who give us pleasure. It is a dilemma our young people will face often enough in the course of their lives.

I'll return to this theme of books for girls and boys after a look at another frequent problem in children's literature: racial prejudice. As an Anglophile Jew who grew up ardently reading English literature, I am an expert in the subject. It would be hard to name an English writer for adults – from Shakespeare to Agatha Christie, Dickens to Chesterton – who did not include anti-Semitic stereotypes as part of the writer's stock-in-trade.

I can't say that it wasn't wounding. Nevertheless, the mere presence of anti-Semitism could not spoil an otherwise good book for me. As I've noted elsewhere, E. Nesbit's *The Story of the Amulet* moved me profoundly by its vision of a utopian society. I chose to ignore, sturdily, the fact that the same book has three extraneous, jarring caricatures of a grossly anti-Semitic nature. I was able to preserve my mood of rapt enchantment, however, because *I knew she was wrong* – we just weren't like that. Note that I was far more vulnerable to slurs against girls because I was growing up in a society which reinforced my inferior position at every turn. This leads me to wonder if a girl today, growing up in just the kind of enlightened family that would bridle at sexism in books, would be nearly as afflicted by these stereotypes as I was. Perhaps she would be proof against them as I was against anti-Semitism.

What about other, less sensitized children? What about boys and girls of Anglo-Saxon background reading, for example, Enid Blyton, whose hundreds of books still maintain their worldwide popularity? I chose a few of her books to read, at random, because I had never read her as a child (my library, I'm glad to say, didn't carry them) and I felt I should know why she is loathed by every intelligent critic in the world and adored by so many children.

The adoration was instantly explained: these are hilariously awful books, exactly parallel to lurid adult thrillers of the Mickey Spillane type. It's pop literature at its most page-turning, breathless, utterly predictable extreme. *The Circus of Adventure*, for example, stars four British children, Jack and Lucy-Ann and their friends Philip and Dinah, all of whom live with Philip and Dinah's mother, Mrs Mannering, who is married to secret service agent Bill Cunningham. One summer this unlikely family must play host to a mysterious eleven-year-old foreign boy, Gussie. The British children are uproariously bloody-minded, aided and abetted by their mother: they are disgusted by timid little Gussie's polite manners, the way he helps carry the bags for Mrs Mannering, and by his 'greasy' black curls and silk pyjamas. They tease, harass and brutalize him, in the most unfair and cruel ways, and all with the blithe approval of the adults: 'I think you can quite safely make young Gustavus toe the line. That won't do him any harm at all,' Mrs Mannering says smugly. 'He seems like quite a spoilt little cry-baby to me.' This, after they have abused him till he, a homeless fugitive, is ready to weep.

British fair play is stunningly absent from these various torments: they trick him, terrify him and then laugh riotously when he is upset. Poor Gussie never learns how he has been duped, but is always slavishly admiring of these true British boys. Only when it turns out that Gussie is the crown prince of Tauri-Hessia do the children complacently change their minds: when Gussie welcomes them as his royal guests to his royal palace at home, 'it seems quite all right somehow' that he should bow to them and kiss their hands.

The anti-foreign bias is staggering (not to mention the homophobia: the worst thing about Gussie's curls is that they make him look like a girl. 'We have enough poofters here,' says bully-boy Jack). Gussie is made to speak in a grotesque parody of immigrant English and the police in Tauri-Hessia are spluttering idiots who wear 'comic flower-pot hats'. Indeed, all the Tauri-Hessians are either greasy villains or greasy fools, and it is up to the invincible, energetic, resourceful, clever, manly Brits to save the whole country. At last, when order is restored, and the British-educated King is on the throne, all look forward to Gussie's eventual rule. 'Gussie was just a silly little boy at present – but perhaps, when he had learnt all that the British people had to teach him, at lessons and at games, he would be as fine a King as his uncle,' Blyton writes.

Needless to say, the gender-stereotyping and the scorn for anything girlish is as extreme as the xenophobia. But children read these books as they read comics, for the sheer preposterous adventure, the physical action, the glorious deeds done by the children themselves, the trying on, in fantasy, of various roles, which may actually be facilitated by the crude exaggeration of the characters.

Blyton books are 'bulk reading'; they would not likely satisfy a sophisticated reader, any more than *Nancy Drew* would, but they may provide a moment of relaxing escapism even for those who are accustomed to better fare. If parents are aware of the far-fetched chauvinism (of both male and British varieties), they can perhaps defuse their silliness by straightforwardly discussing the issues of literary stereotypes with their children. But it would be a phlegmatic parent indeed who would willingly *buy* these books for children, knowing what's in them. If children beg for them, however, there is not much sense in an outright ban. In that situation, I would consider the Blyton (or whatever) as just one rung on what has been called 'the reading ladder'; buy the Blyton if you must, but sandwich it between two or three more highly recommended books with strong reader appeal.

A far more contentious issue arises when books that are deemed racist turn up in school libraries and in school curricula. I loved *Little Black Sambo* when I was a child; that African family seemed as wonderfully warm, endearing and admirable to me as the family of Peter Rabbit. I can still see, in my mind's eye, that delicious moment when the tigers melted into butter; I can still see the enviably radiant colours of Little Black Sambo's clothes. Nevertheless, we have the word of black children that the book can lead to humiliation for them; that when it is read aloud in school, they are singled out on the playground and called 'Sambo' – not affectionately. No sensitive teacher would insist on reading this book in a class with black children present unless she had some malicious motive. There are too many wonderful alternatives – think of Ezra Jack Keats's *The Snowy Day* or *Why Mosquitoes Buzz in People's Ears* by Verna Aardema – which have the same warmth, but implicitly affirm the dignity of black people and do not inadvertently abet the playground bullies.

That's true, also, of *Huckleberry Finn;* of course it is a classic, a great and wonderful book, and it grieves me to think that many black parents think it is racist when it is, in fact, the opposite. Nevertheless, why would a school insist on using it as a text in the early years of secondary school in big city schools heavily populated with blacks who protest against its use? With so much to choose from, why be rigid about using the one book that hurts and humiliates these vulnerable youngsters who are struggling for a sense of their own worth in an alien school system?

We can never have a sterilized literature, free from all offensive racist and sexist references, but we can use common sense in choosing which books to put on school curricula, and which to reserve for the privacy of home, where parents can counteract any mistaken impressions.

Books are powerful; even illiterates acknowledge the power of the printed word when they demand the banning of fine novels. Their power is not the same as the direct impact of visual images, however, and they work in strange and oblique ways: I cite my own experience with Nesbit to show how unforeseen their influence can be. We cannot predict and control the ways in which books will affect our children. Art bursts free of our grasp or it is not art, and those who seek to censor their child's reading will either fail, or deprive their child of the riches of literature altogether, by poisoning the intellectual freedom without which reading is a stifling mechanical chore.

Even the most enlightened, progressive parents can fall into the trap of thinking of children's books as just another dose of moral cod-liver oil. There may even be a danger that some dedicated parents would consider each book another investment in the careful grooming of their little achiever. Undoubtedly, they would make sure to avoid stories tainted with sexism. I have noticed, though, that some feminist mothers are more scrupulously liberated about daughters than sons. Mothers are still wary about that tender male ego and the possible damage it may suffer from too much dishwashing or doll playing. Perhaps they are made nervous, too, by the chorus of masculine voices insisting on the basic male need for aggressive play, sports fanaticism and male bonding. How can we women really know if these traits are inherent in boys, or just the product of conditioning?

I've been particularly perplexed, in writing this book, about the fictional portrayal of boys in modern novels. As a feminist, I am repelled by the crudely aggressive heroes of Cormier, Major, Westall and Southall. It is true that we are long past the age of idealism; Nesbit's boys could try to model themselves on highly principled men of action, but that conscious nobility would seem idiotic in the post-Hitler, post-Vietnam world. It is also true that novels about alienated youth win an automatic response from literate teenage males; a certain veneer of tough cynicism, a determined anti-sentimentality, is the uniform of the modern hero. That leaves me with a gnawing self-doubt; could my criticism of these novels be unduly influenced by my female bias?

My conclusion, after much soul searching, is that a critic is entitled to demand more of a novel than a one-dimensional portrait of masculinity. Literature, from its beginning, is filled with virile heroes who nevertheless have space in their lives for more than aggression or sex obsession. Only the most emotionally limited teenage boy is as callously contemptuous of girls and as single-mindedly bent on macho aggression as the heroes of some of the teenage novels I've discussed. This stereotype, in other words, is as unfair to boys as its opposite is to girls.

Browsing in a book shop one day, I met a woman who complained bitterly to me that 'there are no books for boys'. She insisted that even in Toronto's Children's Book Store, the largest such store in the world, 'all the books' had girls on the cover and 'boys just won't read a book with a girl on the cover'. Her own husband, she told me proudly, had solved the problem by encouraging their son to read the hockey scores in the newspaper every night.

Anyone who haunts an excellent book shop looking for good fiction for herself, but assumes that a child's reading is so mechanical a business that the hockey scores will do as well as a novel, has just not taken children seriously. Nor has she tried to resist making a ghetto of her son's mind;

she seems to concur with the perverse idea that boys should not be forced to read about anything but boys.

The opposite is true. I wish that woman had read *We've All Got Scars*, by Raphaela Best, a stunning exposé of the kind of macho conditioning which ordinary primary-school boys enforce upon each other. Best stayed with a class of children for five years, minutely recording their daily interactions. By the age of seven or eight, the boys had established a clear-cut in-group. To belong, a boy had to be willing to fight – physically and painfully; had to defy female authority; refuse to be seen obeying mother's orders; avoid the company of girls at all costs; insist, in the face of all evidence to the contrary, that boys were physically and mentally superior to girls. It's a hideous picture of boyhood, violent, brutish, narrow, egotistical and frighteningly lonely. In their constant jockeying among themselves for supremacy ('Me first! I'm boss!' was their constant cry), these boys missed out on affection, curiosity, co-operation and many special moments in the classroom which the girls, more relaxed, were able to share and enjoy to the full.

Nothing – not argument, persuasion, example or the teacher's interference – affected the boys' image of themselves as two-fisted warriors or shook their rigid power hierarchy. Already, at the age of seven, the boys refused to help clean blackboards or wash paintbrushes; they denied that they would ever do housework, insisting that their wives would do all that dumb stuff. They would rather die of starvation, they said, than cook for themselves. They were adamant that girls could never be strong enough to be police officers. Confronted with evidence of real live female police, they nevertheless refused to change their fixated ideas.

Not only were these stereotypes repugnant in themselves, but they were, Best revealed, devastating to the boys who were not accepted into the macho in-group. One of her most surprising findings was that school achievement for boys in this school (a typical middle-class suburban school in the eastern United States) was linked chiefly to membership in the macho group. Boys who were excluded were so crushed that they simply lost heart; they had no will to learn, gave up ambition, and fell behind irrevocably.

What Best discovered was that the friendship of girls finally broke down some of the boys' defences and allowed them to be less aggressive, more co-operative and open to all kinds of experience. It did not happen automatically. Best intervened, when the boys were ten years old, to set up a co-educational discussion group. For the first time, the fanatical, self-imposed sex segregation of the classroom was breached. The girls began to blossom into independence and less feminine-stereotyped ambitions, and the boys became more human.

When I investigated the local situation for a radio series based on Best's book, I found that the same conditions, the same ferocious taboos and rigidities, were duplicated in most classrooms. I checked with teachers at homogeneous middle-class schools in affluent neighbourhoods, at inner-city schools, suburban schools with many immigrant children. All confirmed, to a greater or lesser extent, Best's observations. Only one teacher, at a very mixed inner-city school, saw a different pattern: many of her students had attended a progressive, kindly day-care centre together from the age of two or three. These children were able to be friends across the gender barrier, and had far fewer stereotypes and prejudices about each other. The boys were able to be openly affectionate, to play with girls, and to enjoy books and stories that did not always focus on male activities.

It seems to me that books can play an important role in the humanizing of little boys. Publishing insiders, teachers and writers have always asserted that boys will read only about boys, but that girls will read anything. Researching this book, racking my memories, quizzing my daughters, I unearthed a slightly different truth: girls do read more widely than boys, but their deepest allegiance, their fondest memories, are always of books about girls in a vigorous, independent central role.

It seems natural to both genders to want an affirmation of their own possibilities in their books. Girls have been better served in this than boys; though modern 'realistic' novelists, paradoxically, have propagated an image of girls as narcissistic, shallow and manipulative, the predominating tone of earlier popular books has often been a liberating one, all the way back to the first half of *Little Women*. Not only are girls depicted in active roles, but boys are welcome participants in the action, warmly and acceptingly portrayed. I don't think I've ever read a girls' book that indulges in the heartless deprecation of the opposite sex that seems so routine in boys' books, even those written by women.

Could it be that the indoctrination of boys, through their literature as well as through films, popular music, television and schools which put such a heavy emphasis on sports, has continued unabated right through the sexual revolution? Having examined my own conscience, I've concluded that most of those books are wrong: the boys I've known are as interested and involved in family relationships, friendships, nature, cooking, music or canoeing, as they are in their admittedly overpowering fascination with sex. They brood, they worry about nuclear war, they plan for the future, they have serious questions about the meaning of life. If we accept the narrow portrait of boys as hardened sexual exploiters that is offered in so many novels, we are acquiescing in that battle-scarred and joyless male ghetto mentality so shockingly recorded by Best.

It would certainly be futile as well as pointless to try to prevent boys from reading boys' books, but it is well within the realm of possibility to search out and provide for young boys of primary-school age a wide range of stories, involving girls as well as boys, that will be just as satisfying to them as the hockey scores.

Books that celebrate the range of life's possibilities, books that acknowledge and delight in the variety of human experience, books that by their virtuosity of language make the reader share in that curiosity and excitement – these are the books that enhance children's lives, that give them food for thought, pique their imaginations and sensibilities, and arouse their sense of wonder.

The adult who takes the time to learn something of children's books, and to pass them on with enthusiasm and care, gives something precious to the child – and gives something priceless to the world: a child deep rooted in language and story, a child with an educated heart.

A TREASURY OF RECOMMENDED READING

A TREASURY

A WORD OF EXPLANATION is in order about the use of this book guide. For the reader's convenience, I've divided the books into age categories, but these are very rough guidelines. A six-year-old may enjoy reading something from the Beginning Readers list, for example, but may listen with equal pleasure and comprehension to a book from the Middle Readers category if it is read aloud. Your understanding of the child's reading skills and emotional level is the best guide of all.

The books listed under Young Fluent Readers (a handy title which I have borrowed from Taylor and Braithwaite's *Good Book Guide*) are appropriate both for talented youngsters reading ahead of themselves, and for older readers of eight or nine who are just honing their reading skills, but who need interesting content along with simplicity and brevity.

Please note that many books in the Middle Readers are challenging both in content and style. They can certainly be relished by youngsters as old as twelve or thirteen. There is a conscious overlap between Middle, Preteenage and Teenage books; the latter two categories have more to do with emotional than reading or age levels and generally have been chosen as apt for the special social and moral concerns of those going through puberty. Many, though not all, of the Teenage books, for example, focus on male-female relationships and are sexually explicit.

In some cases, a book is suited for a narrower age range than others in that section, and this is noted in brackets (e. g. 4–6). Many of the titles are available as both hardback and paperback although some can be found only in one edition or the other. Some books are part of a series. Occasionally books may be listed as out of print although this is not the final word. Many out-of-print works can be found in libraries or secondhand book shops, or may suddenly become available again. Keep looking.

Most of the authors are represented here by only one or two of their works. If you enjoy one book, search out the others by that author; you are bound to make some wonderful discoveries.

THE WORLD OF CHILDREN'S BOOKS

Beginning Readers: Ages 4 to 8

These picture books and stories are chosen for their special qualities of stimulating and helping children to want to learn to read.

Alexander and the Terrible, Horrible, No Good, Very Bad Day, by Judith Viorst. A perennial favourite because of the hip-urban tone in which Alexander tells of his all-too-familiar middle-class aggravations on a day in which he trips on his skateboard, the shop is all out of snazzy sneakers, and there's kissing on television. (5–8)

Alfie Gets in First by Shirley Hughes. A deserved classic, this drama of a small crisis in a preschooler's life has wonderfully warm and naturalistic drawings of neighbourhood life, suspense, affection, humorous observation of emotional and physical expression, and a small child's triumphant overcoming. *Alfie's Feet* and *Alfie Lends a Hand* are equally good.

Anno's Journey by Mitsumasa Anno. An adventure in close reading of a richly detailed 'text' without words. A man travels across a Europe peopled by famous fairy-tale, contemporary, artistic and musical characters; the reader can follow a dozen interwoven wordless narratives as well as spotting familiar references.

Applebet, An ABC by Clyde Watson. A rollicking, affectionate alphabet that tells a story of a little girl's day at a country fair, in lilting rhyme and richly sensuous language. Appropriately glowing pictures by Wendy Watson. (4–6)

Are You My Mother? by P. D. Eastman. A classic of separation anxiety and its soothing resolution, as a cartoony little bird tries to find his mother. Very simple, repetitive text. (4–6)

Arthur's Prize Reader by Lillian Hoban. Not just one of the excellent *I-Can-Read* series for beginners, but one of the very few stories in which reading is depicted in the plot as a natural and interesting part of children's lives. (5–7)

The Baron's Booty by Virginia Kahl. A deliciously absurd reworking of the old rueful-kidnapper story; this time it's a Baron who kidnaps thirteen boisterous little girls. Told in irresistible, linguistically rewarding rhyme, with sprightly drawings.

Ben's Trumpet by Rachel Isadora. A little black city boy yearns for a trumpet so he can play like the jazz musicians at the Zig Zag Club. Music practically sizzles out of the elegant, black and white art deco illustrations. (6–8)

Bimwili and the Zimwi by Verna Aardema, illustrated by Susan Meddaugh. Another lovely African tale by an accomplished writer. Bimwili, the youngest of three sisters, is captured by a wicked Zimwi who keeps her in his giant drum and makes her sing when he performs. At last Bimwili outwits her magical captor and is reunited with her loving family. Glowing pictures accompany the vivid, often onomatopoeic narrative. (5–6)

Bonnie McSmithers You're Driving Me Dithers by Sue Ann Alderson. Appealing red, inky black and creamy white book, with a catchy refrain, about a rambunctious girl and her distracted, exasperated mother . . . who later repents.

Brave Irene by William Steig. Irene struggles through the snowstorm to deliver the dress her seamstress mother has made for the duchess. This is a recent work of Steig's, his only one with an active heroine, and among his most radiant and tender. He captures Irene's predicament – her courage, her uncertainty, her loneliness and loyalty – with his usual uncanny emotional precision, lending satisfying depth to a simple tale of overcoming.

Bread and Jam for Frances by Russell Hoban, with pencil drawings by Lilian Hoban. Witty verses enliven the sympathetic story about a little girl badger who will eat only bread and jam . . . until her family finds a clever solution.

Brenda and Edward by Maryann Kovalski. Two happily married dogs who live in a cosy crate behind a French restaurant are parted by an accident, only to reunite years later in their old age. A small, offbeat story with appealing illustrations.

The Bunyip of Berkeley's Creek by Jenny Wagner. Huge, homely and engagingly vulnerable, the bunyip searches for his identity and finds the true answer in love. Wonderful rich and humorous drawings by Ron Brooks.

Cannonball Simp by John Burningham. A homely, forlorn little dog survives abandonment and danger to find a warmly lit, thrilling new home in the circus. A tale of courage and survival by a gifted artist whose pictures are a marvel of subtle colour and suggestion.

Cat on the Mat by Brian Wildsmith. The artist turns this elemental 'cat on the mat' text into a charming visual joke with his usual deep, tantalizing colours. (4–5)

CDB! by William Steig, a piquant word game for those who are firmly in control of the alphabet. (7–8)

Cherries and Cherry Pits by Vera B. Williams. Bidemmi, a little black girl, visits the artist and draws these enchanting stories-within-a-story. Her impromptu fantasies achieve a remarkable blend of nature and urban life: cherries sprout everywhere! The watercolour and felt-marker illustrations, as juicily colour-drenched as the cherries themselves, ought to inspire a host of young artists in word and colour.

Chin Chiang and the Dragon's Dance by Ian Wallace. Brilliant and delicate paintings of Vancouver's Chinatown add to the realism of this story about a shy boy's nervousness at participating in the Dragon Dance, and the unexpected encouragement he gets from an old woman.

Clams Can't Sing by James Stevenson. Lots of funny sound effects in this encouraging story about two derided clams, Benny and Beatrice, who prove that they can participate (clap, fooosh, oosh, ba-loop) in the beach concert. (4–6)

Come Away from the Water, Shirley by John Burningham. While Shirley's parents absent-mindedly nag at her from their beach chairs, Shirley's full-colour piratical daydreams are dramatically but wordlessly illustrated on the facing pages. A delightful exercise in reading between the lines. (5–7)

Corduroy by Don Freeman. A much-loved, optimistic and tender picture book about how a little black girl and a department-store teddy bear find each other.

Could Be Worse by James Stevenson. A deadpan tall tale, told by a sleepily imperturbable grandpa. Sparkles with the wry, laconic wit and laugh-out-loud visual humour of an accomplished New Yorker cartoonist. Despite his sophisticated style, Stevenson's books have a warm undercurrent of sympathetic acknowledgement of childhood emotions.

Curious George by H. A. Rey. Children never tire (though adults do) of the antics of this harum-scarum monkey. Simple prose and fresh, lively illustrations.

Dionysos and the Pirates by Penelope Proddow. Barbara Cooney's translucently lovely paintings, with the authentic light and colours of Mediterranean Greece, are the backdrop for the equally fascinating translations of Homeric hymns. A lyrical and dramatic retelling of Greek myths. (6–8)

Do Not Open by Brinton Turkle. Intrepid old Miss Moody, a beachcomber, and her cat, Captain Kidd, find a terrifying genie in a bottle. Superbly told story, full of surprises, sly humour, quiet courage. Outstanding illustrations. (6–8)

Don't You Remember? by Lucille Clifton. An appealing story about a little black girl in a working-class family. Desire Mary Tate is afraid that her busy family is going to forget her birthday cake. Told with verve and sensitivity, and strongly illustrated by Evaline Ness.

Duffy and the Devil by Harve and Margot Zemach. Duffy, a feckless Cornish girl, makes a Rapunzel-type pact with the devil. With the help of witchy old Jone, she wins in the end. Exuberant, dazzling language, Zemach's most appealing pudgy dogs and gnarled faces, and a robustly life-affirming story.

Each Peach Pear Plum by Janet and Allan Ahlberg. Familiar nursery characters are slyly hidden in each sunny pastel picture, with a rhyming couplet on every page. Quickly becoming a classic of 'lap books'. (4–6)

Ellen's Lion by Crockett Johnson. These twelve tender but unsentimental stories about Ellen's imaginary dialogues with her fond, grumpy stuffed lion sensitively illustrate the quality of play which is superior to mechanical amusements. (6–8)

Everyone Knows What a Dragon Looks Like by Jay Williams. A small boy (like the one who saw that the Emperor had no clothes) saves his mountain village from destruction by the Wild Horsemen while the pompous elders panic. Surprise ending and gorgeously Chinese illustrations by Mercer Mayer.

The First Books by M. B. Goffstein. A collection of artfully simple tiny stories, with astonishingly laconic and expressive small line drawings. The exceptional spareness and evocativeness of the first five stories ('Brookie and Her Lamb', 'A Little Squirrel Went Walking', 'Across the Sea', 'The Gats!' and 'Sleepy People') make them perfect for beginners. (5–8)

The 500 Hats of Bartholomew Cubbins by Dr Seuss. An offbeat masterpiece. An imperious king is taught a sharp lesson by a polite small boy whose shabby hat assumes a mysterious multiplicatory life of its own. Other deservedly loved Dr Seuss classics for beginning readers are *Fox in Socks* and *Green Eggs and Ham*. (6–8)

Five Minutes' Peace, by Jill Murphy. 'The children were having breakfast. This was not a pleasant sight.' So Mrs Large (an elephant) retreats to the bathtub for five minutes' peace. Her three youngsters enthusiastically invade her privacy, each using different wiles. The sardonic humour will appeal to harassed parents, while the adorably expressive pastel pictures and tone of amused resignation will delight and reassure the young.

The Fool of the World and the Flying Ship by Arthur Ransome. A classic Russian folk tale about the foolish younger son who triumphs against the odds. An ample, lively retelling by Ransome and richly illustrated by Uri Shulevitz. (6–8)

Fred by Posy Simmonds. An affectionately humorous story in a highly effective melding of comic-strip and picture-book formats. When Sophie and Nick's lazy cat dies, they learn that he has been leading a secret outdoor life as a feline rock star, and attend his hilarious funeral rites conducted by the neighbourhood cats. The picture panels, stretching out to straddle the pages, expanding to full page sizes or shrinking to quick, successive action sketches, are a triumph of wit and visual expressiveness. The story, too, brings insight, humour and solace to a common domestic crisis.

The Funny Little Woman by Arlene Mosel. A Japanese tale about a little old woman who pursues a roll-away dumpling into the land of demons, and outwits her captors. The many-layered drawings by Blair Lent are a tantalizing addition to an enduringly fine story.

George and Martha by James Marshall. Five simple but funny and pertinent stories about the friendship of two endearingly childlike hippos. Marshall has a gimlet eye for the small conflicts that lead to wounded feelings between friends, and for the affectionate honesty that can heal the hurt. The drawings amplify the plot with broad comic details. (4–7)

Ghost's Hour, Spook's Hour by Eve Bunting. On a scary autumn night, a small boy wakes to find that the lights won't go on and his parents are missing from their bed. Carrick's atmospheric paintings beautifully evoke both night fears and the reassurance of parental comfort at the end, as the boy tiptoes through the house with his dog. Of all the 'scared at night/ monsters under the bed' books, this is my favourite because it so gently acknowledges the fear without belittling it, lightens its depiction by the humorous projection of anxiety onto shaggy dog Biff, and communicates a glow of safety and love both verbally and visually.

Go, Dog, Go by P. D. Eastman. Basic vocabulary, but riotously funny with energetic cartoon-like illustrations and a captivatingly nonsensical series of events. Perfect for learning to read. (4–7)

Goggles! by Ezra Jack Keats. A sympathetic and realistic story of two little boys who outwit some bullies, enhanced by Keats's impressionistic collages and his characteristic intuitive feel for children's vulnerability and resilience. (5–7) Of course, no child should miss Keats's other immortal picture-books, *Whistle for Willy* and *A Snowy Day*.

Gorilla by Anthony Browne. A sophisticated and allusive work of art. Hannah loves gorillas but her father is always too busy to take her to the zoo. The night before her birthday, Hannah's new gorilla doll suddenly grows into the immense real thing. The superb artwork perfectly captures the child's-eye view of the gorilla's disturbing size and power and gentle, mesmerizing eyes. The gorilla dresses in father's coat and hat and takes Hannah on a midnight expedition to the zoo, a restaurant and a moonlit dance on the lawn. The eerily beautiful (and sometimes faintly sinister) pictures fuse unconscious wishes, images and emotions with a simple and satisfying storyline. (5+)

Grandma Goes Shopping by Ronda and David Armitage. While a parent reads aloud Grandma's gorgeously nonsensical cumulative shopping list ('an amiable alligator, a variegated vicuna'), the child will be able to 'read' the virtually inexhaustible details in these bright, bumptious illustrations. As Grandma pedals her bike along, a little mouse keeps popping up to tantalize the alligator, nursery-rhyme characters appear inscrutably in the landscape, the zoo has a lion and a unicorn and children playing on the monkey bars . . . surrealistic tricks and teases to reward numerous rereadings.

Harquin, the Fox Who Went Down to the Valley by John Burningham. Harquin is too daring, and brings his family into danger . . . but, after a cinematically thrilling chase scene, leads them out again. Burningham at his most vibrant.

Harry the Dirty Dog by Gene Zion. Harry is alarmed when his owners don't recognize him under a layer of dirt, but all comes right in the wash. A deceptively simple, reassuring and much loved story about identity. (4–6)

Herman the Helper by Robert Kraus. Irrepressibly perky Herman the octopus finds more than eight ways of helping. Humanely supportive of a child's need to feel useful, without preachiness. Lively, colourful and humorously detailed pictures by Jose Aruego and Ariane Dewey. (4–6)

Hey, Al by Arthur Yorinks, illustrated with witty panache by Richard Egielski. Al is a New York janitor. When he and his dog Eddie are transported to a faintly eerie bird-inhabited paradise, they learn that 'ripe fruit soon spoils' and there's something rotten about this avian nirvana. Sharp young readers will spot, in the picture of the dodo, an early clue to the goings-on. The acclaimed wit and modern edge of this award-winning duo are anchored by strong and humane feeling.

THE WORLD OF CHILDREN'S BOOKS

Hey Diddle Diddle illustrated by Randolph Caldecott. A reissue of the first, never surpassed, children's illustrator. Caldecott's endlessly inventive interpretations of familiar nursery rhymes are a delightful education for the eye.

The House on East 88th Street by Bernard Waber. 'Every home should have a crocodile,' conclude the Primms, who moved home to find lovable Lyle in the bathtub. Wryly uproarious, with enchantingly witty drawings by the author.

How Tom Beat Captain Najork and His Hired Sportsmen by Russell Hoban. The glorious victory of Tom, that fidgety, fool-around boy, over the smarmy 'sportsmen' sicked on him by his grim Aunt Fidget Wonkham-Strong. Wickedly funny language, hilarious pictures by Quentin Blake, and balm for the soul of every child who's been scolded for idleness. (5–8)

I'm Not Frightened of Ghosts by Juliet and Charles Snape. Lizzie boldly accepts a dare to explore a haunted house; full-page illustrations show how a frustrated little ghost tries to frighten her, while Lizzie calmly finds a practical explanation – a mouse, a breeze, a trapped bird – for every scary rattle and rustle. The pictures neatly sustain the ambiguity, showing both the ghost and the fluttering bird, for example, while the minimal, deadpan text sticks to the matter-of-fact. (5+)

The Island of the Skog by Steven Kellogg. A band of mice cast away on an island find that the mysterious monster Skog is a timorous, rumpled little animal who was afraid of them. Boisterous humour, intricate drawings and a gentle message.

It's Your Turn, Roger! by Susanna Gretz. Bright, crisp colours, surprises in layout and dialogue. Balloons add reading stimulus to this hilarious story of Roger the pig, who doesn't want to take his turn setting the table for supper. Roger sulkily stomps off to see what the rules are in the other flats in his building. Each visit affords satisfying repetition and cumulative humour, until Roger decides home is best. The tough-minded will relish the 'gross' touches, like Roger's favourite dessert, all too realistically illustrated: worm pie.

Johnny Crow's Garden by L. Leslie Brooke. A Victorian classic, still fresh, crammed with fascinating details in superb pen-and-ink drawings of Johnny Crow, who is the amiable host of an animal garden party that sometimes threatens to get out of control. With brisk and engagingly odd rhyming couplets that stick in the mind.

The Judge by Harve Zemach. A cumulative story with bubbling language, in rhyme and breathless rhythms, about an imperious judge who gets his comeuppance in a marvellous visual surprise. Margot Zemach's sketchy pastel drawings are as swift, comic and rich in observation as ever.

Katie Morag Delivers the Mail by Mairi Hedderwick. Katie Morag makes a muddle of delivering five parcels on the little Isle of Spruay, but her sturdy, overalled Grandma helps her sort out the mix-up by herself, and gives her a ride home on the tractor. Lively, double-spread watercolour illustrations are filled with the fresh and homey detail of island life, adding charm, interest, and lots of incidental print (signs, boat names, labels) to a delightful story of self-reliance.

Lily Takes a Walk by Satoshi Kitamura. Lily blithely saunters through field and town, while her goggle-eyed dog, Nicky, defies the monsters which he imagines lurking everywhere. A neat displacement of ordinary childhood fears, and a comical invitation to the lap-sitter to spot all the action that isn't mentioned in the text.

Little Bear by Else Holmelund Minarik. The first and among the best of all the excellent I-Can-Read books, these affectionate, insightful stories of a small bear, his family and animal friends are illustrated by Sendak at his most tenderly expressive. The economical but richly evocative text is an artistic triumph. (4–7)

Madeline by Ludwig Bemelmans. Urbane and delightful drawings of Paris and an irresistible rhymed story about the youngest (and naughtiest) little girl in the orphanage. (6–8)

Mama Don't Allow by Thatcher Hurd. An absolutely unmissable picture book, alive with rhythmic language and glowing with the richest greens, blues, reds and purples that the Mississippi swampland ever saw. Miles Possum gets a saxophone for his birthday, but mama and papa object to all the noise. So down he goes to the river with the Swamp Band, where a wild party lights up the riverboat and alligators come from miles around to hear Miles and the boys play 'Mama Don't Allow No Music Playin' Round Here'. But the alligators have some nasty plans for dinner, so Miles and the boys put them to sleep with a swampland lullaby and tiptoe back home, playing so softly that Mama says, 'Oh, how nice'. The liberating humour, the energy, the swing of it all are a delight. Lots of reading fun for beginners in the amusing dialogue balloons and uproarious illustrations.

Mary Alice, Operator Number Nine by Jeffrey Allen. A seemingly simple story about a duck who stays off sick and turns out to be irreplaceable. Reassuring and hilarious, with drawings by James Marshall.

Meg and Mog by Helen Nicol. Meg is an amiable witch whose amusing spells . . . frog in a bog, bat in a hat . . . make reading practice fun. Jan

Pienkowski's black stick-figures on vibrant coloured backgrounds add to the allure. (4–6)

Millions of Cats by Wanda Gag. Hundreds of cats, thousands of cats, millions and billions and trillions of cats, in Gag's unforgettable bold black and white woodcuts and equally memorable rhythmic text.

Mister Rabbit and the Lovely Present by Charlotte Zolotow. A rabbit helps a little girl find a lovely present of fruit in every colour for her mother's birthday. Dreamy, luminous illustrations by Maurice Sendak. (4–6)

Moonlight by Jan Ormerod. A remarkable, beautiful, wordless picture book tells a subtle and perceptive story of a little girl's bedtime rituals in a warm family setting. These pictures may well spark a thousand words. By the same author, about the same child, *Sunshine*.

The Most Amazing Hide-and-Seek Alphabet Book by Robert Crowther. Every big, black lower-case letter hides a pop-up matching animal. Unsurpassed for wit and inventiveness. (4–6)

The Napping House by Audrey Wood. A rainy day, and everyone's napping ... granny, boy, dog and cat. Alert lap-sitters will spot a hidden mouse and a flea, who will create uproarious chaos in this cumulative rhyming story. Gentle, light-drenched illustrations by Don Wood create a magical atmosphere, moving from drowsy cosiness to wide-awake energy.

Noisy Nora by Rosemary Wells. Nora is the neglected middle child who feels left out as father plays chess with big sister and mother fusses over baby brother. Her revenge: noise, and lots of it. An amusing, small-sized book, with the simple story told in fluid and appealing rhyme.

One Monday Morning by Uri Shulevitz. A comic juxtaposition of urban reality and make-believe, with a spare, cumulative text. Gorgeously arrayed playing-card royalty come to visit a daydreaming boy. (5–7)

Our Snowman by M. B. Goffstein. The soft, evocative pastel illustrations are a triumphant new departure for Goffstein. In an understated but richly nuanced story of family life, a brother and sister celebrate the first snowfall by building a snowman. The deceptively simple plot has true fictional impact: every image and every sentence resonates with sensory perception and emotional insight.

Papagayo, The Mischief-Maker by Gerald McDermott. Sizzling-hot, almost fluorescent colours make the jungle spring alive in this story about a naughty parrot who is vindicated when he turns his energies to leadership against a common enemy.

The Paper Bag Princess by Robert Munsch. Elizabeth is a modern princess who rescues her preppy prince from a dragon and concludes that he is a 'bum' when he objects to her untidy appearance in this broadly farcical fairy-tale update.

Parrot Told Snake by Harry Stevens. A large baby board book that tells a starkly simple, funny 'chain' story (snake told bear, bear told giraffe), comic punchline and all, in exactly twenty-nine words. Bright, appealing colours and bold, cartoon-like animals.

Polar Bear Cat by Nicola Bayley. A little black cat peers out at the snow and imagines a life among the polar bears, with a quick retreat to snug reality when the daydream becomes too vivid for comfort. The small size of the book, its gem-like framed illustrations, and the perfect coherence of very simple text and picture on each page, make this a particularly satisfying example of picture-book art for the very young. The thrilling beauty and danger of the polar daydream, and its comforting conclusion, are a wonderful metaphor for the pleasures of journeys-through-books.

The Rescue of Aunt Pansy by Lisa Campbell Ernst. The split-page is put to excellent use here, as brave mouse Joanne tries to rescue what she thinks is her Aunt Pansy from Russell the cat. Each turned half-page reveals a funny new quirk in the cat-and-mouse game. The richly coloured artwork, with its excitingly focused close-ups, intensifies both the suspense and the humour; the moment when the cornered Joanne smiles quaveringly up at bemused Russell is a small epiphany of the illustrator's art.

Rosie's Walk by Pat Hutchins. A hen takes a nonchalant walk through a bright Pennsylvania Dutch landscape, slyly followed by a fox who comes to grief in a series of hilarious mishaps. The child 'reads' the pictures as well as the text to get the joke. (4–6)

Sally Go Round the Sun by Edith Fowke. Three hundred skipping rhymes, singing games, finger plays and familiar chants and jingles, with music and bright decorations. A wonderful aid to active play.

Sally, Where Are You? by Yvette Mintzberg. An uproariously funny hide-and-seek book. Mother searches everywhere, but a pair of bright black eyes are the only clue to mischievous Sally's hiding places. Vivid colours and wittily stylized graphics are used to convey suspense and mood. Even the youngest pre-reader will 'read' the signs in this clever book with triumphant glee.

17 Kings and 42 Elephants by Margaret Mahy, illustrated by Patricia MacCarthy. 'Seventeen kings on forty-two elephants, Going on a journey through the wild, wet night, Baggy ears like big umbrellaphants, Little eyes a-gleaming in the jungle light.' The batik paintings that accompany this story poem are as lushly evocative, funny and shivery as the language; simply wonderful to read aloud.

Shadow by Blaise Cendrars. An eerie, imaginatively provocative African prose poem, for stalwart readers, with brilliant collages by Marcia Brown which reward long moments of mesmerized scrutiny. (7–8)

Sid and Sol by Arthur Yorinks. Startling close-ups, zoom and distance 'shots' in black and white make this one of the most convincing (and contemporary) portraits of a giant in picture books. Sol, the boastful giant in a cardigan, towers over the skyscrapers. But Sid, 'a short guy', as archetypal as the 'youngest son' of fairy tales, triumphs over the giant. Richard Egielski's mordantly modern illustrations are stunning.

The Story About Ping by Marjorie Flack. A Chinese duck's first adventures in independence include friendship, loneliness, and a welcome retreat to his huge family at the end. Kurt Wiese's glowing and sensitive pictures are masterful and ensure this story's status as a classic.

The Story of Ferdinand by Munro Leaf. This book celebrates its fiftieth birthday this year, and is still going strong, thanks to its gentle, life-affirming story and the charmingly funny black and white drawings by Robert Lawson. Ferdinand is a bull who refuses to participate in bullfights, despite the rip-snorting enthusiasm of his peers. His mother worries, but she understands that Ferdinand 'just likes to sit quietly under the cork tree and smell the flowers'.

Sylvester and the Magic Pebble by William Steig. A poignant and beautifully illustrated story about a donkey child who gets turned into a stone, to the grief of his parents . . . until they are reunited. By one of the great, humane picture-book artists of our time, whose language is always as rich as his art.

The Tale of Peter Rabbit by Beatrix Potter. An indispensable hand-sized classic, with suspense, vigorous prose, exquisitely precise and memorable watercolours. Read aloud the whole series. Like most adults, you'll probably most cherish *The Tailor of Gloucester*.

Tell Me a Mitzi by Lore Segal. Warm but chaotic family life, in which the parents are as realistically depicted as the competent little girl and her brother Jacob. A funny, wise and wonderful 'shaggy dog' story, with equally wonderful homely illustrations by Harriet Pincus. Also, *Tell Me a Trudy*.

Thank You for the Tadpole by Pat Thomson and Mary Rayner. A conversation between father and son about what to take Becky for a birthday present. Dad, as he does the housework, makes outrageous suggestions (a tadpole, an alligator) – all amusingly illustrated – and finally the boy realizes that the first letters of Dad's suggestions spell 'tea set'. The conversation has a gentle, naturalistic charm, but what's really unusual about the book is that it has been designed to be read aloud alternately by parent and child, as part of the ingenious *Share-a-Story* series.

Three Big Hogs by Manus Pinkwater. Three big hogs lose their cosy home, but overcome their fears to survive happily as 'tough, hairy, regular forest hogs'. An invigorating modern twist on the old *Three Little Pigs* tale. Wittily illustrated by the author, written in his usual jaunty and endearing style.

Three Strong Women by Claus Stamm. A charming tall tale from Japan about an impish girl, her mother and grandmother, who secretly coach a Sumo wrestler. An unusually unforced and liberated folk tale, brilliantly and good-naturedly illustrated by Kazue Mizumura.

Tikki Tikki Tembo by Arlene Mosel. The story of how a too favoured older brother nearly comes to grief because of his inflated name, which just happens to be a favourite, rollicking tongue twister. A classic, perfectly illustrated by Blair Lent.

The Trek by Ann Jonas. A little girl turns her morning walk to school into a fantastic safari of the imagination. Every shrub, grocer's display and shadow on the way hides a lurking and possibly dangerous jungle beast – but her 'amazing skill' as a pretend-trekker 'saves her day after day'. Some of the hidden animals are a miracle of witty artistry; discovery and triumphant laughter will accompany each re-reading. Best of all, the text acknowledges a young child's fears while helping to transcend them.

The Vingananee and the Tree Toad by Verna Ardema. A vivid and exciting Liberian tale about how tiny Tree-Toad saves her bigger friends from the hairy monster. Satisfying sound effects for the reader-aloud, a suspenseful cumulative plot and charming illustrations by Ellen Weiss.

Where the Wild Things Are by Maurice Sendak. Every word is perfect in this justly famous and reassuring story of a small boy conquering his own aggressions in the wild monster-kingdom of his mind. Sendak's full-page artwork is dazzling.

Where's Julius? by John Burningham. On each page, Mr and Mrs Troutbeck wonder 'Where's Julius?' as they prepare to serve another delicious meal, described in mouth-watering detail. But Julius is too busy digging an imaginary hole to the other side of the world, or riding a camel to the top of a pyramid. . . . so obliging dad brings him his meals on a tray. Burningham's spacious pictures rejoice, as always, in the wonderful and various colours of the world and the powers of the imagination.

Whose Mouse Are You? by Robert Kraus. A splendidly swift, evocative story of a little mouse's anger (and reconciliation) when a baby brother is born, with bold, brilliant pictures by Jose Aruego. The genius of the narrative is that the reason for the little mouse's unhappiness is revealed only obliquely. Equally vivid and subtle sequels are *Another Mouse To Feed* and *Where Are You Going, Little Mouse?* about running away from home. (4–5)

Why the Chicken Crossed the Road by David Macaulay. A deliciously rambunctious cause-and-effect story of preposterous chain-reaction events when a chicken startles some cows, who stampede the bridge, which crashes onto the train . . . The brilliant, crowded pictures repay close attention with dozens of visual jokes. (When the cows crash through the roof of the dining car, one passenger asks, 'Who ordered their beef rare?')

Why Mosquitoes Buzz in People's Ears by Verna Ardema. A familiar nuisance amusingly accounted for in a West African chain-reaction tale, rich in onomatopoeia. Vivid, stylized illustrations by Leo and Diane Dillon. (4–7)

The Wild Washerwomen by John Yeoman. A good-natured tall tale, proletarian style, about some washerwomen who rebel against drudgery, marry seven woodsmen, and share the work. Spiked with quirky, eccentric, hyperactive drawings by Quentin Blake.

Would You Rather? by John Burningham. Would you rather be covered in jam, soaked with water or pulled through the mud by a dog? Riotous and sometimes fiendish alternatives (as well as large illustrations) encourage readers to engage in conversation with the book or the person reading aloud. (4–6)

Zoom at Sea by Tim Wynne-Jones. Soft full-page pencil drawings by Ken Nutt add tender humour and mystery to this enchanting, evocative story of Zoom, the kitten who longs to go to sea. His dream is thrillingly fulfilled by the mysterious, maternal Maria, who conjures up an ocean out of the boxes and drawers in her magical house. An exciting story whose hints and overtones of symbolic meaning add depth to the reader's pleasure.

Young Fluent Readers: Ages 5 to 8

Stories and picture books with ample text – good for skilful young readers or older children who need stimulating content with which to hone their reading skills.

Alligator Pie by Dennis Lee. These fresh, contemporary Canadian variants on old nursery rhymes are already on their way to becoming 'classics', thanks to their infectious rhythms, uninhibited humour and inspired word play. Canadian place names, often sounding satisfyingly bizarre and nonsensical, are used to excellent effect. Illustrated by Frank Newfeld.

The Amazing Bone by William Steig. Pearl the pig is befriended by a magic bone with the gift of tongues. Steig's pictures are drenched with colour and his language alive with wit, invention and variety. This book contains one of the best sustained passages of gibberish ever invented. A picture book for readers.

Amelia Bedelia by Peggy Parish, illustrated by Fritz Siebel. A favourite series about a naïve, good-humoured housemaid who constantly misinterprets her employer's instructions. Asked to draw the curtains, she takes pencil and paper to make a picture. Children who are beginning school, and often embarrassed by not understanding instructions, love this simple comedy of errors.

Arabel's Raven by Joan Aiken. Wildly funny and verbally inventive adventures of Mortimer, the raven, adopted by Arabel's unsuspecting working-class family. His escapades lead them into Monty Pythonesque lunacies that are irresistible. Slapstick, satirical, deadpan, ironic . . . Aiken is a genius of every kind of humour. (6–8)

Aurora and the Little Blue Car by Ann-Cath. Vestly. Aurora's father, a PhD student, looks after her and baby Socrates while mother works. The small storms, anxieties and gaieties of contemporary family life are seen with marvellous accuracy through the eyes of Aurora, a resourceful preschooler, who helps her father learn to drive.

The Bat-Poet by Randall Jarrell. A little brown bat stays in the outside world when his relatives go to hibernate; he turns his dazzled perceptions of the world's beauty into poems, but 'the trouble's finding somebody that will listen to them'. An unusually literate, charming allegory about making and listening to poetry, with wonderfully soft, mysterious drawings by Sendak. (7–8)

Beats Me, Claude by Joan Lowery Nixon. Illustrated by Tracey Campbell Pearson. A splendidly funny, laugh-out-loud Texas tall tale. Shirley, rancher Claude's unconventional wife, gamely tries to make apple pie. The slapdash results are so explosively awful that her successive pies help to defrock a con-man preacher, capture a bank robber, and trap some army deserters. Alongside the slapstick, there runs a warm hearted and satisfying story of orphan Tom, whom Shirley rescues from the con man, and who eventually bakes his way into Claude's affections. The perfectly paced narrative has great fun with terse rural understatement and Texas slang, and the sketchy, lively illustrations add to the hilarity with inventive dash. The equally funny 'prequel', about Shirley's comically liberated approach to marriage, is *Fat Chance, Claude*.

The Bee-Man of Orn by Frank Stockton. This turn of the century fable about an eccentric old beekeeper who wants to find out what he was 'transformed' from has its *longueurs* in the middle, but is redeemed by its gentle integrity, surprise ending, and Maurice Sendak's ugly-hilarious illustrations.

Blue Moose by Manus Pinkwater. A quirkily charming short novel about an urbane talking moose who emerges from the north woods to serve as headwaiter at the isolated restaurant of flustered little Mr Breton. The story and pictures are among Pinkwater's wittiest and most endearing. (7–8)

The Brave Little Toaster by Thomas M. Disch. Five 'minor appliances' run away from their dear little cottage near the forest to find their master in the big city. This comic updating of a folk tale follows the adventures of a vacuum cleaner, an electric blanket, an AM radio, and a lamp, led by a stout-hearted two-slice Sunbeam toaster. Delightfully tongue-in-cheek without spoiling the suspense of the story. With drawings by Karen Lee Schmidt.

Bridget and William by Jane Gardam. Two short, simple large-print stories about horses and girls. One is Bridget, who gets a pony who later saves a life; the other is Susan, age six, who cares about the local chalk horse, grown over and threatened by a government fir tree plantation. The stories are lively, swift and told mostly in dialogue.

Burglar Bill by Janet and Allan Ahlberg. Burglar Bill unsuspectingly steals a baby in a box. An affable miscreant, Bill feeds the baby, amuses it and changes its nappies . . . until Burglar Betty turns up and declares herself the mother. When Bill and Betty marry, they 'see the error of their ways' and return all the stolen goods. Each page of text is illustrated with pictures of rosy good nature and abundant comic detail (Bill's portrait on the wall, for example, is a police mug shot). The *pièce de résistance* comes at the end when we see the reformed duo cheerfully returning pianos, toothbrushes and even a policeman's helmet.

A Candle for Christmas by Jean Speare. Tomas lives on a northern Indian reserve and the whole texture of life there is felt through Tomas's perceptions in this simple, satisfying story. He anxiously waits for his parents to return from a journey in time for Christmas; his yearning and joy are warmly conveyed in lovely full-page paintings by Ann Blades.

The Castle of Yew by Lucy Boston. Joseph finds his way into a magic garden where he becomes page to an older boy playing knight, lives in a castle carved from a yew tree, and yearns to ride Emerald, the chess-piece horse. Despite the poetic nature of the fantasy, the language is crisp, clear and forceful and the emotions – especially the jockeying for position between the two friends – strongly delineated. (7–8)

The Cat's Elbow by Alvin Schwartz. Not fiction, but unique and desirable: a handsome compendium of secret languages, most of them variants on English that will mystify eavesdroppers. (They work: my family has used one of these languages for two generations.) With exercises, word lists, illustrations by Margot Zemach and lots of stimulus to play with language. (7+)

Charlotte's Web by E. B. White. Wilbur is the runt of the litter, but he is saved from death first by the girl, Fern, and later by Charlotte the remarkable spider. Rightly considered a classic of elegantly precise, moving prose and luminous insights. And it's the single most popular children's book in America.

Clever Gretchen and Other Forgotten Folk Tales retold by Alison Lurie. Fifteen authentic old folk tales in which the girls are as clever, brave and active as the boys . . . including a Spanish role-reversal version of *The Sleeping Beauty*. Illustrated in pen and ink by Margot Tomes.

Clever Polly and the Stupid Wolf by Catherine Storr. Twelve slyly hilarious stories in which calm, composed Polly outwits the scheming, childish wolf. An added pleasure is that many of the episodes are modern twists on favourite stories and nursery rhymes. Great fun to read aloud.

Cliptail by Gabrielle Roy. Cliptail is a cosily purring cat in Berthe's old farm house until she realizes that a certain rural ruthlessness is intended toward her kittens. Her adventures in saving her next litter from a winter storm emphasize her fierce courage rather than her motherliness. A distinctively French-Canadian style of folk narrative gives this book a special flavour. Illustrated by Frances Olivier.

D'Aulaire's Book of Greek Myths by Ingri and Edgar D'Aulaire. For ambitious readers, this is a handsome, large format, forthright retelling of fifty-six essential Greek myths, with many colour illustrations. (8+)

Dawn by Molly Bang. The little girl, Dawn, unravels the mystery of her mother's disappearance in this poetic, haunting refashioning of the Japanese folk tale, *The Crane Wife*. Extraordinarily beautiful and evocative full-page illustrations by Bang, which reward close observation. (6–8)

The Devil's Storybook by Natalie Babbit. Ten original and vigorously told stories about the Devil and his plans to cause mischief in the world. They read like folk tales, swift, wise, illuminating and sly. (6–8)

The Fairy Tale Treasury by Virginia Haviland. Wonderful for browsing – here are thirty-two world favourites, with their verses and incantations intact, from the *Gingerbread Man* to *Molly Whuppie*. Splendidly humorous, robust colour or black and white illustrations by Raymond Briggs on every page.

Fanny and the Monsters by Penelope Lively. Three excellent stories about nine-year-old Fanny, the oldest of eight children in a Victorian family. She wishes that God might take back the newest baby, and then makes a desperate, comical atonement when she fears God might oblige. She longs to be a paleontologist, and actually discovers dinosaur bones. And she takes part in a rip-snorting play battle against the family next door. Artful, funny, with sophisticated vocabulary and delightful line drawings by John Laurence. (7–8)

Five O'Clock Charlie by Marguerite Henry. One of those old fashioned mass-market books that deservedly find a niche in young readers' hearts – a bookshop assistant recommended it to me with tears of remembered passion in her eyes! Charlie is an old work horse who breaks out of his lonely retirement pasture to reclaim the friendships and pleasures he used to know. Spacious watercolours and black and white drawings by Wesley Dennis add immensely to the good-hearted charm of the story.

Flat Stanley by Jeff Brown. Stanley Lambchop has been flattened by a noticeboard falling off his wall, a convenient catastrophe: now his parents can mail him to California, his brother can fly him like a kite, and he can prove his mettle in solving an art theft. Simple enough for the youngest reader; funny enough for all. Engaging drawings by Tomi Ungerer.

The Fools of Chelm by Isaac Bashevis Singer. Eight exuberantly funny and universally appealing folk stories about the 'shmendricks' (idiots) who live in the legendary town of Chelm. Outstanding illustrations by Uri Shulevitz. (American, H)

Freddy the Detective by Walter R. Brooks. This prewar series of books about a self-impressed pig and his barnyard friends is still popular because of its dry New England humour and genial inventiveness, and despite its leisurely pace and sometimes smugly reactionary tone. Illustrated splendidly by Kurt Wiese. (7–8)

Good-bye, Sarah by Geoffrey Bilson. The Wright family suffers hardship during the Winnipeg General Strike, and Mary has a painful parting of the ways with her closest friend. The best part of the story is the way the two children struggle to make sense of adult disputes, take sides, quarrel and yet realize the value of what they are losing. Illustrated by Ron Berg.

The Happy Orpheline by Natalie Savage Carlson. The gentle adventures of a group of little girls in Paris emanate a cosy quaintness and a real tang of Paris life. Orphan stories satisfy an old-fashioned but not outmoded thirst among young readers; those about girls are relatively rare. Illustrated by Garth Williams.

Harald and the Giant Knight by Donald Carrick. Harald admired the baron's fierce, leather-clad knights (who bear an uncanny resemblance to a modern motorcycle gang) until they ravaged his own father's farm. Then Harald had to come up with a plan to oust them. A richly illustrated picture book with a strong story.

Higglety Pigglety Pop! or, There Must Be More to Life by Maurice Sendak. Jenny, the dog, thinks there must be more to life than having everything, so she leaves home on a quest that leads her to strange, frightening and mystical experiences. Both the superb pictures and the gripping narrative show Sendak's genius for teasing eeriness and humour that tingles with elusive meanings. (6–8)

The Hoboken Chicken Emergency by D. Manus Pinkwater. Arthur's immigrant family is startled when he buys a 280-pound hen (with a tenor cluck) from Professor Mazzocchi, Inventor of the Chicken System. A favourite among the fans of Pinkwater's good-hearted spoofs of American clichés, con men and cops-and-robbers conventions. (7–8)

Hugo and Josephine by Maria Gripe. Six-year-old Josephine is lonely at first, but discovers friendship with the help of Hugo, a woodsy free spirit. A sensitive, amusing and warm-hearted story, with an intriguing taste of strangeness and a fine understanding of children's concerns and misconceptions. (6–8)

The Hundred Dresses by Eleanor Estes. A lovely, sensitive story about a crisis of conscience. Maddie reluctantly joins in the teasing of an outsider in class . . . but what can she do when her conscience needles her too late, after Wanda has moved away? Not a 'problem novel' with prefabricated conclusions, but a real novel delicately exploring profound questions of mischief, guilt and reparations. Finely illustrated by Louis Slobodkin. (8+)

The Iron Man, A Story in Five Nights by Ted Hughes. The boy, Hogarth, makes friends with the terrifying huge robot that comes out of the sea, and learns how to tame the giant's powers. In one of these linked stories, the robot saves the world from an outer-space threat. A scary, amusing, gripping story, told with hair-raising poetic intensity and powerful imagery. An absolutely sure-fire read-aloud. (7–8)

Jacob Two-Two Meets the Hooded Fang by Mordecai Richler. Jacob is the youngest of five brothers and sisters, some of whom help to rescue him after he is convicted of rudeness to adults (his lawyer is named Louis Loser) and sentenced to prison on Slimer's Isle, where he finds the wit and courage to unmask the Hooded Fang as a big softie.

Jenny and the Cat Club by Esther Averill. Jenny is Jenny Linsky (and the idea of giving a cat a surname is indicative of the grave charm of the whole); she is a shy little orphan cat in turn-of-the-century New York. These five simple stories of her adventures in overcoming her shyness in order to join the Cat Club are tenderly whimsical, with an intuitive feel for child nature, the cherished joys of friendship, the small anxieties and reassuring comforts of family life. The black ink drawings, spare, wry and affectionate, have been loved for years.

The Jolly Postman, or Other People's Letters by Janet and Allan Ahlberg. The inexhaustible Ahlbergs spin a fresh enchantment from well-known nursery tales and rhymes. The jolly postman brings letters – real ones, tucked into envelopes that form pages of the book – to storybook characters. There's a pompous solicitor's letter for B. B. Wolf (threatening suit on behalf of Little Red Riding Hood and the Three Pigs), a birthday card for Goldilocks, a publisher's proposal (complete with miniature book) for Cinderella, and an advertising circular from Hobgoblin Supplies for the Wicked Witch. The jaunty spoof will tickle the most literate young readers and the allure of the letters will be irresistible to even the most reluctant.

The Julian Stories by Ann Cameron, illustrated by Ann Strugnell. Six simple, unusual, funny and emotionally rich stories about an imaginative black boy, Julian, and the scrapes he gets into with his little brother Huey. The mingled fear and excitement the boys feel when their dynamic, unpredictable father teases them or gets angry is particularly fine: true to life, but so rarely evoked in children's books. Throughout, there's some wonderful language and a powerful feeling of family love.

Just So Stories by Rudyard Kipling. The cat who walked alone and Yellow-Dog Dingo are still bywords in many families. Read these hypnotically cadenced stories aloud; they are the prototype, and still the best, of modern 'how things came to be' fables.

Kit in Boots by Jane Gardam, illustrated by William Geldart. Kit's hot-tempered father, a Yorkshire farmer, thinks 'only muscle work counts' and Kit is afraid he will chase away the appealing artist who has camped in their field. Instead, the family warily makes friends with 'Lonesome Jones', who encourages Kit in her efforts to draw. Over the course of three summers, the chance acquaintance with the artist brings excitement, surprise and transformation into the lives of Kit and her family. Gardam is a genius; this short beginners' novel is as packed with sparkling language, character-revealing dialogue, affectionate wit and shrewd insight into clashing but mutually enriching cultures as her more sophisticated work for older readers.

Little House in the Big Woods by Laura Ingalls Wilder. A sturdy favourite. We feel the rhythm of the year, the beauty of the wilderness, and the purposefulness of pioneer life, its excitements, fears and family love, through the sensibilities of lively five-year-old Laura. Detailed, informative line drawings by Garth Williams. (6–8)

Little Tim and the Brave Sea Captain by Edward Ardizzone. Tim runs away to sea where he overcomes fear, is competent and brave when the ship goes down in a raging storm, and returns a hero. The charm of Ardizzone's busy, sketchy drawings is undying, and Tim's fantasy of grown-up risks is lightened by humorous daily details and cocoa comforts.

Lost and Found by Jean Little. Lucy is lonely in her new neighbourhood until she finds a fluffy little lost dog. She yearns to keep him, but a new friend, Nan, maddeningly persists in trying to find the dog's true owners. A touching story written with extreme simplicity and emotional honesty.

The Lost Umbrella of Kim Chu by Eleanor Estes. A not-to-be-missed suspenseful adventure, told with delicate observation and wit, of how a desperate but ever-ingenious Kim Chu tracks her father's missing prize umbrella from New York's Chinatown to Staten Island. (7–9)

Louhi, the Witch of North Farm by Toni de Gerez. Louhi, more puckish than fearsome, steals the sun and the moon, plunging the world into darkness, in this splendidly lively retelling of an ancient Finnish epic. Barbara Cooney's magnificent pictures glow with snow-light and firelight and the fresh spring beauty of the Finnish landscape. Rarely has a folk tale been revived with such magical immediacy of detail in both language and picture.

Mary of Mile 18 by Ann Blades. The author's light-washed watercolours of the bleak, dramatic northern landscape are an integral part of this touching story about a Mennonite girl who yearns to adopt a homeless pup. (7–8)

Maurice's Room by Paula Fox. The grown-ups don't understand that eight-year-old Maurice doesn't want a dog or trumpet lessons; he just wants to collect bedsprings, stuffed bears and other junkyard treasures in his already crammed bedroom. A wryly funny portrait of a curious, self-contained and interesting boy and his baffled, if kindly, parents. (7–8)

McBroom Tells a Lie by Sid Fleischman. A rollicking tall tale about a world champion liar; with narrative and dialogue in the hillbilly idiom and humour based on zany exaggeration.

The Moffats by Eleanor Estes. Intense, imaginative Jane, aged nine, is the central figure in this enduringly popular series about prewar family life in a small town. Rufus, Joel and Sylvie also have lively, sympathetic roles. Estes's assured and intimate understanding of children's feelings lends a unique warmth and veracity to the series.

Mountain Rose by Patti Stren. Rose, daughter of the Flying Flushmans, was so big the other kids said she needed her own post code. Stren decorates every page with her appealing, wittily captioned cartoons that add to the story of how Rose, a wrestler, wins the world championship and finds her long-lost brother. The tone is urban-hip, funny and sweet.

Mrs Dunphy's Dog by Catharine O'Neill. A hilarious, captivating picture book that tells a fine tale and also celebrates the joys of reading. Mrs Dunphy always reads the newspaper, and James, her dog, always shreds the discarded pages. One night, he stops long enough to read a headline (GIANT FLYING CAT TERRIFIES TOTS) and is hooked. The watercolour illustrations are rosy with wit, charm and merriment. All are choc-a-bloc with funny headlines to tantalize the young reader, and all add visual amplification of the amazing things James reads about. James progresses from enthralment with the sensational press, to disillusionment, to the discovery of the joys of fiction. But he always keeps a soft spot for junk reading. This accomplished first book radiates a generous, amused spirit, and, for sheer pleasure, is not to be missed by anyone.

Mr Popper's Penguins by Richard and Florence Atwater. Mr Popper, with his little-boy fascination with explorers and the Arctic, has a dream come true: Admiral Drake sends him some penguins. The story is as bouncily good-hearted and uproarious today as it ever was; what seems dated to adults is merely fresh to new readers. Illustrated by Robert Lawson.

The New Golden Land Anthology edited by Judith Elkin. A banquet of very well and widely chosen poems and stories, both old and very new, from a brief page's length to the more leisurely, from Greek myths and Wordsworth to Ogden Nash and Shel Silverstein. Delicious for browsing or bedtime.

The Olden Days Coat by Margaret Laurence. A simple but affecting time-shift story, by one of Canada's greatest novelists, about ten-year-old Sal, who slips into her grandmother's past to discover a wonderful Christmas present – and a memory of snowy woods and sleigh bells – they can share. Warm and richly coloured naturalistic illustrations by Muriel Wood. (6–8)

Outside by André Norton. A simply written but very popular future-fantasy for the young, about nine-year-old Kristie who finds the secret way out of the ruined, domed city where survivors of a polluted world live in resigned misery. Bravely venturing outside, she discovers the world has been reborn. (8+)

Penny Candy by Edward Fenton. Little Paul can't quite keep up with his bossy big sister Lily and her gang . . . but he gets his revenge in the Widder Shinn's sweetshop, where the delicious penny treats mysteriously give you magical fantasies. The writing is superb, the whiff of misogyny less so, and Edward Gorey's drawings are among his most forgiving.

The Piemakers by Helen Cresswell. Set in a rural English past of the imagination, this is a funny, exciting story about Gravella Roller, a rebellious member of a family of piemakers, who nevertheless gets caught up in the frenzy of baking a giant pie to win a royal contest.

Pippi Longstocking by Astrid Lindgren. She's the strongest girl in the world, and lives in a house of her own where she rolls biscuit dough on the floor and keeps her horse on the porch. Pippi is a classic figure of childhood's anarchic energy and imaginative spirit; her self-confidence, tomfoolery and fertile inventiveness at play are liberating for both boys and girls.

The Rain Door by Russell Hoban, illustrated by Quentin Blake. Harry, a spiritual descendant of Hoban's fidgety hero Tom, follows the mysterious rag-and-bone man out of the London heat wave and through the 'rain door' into the desert, where he cleverly makes a clockwork dinosaur to help the rag-and-bone man bring rain back to the parched city. Curious, jaunty and ingenious, Harry is matter-of-fact about his bizarre adventure. The language is playful, poetic and colloquial by turns. A richly satisfying picture book for readers.

Ramona the Pest by Beverly Cleary. A warmly amusing and sympathetic episodic novel about a rambunctious little girl's difficult and sometimes embarrassing first experiences of school; though it reads quickly and easily,

THE WORLD OF CHILDREN'S BOOKS

it is filled with incident, humour and intimate perception of a child's feelings.

The Real Thief by William Steig. Gawain the Goose is falsely accused by his loved monarch of theft from the royal treasury. Gawain undergoes bitter exile before the surprising culprit confesses. A richly told and complex story of friendship, betrayal, exculpation and glorious reconciliation, it will sound familiar emotional chords for any child. (7–8)

The Rocking Horse Secret by Rumer Godden. The housekeeper's six-year-old daughter, Tibby, finds a lost will in the rocking horse, and saves Pomeroy Place from auction. An exciting adventure for young horselovers. (6–8)

Saturday by Seven by Penelope Farmer. Peter hasn't saved the money for his school camping trip, and now he has to earn it all in one day. The story is simple but perfect; we follow Peter's anxious, busy day and the flux of his emotions, as he is by turns humiliated and triumphant. Unusual in its unflinching assumption of a small child's responsibility and capability.

The Secret Language by Ursula Nordstrom. Rebellious, prickly Victoria, age eight, a new girl at boarding school, slowly discovers the rewards (and torn loyalties) of friendship. The secret language, the secret hideout, the 'playing house' games of two best friends are very convincing and freshly conveyed, though the smarmy house mother is hard to take. (7–8)

The Shrinking of Treehorn by Florence Parry Heide. A mordantly witty satire on the banalities and inattention with which adults treat children's problems. Treehorn is shrinking; his parents exhort him to sit up straighter at the table; his teacher tells him, 'We don't shrink in this class.' Drawings by Edward Gorey. (7+)

Song of the Trees by Mildred Taylor. Eight-year-old Cassie's first-person story, lyrical and suspenseful, of a black family's battle to save the trees on their Mississippi farm from the schemes of white racists. (7–8)

Stig of the Dump by Clive King. Barney is eight and lonely when he discovers a stone-age man living in a chalk quarry. The lively story of their shared adventures is particularly rich in graphic descriptions of their ingenious inventions and hair-raising escapades. Illustrated by Edward Ardizzone. (7+)

Stone Fox by John Reynolds Gardiner. A gaspingly tense, terse, exciting story about Willy, aged ten, who tries to save his ailing grandpa and his threatened farm by winning the cash prize in a dog-sledge race. His chief competitor is a giant, unspeaking Indian. Exhilaration, surprise and sadness go hand in hand. Illustrated by Marcia Sewall. (7–10)

Thing by Robin Klein. A funny story about a girl who lives in a flat and can't have pets. When Emily accidentally hatches a baby stegosaurus from a round 'stone', she has to invent all sorts of subterfuges (abetted by Thing's own genius for disguise) to hide his presence from the landlady.

The Tin-Lined Trunk by Mary Hamilton. Polly and Jack are wretched London street urchins who are 'rescued' – a bit of a mixed blessing – by Dr Barnardo and sent off to Canada, where their endurance, courage and fierce determination slowly win them the friendship of dour Ontario farmers. An orphan story anchored in reality. (7–8)

Very Last First Time by Jan Andrews. A haunting yet reassuring picture book with a unique story. Eva, a contemporary Inuit girl, tries, for the first time, an annual rite in her village: going beneath the sea ice, when the tide is out, to harvest mussels. Danger, mystery and triumph are reflected in full-page, evocative paintings by Ian Wallace.

The Violin by Robert Thomas Allen. Misty full-page photographs by George Pastic and Andrew Welsh dramatize the story of two boys who live on Toronto Island. They become friends with a gentle, crumple-faced old man (the real-life violinist Maurice Solway) and one of them satisfies his heart's desire: to learn to play the violin. The ending of this dreamy, mysterious story is particularly poignant.

Walter the Lazy Mouse by Marjorie Flack. Walter is so lazy that he gets left behind when his family moves, and has to survive by himself on an island in the woods for a year. Comic-rueful adventures in independence. Amusing drawings by Cyndy Szekeres.

Whiskers Once and Always by Doris Orgel, illustrated by Carol Newsom. Even the realistic 'problem novel' form can be treated with sensitivity and insight. This short novel, with full-page illustrations, has the requisite elements of the form: Becky, a middle-class eight- or nine-year-old Brooklyn girl, is angry about her divorced mother's new boyfriend. When her beloved cat Whiskers dies, Becky's grief is complicated by guilt: for one brief moment, she'd imagined her mother dead instead of her cat. The story, with its satisfying resolution, is funny, touching and told with tolerant affection for the adults as well as the children. An added dimension is the solace that Becky finds in artwork.

Wingman by Manus Pinkwater. The author's heavy black-ink cartoon illustrations are the perfect witty complement to this superbly told story about a Chinese boy in New York who skips school every day to climb the George Washington Bridge, read comics, and dream about a Chinese superman. It's one of those stories with layers and layers of felt life and deep emotion behind them; a classic. (6–8)

The Worst Witch by Jill Murphy. Mildred is a hapless first-year student at Miss Cackle's Academy for Witches, where the school uniform is all black, right down to the hobnail boots. The gentle humour derives from the transposition of all the familiar school routines and escapades (outsmarting the teacher's pet, a run-in with a mean teacher) into a witchy setting. In the 'potion class', for example, it's 'two girls to a cauldron'. A popular series.

The Yellow Aeroplane by William Mayne. Rodney finds a wonderful model aeroplane that flies into his grandparents' garden, discovers a tree fort, joins a gang called the Three Bad Eggs and wins over Maureen, the local bully. Mayne is an artist in prose, able to see the world through the child's eyes and recreate it with elegant precision. A perfect story for a young, accomplished reader.

Zlateh the Goat and Other Stories by Isaac Bashevis Singer. Seven wonderful stories, some about Chelm, the mythical village of fools, all told with the economy, eccentric detail and humour of a masterful storyteller. The title story is particularly touching. Fine illustrations by Maurice Sendak.

A TREASURY

Middle Readers: Ages 8 to 12

The Adventures of Robin Hood by Roger Lancelyn Green. The most straightforward and comprehensive retelling of the indispensable Robin Hood legend, free of forsoothery, and with excerpts of old ballads to head the chapters.

All-of-a-Kind Family by Sidney Taylor. The sympathetic story of five Jewish sisters (ages four to twelve) who live on the Lower East Side of New York in the early days of this century, with lovingly realistic descriptions of the library, Papa's rag business, school, the street pedlars, family hardships and feasts, and a wonderfully romantic grown-up love story seen through the children's eyes.

Angel Square by Brian Doyle. Angel Square is where the kids from the Jewish, Catholic and Protestant schools meet to fight every day in this high-spirited, tough-talking, tolerant and nostalgic farce about Ottawa's Lowertown after the war. But the kids all get together to track down the real anti-Semite who beat up Sammy's father. Doyle's most accomplished book yet.

Anne of Green Gables by L. M. Montgomery. Anne is an unconventional orphan, much given to self-dramatization. But the tart humour and reticence of the adults, Matthew and Marilla, save the book from mawkishness. Anne's unusual character and the author's palpable, sensuous love of the Prince Edward Island landscape, have made the book a worldwide favourite.

The Baby Project by Sarah Ellis. Jessica, eleven years old and the youngest of three, is elated when her parents announce that a new baby is expected. This is an unflaggingly funny, warm and insightful story about a contemporary family in which all the characters – spunky friend Margaret, the hip hairdresser who lives downstairs, Aunt Eileen who sends stocks to the new baby ('Nothing gives a woman more confidence than her own financial portfolio') – are vivid, complex yet lovable. The tragedy at the book's climax is heartbreakingly poignant, but the resolution is both touching and optimistic. This is a perfect book to tempt readers of 'problem novels' because it is swift, accessible and realistic without any sacrifice of depth.

The Battle of Bubble and Squeak by Philippa Pearce. The battle is really between unhappy Sid and his resented though affable stepfather. Sid's mother, Peggy, who doesn't want him to have gerbils, is another combatant. A sympathetic and piercingly intuitive story about the feelings of a working-class family as they move towards a resolution. On the surface, delighted attention is paid to the gerbils' antics and crises.

Beowulf by Kevin Crossley-Holland. In this electrifying translation of the Anglo-Saxon epic, young Beowulf sails over the whale's way to fight the clawed monster Grendel and his mother the sea-wolf. The harsh northern background springs to life in marvellous imagery, and Charles Keeping's full-page black and white drawings are appropriately sinister.

Black Hearts in Battersea by Joan Aiken. When Simon comes to nineteenth-century London to be an artist, he meets Dido Twite, the most appealing guttersnipe in fiction, and the two of them are dragged into a wildly complicated and comic 'Hanoverian' plot. The story joyfully sends up all the clichés of missing heirs, meaningful tapestries, and royal jewels. Don't miss the wonderful sequels, up to and including the most recent, *Dido and Pa*.

Blue Willow by Doris Gates. An exceptionally sensitive and evocative story of a too thin, lonely, guarded child, ten-year-old Janey Larkin, the daughter of Dustbowl migrant farm workers in America's Depression years. Bible phrases are woven into the story with great poetic force. Janey survives, and believably saves her family and wins them a home, by her defiant courage and one great act of generosity.

The Bongleweed by Helen Cresswell. Rebellious Becky Finch plants a mysterious seed in the manicured Pew Gardens where her father is head gardener. The analogy with Eden is no mistake; while the Bongleweed takes over the gardens, Becky is bursting with new intimations of creativity and freedom. A perfectly written, poetic and humorous fantasy.

The Borrowers by Mary Norton. Pod and Homily Clock and their thirteen-year-old daughter Arietty are 'borrowers', those little people who live hidden in houses and whisk away useful small things like thimbles. Their miniature world is worked out with great imaginative vigour, and the clash of their world with the larger one – when a Boy intervenes – is not only comic and wise about the energies of youth, but filled with perceptions about the nature of reality.

Bows Against the Barons by Geoffrey Trease. A romantically radical version of Robin Hood, in which the struggle is not so much Saxons against Normans but peasants against overlords. The political idealism gives new vigour to the story.

Charlotte Sometimes by Penelope Farmer. Charlotte, a lonely thirteen-year-old at boarding school, shifts back in time to 1918; the tone is sombre and often haunting, but this is a subtle, provocative and touching book about finding one's identity.

Cloud Horse by Jill Pinkwater. Arnora, a Viking girl in Iceland, has an instinctive bond with animals . . . especially her beloved Icelandic pony, Skyfaxi. But she is restless, too, longing to journey like her brothers to distant Vinland. Nearly 1000 years later, Kate, an American girl, is haunted by dreams of cloud horses, a vision bequeathed her by Arnora. And in Vinland – Maine – she gets her chance to work with a herd of Icelandic ponies. Viking life has wonderful immediacy in this book, and the lovable little horses, their characters and their training, are brought to life in enough sympathetic detail to gratify the most passionate young horselover.

Come Sing, Jimmy Jo by Katharine Paterson. Eleven-year-old James struggles to cope with the strains in his family and with his own frightening new fame as a TV country singing star. His strong relationship with his Appalachian grandmother helps him to deal with complexities in this fresh, funny and touching story.

The Cricket in Times Square by George Selden. A cheerfully urbane story about Chester, the cricket, who makes a fortune for the Bellini family's subway newstand in New York by playing classical music. But fame isn't enough; Chester is homesick for the country, so his streetwise pals, Tucker Mouse and Harry Cat, help him escape.

The Dark Is Rising by Susan Cooper. This five-book series, beginning with *Over Sea, Under Stone*, in which children battle against the forces of darkness, is a gripping, complex fantasy based on Welsh legend. For excellent writing and imaginative depth, this cycle is head and shoulders above most of the fantasy genre.

Dawn of Fear by Susan Cooper. Seven days in the life of Derek, a young boy in surburban London during the Blitz. The fort he and his friends build, and their own war with a gang of bullies, are more real to him than the nightly bombardment – until the heartrending end. Stunningly vivid evocation of the Blitz, and superb perceptions of childhood feelings.

The Devil's Children by Peter Dickinson. One of Dickinson's three excellent novels about the Changes (a future time when all the English turn against machinery and revert to a kind of chaotic mediaevalism), this story features twelve-year-old Nicky and a band of wandering Sikhs with whom she finds sanctuary. Dickinson is an outstanding storyteller, whose swift, engrossing narratives are always as intellectually stimulating as they are exciting.

The Diamond in the Window by Jane Langton. Edward and Eleanor, who live in a 'Gothico-Byzantine' house in Concord, Massachusetts, solve an old mystery involving their lost aunt and uncle, Prince Krishna, a magic mirror, a secret code and a fabulous treasure. This book has everything, including rich literary allusiveness and a naturalistic family background, that makes an enthralling read.

The Diddakoi by Rumer Godden. Kizzy is a seven-year-old gypsy girl, tormented by the others at school, left alone when grandma dies. This is the ultimate outsider fantasy for girls, which perhaps accounts for its persistent popularity. A covey of distinguished village gentry hover over Kizzy, adopt her, adore her, and even make her a child-sized gypsy wagon with all the 'little fitments'. She, fierce, wayward and with a wild integrity, is at centre stage through several melodramas. Rotten with sentimental fantasy, shot through with a weird streak of misogyny, this is still a mesmerizing story to multitudes of little girls.

A Dog So Small by Philippa Pearce. What happens when you finally get your heart's desire – and reality falls short of the dream? Ben Blewitt, the middle child in a large working-class family in London, yearns passionately for a dog of his own. Of all yearning-for-a-pet stories, this one ranks with *The Yearling* in sheer intensity. The drama of the plot is matched by the subtlety of Ben's inward struggle to relinquish a dream and take pleasure in reality.

Dominic by William Steig. Dominic is an anthropomorphic dog who sets out to satisfy his need for adventure. Filled with the ardour, restlessness and reckless generosity of youth, he befriends hapless animals, conquers the ruthless Doomsday Gang and finds his true love. A romantic, exuberant, satisfying story, crackling with energy, love of life and Steig's dazzling breadth of both vision and vocabulary.

The Egypt Game by Zilpha Keatley Snyder. An imaginative game of Egyptian queens, priests and oracles, that takes place in a junkshop yard, turns into something spookier and more exciting than even the gang of eleven-year-old players could have dreamed up when a child molester threatens the neighbourhood.

The Eighteenth Emergency by Betsy Byars. Benjie, nicknamed 'Mouse', is pursued by an angered Marv Hammerman, the Neanderthal of the eleven-year-olds. Wry and wisecracking, this short novel by one of America's most skilful and popular writers perfectly captures the fear and hopelessness – and eventual relief – of anyone hounded by a bully.

Emil and the Detectives by Erich Kästner. A rousing and delightful story about how Emil is robbed of his mother's hard-earned money while on his first solo train trip to visit relatives in prewar Berlin. Quick-witted Emil follows the thief, and is aided by a friendly gang of city kids. Together they form a clever plan to get the money back. Swift action and warmly believable characters and settings have made this an enduring favourite.

Emily Upham's Revenge by Avi. Prim little Emily, aged seven, ends up as the bank-robbing accomplice of Seth Marple, alias Deadwood Dick, aged eleven, in this fast-moving, plot-twisting, good-natured Massachusetts send-up of the Wild West.

The Empty Schoolhouse by Natalie Savage Carlson. A simple but affecting story about clever, ten-year-old Lullah's passionate desire to attend a white school, as told by her teenager sister. The children struggle against southern racism and win . . . though the book itself is not entirely free of some racial stereotypes. Still, the malevolence of local bigots is creepily convincing, as is the child's longing for a less shackled life.

Five Children and It by E. Nesbit. The five children are a triumph of affectionate observation: decent, funny, quarrelsome and occasionally grubby, and their dialogue, written at the turn of the century, still crackles with spontaneity. Nor can age wither the fresh inventiveness and satirical snap of their adventures with the cranky sand fairy who grants wishes. All the sequels are as good or better; these are classics of British children's fiction.

From Anna by Jean Little. Anna is the clumsy, ten-year-old outsider in her warm but sometimes insensitive family. When her idealistic father insists that they flee from Hitler to Toronto in 1933, Anna resists . . . but in Canada she comes into her own. When it's discovered that she is nearly blind, a special class is found for her and we see her begin to bloom. A moving, honest and strong story.

From the Mixed-Up Files of Mrs Basil E. Frankweiler by E. L. Konigsburg. When twelve-year-old Claudia and her younger brother, James, run away from home to live in the Metropolitan Museum of Art, they not only survive with great ingenuity but also solve a museum mystery. Sophisticated, fun and convincing.

Gaffer Sampson's Luck by Jill Paton Walsh. Just possibly the best novel yet from this fine writer. When James's family moves from familiar Yorkshire to the strange, watery flatness of the Fens, he feels stranded – and at school, he *is* stranded between the rival cliques of tough villagers and snobbish suburbanites. Worse, in his attempt to help a marvellously crotchety old neighbour to find a long-lost lucky charm, James runs foul of the local bully and has to accept a hair-raising dare – a scene that will set adult pulses racing along with the children's. Walsh's swift, polished and drily humorous prose make this an immensely evocative story for a skilled reader. At the same time, the realistic scrapes and adventures of boyhood provide a lively read for the action-oriented.

The Ghost of Thomas Kempe by Penelope Lively. Ten-year-old James is uproariously and maddeningly haunted by the ghost of a cantankerous seventeenth-century apothecary. A wonderfully funny and intelligent, many-layered story about a boy's perception of time.

Ginger Pye by Eleanor Estes. Jerry and Rachel Pye, aged ten and nine, live in a small town in prewar America. The story of their amazing dog, Ginger, how he was lost, and how he was finally recovered, is full of warm family feeling, telling detail, humour, suspense and the leisurely, incident-filled childhood of other times.

Goldie the Dollmaker by M. B. Goffstein. A touching and original story about a girl who lives alone in the forest, making wonderful dolls, and who comes to realize that her craft and independence are more precious than a disappointing boyfriend. The author's wiry line drawings add a folk-tale atmosphere and are an expression of distilled tenderness. (6–10)

Gone-Away Lake by Elizabeth Enright. Portia and her cousin, Julian, discover a long-abandoned summer village at the edge of a swamp, and learn that some old people are secretly living there. A lovely, sympathetic and believable family story of exploration.

A Handful of Thieves by Nina Bawden. Fred tells how he and his gang track down the lodger – a sanctimonious fraud artist – who stole Granny's life savings from her teapot. An exciting and often funny 'detective' story, with understated and tolerant affection among working-class friends and relatives.

A Handful of Time by Kit Pearson. A touching and exciting time-shift story in which twelve-year-old Patricia, angry with her distracted, careerist mother, and unhappily in the midst of a family divorce, is sent to stay with relatives at an old family cottage. Plump and awkward, she doesn't fit in with her boisterous cousins. But an old watch she finds under a floorboard mysteriously takes her back in time to the summer when her mother was an unhappy teenager, too, and Patricia begins to work out the family constellation, how it shaped her mother, and where she herself fits in. A subtle and sympathetic story about a youngster's growing under-standing and confidence.

Harriet the Spy by Louise Fitzhugh. A colloquial and still disturbingly funny story about a headstrong eleven-year-old, Harriet, who lives in Manhattan, New York, with her parents and Ole Golly, her eccentric governess. Harriet records in her notebook her devastating observations about schoolmates and neighbours – until her scathing honesty backfires.

The Haunting by Margaret Mahy. Eight-year-old Barney fears that he has inherited the Scholar family magical powers when he begins to be haunted by a missing uncle. But his silent twelve-year-old sister Troy is guarding a secret. A tense psychological thriller with a background of family affection.

Heidi by Johanna Spyri. Like Anne of Green Gables, this little free spirit wins over a crotchety old man; the sensual beauty of life in the Swiss Alps – the wildflowers, sunsets, bed of sweet hay, bowls of milk and toasted cheese – is still captivating.

Henry's Leg by Ann Pilling. Henry Hooper is an avid collector of junk, but when he helps himself to a plastic leg from the rubbish outside a dress shop, he falls into the middle of a hair-raising detective adventure. This is an unclassifiable book: a realistic comedy of contemporary family life, a thriller, a school story and an adventure. A rich and believable cast of characters, and Henry's own quirky, street-smart, wistful personality, help make this an exceptionally winning story.

The Hobbit by J. R. R. Tolkien. Bilbo Baggins sets out, at the urging of the wizard Gandalf, to help the dwarves recover their lost treasure from the dragon Smaug. A suspenseful, exciting treasure-quest, with plenty of apple-cheeked rural cosiness to pace the adventure. A much-loved tale, told in an avuncular, fireside tone.

The Hounds of the Morrigan by Pat O'Shea. Pidge and his five-year-old sister, Brigit, are drawn into an epic quest to defeat the Goddess of Death and Destruction and her sinister pack of hounds. Like children in a fairy tale, they're aided by talking frogs, fairies, tinkers and nearly all the heroes of Irish legend. An immensely long book (465 pages), it maintains its urgency and believability throughout by the lively naturalism of the children's speech (especially spunky Brigit), the wit and cosy humour of many of the episodes, the strong magical appeal of its fairy-tale characters and the frequent peaks of excitement and danger in the chase. A welcome glossary provides the meaning and pronunciation of Gaelic names. The dialogue comes in many savoury varieties, so this adventure would make a splendid read-aloud.

The House of Sixty Fathers by Meindert DeJong. A richly imagined, touching and powerful World War II story about a Chinese boy and his pet pig, Glory-of-the-Republic, who make a frightening, desperate journey to find the boy's family while eluding the advancing Japanese troops. Danger, hunger and anxiety are offset by Tien Pao's resilience, courage and love. The emotion of Tien Pao's search for his mother builds to a heart-bursting climax.

The House with a Clock in Its Walls by John Bellairs. Lewis Barnavelt, a chubby ten-year-old orphan, goes to live with his jaunty Uncle Jonathan in a strange mansion haunted by the ghost of a warlock. It turns out that Jonathan and his friend, Mrs Florence Zimmerman, are magicians too.

Spooky, exciting, funny and sweet. Cosiness and cocoa always balance the ghoulishness.

How Many Miles to Babylon? by Paula Fox. A bleakly convincing but ultimately optimistic story of how ten-year-old James, a black boy in Brooklyn, is kidnapped and terrorized by a teenage gang in an abandoned fun-house, and manages to escape.

Hurry Home, Candy by Meindert DeJong. The suspenseful, empathetic story of an abused puppy who becomes a stray, its year-long hardships on the loose, and its eventual happy homecoming to a retired sea captain who understands him. Illustrated by Maurice Sendak.

The Indian in the Cupboard by Lynne Reid Banks. An extraordinary book, exciting and thought-provoking, about Omri, whose plastic Indian comes alive when it is shut in a special cupboard. Both the thrill and the growing burden, physical and moral, of caring for living, miniature, recalcitrant people are astonishingly well conveyed. The sequel, *The Return of the Indian*, is just as tense, thrilling and provocative, as Omri is tempted to travel through time to provide 'his' Indians with modern weapons.

Into the Dream by William Sleator. Paul and Francine, twelve-year-old classmates, learn they have telepathic powers and are reluctantly drawn into a nightmarish CIA plot to kidnap a four-year-old with even greater psychic gifts. This popular, easy-to-read thriller is written with urgency and conviction.

Jasmin by Jan Truss. Jasmine, defiant and depressed by her chaotic rural-slum family and her imminent failing of her school year, runs away into the Alberta bush where she survives alone in a cave, is swept away by floods, and is rescued by new friends who show her a way to independence and happiness.

Jennifer, Hecate, Macbeth, William McKinley, and Me, Elizabeth (UK title *Jennifer, Hecate, Macbeth and Me*) by E. L. Konigsburg. Elizabeth is lonely in her new suburban apartment until she meets Jennifer, a tall, skinny, fierce and imaginative black girl who claims to be a witch. An air of mystery hangs over Jennifer's amazing feats, and much ghoulish humour attends Elizabeth's apprenticeship in make-believe witchcraft, but the real story is of their growing friendship and confidence.

The Juniper Tree, and Other Tales from Grimm translated by Lore Segal and Randall Jarrell. An indispensable collection of the eeriest and most powerful Grimm stories, translated with riveting clarity and illustrated with haunting strangeness by Maurice Sendak.

A Lemon and a Star by E. C. Spykman. An unusually vibrant depiction of a high-spirited, wealthy New England family at the turn of the century. The motherless children have uncommon freedom, and Edie, the youngest (at five) is the boldest and most interesting, though most vulnerable to her brothers' teasing. In a sequel, *Edie on the Warpath*, Edie at eleven rebels against 'ladylike' restrictions and joins the suffragettes. Funny and wonderfully perceptive.

The Lion, the Witch and the Wardrobe by C. S. Lewis. The best of the popular *Narnia* series (the symbolism does not weigh too heavily on the plot), this is the story of how Lucy, her brothers and sisters go through the back of the wardrobe in the old Professor's house and into a kingdom where, because of a spell cast by the White Witch, it is 'always winter but never Christmas'.

Lisa and Lottie by Erich Kästner. There is something uniquely satisfying about the reunion of twins who have been separated from birth: perhaps we all long for a double, a perfect soul-sister? This charming and light-hearted novel is emphatically a girls' book, and almost quaint – but still imperishably delicious. The nine-year-olds discover each other's existence accidentally, at a summer camp, and contrive to reunite their divorced parents by secretly switching places. Despite the lively pace and sustained suspense, the atmosphere is sunny and loving.

The Little Bookroom by Eleanor Farjeon. Fairy-tale-style short stories by the unusually imaginative, humorous and lyrical Farjeon. 'And I Dance My Own Child' and 'The Connemara Donkey' are particularly touching and splendid, with strongly drawn child characters and a vivid feel for long-gone rural ways. Lovely drawings by Edward Ardizzone.

The Magic Adventures of Pretty Pearl by Virginia Hamilton. A stunning book, perhaps even an indispensable one: I don't know any other children's book that lends such mythic force to the black experience in America. Pretty Pearl is a 'god chile' who comes down from Mount Kenya to help the black people during the painful persecutions of Reconstruction times. She finds a clan of 'inside people', hidden away in a magically self-sufficient and beautiful secret world in a huge forest in Georgia, and her fate becomes intertwined with theirs. Hamilton renders black speech so lyrically that it mesmerizes the reader; she makes folk-tale tricksters and heroes vibrant with life. There is strangeness, 'otherness', here for the white reader unfamiliar with African lore; Hamilton makes it glorious, with great emotional warmth and depth. The book is beautifully produced, with a Romare Bearden painting on the cover and elegant African decorations throughout. (11+)

Marianne Dreams by Catherine Storr. Two convalescent children, a ten-year-old girl and a teenage boy, who have never met, come together in a terrifying dream from which they gradually free themselves. An eerie, sometimes frightening, psychologically convincing and ultimately reassuring story.

Me and My Million by Clive King. A gimlet-eyed illiterate urchin, Ringo, is led into crime by his older brother, Elvis, and ends up on the run in London with a priceless Pestalozzi painting of the Madonna ('some mum and her kid'). Ringo is unexpectedly aided by an amiable art forger who lives on a canal boat. Suspenseful, satirical, funny and fine, puncturing the pretentions of everyone from art experts to animal liberationists and posing some subtle questions about art and truth.

Mouldy's Orphan by Gillian Avery. Mouldy is the dreamer and the reader in a realistically rendered cottager family; she longs to adopt an orphan, just like in the sad books she reads, but things go maddeningly wrong when, on a rare school outing to town, she actually finds a homeless boy. Avery brilliantly conveys the gritty texture of Victorian rural life – mud, chilblains and all – in this short novel. And though Mouldy gets a brisk education in unsentimental realities, her idealism remains unshaken: in the end, her down-to-earth family does help her to rescue her orphan.

The Mouse and His Child by Russell Hoban. This poignant and absorbing story of a clockwork mouse and his father – their journeys, perils and adventures, rich in symbolism – has become something of a cult favourite among adults. Teenagers will also appreciate its philosophical, humanistic underpinnings.

Mrs Frisby and the Rats of NIMH by Robert C. O'Brien. Some super-intelligent rats escape from an experimental lab and, with the help of a courageous mother mouse, attempt to found a new rat civilization based on self-sufficiency instead of stealing. An absorbing and ingeniously worked-out fantasy.

The Mysterious Disappearance of Leon (I Mean Noel) by Ellen Raskin. Mrs Carillon seeks her long-lost husband with the help of adopted twins Tony and Tina. A widely loved, funny and satisfying detective adventure, complete with puzzles, riddles, codes and visual clues, it also resonates with meaning: the mystery is solved when everyone's true name is known and false roles and identities discarded.

The Night Watchmen by Helen Cresswell. Henry meets two strange tramps, Josh and Caleb, who come from There by the mysterious night train. But the Green Eyes, a frightening enemy, appear, and Henry begins to realize that the world is filled with infinite possibility. A suspenseful story with an unusual wistful flavour.

Ninny's Boat by Clive King. 'Bat bee iroo low' . . . that scrap of a forgotten language is Ninny's only clue to his identity. He is a thrall to a primitive

Anglish tribe, a funny, shaggy, kind-hearted and resourceful boy. It's a marvel how thoroughly King makes us see and hear everything through Ninny's sensibility. The saga of his quest is exciting, uproarious, and linguistically rich; just unmissable.

No Way of Telling by Emma Smith. Amy and her grandmother are isolated by a blizzard in their remote Welsh farmhouse when a frighteningly huge wounded stranger blunders in. Whom should they help: the fugitive or the smooth-talking men on skis who pursue him? An extraordinarily believable and superbly written heart-thumping tale of tension, character, intuition and courage.

Nurse Matilda by Christianna Brand. Nurse Matilda, with a nose like two potatoes, is brought in to teach seven mysterious, magical lessons to the completely unruly Brown children, an innumerable Victorian family. Accurately captures both the anarchic fun and ultimate misery of being out of control. A wonderfully strange and memorable fantasy. Illustrated by Edward Ardizzone.

Ordinary Jack by Helen Cresswell. Jack is eleven, the only 'ordinary' member of the wildly competitive, over-achieving Bagthorpe family, which is mercilessly and hilariously spoofed. The slapstick, fast-paced comedy is up-to-date and Pythonesque, though it always stops short of the grotesque.

Owls in the Family by Farley Mowat. A lovable and funny autobiographical novel about boyhood in Saskatoon and a family's unusual pets. Mowat, who also immortalized his comical dog in *The Dog Who Wouldn't Be*, here describes the endearing and ludicrous antics of two owls, Wol and Weeps. Abounds in physical comedy and affection.

The Peppermint Pig by Nina Bawden. Nine-year-old Poll has an amusing pet, a riotously disruptive pig, to console her during a difficult year in her family's life. Through this unconventional family – strong-willed aunts, a mother who loves to tell ghoulish stories, an hysterical younger brother – themes of betrayal, family trust, loss and reaffirmation are touched on with vivacity and wit.

The People Could Fly; American Black Folktales by Virginia Hamilton, illustrated by Leo and Diane Dillon. Wonderfully strange, funny and reverberant tales, all of them fresh to our ears, and told in a unique version of black dialect that is both understandable and richly alive: 'Say that he Lion would get up each and every mornin. Stretch and walk around. He'd roar "ME AND MYSELF. ME AND MYSELF", like that.' Tall tales, ghost tales, animal fables with bits of African magic patter – and some poignant true tales of escapes from slavery – all seem to gain extra vitality from the extraordinary language, which rolls across the page as though a magical storyteller is sitting right there. The Dillons' black and white illustrations are magnificent.

The Phantom Tollbooth by Norton Juster. The picaresque adventures of Milo, tootling through Dictionopolis in his electric car to rescue the 'fair' princesses, Rhyme and Reason. The whole story is a light, airy juggling of wordplay and witty abstractions, with some luminous moments of imagery, as when an orchestra 'plays' the sunset.

The Pinballs by Betsy Byars. Written with extraordinary simplicity, directness and wisecracking humour, this story of how three preteenage foster children come to terms with their hurts nevertheless avoids slickness and rings true emotionally.

A Pocket Full of Seeds by Marilyn Sachs. A strongly moving and emotionally honest fictionalized account of a real girl, Nicole, aged thirteen, who is left behind in a French town when her parents and sister are deported by the Nazis. The moral confusion of the times is vividly conveyed, and the sometimes stormy but deeply loving relationship between Nicole and her mother is heartbreakingly real. Illustrations by Ben Stahl.

The Princess and the Goblin by George MacDonald. A wonderful, large-spirited and vigorous Victorian fairy tale that remains in the memory for years. Gallant Curdie, a miner's son, fights back against the sinister underground goblins; at one point, his life is saved by the King's little daughter Irene, helped by her magical great-great-grandmother. The children's tender friendship, and some delicate issues of trust and belief, are beautifully conveyed.

The Riverside Anthology of Children's Literature edited by Judith Saltman. A remarkable collection, of nearly 1400 pages: international folk and fairy tales, myths, legends, hundreds of poems, excerpts from the finest children's novels and picture books, coloured illustrations, riddles, singing games, poetry by children, science fiction, and even a large selection of excerpts from biography, history and science writing for children. A unique resource for parents, and one of the best rainy-day browsing books I can imagine for the middle reader.

Sadako and the Thousand Paper Cranes by Eleanor Coerr. A very simply written, sombre but sensitive and honestly told true story of a twelve-year-old Japanese girl who died from the after effects of Hiroshima. Her courage and faith during her illness endeared her to Japanese schoolchildren and these qualities shine through this unaffected account. Gentle black and white paintings by Ronald Himler.

The Saga of Erik the Viking by Terry Jones. Sea demons, mischievous trolls, islands of bleak rock and dog-headed warriors – this series of new stories seems to capture all the fantastic magic and rugged conflict of Norse legend in swift, gripping prose. A perfect read for super-hero addicts, and a civilizing one, too: these heroes are capable of fear, tenderness and foolishness as well as great boldness. Abounding invention and superb full-colour illustrations by Michael Foreman.

The Sea Egg by Lucy Boston. Two boys on a seaside holiday find a mysterious rock that hatches into a 'triton', a sort of youthful merman who leads them on exhilarating magical adventures in the sea. Intensely poetic and beautiful writing.

The Secret Garden by Frances Hodgson Burnett. Mary, a sickly, self-centred orphan, discovers a locked garden on her uncle's Yorkshire estate, where she finds emotional and physical healing through her closeness to nature and through her friendship with Dickon and Colin. Despite some religiose posturing at the end, this book has never lost its power to enchant.

Shadow of a Bull by Maia Wojciechowska. Manolo, at twelve, must face his first bullfight, and all because his father was Spain's most famous torero. Secretly, Manolo is torn by doubts and fears. A vivid, convincing and dramatic story of a boy's difficult choices.

The Sheep-Pig by Dick King-Smith. A perfectly accomplished animal story for all ages over six. An orphan piglet, Babe, learns the essentials of sheep-herding from his canine foster mother. But because he combines gentle courtesy with eager intelligence, he wins the loyalty of the sheep and outdoes all doggy contenders to become a grand champion in the sheep-dog trials. The reticent Farmer Hogget and his loquacious wife are carica-tures, but endearing ones, as are the unexpectedly refreshing depictions of the farm animals. The whole story bubbles with gentle satire, affection and the delightful triumph of the underpig. Mary Rayner's witty line drawings add to the charm.

Smith by Leon Garfield. Smith, a grubby eighteenth-century urchin and pickpocket, witnesses a murder, befriends a blind Justice, unravels a mystery and finds a treasure in this brilliant novel. Garfield dazzles with his speed, sardonic wit, Gothic plots and mastery of the language, but beneath the dazzle there is also irony and subtle moral discrimination.

Smoky, the Cow Horse by Will James. A rambling old-fashioned narrative about the birth, adventures and misadventures of a cow pony who is adopted by Clint, the cowboy, on the cattle ranges of the old West. The story is told in cowboy lingo, and tinged with the casual racism of its day (the villain is a 'half-breed'), but the narrator's impassioned empathy with the horse, and the authentic, unromanticized details of rodeo and range life, make this 1926 tale a sturdy old favourite, particularly for young horselovers.

Snow Treasure by Marie McSwigan. Despite its somewhat simplistic style, this true action story has been loved by generations of schoolchildren. Sledging right under the noses of Nazi occupation troops, Norwegian children smuggle nine million dollars of Norwegian gold bullion to a waiting ship for transport to America. Their courage and steadfastness, and the swift, suspenseful plot, make the story almost cinematically gripping.

Soup by Robert Newton Peck. A classic 'boys' book' about a New England boyhood, complete with fistfights, escapades, moral revelations. The prose is crisp, wryly observant, unsentimental.

The Stone Book by Alan Garner. Mary's father is a stonemason in a Cheshire village; he takes her to the dizzying top of the steeple on a church he has helped build, and deep to a hidden underground cave where he shows her a family secret: a prehistoric painting. This is the first of four very short, intense and poetically powerful novels in which different generations of craftsmen and their children in Garner's family are glimpsed in a mesh of criss-crossing relationships and tasks. They are beautiful, demanding and unique.

The Story of the Treasure-Seekers by E. Nesbit. Unforgettably funny and charming book about the struggles of the Victorian Bastable children – all of them distinct characters in their own right – to restore 'the fallen fortunes' of their motherless family. Part of the delight is the tone of the supposedly anonymous narrator, Oswald, who can't resist giving away his identity through some not-so-discreet boasting.

The Summer of the Swans by Betsy Byars. A down-to-earth and affecting story about a summer in the life of a fourteen-year-old American girl who worries about her looks, loves her retarded brother Charlie, and makes some important discoveries on the heart-stopping day when Charlie gets lost.

Swallows and Amazons by Arthur Ransome. This series about two families of children who sail their dinghies and camp out on an island on Lake Windermere were the first and for ever the best of the 'children on holiday' books. The novels are about the developing character, spirited independence and imaginative play of the Walker and Blackett children; Ransome tells their story with a journalist's feel for humour, dialogue and concrete detail. At their best (*Missee Lee* and *We Didn't Mean to Go to Sea*), they are exciting, dramatic and liberating.

That Scatterbrain Booky by Bernice Thurman Hunter. A warm-hearted, fictionalized account of a skinny, spirited little girl growing up in a real

Depression in Toronto. Rich in recollected detail of city life, hardship, family struggle and improvised fun.

Tom Tiddler's Ground by John Rowe Townsend. A straightforward 'summer adventure' story in a modern industrial setting of unusual charm. Victor and Brian live beside an old, unused canal where, tagged after by some pesky girls and an unpopular boy, all of whom soon become valued members of the gang, they discover a half-sunken barge. There's treasure, warfare with crooks, and an old family mystery to unravel in this lively, naturalistic and appealing story.

The Three and Many Wishes of Jason Reid by H. J. Hutchins. Eleven-year-old Jason tricks an 'elster' – a kind of elf – into giving him unlimited wishes, but all the magical toys (a homework machine, a dinosaur book with living pictures) begin to pale. Jason and his friend Penny try to invent a really worthwhile wish and end up saving the local park from development.

The Three Royal Monkeys by Walter de la Mare. The immense odyssey of the three monkeys, Thumb, Thimble and Nod, to the secret kingdom of Tishmar, has been called 'one of the most imaginative and poetic stories ever written for children'. Rich, strange and wonderful, it is a rewarding challenge for good readers.

Thunder and Lightnings by Jan Mark. Two boys of very different backgrounds, living in Norfolk, form a friendship around a fascination with aeroplanes from a local air base. Andrew, the middle-class boy, learns some subtle lessons of friendship. Sharply observant, verbally inventive and emotionally rewarding.

Tikta'Liktak by James Houston. Adrift on an ice floe, and then marooned on a barren island, the young Inuit hunter Tikta'Liktak resigns himself to death – and then resolves to live. His ingenuity, skill and daring, and eventual reunion with his family, make a realistically detailed and exciting story of survival. Excellent drawings by the author.

Tom's Midnight Garden by Philippa Pearce. Tom is bored at his aunt and uncle's flat, until he discovers a door that opens to an enchanted garden whenever the hall clock strikes thirteen. The story gains unusual emotional depth from the superb imagery and from the evolving friendship between Tom and the mysterious Hatty, a girl who lives in another time. The resolution of the story is uniquely satisfying. This is widely regarded as the finest, most poignant and exhilarating time-shift fantasy ever.

Tuck Everlasting by Natalie Babbit. A beautifully written fable about over-protected Winnie Foster, aged ten, who stumbles on the Tuck family's secret: a fountain of eternal youth. Winnie rebels, discovers the joys of freedom, and has to make a profound choice.

The Twelve and the Genii by Pauline Clarke. Under a loose board in the attic of the farmhouse, eight-year-old Max finds twelve faded wooden soldiers. And then they come to life, under the leadership of their 'patriarch', Butter Crashey. They are, in fact, the famous lost soldiers of the Bronte children. The engagingly intense Max and his sister Jane must negotiate perilously between the 'real' adult world and the fascinating miniature one they are trying to protect and preserve. The story is written with crackling vitality, mesmerizing drama, and a vigorous moral dimension.

The Twenty-One Balloons by William Pene du Bois. This elegant and marvellously fresh Robinsonnade, set in 1883, was first published in 1947. Professor Sherman tells how he left San Francisco for a leisurely year of balloon travel, only to crash-land on the South Pacific island of Krakatoa. There he discovers a boyish utopia in which twenty families, blessed with fabulous wealth and a Gourmet Government, revel in inventions of great mechanical ingenuity, rotating feasts and tropical indolence. A swift and good-humoured story, with the added zest of science-fiction marvels and balloon-lore, all made clear by the author's extraordinarily witty and appealing black and white drawings.

Two Piano-Tuners by M. B. Goffstein. Debbie wants to be a piano tuner like her grandfather; he wants her to be a concert pianist. An empathetic story about love and individuality, with Goffstein's characteristic vividness of homey details.

Warrior Scarlet by Rosemary Sutcliff. Drem, a nine-year-old boy in a Bronze Age village, grows to manhood but fails his crucial 'wolf-slaying' test because of his withered arm. Heady, Kiplingesque language and a powerful, emotional evocation of a distant time.

We Couldn't Leave Dinah by Mary Treadgold. A fast-moving, exciting adventure story about a brother and sister who are accidentally left behind when Jersey, in the Channel Islands, is evacuated as the Nazis invade. The children engage in a daring plot to rescue their beloved pony from the Nazi occupiers before they flee. Believable and tense, and a favourite of horselovers.

The Way to Sattin Shore by Philippa Pearce. Nine-year-old Kate Tranter's family has too many secrets. Brooding and reserved, she puzzles over her missing ... dead? ... father. In solving the mystery, Kate begins to move out of childhood's self-centredness. This is a subtle, splendidly written story of family relationships and reconciliation; unsentimental, lucid and challenging.

When Marnie Was There by Joan Robinson. A dreamy, leisurely paced story of haunting beauty and great emotional resonance. Anna is a shy, withdrawn foster-child, cut off from easy friendships by her bottled-up anger against both the mother who died and the grandmother who she thinks abandoned her. Sent down to a Norfolk village for several months, she meets a strange, exciting, will-o'-the-wisp kind of girl who becomes her secret friend. In the intensity of the friendship with Marnie, the icy anger in Anna thaws. When a lively, affectionate family comes to stay in the romantic old Marsh House, Anna is drawn easily into the warmth of their circle. It's a wonderful portrait of natural healing and the gaiety of play. The ending, in which all the threads are drawn together, the mystery of Marnie explained and Anna's link with Marsh House revealed, is unforgettably satisfying.

Wildcat Under Glass by Alki Zei. Two little girls in a Greek village are caught up in wrenching political controversies as fascism poisons prewar Greece. The younger, Melia, influenced by her sage-like grandfather, chooses democracy, and helps to hide her fugitive freedom-fighter cousin, Niko. A rounded and fascinating portrait of both child and adult characters; play and friendship go on during the tense excitements and moral dilemmas of the times.

The Wind in the Willows by Kenneth Grahame. This arcadian reverie is not only a wonderfully well-written celebration of rural bliss, but is peopled with endearing, comic childlike characters (Mole, Ratty and Toad of Toad Hall) whose affections and escapades are unforgettable. With the familiar E. H. Shepard drawings, far preferable to most later versions.

Witch Week by Diana Wynne Jones. In a world where witchcraft is common but absolutely illegal, two students in a boarding school are persecuted for their suspected witchery. As usual in Wynne Jones, there is spirited comedy, a plot filled with twists and surprises, vigorous action, and a deeper, unstated and valuable message. In this case, it's that growing to adult power is all the revenge you need for childhood injustices.

The Yearling by Marjorie Kinnan Rawlings. The story of a lonely boy, Jody, and his pet deer, Flag, won a Pulitzer Prize in 1939, and retains all its power to seize the reader by the imagination and the heartstrings. This is an unparalleled recreation of the primitive, beautiful Florida wilderness and the hard lives of its inhabitants. Jody's intense, sometimes heartbreaking, relationships with his father, his fawn, and his crippled friend, Fodder-wing, are drawn with compelling force. A recent Charles Scribners' Sons edition has the original N. C. Wyeth colour illustrations.

Preteenage Readers: Ages 10 to 12

Reading levels overlap with those of older 'middle readers', but the content tends more to the introspective and social concerns of the prepubescent.

Alan and Naomi by Myron Levoy. When thirteen-year-old Alan is asked to befriend a disturbed girl who is a refugee from Nazi-occupied France, he is afraid of losing his street-smart best buddy, Shaun Kelly. Levoy brilliantly captures the conversation, games and complex feelings of the three youngsters and the atmosphere of wartime New York.

Alan Mendelsohn, the Boy from Mars by Daniel M. Pinkwater. When portly Leonard Neeble goes to Bat Masterson High, he is definitely odd man out – until he meets Alan and the two of them embark on a zany exploration of the occult, including a solemn study of Samuel Klugarsh's Mind Control Method. The story is thickly populated with Pinkwater's most inspired eccentrics, and riotous with his off-the-wall deadpan humour. Humane values underlie this lovable spoof-cum-fantasy.

And Now Miguel by Joseph Krumgold. A remarkably fresh, realistic and sympathetic first-person account of Miguel, the middle son in a large New Mexico sheep-herding family. Miguel is impatient for adulthood to arrive, so he can be allowed to join the men who drive the sheep up into the Sangre de Cristo Mountains for their summer grazing. The setting of a warm, traditional family structure and Spanish culture is intensely particular; the tumult and the longings are universal.

Ask Me No Questions by Ann Schlee. Stifled by the Victorian respectability of her aunt's village house, Laura is unable to make anyone listen to the truth about the ghastly conditions she has observed in the 'baby farm', or paupers' orphanage, next door. At last she takes desperate action to deal with the moral dilemma herself.

Badger on the Barge by Janni Howker. Five brilliant, deeply engaging stories about youngsters' strange and rewarding encounters with old people. Like Mayne, Pearce, Walsh, Mark and Gardam, Howker's literary bravura can be relished on a thoroughly adult level. Dazzling technical facility combines with a depth of insight, emotional honesty and originality to make her stories as gripping to young readers as they are to adults. Her characters are vitally, individualistically *present* from their first utterance; the swiftly developed plots resonate with dreamlike eeriness or the grittiness and impetuosity of daily life, and yet flow with seeming effortlessness. Her themes are large (pain, loss, ageing, death, youth's troubling intimations of adult sexuality, class resentment, economic hardship, racial and sexual bigotry) but they always emerge through speech, action and character, in all their human complexity. The reader ends up, not with a 'message', but with a sharp, exhilarated sense of being more intimately involved with life.

The Baitchopper by Silver Donald Cameron. The liveliest part of this boys' story, about a fishermen's strike in Nova Scotia and the rancorous divisions among the townspeople, comes at the climax when two boys, sons of strikers, rescue a fishing boat that has been set adrift in a storm.

The Book of Three by Lloyd Alexander. Taran is an assistant pig keeper who finds himself helping a prince to save the land of Prydain from the Horned King and the forces of evil. The sturdy, open honesty of Taran's youthful character, the humour and the natural dialogue save this Welsh-legend-based five-volume fantasy from seeming derivative.

Bridge to Terabithia by Katharine Paterson. Eleven-year-old Jess's family is rural, poor and harsh. But his life changes for ever when Leslie, a bright, independent city girl, moves nearby. Together they create an imaginary kingdom where Jess absorbs enough of Leslie's courage to enable him to deal with the tragedy that ends their idyll. An intensely moving and widely loved book.

Carrie's War by Nina Bawden. Carrie, now grown up, brings her own children back to the Welsh village to which she was evacuated as a twelve-year-old during the war. The novel is a flashback to dramatic events and powerful emotional ties which have haunted Carrie ever since. The ending, back in Carrie's adult present, provides a deeply satisfying conclusion to the story of a lost friendship.

A Chance Child by Jill Paton Walsh. An especially gripping time-shift fantasy in which Creep, an abused child, escapes down a Northern England canal and slips back a century, to a time in which seven- and eight-year-old children worked in mines and smithies. Creep, a shivering, bewildered ghost, can be seen only by children as hungry as he is – and they befriend him despite their own horrifically convincing misery. Poignant and memorable.

Comfort Herself by Geraldine Kaye. Comfort is a bright, self-sufficient eleven-year-old, half-English and half-Ghanaian. When her flower-child mother is killed in an accident, Comfort must use all her wits and courage to adapt to drastic circumstances. First she lives with her middle-class English grandparents in a village; then with her father's family in rural

Ghana. The contrasting cultures are brought swiftly, sympathetically and convincingly to life. Comfort emerges as a uniquely resilient, believable character in this satisfying and accessible story.

The Court of the Stone Children by Eleanor Cameron. Nina, new to San Francisco, spends her time daydreaming in the French Museum – and finds that her life overlaps with that of a mysterious French girl from another century. Together, they help the museum curator unravel a romantic mystery from the past. A love story and time fantasy expertly woven together.

Dear Mr Henshaw by Beverly Cleary. A lightly and skilfully written epistolary novel. Leigh Botts, age ten, writes a series of letters to the author of his favourite book, *Ways to Amuse a Dog*. Obliquely, through their correspondence, we watch Leigh come to terms with his distress about his divorced and negligent truck driver father. (9+)

Death Over Montreal by Geoffrey Bilson. A Scots immigrant boy, teenager Jamie Douglas, finds himself in the midst of a cholera epidemic in the new country. A vivid story of the confusion, the squalor, and the riff-raff who preyed on new immigrants – and of Jamie's growing courage and competence.

Dogsbody by Diana Wynne Jones. An astonishingly original account of how hot-headed Sirius, the dog star, is cast down to earth in the shape of an Irish setter puppy and adopted by the lonely daughter of an imprisoned IRA member. The entire story of Sirius's search for a lost 'zoi', or magical power, and his eventual return to his status as a heavenly Luminary, is told from inside his doggy persona. Parallel to the exciting fantasy is the touching story of the girl's affection for Sirius and her growth to independence.

Drift by William Mayne. An extraordinarily believable adventure, in which Rafe, an American boy of early settler times, is lost in the wilderness when he follows an Indian girl to see a bear. We see Rafe's frightening odyssey through his own baffled eyes and then through the eyes of Tawena, the resourceful Indian girl, who helps him to save himself. The clash of cultures and the strange bond between them is beautifully evoked through the youngsters' reactions to each other and to crisis.

Earthfasts by William Mayne. When Nellie Jack John, drummer boy, comes marching out of a crack in a Cumbrian hillside before the astonished eyes of two contemporary schoolboys, he opens a 'leak' in time: soon the neighbouring farms are beseiged by walking stones, giants, boggarts, wild boars and the clatter of King Arthur's troops. Told with hallucinatory clarity by a master of English prose.

A TREASURY

The Eight Days of Luke by Diana Wynne Jones. Twelve-year-old David has to live with ghastly relatives until he accidentally conjures up a mysterious boy, Luke, who has strange powers – and powerful enemies. A suspenseful, comedic fantasy with elements of Norse legend.

The Emperor's Winding Sheet by Jill Paton Walsh. Young Piers is kidnapped from a British merchant ship by Turkish pirates, escapes, and ends up as a sullen captive mascot to the Emperor Constantine in the exotic, doomed city of Byzantium. As the Turkish siege tightens around the city and the gruesome last battle begins, Piers learns to see the world through changed eyes. A subtle, intelligent and highly charged historical novel.

The Endless Steppe: A Girl in Exile by Esther Hautzig. Like *The Diary of Anne Frank*, only less tragic, this true story of a Jewish girl and her family who are deported to Siberia during World War II is inspiring, rather than gloomy. Despite overwhelming hardship, Esther approaches her experiences with the buoyancy, freshness and optimism of youth; her concerns and triumphs are those of adolescence, not those of a starving refugee.

Fireweed by Jill Paton Walsh. Runaway teenagers Bill and Julie meet during the London Blitz and try to survive together in a bombed house. The Blitz is evoked with eerie sensual power, and the tensions, the growing bond and the eventual heartbreaking gulf between the young people is handled with moving delicacy. (12+)

A Flute in Mayberry Street by Eileen Dunlop. A teenaged brother and his sickly sister in Edinburgh stumble on a family mystery. The solution, with fantasy elements, is gripping, and the character development is strongly integrated with the plot.

Freaky Friday by Mary Rodgers. Annabel Andrews, thirteen, 'metal-mouthed killer ghoul of Central Park', wakes up one morning to find herself in her mother's body. All set to savour the delights of adulthood, she runs into a Marx Brothers kind of mayhem instead. Spying on her own life, however, she finds out some ego-bolstering truths. Hilarious.

Frozen Fire by James Houston. Matthew Fraser, thirteen, and his Inuit friend Kayak get lost in the Arctic winter in a search for Matthew's missing father. The story is strong on information and excitement; the style is the usual brisk journalism of all these Canadian-boy-and-native-friend adventures.

The Ghost Belonged to Me by Richard Peck. Thirteen-year-old Alexander, living in a Midwest town in 1913, gets a rural, folksy, funny education in the interesting subject of girls – via a ghost of a Southern belle with whom he falls in love, and also via the all-too-real, skinny, snap-eyed Blossom Culp, his unwanted but tenacious accomplice in solving the mystery.

Gideon Ahoy! by William Mayne. Only Mayne could have written this extraordinarily evocative, moving and intensely observed story of family life. Eve, twelve, is the sensible, reliable one; her teenage brother, Gideon, is brain damaged and deaf and her small brother and sister are impish, wildly imaginative toddlers. In his usual demanding, finely calibrated prose, Mayne makes us feel the warm humanity and individuality of each of the characters (Gideon no less than the others). We rejoice in Gideon's new-found independence when he gets a job as a helper on a canal-boat, hold our breath when he falls into danger, share Eve's loving exasperation and feel moment by moment the terror of the book's climactic episode. 'One touch of nature makes the whole world kin,' says Dad, as Gideon hovers near death. Mayne's books do the same for the accomplished reader.

The Granny Project by Anne Fine. Four brothers and sisters of distinctive character decide to fight their parents' decision to put Granny in a home – by fair means and foul. The novel does not shirk the truth about the demands of caring for an elderly relative, but it tackles the subject with wit, energy and compassion. Particularly interesting is the intellectual debate between the two teenage siblings, Sophie and Ivan, that brings abstract political ideas into the realm of personal behaviour.

The Great Gilly Hopkins by Katharine Paterson. Gilly, the eleven-year-old abandoned daughter of a flower child, is tough, smart and hostile. Too late, she realizes that the freakish foster home she has rejected is a loving haven. Though the ingredients are the familiar ones of contemporary 'problem novels', Paterson writes with such skill and sensitivity that her characters are alive with stubborn complexity; they are both moving and memorable.

The Hand of Robin Squires by Joan Clark. An eighteenth-century English boy is brought to Oak Island, off Nova Scotia, by his piratical uncle. The boy is forced to work with pitiful black slaves to dig the shafts where treasure is to be buried, and escapes only with the help of a Micmac Indian friend. This is an ingenious fictional explanation for the real Oak Island diggings.

Handles by Jan Mark. The deliciously funny story of eleven-year-old Erica's holiday with sluglike country relatives. Erica, miserably exiled from town life, consoles herself with imaginative stream-of-consciousness private jokes. Then she discovers the motorcycle garage in the village. Erica, mad for motorcycles and determined to be a mechanic, finds a kindred soul in the man who owns the garage and who bestows witty 'handles', or nicknames, on everyone and everything. Jan Mark creates a vivid private world in the life of the garage.

Harpoon of the Hunter by Markoosie. Canada's most thrilling, poignant and poetically intense story of Inuit life. Kamik, sixteen, must survive alone in the wilderness after his father's hunting party is wiped out. We see how Inuit resourcefulness and courage are born of desperation and fear. There are convincing portraits of the women's strength, too, and a touching but tragic love story. Illustrated by Germaine Arnaktauyok.

The Hill of the Red Fox by Allan Campbell McLean. Alasdair, twelve, is a big-city bookworm and daydreamer when he visits his dead father's former home on the Isle of Skye, where he forms a strong and heartening bond with his father's rugged friend, Duncan Mor. This is a wonderful, suspenseful spy thriller, with lively Scots background and affecting relationships worthy of R. L. Stevenson.

Homecoming by Cynthia Voight. A long, naturalistic and very compelling novel about strong-minded, resilient thirteen-year-old Dicey. She shepherds her younger brothers and sisters from Cape Cod to Maryland, mostly by foot and mostly hungry, to find a relative who will take them in after their confused mother deserts them. Vivid, believable characters, a suspenseful quest, and a deep feeling for the contemporary landscape.

Homesick by Jean Fritz. A memoir of Fritz's missionary childhood beside the Yangtse River in turbulent pre-revolutionary China. Fritz's account of colourful experiences, fascinating people and dramatic events are told so freshly, from within a lively child's keen sensibility, that the memoir reads like fiction.

The Homeward Bounders by Diana Wynne Jones. A dazzlingly complex and suspenseful fantasy about Jamie, aged twelve, who is doomed to be an exile from his own time after he becomes a Random Factor in a world-dominating war game played by shadowy evil figures. Especially thought-provoking for Dungeons and Dragons devotees. Strands of mythology (Prometheus, the Flying Dutchman) and original characters like Joris the Demon-Hunter enrich this mysterious and surprising story. (12+)

I, Juan De Pareja by Elizabeth Borton de Trevino. A strange, fascinating fictional 'autobiography', by turns stoic and lushly exotic, of a black slave in seventeenth-century Spain, who became an apprentice to the great painter Velasquez. (A famous portrait of De Pareja exists.) Only in middle age, when he goes to Italy, does De Pareja realize his dream of becoming a painter himself, since Spain forbade slaves to practise any art.

I Own the Racecourse! by Patricia Wrightson. Andy, who is slightly retarded, is the mascot of a good-hearted gang of working-class boys in

Sydney. When a tramp 'sells' the local racecourse to the gullible Andy, they are indignant on his behalf and finally confused about just what is real and what isn't. An extremely unusual, rounded and luminously written story.

Island of the Blue Dolphins by Scott O'Dell. A poignant and dramatic story, restrained in tone but powerful in impact, about the resilience of the human spirit. Karana is only twelve when she is accidentally abandoned on a wind-scoured Pacific island by her departing tribe. Her lonely survival into womanhood is both heartbreaking and triumphant.

Jellybean by Tessa Duder. Geraldine, nicknamed 'Jellybean', resents her single mother's preoccupation with her career as a classical cellist, so she hides her own growing interest in music. Then a mysterious stranger, also a cellist, arrives on the scene, and he seems to know all about Geraldine and her mother. Could this be her missing father? The backstage scenes at a production of *The Nutcracker*, and Geraldine's secret dreams and public triumph as a junior conductor, add an extra dimension of interest to this competently told story.

Jeremy Visick by David Wiseman. Matthew, twelve, works on a 'boring' history assignment and finds himself caught up in a Cornish mining tragedy of a century before, in which another twelve-year-old boy was buried in a now-lost mine shaft. A tense, adventuresome time-shift story.

Johnny Tremain by Esther Forbes. An enduringly spacious, detailed and lively historical novel about an arrogant and talented silversmith's apprentice in Boston just before the Revolution. Johnny becomes an outcast after a crippling accident, but it is the making of his character, and he goes on to become an idealistic young acolyte of the Revolutionaries.

Journey of the Shadow Bairns by Margaret J. Anderson. Elspeth, suddenly orphaned in a Glasgow slum, is only twelve, but she manages to bring her four-year-old brother all the way to Canada, following a charismatic leader who takes a group to the North Saskatchewan territory. An added dimension is the way Elspeth stubbornly works out for herself whether to continue to follow the group's leader after the other settlers become disillusioned with him. A believable and dramatic story of pioneer days.

Julie of the Wolves by Jean Craighead George. An implausible yet convincing and touching story of a thirteen-year-old Inuit girl who runs away from an arranged marriage. She is lost on the tundra, survives with the help of a wolf pack and the memory of her father's lore, only to arrive at safety in a bittersweet conclusion as she realizes 'the day of the wolf and the Eskimo is gone'.

The Keeper of the Isis Light by Monica Hughes. Sixteen-year-old Olwen has kept the lighthouse on the planet Isis for years, alone with her mysterious Guardian, just in order to guide Earth refugees to a haven. But when fellow humans do arrive, her happiness is shattered as they recoil from the strange adaptations she has been forced to make to live there. Easy-to-read science fiction, but thought-provoking, with much more scope for emotional empathy than is usual in this type of fiction.

Kim by Rudyard Kipling. The great adventure of Kim, the Irish-Indian bazaar urchin who speaks a dozen dialects, goes on a pilgrimage with a Tibetan Lama, is master of a thousand disguises, lives by his wits and is trained to be a spy, is told in the rolling, rhythmic, highly coloured language that makes it irresistible.

The Lantern Bearers by Rosemary Sutcliff. In a time of wrenching dislocation in Britain's history – brutal pillaging by Saxon 'sea wolves' and the departure of the last Roman troops – Aquila and his younger sister make painful decisions about their destiny. Aquila, after escaping from Saxon slavery, takes arms under Artos, British warlord. His sister marries a Saxon. Sutcliff gives a human face to history in this and her other fine novels, like *The Eagle of the Ninth*.

Let It Go by Marilyn Halvorson. Fifteen-year-old Jared and his friend, Lance, are buddies, but they each hide one secret. Jared has a brother in a drug-overdose coma, and Lance's absent mother is a country singing star who has reappeared suddenly, threatening Lance's happy life with his father. A 'problem novel' that is saved from being an S. E. Hinton clone by a strong evocation of adolescent emotions and of Alberta wilderness living.

Little Women by Louisa M. Alcott. The adolescent sisters and their 'Marmee' (Smarmee, as one biting critic called her) still hold fascination, mostly by virtue of their moral ambition – their ongoing game is to act out Pilgrim's Progress – and the rebellious character of Jo. The eventual 'taming' of Jo into ladylike behaviour is a letdown but central to the purposes of anti-feminist Alcott.

Madame Doubtfire by Anne Fine. A lesson in how a contemporary novel, complete with divorced and warring parents, joint custody, a working mum, unemployed dad and other up-to-date problems, can achieve more than relevance. Lydia, Christopher and little Natty shuttle tensely back and forth between their angry parents until a crisis blows up. Their mother needs a housekeeper. And their father, Daniel, an actor, needs more time with them and more money than he earns by part-time nude modelling. Anne Fine carries off his masquerade, and its slapstick consequences, with great flair. And when the charade explodes in open parental warfare, the children teach the parents how to negotiate a ceasefire. The writing is hilarious, poignant and ultimately both sane and hopeful.

Mama's Going to Buy You a Mockingbird by Jean Little. After his father's lingering death from cancer, Jeremy, eleven, must cope with repressed rage and grief, his mother's new life, and the tall, embarrassingly unconventional girl his father wanted him to befriend. A touching, naturalistic novel.

Midnight Is a Place by Joan Aiken. Cruel child labour in a nineteenth-century carpet mill provides the vivid background to this lively Gothic adventure, in which two orphans, Lucas, thirteen, and waiflike Anne-Marie, are cast down from cold privilege to hard times. Independence, comradeship and an enlightened conscience are their reward for their determined survival in the slums. Aiken can infuse the grimmest situation with humour, and her characters are always warmly appealing.

The Moves Make the Man by Bruce Brooks. Jerome is witty, endearing, a brilliant student, a basketball whiz, a thirteen-year-old who unabashedly takes cooking lessons at school so he can feed his older brothers while Momma is ill. He is also hearteningly impervious to the crude racism he meets at his all-white school. But he's completely convincing, partly because Brooks can write about Jerome's solitary basketball practice in a way that makes the reader feel the exhilaration of physical mastery. Jerome, whose wily trickster 'moves' in basketball are a metaphor for methods of black survival, befriends a white athlete, Bix, who is neurotically fixated on an ideal of 'truth', however narrowly defined and destructive. Their strange friendship illuminates the black–white culture gap, while the story never loses momentum.

Nkwala by Edith Lambert Sharp. Nkwala is a Salish Indian boy of twelve, who must undergo a lonely manhood vigil on the Canadian prairies. His trials of endurance and skill are fascinating; this is one of the few Indian stories written by a non-Indian that can make us feel from within the awe, the mystery, the prickle of fear a native youth experiences in the primordial forest. The story of his tribe's trek into danger is both dramatic and touching.

No Beat of Drum by Hester Burton. A vigorous, absorbing and beautifully written historical novel about Joe Hinton, a sturdy and optimistic youth who is caught up in the farmers' riots of 1830 and transported to Van Diemen's Land. The crushing injustices of the times are conveyed with unsparing vividness: starvation on the farm, hopelessly biased courts, convict ships and brutish life in the colonies. But Joe, doggedly faithful to decent rural values, perseveres, finds his childhood sweetheart, and flourishes at last.

Nobody's Family Is Going to Change by Louise Fitzhugh. Eleven-year-old Emma is a 'fat brown girl' determined to be a lawyer like her father; her little brother Willie is equally determined to be a dancer. Her tough-minded rebellion against her parents' stereotyped expectation leads her at last to an understanding that time and hope are on her side. An unsentimental, vigorously written and optimistic story.

The One-Eyed Cat by Paula Fox. Ned is haunted by guilt: did he shoot the one-eyed cat that night in the dark with his forbidden Daisy air rifle? A subtle, controlled and moving story about a boy's conscience and expiation. Comic relief is provided by a savage satiric portrait of a repulsive housekeeper.

Pat of Silver Bush by L. M. Montgomery. Another thick, sweet fudge of a Montgomery book, filled with stage Irish, ardent innocent girlhood and rural nostalgia, still a potent (and reactionary) mixture. Pat grows from a tradition-loving seven-year-old to a tradition-loving young woman who is taken in by several different meretricious styles of manhood before she settles for her childhood chum.

Philip Hall Likes Me, Maybe I Reckon by Bette Green. A black eleven-year-old, Beth, in rural Arkansas has a crush on the boy next door, but has to let him win every contest to keep his friendship – until she gets fed up. A short, jaunty and good-humoured novel of budding boy–girl relationships.

Playing Beatie Bow by Ruth Park. Spiky and resentful Abigail, age fourteen, quarrels with her divorced parents just before she is led into the past by a mysterious little girl. Her year with the Bow family in nineteenth-century Sydney is an amazingly vivid and poignant recreation of the hardships of working-class life in the slums. An extremely absorbing, exciting and touching account of growing maturity and first love. (12+)

Roll of Thunder, Hear My Cry by Mildred D. Taylor. Cassie is the middle child in a proudly independent black family which struggles to hold on to its own land in Depression-era Mississippi. This is a richly detailed, powerful and unflinching family drama of a girl's confrontation with brutal racism.

The Root Cellar by Janet Lunn. An unusually fine time-shift fantasy about Rose Larkin, a lonely thirteen-year-old orphan, who slips back in time to Upper Canada where she is befriended by a warm-hearted servant girl and a restless, sensitive boy. During a graphically realistic search for Will, lost somewhere in the American Civil War, Rose discovers compassion, roots and the warmth of friendship.

Runaway to Freedom by Barbara Smucker. (Originally *Underground to Canada*.) Tall, strong Julilly, twelve, and thirteen-year-old Liza, who is crippled from cruel beatings, escape from slavery in Mississippi and travel to safety in Canada by the underground railway. This immensely strong story is told with honest simplicity and real emotion. The girls have dignity and resourcefulness, and those who hinder or help them along the way are sharply drawn.

The Sign of the Beaver by Elizabeth George Speare. Twelve-year-old Matthew is left to fend for himself in a Maine cabin when his pioneer father unaccountably doesn't return from a trip to town. How he copes with difficulties – and his dawning awareness of injustice as he forms a prickly, tentative friendship with Attian, an Indian boy – make a strong and provocative story.

The Slave Dancer by Paula Fox. A horrific and illuminating story of Jesse, a twelve-year-old boy who is kidnapped from New Orleans to serve as a fife player on a slave ship. Perfectly pitched to the understanding of young readers without shirking or exploiting the gruesome reality and moral horror of the slave trade.

The Snow Spider by Jenny Nimmo. Gwynn's sister vanished mysteriously on his fifth birthday; now, four years later, his grandmother gives him a handful of strange birthday gifts that will bring him his heart's desire and heal the grieving, divided family. This strong fantasy is anchored in daily life in rural Wales, with its farm chores and routines of school and friends. The icy menace and eerie beauty of the magic Gwynn invokes – as well as his faltering progress toward greater maturity – are powerfully written.

Soumchi by Amoz Oz. An ancient quarter of postwar Jerusalem, crowded with exotic cultures and political passions, is the colourful background for this lovely, funny story of a day in the life of eleven-year-old Soumchi. He trades his new-old bike for an electric train, acquires and loses a dog, runs away from home, falls in love, and tastes the first nostalgia for swiftly passing childhood. Superbly translated from the Hebrew by Penelope Farmer.

A Stranger Came Ashore by Mollie Hunter. Robbie, twelve, is suspicious when handsome Finn Lerson is washed ashore on their Shetland island and courts his pretty sister, Elspeth. Hunter, a vigorous and compelling storyteller, draws on Scottish legend for this swift-moving, suspenseful story.

Summer of My German Soldier by Bette Green. Patty, an abused twelve-year-old Jewish girl in a racist Arkansas town, daringly hides an escaped German prisoner-of-war. The unmitigated cruelty of her parents and the unbelievable nobility of the prisoner make this story into a melodrama, but it is undeniably powerful, especially in the relationship of Patty and Ruth, the family's black servant.

A Summer's Lease by Marilyn Sachs. Gloria, fifteen, is mercurial, prickly and gnawingly competitive; she is determined to overcome her bleak and limiting home life to become a great writer. A summer with a group of youngsters at the country home of her English teacher takes her through some alternately blissful and agonizing steps to maturity. A compelling insight into the abrasive egotism and wounding vulnerability of adolescence.

The Sword in the Stone by T. H. White. The first book in the *Once and Future King* trilogy, and by far the best; the sequels are marred by White's bitter misogyny. The Wart (to rhyme with Art) is just a scruffy orphan, fated to be squire to the arrogant young knight Kay, when a scraggly, wise, mysterious Merlin singles him out for a magical education. This comic, fantastic and capacious recreation of the King Arthur legend is not just a classic, but also a deserved favourite.

Tex by S. E. Hinton. This immensely popular story of two brothers in Oklahoma is a sort of Mills and Boon romance for boys; beneath their tough, macho swagger and narcissism, the boys are sensitive, loyal and have well-scrubbed middle-class values. No prizes for the Rebel-Without-a-Cause prose, but the emotional bond of the brothers and the reconciliation with their father are strongly evoked. (12+)

Torch, by Jill Paton Walsh. A strange and challenging story of a band of teenage youngsters with fragmentary Greek names . . . Cal, Cassie, Dio . . . who carry a mysterious torch on a quest that takes them from the Greek village of Olim, across deserts and seas, in search of 'The Games'. They are bearers of ancient meanings in a neoprimitive time that has lost books, history and technology. The story is carried along by the urgency and mystery of the quest. The author's provocative ideas about the rise and fall of civilizations, the central importance of memory, stories and continuity, and the divine spark that survives in darkest times are an added strength.

A Traveller in Time by Alison Uttley. Penelope Taberner steps through a door in an old farmhouse and finds herself in Tudor times, in the midst of a plot to save Mary, Queen of Scots. A dreamy, romantic time-travel story, drenched in pastoral colours and fragrances, combining the sturdy domestic comforts, affections and intrigues of a prosperous Elizabethan farmhouse with a shimmering kind of time-magic.

Treasure Island by R. L. Stevenson. Blind Pew, Long John Silver, Dr Livesey, Squire Trelawney – and yo-ho-ho and a bottle of rum! – who can forget any of these provokingly ambiguous characters, or the magnificent story of piracy, the sea, buried treasure and the disillusionment of its pursuit? An essential book, especially in the facsimile edition with superb N. C. Wyeth oil paintings.

The Twenty-Two Letters by Clive King. A perfect novel for those youngsters who long to know the beginnings of things, to spy on the past. A family of one sister and three brothers living in Byblos 3500 years ago – Aleph, Beth, Nun and Zayin – are caught up in the great events of their day. Almost accidentally, they invent the practical use of the alphabet, discover the secret art of horse riding, and learn how to navigate by the stars. King makes us feel how difficult and how momentous these mental steps were in that time and place; humour and grand adventure carry the story swimmingly along, and a subtler message ('What you carry in your mind is of far greater value than your material possessions') is brought home convincingly after the apocalyptic volcanic eruption that nearly wipes out civilization at the book's climax.

Up a Road Slowly by Irene Hunt. The great strength of this story about Julie, who goes to live with her austere Aunt Cordelia in New England when she is seven and stays until she graduates from high school, is the sensitive observation of both adult and teenage male–female relationships in all their variety, and the sometimes agonizing struggle of a strong-willed, talented girl to conform to the expectations of male society. The tone is restrained, adult and optimistic. (12+)

Up to Low by Brian Doyle. A rollicking story of pubescent love in the Ottawa Valley, told with an Irish lilt, genuinely funny grotty humour and an economy and freshness of language and imagery that distinguishes this writer among his contemporaries.

The Village By The Sea by Anita Desai. A superbly written novel about an Indian brother and sister who struggle to keep their family alive in an impoverished but heartbreakingly beautiful village near Bombay. Hari, twelve, runs away to the city where he endures cruel deprivation but does find work and learn a trade. This novel has all the texture and drama of Indian life and the believable emotion and yearnings of youth. (12+)

Walkabout by James Vance Marshall. The prose is too didactic, but this is a taut, tense and provocative story of how Mary, a prudish thirteen-year-old from South Carolina, and her more free-spirited six-year-old brother, are rescued by an Aboriginal boy when their plane crashes in the Australian desert. Mary's inability to overcome her racism and passive conditioning leads to doom for the boy who saves them.

Where the Lilies Bloom by Vera and Bill Cleaver. Mary Call, fourteen, struggles with all her ferocious determination to keep her Tennessee mountain family together after their father dies, and to prevent her 'cloudy-minded' older sister from marrying a boorish neighbour. By teaching her brothers and sisters to wildcraft – gather local herbs and roots – she keeps a roof over their heads despite all odds. (12+)

The White Mountains by John Christopher. Europe has been returned to a kind of ruined feudalism by the mysterious, menacing Tripods from outer space, who keep people ignorant and docile by the 'capping' ceremony. Will Parker, thirteen, flees with a friend to join a group of rebels. Effective, stripped-down prose and dramatic action for young science fiction addicts.

Words by Heart by Ouida Sebestyen. Lena's fierce pride is tempered by her father's gentle dignity in this well-written, moving story of a black family's struggle to establish themselves in the rural Midwest.

Teenage Readers: Ages 13 and Over

The emphasis in these books is on relationships of all kinds, some explicitly sexual, and on the spiritual and moral struggles of adolescence.

Across Five Aprils by Irene Hunt. Jethro, an Illinois farm boy, is only nine when the American Civil War begins. Over the next five years, his large, affectionate family is wrenched and buffeted by the strains of war, brought home to the reader in an intensely personal way. A growing-to-manhood story of unusual depth and solidity.

Across the Barricades by Joan Lingard. The working-class families, Belfast streets and constant poisonous pressure of religious hatreds add interest to the simple story of a Protestant girl who dares to love a Catholic boy.

The Adventures of Huckleberry Finn by Mark Twain. Around the basic adventure story of two runaways rafting down the Mississippi – a boy and an escaped slave – Twain exuberantly weaves this high-spirited, satirical, complex story of growing up. He exposes every variety of hypocrisy and human self-deception, and shows us how Huck learns to choose between good and evil, truth and lies, cruelty and compassion. His innate decency constantly bursts through the smokescreen of his learned 'morals'. Unforgettable.

The Apprentices by Leon Garfield. These twelve stories sparkle with scintillating imagery, much of it drawn from the Garden of Eden and Song of Songs, as they follow the linked destinies of twelve variously grimy, wretched but chipper London apprentices through the cycle of the year and the cycles of adolescent love and hope. Only Garfield could combine so much tenderness with so much glittering wit and verbal dash.

At the Sign of the Dog and Rocket by Jan Mark. Mum's on holiday, Dad's confined to bed with a slipped disc, and Lillian has to run the family pub by herself. What a shock when the new summer help turns out to be the student teacher she had mocked at school! Super-confident and combative Lillian learns some hard lessons before her relationship with 'Old Collins' starts to become interesting. The story is swift and hilarious as the job of running a busy pub veers close to chaos. Mark is in brilliant control, bringing us tantalizing hints of character and emotion in speech and action.

Her touch is uncannily deft and light and her insights and ear for dialogue razor-sharp.

Bilgewater by Jane Gardam. As sophisticatedly satirical and insightful as – and certainly better written than – most adult novels, this is the funny, oblique and many-layered story of Bilgewater's education of the heart. A pudgy, bespectacled, eccentric child growing up in the boys' boarding school where her father teaches, Bilgewater barely notices when she turns into a leggy adolescent. And she's just as myopic in her choice of boyfriends, falling for a handsome lout and then a poetic cheat while sturdy, unnoticed Boakes trots loyally at her heels. Meanwhile, the adults around her – from ageing professors to the wonderful matron – are engaging in their own foolish, wrong-headed or downright peculiar affairs of the heart. Bilgewater makes the right choices at last, but, years later, her backward look at her youth is tinged with the inevitable regrets.

A Bird in the House by Margaret Laurence. Eight beautifully written, resonant stories about the young Vanessa MacLeod and her tough, wry, domineering or defiant relatives – especially some wonderful aunts – in Manawaka, Manitoba. Through layers of the narrator's memory and Vanessa's growing awareness, we taste the irreducibility of early experience and the moral complexity that haunts us in the best fiction.

The Blue Hawk by Peter Dickinson. The remarkably convincing and vivid story of a priestly culture resembling ancient Egypt. Tron, a boy marked for the priesthood, begins to doubt, and is gradually moved to a daring rebellion. Dickinson makes the desert air crackle, the temples echo with hidden menace, and his characters live and breathe in an atmosphere charged with tension and awe.

The Book Lovers by Leon Garfield. A shy young man woos a pretty librarian by offering her this glorious compendium of love scenes from famous literature – Turgenev, Dickens, Balzac, Tolstoy, Austen and more. The playful intertwining of the nameless young couple's courtship with apposite selections from literature makes this a double treat.

Candy for King by Robert Leeson. Leeson uses a marvellous device to send up British institutions including public schools, trade unions and the army: Kitchener 'Candy' Candeford is a lumbering tabula rasa, a big, bumbling teenage orphan who is totally, riotously innocent. He takes the hypocritical cant of headmasters, officers and officials with complete Boy Scout earnestness and carries them to their idealistic extremes, thus showing up their hollowness in a series of rowdy adventures set in the 1950s. Leeson manages to make Candy a sympathetic and engaging hero-buffoon; though the novel shambles a bit, a satirical look at society is a breath of bracing air in the claustrophobic world of the teen novel.

Come to Mecca by Farrukh Dhondy. Six particularly sharp, colloquial and alert short stories that speak straight from the sensibilities of Bengali, Chinese and Caribbean teenagers in London. Dhondy is especially good at evoking the insecurity and panic that lie just below the surface of the young men's swaggering macho, and the anguish of youngsters caught between two cultures.

Dance on My Grave by Aidan Chambers. A first person story of homosexual love and tragedy, in which sixteen-year-old Hal confides to his journal (in a brittle, defensively cynical tone) the course of his shattered love affair with Barry, and why he had to keep the bizarre vow he had made to dance on Barry's grave. Through scraps of news reports, social workers' notes, court records and Hal's flashbacks, we watch him come to terms, painfully but with growing strength, with his own character.

Dogsong by Gary Paulsen. Paulsen is an exciting new writer and this novel about an Inuit boy, Russel, who chooses to live 'the old way' with the help of a dying shaman, is gripping, intense and completely convincing. Though Paulsen gives full measure to the harshness and beauty of the Arctic landscape, he manages not to romanticize Inuit life. In fact, his unflinching realism about Inuit ways is sometimes shockingly direct. When he describes the shaman eating frozen caribou eyes, or the way Russel trains a wolfish sled dog by matter-of-factly biting its nose, we are brought sharply against the otherness of the Inuit. It's a confrontation that stirs a respect born of awareness.

The Donkey's Crusade by Jean Morris. This is terra incognita for the children's novel: Asia in the thirteenth century. And so it breathes an exhilarating tang of strange deserts and icy mountain passes, as young Thomas, a Syrian 'Traveller' or professional guide, leads a Crusade of one English friar and one runaway boy across the Mesopotamian desert and along the ancient Silk Road in search of the mysterious Prester John. Even Thomas's imperious talking donkey, or the lonely desert ghosts they meet, do not seem implausible in such exotic climes. Despite the vast scope of their travels and the chaos of the times, with a Christian empire riven by schisms and crumbling under Mongol attack, the characters are endearingly individual and lively. Their long journey makes an absorbing story.

Dragonsong by Anne McCaffrey. On a planet menaced by deadly spores, where society is highly structured, a young girl, Menolly, breaks through taboos because she is the only one talented enough to take up the duties of Harper. One of the strongest of a very popular series of dragons and space fantasies.

The Druid's Tune by O. R. Melling. A melodramatic but effective first novel by a young Canadian in which a Toronto brother and sister, Rosemary, seventeen and Jimmy, fifteen, visit Ireland and are taken into a battle in prehistory, at the side of the legendary hero Cuculann, through the medium of a hired hand who turns out to be a wandering Druid.

The Ennead by Jan Mark. Isaac, a fifteen-year-old house steward on the bleakly authoritarian planet Erato, is a scrawny, nervous boy, as self-seeking and pettily corrupt as those he serves. Two immigrants – the silent, prophetic Moshe and a gangly, defiant artist, Eleanor – shake him out of his complacency and force him to make a desperate choice. Crisp, challenging prose and a thought-provoking story.

A Fabulous Creature by Zilpha Keatley Snyder. Vacationing in the Sierra Nevada mountains, fifteen-year-old James falls in love with a dazzling bikini-clad flirt, daughter of a trophy hunter, and, from the basest of motives, betrays to her the secret that only he and the imaginative thirteen-year-old Griffin know: an incredible stag is living nearby in a secret valley. An honest and sensitive look at teenage infatuation.

Far From Shore by Kevin Major. It's a rotten year for fifteen-year-old Chris. Dad is out of work and drinking, his older sister does well in school while he is failing, and Chris drifts into bad company with disastrous results. The story of his troubles – and recovery – is believably and sympathetically told through the interior monologues of each family member, with an earthy and amusing use of Newfoundland dialect and humour.

Father Figure by Richard Peck. Upper-class New Yorker Jim Atwater, seventeen, is too controlled, too sardonically defensive, to grieve openly over his mother's death. But when he and his precocious little brother Byron are forced to spend a summer in Florida with their shabby, estranged father (and his friend, the warm-hearted Marietta), Jim learns some hard lessons about his own sexual uncertainty, rivalry and defensiveness. Peck is at his urbane, witty and compassionate best in this excellent novel.

The First of Midnight by Marjorie Darke. Jess is a truculent, benighted poorhouse urchin in eighteenth-century Bristol; her growth into some kind of personal freedom is accomplished when she helps, and then falls in love with, an educated runaway Ibo slave. Dickensian settings, lively prose, and a believable, sensitive though explicit rendering of Jess and Midnight's delighted discovery of sexual joy.

Frost in May by Antonia White. An adult work of art perfect for adolescent reading, this is the story of Nanda Grey, who arrives at a rigorously authoritarian English convent boarding school at the age of nine. Through restrained, elegantly precise yet quiveringly intense prose, we re-live the passionate (and corrupting) desire of childhood to belong utterly. A riveting study of atmosphere and character.

THE WORLD OF CHILDREN'S BOOKS

A Game of Dark by William Mayne. Donald Jackson, fourteen, leads a disturbing double life: in his cold, rigid family, he struggles against his mother's sternness and his father's hysterical fundamentalism; in his fantasy, he is a beleaguered medieval squire doomed to fight the loathsome giant Worm, or dragon, who threatens a town. Gradually, Donald integrates his conflicting yearning for and rage against the different father figures in his life. A strange, surreal and powerful novel.

Gentlehands by M. E. Kerr. Buddy Boyle, a working-class local in a wealthy resort town, tries to impress the glittering Skye Pennington with his only social asset: his remote, elegant German grandfather. The fantasy begins to falter when a reporter unearths the truth that grandfather Trenker was the vicious 'Gentlehands', an SS officer at Auschwitz. Kerr is an excellent contemporary writer with an ear for dialogue that makes all the characters, of every age and social class, thoroughly believable.

Goldengrove by Jill Paton Walsh. Goldengrove is Gran's house in Cornwall, where Madge and Paul, who think they are cousins, spend every summer together. Walsh's finely controlled yet sensuous, colour-washed prose is the perfect translucent medium for this delicate novel about childhood's last summer and the misguided passions of adolescence. The sequel, *Unleaving*, is equally strong.

Goodnight, Prof, Love by John Rowe Townsend. Graham Hollis, the sardonic but well-behaved son of an accountant, dreams of rescuing pale maidens – and ends up rescuing, and running away with, a good-hearted tart of a waitress from the local café. With wry wit and dead-on dialogue, Townsend moves his awkward hero from blushing daydreams through a tender and funny first sexual encounter to a more mature self-awareness.

Grow Up, Cupid by June Oldham. Seventeen-year-old Mog is a tough-minded working-class comic terror with an unfettered imagination. Blithely indifferent to both authority and convention, she dashes off a romance novel while simultaneously running down men, starts a crèche at her technical college and meddles creatively in lives all around her. A male student with rainbow hair and similar rebellious tendencies provides prickly romantic interest. The offbeat characters are engaging, and though the hip, hectic prose is a little exhausting, this is a valiant effort to inject the contemporary realistic novel with wit, energy and iconoclasm.

Howl's Moving Castle by Diana Wynne Jones. Jones can wrap a light-hearted love story in such a dazzle of mystification, magic and swift-moving plot that young romantics, fantasy-lovers and adventure addicts will all be captivated. Her characters and settings always have strong appeal. In this story, timid Sophie is cast under a spell by the Witch of the Waste, and is changed into an ancient crone, in which guise she seeks work in the moving castle of the fearsome wizard Howl – who is not what he seems, either. Hidden in her ancient body, young Sophie finds herself becoming stubborn, tough and tart-tongued. Irresistibly funny and charming.

The Ice Is Coming by Patricia Wrightson. A remarkably original fantasy trilogy about Wirrun, an Aborigine youth who is called upon to save the land from a conspiracy of ice. Wrightson's free-flowing prose compels our utter belief in the spring-kneed possum-eyed Mimi, a rock spirit who helps Wirrun on his quest; the creaking Ninya, men of ice, and dozens of other fresh and fascinating earth spirits bred of Australian aboriginal folk lore. *The Dark Bright Water*, the second in the trilogy, is a fine work about the complexities of passion and love. Humour, imagination, suspense, depth and beauty.

In Summer Light by Zibby Oneal. A beautifully crafted story about seventeen-year-old Kate, whose artistic talent has been strangled by rage at her domineering father, a famous painter. Shimmeringly evocative landscapes of summer on a New England island are the backdrop for Kate's growing self-awareness. Best of all is the way in which Kate's musings on Shakespeare's *The Tempest* obliquely illuminate her working-out of the Oedipal struggle.

Isaac Campion by Jannie Howker. A tour de force by one of England's most gifted new writers. Isaac, aged ninety-six, reminisces about his hard Lancashire boyhood at the turn of the century – a time of grinding labour, harsh relationships, superstitions and dour religion. An unpromising scenario for a story? Yet Isaac's voice is a marvellous vehicle: rueful with the wisdom of hindsight, stoic, tender, wrenched with pity, grimly humorous. The voices, the sounds and sights of stableyards, streets and mean kitchens all spring to life in Isaac's terse, unsentimental Lancashire idiom. Above all, we feel his hurt at life's cruelty and see through his own wondering eyes the dramatic events of one brief spring that changed his life.

The Islanders by John Rowe Townsend. A tiny community clings to life on a windswept South Pacific island, reinforced by rigid, if half-understood, traditional laws and customs. One iron rule says that all newcomers must be killed. But when two young strangers are swept ashore, apocalyptic changes come with them. Molly, a teenager who rebels against the restrictive laws of the colony, is a key figure, along with her brother Thomas. A gripping adventure that poses thorny but essential questions about the nature of society and change.

It's My Life by Robert Leeson. When Mum suddenly disappears, teenage Jan is left with the burdens of housekeeping for her father and younger brother, plus confused feelings of anger and muddle about school, family and work. A love affair with the popular Peter gives her a brief illusion of womanly power, but proves a dead end. Only as Jan gradually pieces together the puzzle of her mother's disappearance do her own feelings and plans for her future come into clearer focus. The writing is simple without simple-mindedness, forthright and true to the complexities of female experience (including an attempt at a homemade abortion), a model of 'realistic' prose for less ambitious readers.

The Jersey Shore by William Mayne. A strange, dreamy, quiet book, flickering with submerged emotion and slanting drama like fish glimpsed in an aquarium. Arthur, a black American boy, visits his grandfather on the sandy New Jersey coast, and shares visions of his English past – some real and some dream memories of the further past – that he can carry on into his future life when, as an American pilot in World War II, he will visit the ancestral English Fen district, joining the generations.

John Diamond by Leon Garfield. William Jones is a twelve-year-old middle-class country innocent when he goes to London to right a family wrong and falls into a wildly complex mystery in the city's menacing slums. Garfield's careless abundance of sparkling imagery and entrancing characters – notably Liverguts, the hook-handed villain, and Shot-in-the Head, a roof-dwelling urchin who lives by 'snick-and-lurk' (pickpocketing) – build an atmosphere of ghoulish hilarity. But underneath is an unmistakably sober conclusion: 'boys and fools dream of treasure'.

The King's Daughter by Suzanne Martel. High-spirited Jeanne Chatel, an eighteen-year-old French orphan, is chosen to join the 'King's daughters', the brides for Quebec's first settlers. Though her marriage is unpromising at first, Jeanne's stoicism, audacity and intelligence at last overcome great hardships in the wilderness and she and Simon achieve an affectionate, fruitful marriage. A naturalistic and lively novel.

The Lark and the Laurel by Barbara Willard. Cecily, sixteen, is a mincing, conventional Tudor aristocrat who is suddenly dumped in the remote forest home of her strong-willed aunt, Dame Elizabeth, who runs an iron foundry. Cecily's liberation, and her love for Lewis Mallory, are vigorously and believably written. The Mantlemass series follows the intertwining fates of subsequent generations in the Ashdown Forest. Willard usually weaves a spirited story of romance into her exciting historical settings.

Let the Circle Be Unbroken by Mildred D. Taylor. A continuation of the powerfully told story of Cassie Logan and her family (*Roll of Thunder*). This richly textured narrative of black life in Mississippi gives a vivid fictional background to the roots of the civil rights movement, from the organizing of tenant farmers to voter registration drives.

A Little Love by Virginia Hamilton. Sheema and Forrest are black teenagers in a vocational high school, but this is no sociological tract. Instead, it is a sensitive, complex and touching exploration of their hopes, daydreams, fears and sexual tenderness, by one of America's finest writers.

A Long Way from Verona by Jane Gardam. A witty, perceptive and finely written novel about Jessica Vye, a teenager on the north coast of England during the war. Her intelligence and literary talent don't protect her from hasty misjudgements, the small betrayals of adolescence, and the rueful experience of falling in love with a handsome but shallow boy.

The Lord of the Rings by J. R. R. Tolkien. By now a rite of passage, the reading of this massive trilogy about the hobbits and dwarves who fight the forces of evil is bound to be thoroughly engrossing. It's like an immense, magical compendium of fairy tales, enriched with wonderful folkloric names, poems, battles and unforgettable archetypal characters.

The Machine-Gunners by Robert Westall. Chas, fifteen, steals a machine-gun from a downed Nazi plane and builds a hidden bunker with his friends. Gradually, the boys are caught up in the hysteria of war; their confused adolescent hatred is directed against the adults who have failed to protect them, rather than against the German enemy. This is an accomplished, overpoweringly effective novel, marred by the boys' panicky misogyny from which the author never dissociates himself.

Memory by Margaret Mahy. Nineteen-year-old Jonny Dart, former child tap-dance star, is not really 'mad, bad and dangerous' – just reckless, confused, and haunted by shifting memories of his sister's death. Searching for the girl who was the only other witness, he falls into a bizarre house-keeping arrangement with muddled old Sophie, whose rare sweetness shines through her crazily clouded memories like shafts of sunlight. Sophie is heartwrenching and amazingly funny, and through his reluctant kindness to her, Jonny discovers just how treacherous memory can be. A wonderfully written novel, energetic, poetic, poignant, funny and, finally, vigorously optimistic.

Moses Beech by Ian Strachan. A strong, forthright novel about teenage Peter, who runs away from a slovenly home and finds refuge with an eccentric old hermit, Moses. Their developing friendship – not to mention Peter's love affair with a local farmer's daughter – bring down catastrophe on Moses, but both of the young people are left with a legacy of self-reliance and saner values.

The Nature of the Beast by Janni Howker. A stark, angry, rivetingly dramatic story of unemployment, social disintegration and an escaped leopard in northern England. Bill Coward, a stubborn, despairing teenager, decides to hunt the 'mysterious beast' on his own: an expression of the rage he feels against the hopeless blows fate has dealt his fragile family (consisting of dad and grandad). There are some blood-chilling scenes of terror on the moors, and a pervading sense of a boy's solitary determination hurled in the teeth of hopeless circumstances.

One More River by Lynne Reid Banks. Leslie Shelby is a spoiled, petulant Canadian fourteen-year-old who sulks when her family moves to an Israeli kibbutz. There, her prickly relationships with her peer group, her tentative distant friendship with an Arab boy on the West Bank, and her observation of the Six Day War, help her to grow in valour, resilience and tolerance.

A Question of Courage by Marjorie Darke. A rare celebration of the courageous battle waged by the suffragettes, amidst the sneers of their contemporaries, the apathy of the majority and the brutality of the authorities. Emily Palmer, a sturdy and rebellious working-class girl, rises above class and the restricted horizons of poverty when she throws in her lot with the middle-class women fighting for the vote. There's humour, friendship, romance and excitement as well as a probing look at the quality of courage, in this lively and readable historical novel.

A Parcel of Patterns by Jill Paton Walsh. The grim true story of Eyam, a lovely English village of 350 people which was almost entirely wiped out by the Plague in 1665, is told here in a graphic and moving fictionalized account of love, tragedy and survival by sixteen-year-old Mall Percival. Such courage and moral perseverance in the face of doom have a particular relevance for today's teenagers.

Pennington's Seventeenth Summer by K. M. Peyton. He's a hulking, working-class thug, a tornado of reckless energy, a thoughtless prankster, loathed by his teachers – and he's a brilliant pianist. This trilogy is a tour de force: hectically funny, written with a flair for dialogue and pell-mell physical action but just as good at evoking the sound of classical music, and the most sympathetic and believable portrait in print of an inarticulate delinquent with genius in his hands. Less breathless, but equally unsentimental, are the sequels about his jail sentence, marriage, fatherhood and musical career.

A Pistol in Greenyards by Mollie Hunter. Connal Ross is a hot-headed fifteen-year-old whose family is shattered by the brutal Highland Clearances of the 1750s. A vivid, fast-moving historical drama with romantic interest.

Raisins and Almonds by Fredelle Maynard. Sharp and sweet as wild berries are these memories – in twelve short stories – of a Jewish girl growing up in a series of tiny prairie towns where coyotes howled at the icy moon outside the bedroom window. The Canadian experience seems more vividly real here, in its harshness, beauty and bigotries, than in much fiction.

Representing Superdoll by Richard Peck. Verna, sixteen, is an ordinary Indiana farm girl who can't help but feel that her life is a little flat –

especially compared to that of her voluptuous classmate, Darlene Hoffmeister, Miss Hybrid Seed Corn. But the future begins to look more expansive than Verna had suspected when she is chosen as Darlene's chaperone on her prize trip to New York. Peck is at his suave, satirical, observant best in this story of Verna's growing self-awareness and triumphant good sense.

The River by Rumer Godden. Harriet, gifted with a restlessly inquiring mind and a passion for writing, teeters on the brink of puberty in this sensuous, piercing and delicately written novel of colonial childhood in Bengal. Few memoirists have captured so keenly the way an imaginative child is drawn to and repelled by the adult mysteries around her, or the sensory intensity of the last days of childhood.

The Runner by Cynthia Voight. 'Bullet' Tillerman has made himself into a sort of early 1960s southern Clint Eastwood: toughly self-disciplined, relentlessly hostile, a superb cross-country runner, totally unconnected with others or with his own emotions. He's also a bigot in a high school undergoing integration. With considerable skill, Voight makes us feel from the beginning what possible strengths and virtues lie below the surface numbness of Bullet's misery. In a story packed with action and incident, yet with careful attention paid to Bullet's evolving self-awareness, Voight draws a moving portrait of a boy coming to terms with himself, his cruel father, his wounded mother and his difficult times – the years of the Vietnam War.

The Secret Diary of Adrian Mole, Aged 13¾ by Sue Townsend. The satire is aimed at the priggish, self-absorbed diarist himself, would-be intellectual Adrian Mole, the kind of person whose nose sticks to his model aeroplane when he tries to sniff glue. Adrian's parents are engaged in a chaotic variety of extra-marital dalliances which he is too naïve to notice; by the end, Adrian has become more human and his family has settled down.

See You Thursday by Jean Ure. A contemporary romance between Marianne, a lonely sixteen-year-old, and the blind lodger, a twenty-four-year-old musician called Abe. Marianne, at first sullen, defiant and unfocused, accused by her teachers of 'immaturity', discovers new talents and depths in herself through her growing relationship with Abe. The strength of the novel is in the believable tension between Marianne and her decent, hard-working mother, and in the slow transition Marianne makes between self-centred adolescence and a more assured, tolerant, dawning adulthood.

Shadow in Hawthorn Bay by Janet Lunn. Mary is a spitfire: a fifteen-year-old Highland Scot, gifted (and, she thinks, cursed) with 'second sight'. When she hears her beloved cousin Duncan calling her from the New World, she sets out on her own to join him – only to find, after a stubborn, arduous journey, that he is dead. Lunn brings alive the clash of cultures between brooding, aloof Mary, with her other-worldly beliefs, and the friendly, practical Yankee settlers with whom she must make a new life on the shores of Lake Ontario. Before she can find new love, she must throw off the shadow of her morbid attachment to Duncan. This is an exhilaratingly many-faceted novel, strongly and unsentimentally written, with a fine feel for the details of daily colonial life.

The Singing Stone by O. R. Melling. A vigorous, action-filled fantasy about a contemporary eighteen-year-old orphan who is unaware of her secret powers as a Mage. Kay Warrick's lonely life is disrupted by a mysterious anonymous present: a package of ancient Celtic tomes. They galvanize her to search for her Irish roots – and she is soon caught up in a terrifying quest for four lost treasures of power. Kay is accompanied by a strange waif of a girl, Aherne, who grows to be an unexpected heroine. This is one of those rare quest novels that turn received conventions on their heads: there are lots of pitched battles and action scenes, but, in the end, it is through betrayal in the name of love, and not through battle, that a people is saved. The contemporary love story that frames the time journey is also appealingly handled.

Skindeep by Toeckey Jones. Rhonda, a spoiled and aimless Johannesburg suburbanite, falls in love with the mysterious Dave, a fellow student with a shaved head and a motorcycle. Their love affair explodes when Rhonda discovers Dave's secret identity. Though the prose often teeters on the edge of teen-novel banality ('His heart was bared to me in his face. My throat swelled up'), *Skindeep* has the rare virtue of making a profound moral issue come alive in the context of a highly accessible teen romance.

Snow Apples by Mary Razzell. A grittily honest and compassionate novel about what it was like to be a bright and pretty sixteen-year-old girl in the 1940s, growing up in a west coast outport of Canada, Sheila's embittered, begrudging mother and her chauvinist brothers do nothing to protect her from the cruel sexual double standard of the times, and only Helga, an old Norwegian woman, comes to Sheila's aid after a horrifying illegal abortion. The tone of working-class realism is reminiscent of *A Tree Grows in Brooklyn*.

A Sound of Chariots by Mollie Hunter. This incandescent and powerfully emotional autobiographical novel traces the life of Bridie McShane from the age of nine to her teens. Bridie, passionate, brave and defiant, with a Celtic sense of the richness of words, is her father's favourite, and her life is shattered – and only slowly remade – when he dies suddenly.

Them That Glitters and Them That Don't by Bette Green. Half-Gypsy, half-Irish, with a derelict family living in a trailer, Carol Ann is an outcast in her Arkansas town, ferociously determined to achieve fame as a country and western star. The local colour, clever characterizations, humour and deft colloquialism lift this novel above the ranks of the merely predictable.

This Strange New Feeling by Julius Lester. Three love stories based on true accounts of slavery days: vivid, direct, easy to read and yet with the sharp flavour of a heartbreaking reality. Though the characters are young, theirs is an adult love, and the heroes and heroines have the courage, dignity and bluntness of survivors.

Two's Company by Catherine Storr. Kathy, fifteen, is envious of her beautiful older sister's success with boys, and resentful of her father's infidelity. On a family holiday in southern France, she falls in love with the broodingly handsome Val, only to discover too late that he is homosexual. This is an intelligent, sympathetic and humane story that captures the temporary frenzy of infatuation and puts it into perspective.

Tulku by Peter Dickinson. Theodore, teenage son of an American missionary in China, is suddenly orphaned and made homeless by the Boxer Rebellion. He falls into the company of an eccentric Englishwoman who is an amateur botanist, and joins her on a perilous journey to Tibet. There, their lives become strangely intertwined with Buddhist monks at a remote monastery, whose lama insists their arrival has been foretold in a vision. Despite the improbably adventurous plot (bandits, warfare, flight across Himalayan rope bridges, riots, assassinations, love affairs), this is a strangely dense, inward, slow-moving novel. Loss of faith and religious revelation are important strands in the story, as is an extraordinarily vivid and complex depiction of Tibetan Buddhism. A gripping novel for thoughtful readers.

A Very Long Way from Anywhere Else by Ursula Le Guin. A sharply perceptive novel about Owen Griffiths, a seventeen-year-old introvert, who finds himself falling in love with another nonconformist, the fiercely dedicated musician Natalie. Too late, Owen realizes that he has warped their relationship by his insistence that love must lead at once to sex. A thoughtful and honest look at teenage relationships.

What About Tomorrow? by Ivan Southall. Sam is fourteen, an impoverished Melbourne schoolboy during the Depression, when he smashes his bicycle and decides to run away. This picaresque story of his startling encounters, the people who befriend him, the girls with whom he falls in love, is told with tenderness and insight through Sam's own vulnerable, optimistic and endearing sensibility. A dimension at once sombre, exciting and satisfying is added by virtue of the flash-forward scenes to his life and death as a World War II pilot.

A Wizard of Earthsea by Ursula Le Guin. The education, spiritual and magical, of the young wizard Ged. This magnificent, powerfully imagined trilogy (the second book, *The Tombs of Atuan*, deals with the emergence to womanhood of a young captive priestess) is more sensitive, intense and original – and certainly more egalitarian – than *The Lord of the Rings*, and its prose is more muscular and polished.

Poetry for Children

Colours by Shirley Hughes. Melodic, sensuous rhyming couplets on every page accompany colour-drenched illustrations in Hughes's most intimate, lyrical mood. 'Syrup dripping from a spoon, buttercups, a harvest moon, Sun like honey on the floor, warm as the steps by our back door,' are the words that go with yellow. *Two Shoes, New Shoes* is another wonderful nursery book in this series. Despite her palpable warmth, Hughes's lively, realistic drawings prevent her from slipping into sentimentality.

The Faber Book of Nursery Verse edited by Barbara Ireson. A standard and invaluable collection of hundreds of poems, nursery rhymes, jingles and finger-plays for the preschool child. Ireson chose poems on the basis of 'pungency, strong and pleasing verbal pattern, economy, humour, incongruity, and pleasing repetition', according to the introduction, and she has ranged widely and refreshingly. Hundreds of readings-aloud will not exhaust the pleasures and surprises of this anthology. Arranged in thematic sections (Playtime, Pets, Sense and Nonsense, etc), with an index of authors and of first lines.

17 Kings and 42 Elephants by Margaret Mahy. 'Baggy ears like big umbrellaphants/Little eyes a-gleaming in the jungle night,' the elephants are rollicking through a wet, wild jungle. This inspired picture book tells a brief, mysterious tale in rhyming quatrains of exuberantly playful, rich, rumbustious language. Rhythm, rhyme, images and story are irresistible, skilfully employing all the most ear-pleasing techniques while creating a tantalizingly exotic atmosphere. Patricia MacCarthy's jewel-bright batik paintings on silk sweep, swirl, march and dance across the page, to joyful effect.

The New Golden Land Anthology, edited by Judith Elkin. Stories, drawings and poems by all the best artists and writers, old and new, for every age group, Wordsworth to Terry Jones, 'Anon' ('Moses supposes his toeses are roses') and Michael Rosen. The poetry has been chosen 'for the pleasure of the language' according to James Reeves, the original editor of this enduringly popular anthology. Most of the poems are on the light or humorous side and can be enjoyed by six-to-eleven-year-olds reading on their own.

The New Wind Has Wings. Poems from Canada by Mary Alice Downie and Barbara Robertston. An ample and fascinating collection, from Bliss Carman to Jay McPherson and many others. With vivid collages by the distinguished Elizabeth Cleaver on every page. (8+)

Oxford Book of Poetry for Children compiled by Edward Blishen, with illustrations by Brian Wildsmith. A large and visually very appealing book: though Wildsmith's pictures are beautiful, richly coloured and sometimes exciting, they do not fight with the poems on the page. This selection is particularly rich in ballads and narrative poems, and lesser-known lyrics by such poets as Jonathan Swift, Lewis Carroll and Thomas Hardy. There are some striking old songs by 'Anon', the wonderful 'For My Cat Jeoffrey' by the eighteenth-century poet Christopher Smart, and dozens of other felicities. Though all the poems are excellent, none are difficult; a rewarding book for middle readers and lovely for reading aloud to children of seven and up.

A Puffin Quartet of Poets: Eleanor Farjeon, James Reeves, E. V. Rieu, Ian Seraillier chosen by Eleanor Graham. An excellent idea: anthologies are the standard poetic fare for children, but there's a special reward in reading a whole body of work by one poet. A substantial collection from each of four poets writing specifically for children is offered here, each section with a brief, fascinating introduction to the author's life and way of working. These are mostly short, easy lyrics, all with some beauty of language or spark of humour, and perfect for children reading on their own. (7–11)

The Walker Book of Poetry for Children selected by Jack Prelutsky, illustrated by Arnold Lobel. The subtitle, 'A Treasury of 572 Poems for Today's Child', reveals this handsome anthology's strength and its weakness. This is an immense selection of short poems, most of them rarely anthologized, to appeal to 'primary school children', according to the editor. But 'today's child', evidently, must be wooed with high-decibel humour and high-voltage scariness. Most of these poems deliver a quick jolt based on familiar themes of contemporary life. It's good to see the poetry of outer space celebrated, but too few of these poems are geared to inner space. Still, this extroverted and eclectic book has wide appeal and some tantalizing surprises.

Gargling with Jelly by Brian Patten. Most of these are of the 'I love snot' variety: silly, aggressive, grotty or grotesque rhymes and jingly quatrains, and with not much in the way of interesting language. But when Patten stops pandering, he can be tense, taut and eerie, or tersely thought-provoking. A collection worth trying with the language-insensitive or poetry-resistant boy. (9+)

A Fourth Poetry Book compiled by John Foster. This is one in a fine age-graded series from Oxford University Press. The *Fourth*, mostly contemporary and short poems, seems perfect for nine- and ten-year-olds, especially boys, with a smattering of serious lyrics and a wide though fairly judicious assortment of the hostile-humour sort. Although the series was designed for use in schools, it is extremely accessible, with coloured illustrations on every page.

Hey World, Here I Am! by Jean Little. A delightful collection of poems written in the voice of 'Kate', the intelligent, curious, ebullient preadolescent heroine of Jean Little's novel, *Kate*. Kate's free-verse reflections are intimate, sharp, honest, funny and touching, and express both the wit and the 'long long thoughts' of an appealing youngster. Kate's poems are recommended not only for their uncanny perceptiveness about intense moments of childhood that are normally overlooked in literature, but also as a model of fresh, unforced writing that might stimulate other young poets to equally original and honest efforts.

Why Am I Grown So Cold? Poems of the Unknowable edited by Myra Cohn Livingston. Though I usually find thematic collections too limiting, Livingston's various anthologies are an exception. She ranges from Shakespeare's songs to American Indian chants in an effective search for that tingle of the mysterious and the unearthly which is one of poetry's joys. A good temptation to put before a child who has not previously enjoyed poetry. (10+)

The Cremation of Sam McGee by Robert Service. The hard-edged, brilliant, rainbow-hued paintings by the Yukon artist Ted Harrison are a perfect complement to the challenging landscape and the memorable rhythms of this familiar poem ('There are strange things done in the midnight sun . . . '). The whole handsome production radiates a spirit of vigour to the point of excess, both in the poem's comic exaggeration and the vibrant paintings, that make it ideal for the restless or reluctant 'middle' reader. Narrative poems in general (like 'The Highwayman', illustrated by Charles Keeping and available as a single picture book) are a grand enticement for those middle and preteenage readers who think they don't like poetry.

Words on Water a collection of poems entered for the Young Observer National Children's Poetry Competition. A stimulating experience: all the entrants (ages four to eighteen) were asked to write on the theme of 'water', yet there is very little repetition in the ideas that emerge. Naturally, some of the poems lack polish, yet there is so much energy, surprising originality and promise here that any youngster interested in poetry might be inspired.

All Day Long compiled by Pamela Whitlock. A favourite anthology of mine; out of print, but search for it. Several hundred excellent poems, chosen for their intensity and excitement, interestingly arranged by hour and season, ranging over the centuries and with many strange surprises – Hopkins and de la Mare, Alice Meynell, John Clare and Vita Sackville-West, and many less conventional, like the Devon postman Edward Capern. A good selection of interesting, little-known women is a definite plus. Each section opens with a hauntingly beautiful tinted wood engraving by John Hassall; there's an index of first lines and a short biography of each poet. A treasure for poetry-lovers. (11+)

The Rattle Bag compiled by Seamus Heaney and Ted Hughes was an instant and deserved success. More than 400 poems are arranged alphabetically by title; this arbitrariness works beautifully, setting up provocative reverberations, connections and dissonances. The poems are so enticing, diverse and unusual – including absolutely none of the 'sweetness and light' variety and none specially written for children – that any serious lover of words and poems will be irretrievably hooked.

A Flock of Words collected and annotated by David Mackay. Even more eclectic than *The Rattle Bag* (it has, for example, a nineteenth-century German poem, 'Night Song of the Fish', composed entirely of curves and dashes), this is another of my out-of-print cherished ones. Rilke, Rimbaud, Roethke, Yevtushenko and Chaucer – despite the richness, most are not too difficult for poetry-lovers over eleven. Though women are drastically under-represented, as happens so often with male anthologists, this collection offers a dazzling sense of breadth. The way these poems 'rub shoulders together' – they are arranged by subtle links in themes or images – provides constant jolts and miracles.

Going Over to Your Place, Poems for Each Other. Selected by Paul B. Janeczko. Janeczko has combed the small literary journals and the collected works of leading contemporary poets for this gem of an anthology. Vigorous, fresh, playful or reflective, these are serious poems, mostly in a speaking voice, on themes of relationships (between friends, lovers, parents and children, people and their clothes, a writer and his outmoded typewriter, a new tenant and the previous ones). Not one poem is over-familiar, not one panders to the inexperienced reader, yet all are immediately accessible and engaging. John Updike, Adrienne Rich, Seamus Heaney and Michael Ondaatje are among the more than 100 poets represented.

A TREASURY

Books About Children's Reading

This is a mere handful of books that I have found particularly useful for the general reader.

Babies Need Books by Dorothy Butler. A trail-blazing and completely accessible book, written with charm, vivacity, and detailed, helpful advice.

Booktalk. Occasional Writing on Literature and Children by Aidan Chambers. Thoughtful, provocative and anecdotal; a very strong and moving account of a new way of studying literature in schools – should be required reading for every teacher.

The Child and the Book by Nicholas Tucker. A wonderfully sensitive and sensible exploration of the connection between children's psychological development and the literature they need and enjoy.

Cushla and Her Books by Dorothy Butler. A dramatic, true and detailed account of how the life of a multiple-handicapped child was transformed through picture books. Indispensible for parents and teachers of handicapped children.

The Marble in the Water: Essays on Contemporary Writers of Fiction for Children and Young Adults by David Rees. Fascinating, contentious, readable essays about some of the leading British and American children's authors of today.

Read-Aloud Handbook by Jim Trelease. Useful and persuasive guide to reading aloud to all age groups, by an American journalist, with 300 suggested books.

Reading for Enjoyment. A series of four pamphlets, each written by a different author, listing the outstanding books for each age group. The capsule reviews are lively, informed and informative. The *16 And Up* booklist is a particularly good and unusual idea, with appealing reviews of a wide-ranging selection of novels.

We've All Got Scars: What Boys and Girls Learn in Elementary School by Raphaela Best. A unique account, filled with startling and illuminating anecdotes, about the sexist conditioning boys impose on each other in primary school, and its effect not only on their play and character but also on their reading ability. Based on a long-term study in an American primary school.

Written for Children by John Rowe Townsend. The most authoritative, sane and gracefully written history and critique of children's literature for a general audience, recently updated.

Index

Aardema, Verna, 77–8, 219, 229, 239, 240
ABC (Wildsmith), 39
Across Five Aprils, 284
Across the Barricades, 196, 284
'Across the Sea', 231
adolescents, books for, 152–3, 183–204
adults, and children's books, 6, 21–2, 41
adventure stories, 119–39
The Adventures of Huckleberry Finn, 137–9, 219, 284
The Adventures of Robin Hood, 127, 253
The Adventures of Tom Sawyer, 27
Ahlberg, Janet and Allan, 35, 51–2, 78–9, 231, 242–3, 246
Aiken, Joan, 58, 81–2, 148, 151–2, 156, 198, 209, 241, 254, 278
Alan and Naomi, 98, 270
Alan Mendelsohn, the Boy from Mars, 154, 155–6, 270
Alcott, Louisa May, 100, 222, 277
Alexander and the Terrible, Horrible, No Good, Very Bad Day, 228
Alexander, Lloyd, 271
Alfie Gets in First, 41–2, 228
Alice in Wonderland, 5
All Day Long, 299–300
All Quiet on the Western Front, 193
All-of-a-Kind Family, 253
Allen, Jeffrey, 75, 235
Allen, Robert Thomas, 251
Alligator Pie, 78, 241
The Amazing Bone, 57–8, 241
The Amboy Dukes, 192–3
Amelia Bedelia, 78, 241
And Now Miguel, 217, 270
Anderson, Margaret, 276
Andrews, Jan, 251
Angel Square, 82–3, 253
Anne of Green Gables, 99–100, 101, 102, 253
Anno, Mitsumaso, 228
Anno's Journey, 228
Another Mouse To Feed, 240
appealing to children, need for, 19
Applebet, an ABC, 228
The Apprentices, 284
Arabel's Raven, 81–2, 241
Ardizzone, Edward, 58, 83–4, 119, 123, 247, 250, 261, 263
Are You in the House Alone?, 191–2
Are You My Mother?, 35, 37, 228
Armada, 3
Armitage, Ronda and David, 233

Arnakyauyok, Germaine, 275
Arthur's Prize Reader, 228
Aruego, Jose, 39, 42–3, 233, 240
Ask Me No Questions, 270
At the Sign of the Dog and Rocket, 284–5
Atwater, Richard and Florence, 248
Aurora and the Little Blue Car, 52–3, 241
Averill, Esther, 120–1, 246
Avery, Gillian, 206, 262
Avi, 257

Babbitt, Natalie, 111–12, 244, 267–8
Babies Need Books, 301
The Baby Project, 253
bad books, 207–23
Badger on the Barge, 270–1
The Baitchopper, 271
Bang, Molly, 244, 265
Banks, Lynne Reid, 110–11, 196–7, 260, 282, 292
The Baron's Booty, 228–9
Barzun, Jacques, 17
The Bat-Poet, 241–2
The Battle of Bubble and Squeak, 65, 253–4
Bawden, Nina, 258, 263, 271
Bayley, Nicola, 39, 237
Beardon, Romare, 261
Beats Me, Claude, 120, 242
The Bee-Man of Orn, 104–5, 242
The Beethoven Medal, 204
Beezus and Ramona, 55
beginning readers, books to encourage, 33–45, 228–40
Behind the Wind, 162
Bellairs, John, 131, 259–60
Bemelmans, Ludwig, 38, 153, 235
Ben's Trumpet, 229
Beowulf, 254
Berg, Ron, 245
Best, Raphaela, 221–2, 301–2
bias in children's books, 138, 207–23
bibliotherapy, 210–11
Bilgewater, 198–9, 285
Bilson, Geoffrey, 245, 272
Bimwili and the Zimwi, 229
A Bird in the House, 204, 285
Black Hearts in Battersea, 151–2, 254
Blades, Ann, 243, 248
Blake, Quentin, 86, 234, 240, 249
Blishen, Edward, 298
Blubber, 212–13, 214
The Blue Hawk, 160, 285

INDEX

The Blue Lagoon, 162
Blue Moose, 72, 74–5, 242
Blue Willow, 100–1, 254
Blume, Judy, 5–6, 184–90, 195, 198, 204, 207, 212–13, 214
Blyton, Enid, 50, 88, 124, 207, 217–19
The Bobbsey Twins, 3, 50, 208
Bond, Michael, 55
The Bongleweed, 154–5, 168, 254
Bonnie McSmithers You're Driving Me Dithers, 229
The Book Lovers, 285
The Book of Three, 271
books about children's reading, 301–2
Booktalk. Occasional Writing on Literature and Children, 301
The Borrowers, 146–7, 156, 254
Borton de Trevino, Elizabeth, 275
Bosmajian, Hamida, 88
Boston, Lucy, 26, 65–6, 243, 265
Bows Against the Barons, 127, 254
boys, and children's books, 49, 220–2
Bradman, Tony, 36
Brand, Christianna, 83–4, 263
Brave Irene, 57, 229
The Brave Little Toaster, 242
Bread and Jam for Frances, 229
Brenda and Edward, 229
Bridge to Terabithia, 210, 271
Bridget and William, 242
Briggs, Raymond, 85–6, 244
Brooke, L. Leslie, 234
'Brookie and Her Lamb', 231
Brooks, Bruce, 278
Brooks, Ron, 229
Brooks, Walter R., 245
Brophy, Brigid, 48
Brown, Jeff, 244
Brown, Marcia, 238
Browne, Anthony, 233
'bulk reading', 207–9
'bum humour', 85
Bunting, Eve, 232
The Bunyip of Berkeley's Creek, 36–7, 229
Burglar Bill, 51–2, 242–3
Burnett, Frances Hodgson, 99, 100, 265
Burningham, John, 74, 104, 229, 230, 233, 239, 240
Burton, Hester, 278
Butler, Dorothy, 301
Byars, Betsy, 65–8, 67, 256, 264, 266, 284

Cabbage Patch Kids, 22
Caldecott, Randolph, 44, 234
Caleb and Kate, 57
Cameron, Ann, 77, 246
Cameron, Eleanor, 272
Cameron, Silver Donald, 271
A Candle for Christmas, 243
Candy for King, 285
Cannonball Simp, 104, 229
Care Bears, 22, 93, 94, 209
Carlson, Natalie Savage, 245, 257
Carrick, Donald, 245
Carrick (illustrator), 232

Carrie's War, 210, 271
A Castle of Yew, 26, 243
The Cat in the Hat series, 37, 75, 82
Cat on the Mat, 230
The Catcher in the Rye, 186
The Cat's Elbow, 243
CDB, 230
Celebrating Children's Books, 182, 206
Cendrars, Blaise, 238
Chambers, Aidan, 6, 286, 301
A Chance Child, 271
The Changeover, 157
Charlie and the Chocolate Factory, 89
Charlotte Sometimes, 168–70, 254–5
Charlotte's Web, 147, 243
Cherries and Cherry Pits, 230
Chesterton, G. K., 217
The Child and the Book, 301
children's reading, books about, 301
Chin Chiang and the Dragon's Dance, 230
The Chocolate War, 112–14, 116
Christie, Agatha, 217
Christopher, John, 283
The Circus of Adventure, 218
A City Out of Sight, 215, 240
Clams Can't Sing, 230
Clark, Joan, 274
Clarke, Pauline, 268
classics, effect of encouraging child to read, 27
Claude, 120
Cleary, Beverly, 55–6, 249–50, 272
Cleaver, Elizabeth, 298
Cleaver, Vera and Bill, 282
Clever Gretchen and Other Forgotten Folk Tales, 243
Clever Polly and the Stupid Wolf, 79, 243
Clifton, Lucille, 94, 231
Cliptail, 243–4
Cloud Horse, 255
The Coal House, 194
Coerr, Eleanor, 264
Colours, 297
Come Away from the Water, Shirley, 230
Come Sing, Jimmy Jo, 255
Come to Mecca, 215–16, 286
comedy, in children's books, 73–90
Comfort Herself, 95–6, 271–2
comics, 207–8
'commodity' books for children, 7, 22
consumerism, and children's values, 12–13
Cooney, Barbara, 40–1, 230, 247
Cooper, Susan, 97, 192, 255
Corduroy, 230
Cormier, Robert, 112–14, 116, 215, 220
cost of books, effects, 7–8
Could Be Worse, 230
The Court of the Stone Children, 272
Crane, Stephen, 175
The Crane Wife, 244
creative power of reading, 17
The Cremation of Sam McGee, 299
Cresswell, Helen, 82, 154, 168, 189, 249, 254, 262, 263
The Cricket in Times Square, 255
criticism of children's books, reaction to, 7, 207

304

INDEX

Crossley-Holland, Kevin, 120, 254
Crowns, 5
Crowther, Robert, 236
Cry the Beloved Country, 193
The Cuckoo Tree, 151–2
Curious George, 35–6, 230
Cushla and Her Books, 301

Dahl, Roald, 87–90
Dance on My Grave, 286
Danziger, Paula, 5–6, 185, 195
Dark Bright Water, 161–2, 289
The Dark Is Rising, 97, 255
Darke, Marjorie, 121, 198, 287
D'Aulaire, Ingri and Edgar, 244
D'Aulaire's Book of Greek Myths, 244
Dawn, 244
Dawn of Fear, 97–8, 255
Dear Mr. Henshaw, 55, 272
Death Over Montreal, 272
Deenie, 188
de Gerez, Toni, 247
DeJong, Meindert, 259, 260
de la Mare, Walter, 267
Demeter and Persephone, 40–1
Dennis, Wesley, 244
de Paola, Tomie, 31
Desai, Anita, 197, 282
The Devil's Children, 255
The Devil's Storybook, 244
Dewey, Ariane, 42–3, 233
Dhondy, Farrukh, 215–16, 286
The Diamond in the Window, 255–6
The Diary of Anne Frank, 273
Dick and Jane, 23
Dickens, Charles, 20, 27, 217
Dickinson, Peter, 160, 255, 285, 295
The Diddakoi, 256
Dido and Pa, 254
difficult books, 28–9
Dillon, Leo and Diane, 240, 263–4
Dionysos and the Pirates, 230
Disch, Thomas M., 242
Do Not Open, 231
A Dog So Small, 256
The Dog Who Wouldn't Be, 80, 263
Dogsbody, 157, 272
Dogsong, 286
Dominic, 256
The Donkey's Crusade, 286
Don't Never Forget, 48
Don't You Remember?, 94, 231
Down the Rabbit Hole, 75
Downie, Mary Alice, 297–8
Doyle, Brian, 82–3, 253, 282
Dragonsong, 286
Drift, 272
The Druid's Tune, 173, 286–7
du Bois, William Pene, 268
Duder, Tessa, 276
Duffy and the Devil, 231
Dunlop, Eileen, 273

Each Peach Pear Plum, 231
The Eagle of the Ninth, 277

early reading, 18, 23, 24
Earthfasts, 28, 172–3, 272
Eastman, P. D., 19, 35, 37, 228, 232
Edie on the Warpath, 261
Egielski, Richard, 233, 238
Egoff, Sheila, 4, 123, 185, 194
The Egypt Game, 256
The Eight Days of Luke, 273
The Eighteenth Emergency, 256
Eliot, T. S., 183
Elkin, Judith, 248–9, 297
Ellen's Lion, 231
Ellis, Sarah, 253
Emil and the Detectives, 256–7
Emily Upham's Revenge, 257
The Emperor's Winding Sheet, 136–7, 273
The Empty Schoolhouse, 257
encouraging a child to read, 24–5, 26–7, 45
The Endless Steppe: A Girl in Exile, 273
The Ennead, 287
Enright, Elizabeth, 258
Ernst, Lisa Campbell, 237
Escape to Persia, 5
The Eskimo Twins, 3, 50
Estes, Eleanor, 55, 56, 213–14, 215, 245–6, 247, 248, 258
Everyone Knows What a Dragon Looks Like, 231
An Experiment in Criticism, 182

The Faber Book of Nursery Verse, 28, 297
A Fabulous Creature, 287
Fairy Books series, 27
fairy stories, 27–8, 59, 78, 152
The Fairy Tale Treasury, 244
Fanny and the Monsters, 244
The Fantastic Imagination, 142
The Fantasists, 21
fantasy, 15, 143–63
Far from Shore, 287
The Far-Distant Oxus, 5
Farjeon, Eleanor, 261, 298
Farmer, Penelope, 168–70, 250, 254–5, 280
The Farthest Shore, 160
Fat Chance, Claude, 120, 242
Father Figure, 200–1, 287
father's role, and reading, 15
female characters, in children's books, 215–17
Fenton, Edward, 132–3, 249
Fine, Anne, 194, 274, 278
Fireweed, 197, 273
The First Books, 231
The First of Midnight, 198, 287
'Fish Is Fish', 42
Fisk, Nicholas, 153–4
Fitzgerald, John D., 131
Fitzhugh, Louise, 201, 258, 278–9
Five Children and It, 3, 149, 257
The 500 Hats of Bartholomew Cubbins, 231
Five Little Peppers and How They Grew, 50
Five Minutes' Peace, 73, 231
Five O'Clock Charlie, 244
Flack, Marjorie, 37–8, 238, 251
Flat Stanley, 244
Fleishman, Ted, 248

INDEX

A Flock of Words, 300
fluent readers, books for young, 241–52
A Flute in Maybury Street, 273
The Fool of the World and the Flying Ship, 232
The Fools of Chelm and their History, 244–5
For Whom the Bell Tolls, 193
Forbes, Esther, 201–2
Foreman, Michael, 265
Forever, 189–90, 195, 198
Forster, E. M., 209
Foster, John, 298–9
A Fourth Poetry Book, 298–9
Fowke, Edith, 237
Fox in Socks, 231
Fox, Paula, 11–12, 114–16, 206, 211, 248, 260, 279, 280
Fraser, Antonia, 127
Freaky Friday, 81, 273
Fred, 56–7, 232
Freddy the Detective, 245
Frederick's Tales, 42
Freeman, Don, 230
Fritz, Jean, 275
From Anna, 107, 257
From the Mixed-up Files of Mrs. Basil E. Frankweiler, 257
Frost in May, 287
Frozen Fire, 125, 273
Fungus the Bogeyman, 85–6
Fungus the Bogeyman's Plop-up Book, 85–6
The Funny Little Woman, 120, 232

Gaffer Sampson's Luck, 257
Gag, Wanda, 236
A Game of Dark, 288
Garbage Delight, 86
Gardam, Jane, 21, 53–4, 198–9, 242, 247, 285, 291
Gardiner, John Reynolds, 65, 250
Gardner, Helen, 183
Garfield, Leon, 127–8, 152, 198, 265, 284, 285, 290
Gargling with Jelly, 298
Garner, Alan, 266
Gates, Doris, 100–1, 254
'The Gats', 231
Geldart, William, 247
Gentlehands, 288
George and Martha, 232
George, Jean Craighead, 103–4, 276, 300
George's Marvellous Medicine, 89
The Ghost Belonged to Me, 273–4
The Ghost of Thomas Kempe, 171–2, 175, 258
Ghost's Hour, Spook's Hour, 232
Gideon Ahoy, 274
Ginger Pye, 258
girls, and reading, 49
Go, Dog, Go, 37, 232
Godden, Rumer, 250, 256, 293
Goffstein, M. B., 58, 231, 236, 258, 268
Goggles, 232–3
Going Over to Your Place, 300
Goldengrove, 288
Goldie the Dollmaker, 58, 258
Gone-Away Lake, 258

Good Book Guide, 227
Goodbye Sarah, 245
Goodnight Prof, Dear, 200
Goodnight Prof, Love, 200, 288
Gorey, Edward, 249, 250
Gorilla, 233
Gorky, Maxim, 10, 16
Graham, Eleanor, 298
Grahame, Kenneth, 145–6, 150, 269
Grandma Goes Shopping, 233
The Granny Project, 194, 274
The Great Brain series, 131
The Great Gilly Hopkins, 274
Greek myths, 40–1, 230
Green, Bette, 108, 196, 279, 280, 294–5
Green Eggs and Ham, 231
Green, Roger Lancelyn, 127, 253
Gretz, Susanna, 74, 234
Grimm, the Brothers, 27
Grinny, 153–4
Gripe, Maria, 245
Grow Up, Cupid, 288
growing up as theme of books, 183–204
Gulliver's Travels, 27, 193

Halvorson, Marilyn, 277
Hamilton, Mary, 251
Hamilton, Virginia, 120, 195–6, 261, 263–4, 290
The Hand of Robin Squires, 274
A Handful of Thieves, 258
A Handful of Time, 258
Handles, 274–5
Happy Family books, 35
The Happy Orpheline, 245
Harald and the Giant Knight, 244
harmful books, 212
Harpoon of the Hunter, 125–7, 275
Harquin, the Fox Who Went Down to the Valley, 233
Harriet the Spy, 258
Harrison, Ted, 299
Harry the Dirty Dog, 104, 233
Hassall, John, 300
The Haunting, 258–9
Hautzig, Esther, 273
Haviland, Virginia, 85, 244
Hawkins, Colin, 36
Heaney, Seamus, 300
Hedderwick, Mairi, 235
Heide, Florence Parry, 84–5, 250
Heidi, 99–100, 101, 259
Hello, Aurora!, 52–3
Henry Huggins, 55
Henry, Marguerite, 244
Henry's Leg, 259
Henty, G. A., 3
Herman the Helper, 42–3, 233
Hermes, Lord of the Robbers, 41
heroism, 126–7
Hey, Al, 233
Hey Diddle Diddle, 44–5, 234
Hey World, Here I Am!, 299
Higglety Pigglety Pop! Or, There Must Be More to Life, 244

INDEX

'The Highwayman', 299
The Hill of the Red Fox, 275
Himler, Ronald, 264
Hinton, S. E., 184, 185, 192–3, 195, 196, 202, 204, 207, 281
historical novels, 127, 132
Hoban, Lillian, 228, 229
Hoban, Russell, 21, 86–7, 229, 234, 249, 262
The Hobbit, 145, 259
The Hoboken Chicken Emergency, 64, 245
Hold Fast, 101–2
Homecoming, 121, 275
Homeric hymns, 40–1, 230
Homesick: My Own Story, 275
The Homeward Bounders, 156–7, 275
Horn Book magazine, 6, 89, 206
The Hounds of the Morrigan, 144, 259
The House of the Sixty Fathers, 259
The House on East 88th Street, 234
The House with a Clock in Its Walls, 131, 259–60
Houston, James, 125, 267, 273
How Green Was My Valley, 193
How Many Miles to Babylon?, 260
How Tom Beat Captain Najork and His Hired Sportsmen, 86–7, 234
Howker, Janni, 21, 270–1, 289, 291
Howl's Moving Castle, 158, 288–9
Hughes, Monica, 276–7
Hughes, Shirley, 41–2, 51, 228, 297
Hughes, Ted, 11, 14–15, 18, 62, 209, 246, 300
Hugo and Josephine, 245
Hull, Katherine, 5
humour, in children's books, 34, 73–90, 199–200
The Hundred Dresses, 56, 61, 213–14, 215, 245–6
Hunt, Irene, 199, 282, 284
Hunter, Beatrice Thurman, 266–7
Hunter, Molly, 280, 292, 294
Hurd, Thatcher, 235
Hurry Home, Candy, 260
Hutchins, H. J., 267
Hutchins, Pat, 43, 237

I, Juan de Pareja, 275
I Own the Racecourse!, 275–6
I-Can-Read books, 35, 235
The Ice is Coming, 158, 161–3, 289
identity, search for, 17, 93–116
I'm Not Frightened of Ghosts, 234
imagination, 11–12, 19–20
In Summer Light, 289
The Indian in the Cupboard, 110–11, 196, 240
intimacy with children, and reading, 20
Into the Dream, 260
Ireson, Barbara, 297
The Iron Man: A Story in Five Nights, 62–3, 246
Isaac Campion, 289
Isadora, Rachel, 229
Island of the Blue Dolphins, 102–3, 276
The Island of the Skog, 234
The Islanders, 289
It's My Life, 193–4, 289–90

It's Too Frightening for Me!, 51
It's Your Turn, Roger!, 74, 234

Jacob Two-Two Meets the Hooded Fang, 76, 246
James and the Giant Peach, 89
James, Will, 265–6
Janeczko, Paul B., 300
Janet and John, 23
Japanese haiku, 210–11
The Japanese Twins, 50
Jarrell, Randall, 10, 209, 241–2, 260
Jasmin, 260
Jelly Belly, 86
Jellybean, 276
Jennifer, Hecate, Macbeth and Me, 260
Jennifer, Hecate, Macbeth, William McKinley and Me, Elizabeth, 260
Jenny and the Cat Club, 120–1, 246
Jeremy Visick, 276
The Jersey Shore, 290
John Diamond, 128, 290
Johnny Crow's Garden, 234
Johnny Tremaine, 201–2, 276
Johnson, Crockett, 231
The Jolly Postman, 78–9, 246
Jonas, Ann, 239
Jonathan Livingstone Seagull, 22
Jones, Diana Wynne, 156, 157–8, 269, 272, 273, 275, 288–9, 309
Jones, Terry, 264–5
Jones, Toeckey, 294
Josh, 106
The Journey of the Shadow Bairns, 150, 276
The Judge, 75–6, 234–5
The Julian Stories, 77, 246
Julie of the Wolves, 103–4, 276
The Juniper Tree, 31, 59, 260
junk reading, 207–9
Just So Stories, 247
Juster, Norton, 78, 264

Kahl, Virginia, 228–9
Kane, Alice, 24
Kästner, Erich, 256–7, 261
Katie Morag Delivers the Mail, 235
Kaye, Geraldine, 95–6, 271–2
Keats, Ezra Jack, 219, 232–3
Keene, Carolyn, 208, 219
The Keeper of the Isis Light, 276–7
Keeping, Charles, 254, 299
Kellogg, Steven, 234
Kerr, M. E., 288
Kim, 95, 118, 119, 124–5, 277
King, Clive, 64–5, 80, 105–6, 209, 250, 262–3, 282
King, Steven, 190
King-Smith, Dick, 76–7, 265
The King's Daughter, 290
Kipling, Auden & Co., 10
Kipling, Rudyard, 95, 118, 119, 124–5, 247, 277
Kit in Boots, 53–4, 247
Kitamura, Satoshi, 235
Klein, Robin, 63, 251

INDEX

Konigsburg, E. L., 209, 257, 260
Kovalski, Maryann, 229
Krantz, Judith, 190
Kraus, Robert, 39–40, 42, 233, 240
Krumbold, Joseph, 217, 270

Landon, Michael, 54
landscape, in children's books, 98–9
Lane, Selma, 75
Lang, Andrew, 27
Langton, Jane, 255–6
The Language of the Night, 92
The Lantern Bearers, 130, 277
The Lark and the Laurel, 290
late readers, 25–6
Laurence, John, 244
Laurence, Margaret, 204, 249, 285
The Lavender Hill Mob, 80
Lawson, Robert, 238, 248
Leaf, Munro, 238
learning to read, 23–4
Ledson, Sidney, 24
Lee, Dennis, 78, 86, 88, 241
Leeson, Robert, 193–4, 285, 289–90
Le Guin, Ursula K., 21–2, 92, 112, 143–4, 149, 158–60, 161, 162–3, 192, 201, 295
A Lemon and a Star, 260–1
Lent, Blair, 77, 120, 232, 239, 258
Lester, Julius, 206, 295
Let It Go, 277
Let the Circle Be Unbroken, 290
Levoy, Myron, 98, 270
Lewis, C. S., 173, 175, 183, 215, 261
Lily Takes a Walk, 235
Lindgren, Astrid, 60, 249
Lingard, Joan, 196, 284
linguistic invention, in children's books, 77–8
The Lion and the Unicorn (periodical), 88
The Lion, the Witch and the Wardrobe, 261
Lionni, Leo, 42
Lisa and Lottie, 261
Little Bear, 35, 37, 235
Little Black Sambo, 219
The Little Bookroom, 261
The Little House in the Big Woods Series, 19, 20, 54, 247
Little, Jean, 107, 247, 257, 278, 299
A Little Love, 284, 290
Little Red Riding Hood, 79
'A Little Squirrel Went Walking', 231
Little Tim stories, 58, 119, 123, 247
Little Women, 93, 100, 222, 277
Lively, Penelope, 171–2, 173, 175, 244, 258
Lives of Girls and Women, 204
Livingston, Myra Cohn, 299
Lobel, Arnold, 298
A Long Way from Verona, 199, 291
The Lord of the Rings, 144, 291, 296
Lost and Found, 247
The Lost Umbrella of Kim Chu, 247
Louhi, the Witch of North Farm, 247
Lunn, Janet, 6, 173–5, 279, 293–4
Lurie, Alison, 243

Macaulay, David, 240

McBroom Tells a Lie, 248
McCaffrey, Anne, 286
MacCarthy, Patricia, 297
McDermott, Gerald, 236
MacDonald, George, 142, 149, 211, 264
The Machine Gunners, 216, 291
Mackay, David, 300
McKee, David, 84
McLean, Allen Campbell, 275
McSwigan, Marie, 266
Madame Doubtfire, 277
Madeline, 38, 235
Madeline and the Bad Hat, 38, 153
The Magic Adventures of Pretty Pearl, 120, 261
Magicians of Caprona, 156
Mahy, Margaret, 157, 237–8, 258–9, 291, 297
Major, Kevin, 101–2, 185, 190–1, 220, 287
The Making of Americans, 182
Mama Don't Allow, 235
Mama's Going to Buy You a Mockingbird, 278
The Marble in the Water, 301
Marianne Dreams, 261–2
Mark, Jan, 96–7, 267, 274–5, 284–5, 287
market for children's books, America, 17
Markoosie, 125–7, 275
Marks, Alan, 120
Marshall, James, 75, 232, 235
Marshall, James Vance, 282
Martel, Suzanne, 290
Mary Alice, Operator Number Nine, 75, 235
Mary of Mile, 18, 248
Mary Poppins, 83–4, 148–9
Masefield, John, 173
Maurice's Room, 248
Maynard, Fredelle, 56, 292
Maynard, Joyce, 189
Mayne, William, 21, 28–9, 97, 150–1, 153, 172–3, 252, 272, 274, 288, 290
Me and My Million, 80, 262
Meddaugh, Susan, 229
Meek, Margaret, 207, 208
Meg and Mog, 235–6
Melling, O. R., 173, 175, 286–7, 294
Melville, Herman, 152
Memory, 291
The Merchant of Venice, 139
Merrill, James, 59
Meyer, Mercer, 231
middle readers (8 to 12), 253–69
The Midnight Folk, 173
The Midnight Fox, 61, 65–8
Midnight is a Place, 278
A Midsummer Night's Dream, 176
Millions of Cats, 236
Mills and Boon romances, 199
Milne, A. A., 4, 5
Minarik, Else Holmelund, 35, 37, 235
Mintzberg, Yvette, 34–5, 237
Missee Lee, 121, 124, 212, 266
Mister Rabbit and the Lovely Present, 236
Mizamura, Kazue, 81, 239
Moby-Dick, 152
The Moffats, 55, 248
Montgomery, L. M., 99–100, 101, 102, 253, 279

308

INDEX

Moonlight, 43–4, 236
Moore, Marianne, 142
More Stories Julian Tells, 77
Morris, Jean, 286
Morris, William, 150
Mosel, Arlene, 77, 120, 232, 239, 263
Moses Beech, 291
Moss, Elaine, 45
The Most Amazing Hide-and-Seek Alphabet Book, 236
Mother Goose, 31
Mouldy's Orphan, 262
Mountain Rose, 248
The Mouse and His Child, 21, 262
The Moves Make the Man, 278
Mowat, Farley, 80, 125, 263
Mr Man series, 37
Mr Popper's Penguins, 63–4, 248
Mrs Dunphy's Dog, 248
Mrs Frisby and the Rats of NIMH, 262
Munro, Alice, 204
Munsch, Robert, 78, 237
Murphy, Jill, 73–4, 231, 252
My Apprenticeship, 10
My Side of the Mountain, 103
The Mysterious Disappearance of Leon (I Mean Noel), 79–80, 262

Nancy Drew stories, 208, 219
The Napping House, 236
Narnia cycle, 173, 195, 215, 261
The Nature of the Beast, 291
need for books, 210–11
Nesbit, E., 3, 79, 122, 148, 149, 169, 215, 217, 219, 220, 257, 266
Ness, Evaline, 231
The New Golden Land Anthology, 248–9, 297
The New Wind Has Wings. Poems from Canada, 297–8
Newfield, Frank, 241
News from Nowhere, 150
Newson, Carol, 251
Nicoll, Helen, 235–6
The Night Watchman, 262
Nightbirds on Nantucket, 151–2
Nimmo, Jenny, 280
Ninny's Boat, 105–6, 262–3
Nixon, Joan Lowery, 120, 242
Nkwala, 11, 125, 278
No Beat of Drum, 278
No More School, 29
No Way of Telling, 135–6, 263
Nobody's Family Is Going to Change, 278–9, 281
Noddy, 50
Noisy Nora, 236
Nordstrom, Ursula, 96, 250
Norton, André, 249
Norton, Mary, 146–7, 150, 184, 254
Not Now, Bernard, 84
novels, for young children, 49–69
Noyes, Alfred, 127, 166
Nurse Matilda, 83–4, 263
nursery rhymes, 44, 77, 234, 297
Nutshell Library, 83

Nutt, Ken, 240

O'Brien, Robert, 262
O'Dell, Scott, 102–3, 276
The Olden Days Coat, 249
Oldham, June, 288
Olivier, Frances, 244
The Once and Future King, 281
101 Things to Do with a Baby, 40
One Monday Morning, 236
One More River, 196–7, 292
The One-Eyed Cat, 115–16, 279
Oneal, Zibby, 289
O'Neill, Catharine, 248
oral culture, decline, 24
Ordinary Jack, 82, 263
Orgel, Doris, 251
Ormerod, Jan, 40, 43–4, 236, 291
orphan stories, 58–60
O'Shea, Pat, 144, 259
Our Snowman, 236
Outside, 249
The Outsiders, 192
Over Sea, Under Stone, 255
Owls in the Family, 80, 81, 263
Oxford Book of Poetry for Children, 298
Oz, Amos, 101, 280

Paddington Bear, 55
Papagaya, the Mischief-Maker, 236
The Paper Bag Princess, 78, 237
A Parcel of Patterns, 292
parents, influence on children's reading, 210
Parish, Peggy, 78, 241
Park, Ruth, 177–8, 279
Parrot Told Snake, 237
Pastic, George, 251
Pat of Silver Bush, 279
Paterson, Katherine, 255, 271, 274
Patten, Brian, 298
Paul, Lissa, 211
Paulsen, Gary, 286
Pearce, Philippa, 21, 65, 108–9, 178–80, 253–4, 256, 267, 268, 307, 312
Pearson, Kit, 258
Pearson, Tracey Campbell, 242
Peck, Richard, 191–2, 198, 200, 273–4, 287, 292–3
Peck, Robert Newton, 87, 216–17, 266
Pennington books, 199, 202–4, 292
Pennington's Heir, 204
Pennington's Seventeenth Summer, 202–4, 292
Penny Candy, 249
The People Could Fly, American Black Folktales, 263–4
The Peppermint Pig, 263
Peter Duck, 121
Peter Pan, 5
Peyton, K. M., 199, 202–4, 292
The Phantom Tollbooth, 78, 264
Philip Hall Likes Me, I Reckon Maybe, 196, 279
The Phoenix and the Carpet, 149
picture books, 34–45, 228–40
pictures, 'reading', 45
The Piemakers, 249

INDEX

Pienkowski, Jan, 235–6
'Pierre', 83
Pilling, Ann, 259
The Pinballs, 264
Pinkwater, Daniel Manus, 6, 64, 67, 72, 74–5, 154, 155–6, 239, 242, 245, 251, 270
Pinkwater, Jill, 255
Pippi Longstocking books, 60, 249
A Pistol in Greenyards, 292
Playing Beatie Bow, 177–8, 279
A Pocket Full of Seeds, 133–4, 264
poetry for children, 28, 297
Polar Bear Cat, 39, 237
Pollyanna, 93
pop-up books, for beginning readers, 36
popular culture, and children's books, 6–7
Potter, Beatrix, 94, 143, 238
The Power of Three, 156
prejudice, against children's books by adults, 21–2
The Prelude, 10
Prelutsky, Jack, 298
The Princess and the Goblin, 264
'problem' novels, 210–11
Proddow, Penelope, 40–1, 230
A Puffin Quartet of Poets, 298
purchase of books, importance, 8
Pyle, Howard, 127

quality, and children's books, 6–7
A Question of Courage, 121

racial prejudice, in children's books, 217
The Rain Door, 249
Raisins and Almonds, 56, 292
Ramona and Her Mother, 56
Ramona the Pest, 249–50
Ransome, Arthur, 20, 121–4, 131–2, 212, 215, 232, 266
Raskin, Ellen, 79–80, 262
The Rattle Bag, 300
Rawlings, Marjorie Kinnan, 269
Rayner, Mary, 77, 238–9, 265
Razzell, Mary, 197–8, 294
Read-Aloud Handbook, 210, 301
reading aloud, 19, 36, 41, 45, 50
Reading for Enjoyment, 301
reading readiness, 25–6
The Real Thief, 250
realism in books, 15, 59, 210–11
The Red Badge of Courage, 175
Rees, David, 184, 187, 301
Reeve, James, 297, 298
Representing Superdoll, 200, 292–3
The Rescue of Aunt Pansy, 237
The Return of the Indian, 260
Rey, H. A., 35–6, 230
Richler, Mordecai, 75, 246
Riddley Walker, 21, 24
Rieu, E. V., 298
The River, 293
The Riverside Anthology of Children's Literature, 31, 264
Robertson, Barbara, 297–8
Robin Hood, 125

Robinson Crusoe, 27
Robinson, Joan, 175–6, 269
The Rocking Horse Secret, 250
Rodgers, Mary, 81, 273
Roll of Thunder, Hear My Cry, 279, 290
The Root Cellar, 173–5, 279
Rosie's Walk, 43, 237
Rousseau, Jean-Jacques, 32
Roy, Gabrielle, 243–4
Rumble Fish, 192
Runaway to Freedom, 134, 279–80
The Runner, 293

Sachs, Marilyn, 133–4, 264, 280–1
Sadako and the Thousand Paper Cranes, 264
The Saga of Erik the Viking, 264–5
Salinger, J. D., 186
Sally Go Round the Sun, 237
Sally, Where Are You?, 34–5, 237
Saltman, Judith, 31, 264
satire, in children's books, 78–9
Saturday by Seven, 250
Schlee, Ann, 270
Schmidt, Karen Lee, 242
school readers, 23, 50
Schwartz, Alvin, 243
science fiction, 156
The Sea Egg, 65–6, 265
Sebestyn, Ouida, 196, 283
The Secret Diary of Adrian Mole, Aged 13¾, 293
The Secret Garden, 99, 100, 265
The Secret Language, 96, 97, 250
See You Later, Alligator, 36
See You Thursday, 194, 293
Sefton, Catherine, 106–7, 131
Segal, Lore, 27, 94–5, 238, 260
selection of books, grounds for, 5, 6–7
Sendak, Maurice, 27, 35, 37, 83, 104–5, 235, 236, 239, 242, 245, 252, 260
Seraillier, Ian, 298
Service, Robert, 299
Seuss, Dr., 24, 37, 75, 82, 231
The Seven Kids, 79
17 Kings and 42 Elephants, 237–8, 297
Sewall, Marcia, 250
Shadow, 238
Shadow in Hawthorn Bay, 293–4
Shadow of a Bull, 265
Shakespeare, William, 139, 176, 199, 217, 289
Share-a-Story series, 238–9
sharing experiences, and reading, 19–20
Sharp, Edith Lambert, 125, 278
The Sheep-Pig, 76–7, 265
Shepard, E. H., 269
The Shrinking of Treehorn, 84–5, 250
Shulevitz, Uri, 232, 236, 244–5
Sid and Sol, 238
Siebel, Fritz, 241
The Sign of the Beaver, 280
Simmonds, Posy, 56–7, 232
Singer, Dorothy and Jerome, 15
Singer, Isaac Bashevis, 31, 244–5, 252
The Singing Stone, 193, 294
16 and Up, 301

310

INDEX

Skindeep, 294
The Slave Dancer, 102, 114–15, 116, 280
Sleator, William, 260
The Sleeping Beauty, 243
'Sleepy People', 231
Slobodkin, Louis, 56, 246
Smith, 127–8, 265
Smith, Emma, 135–6, 263
Smoky, the Cow Horse, 265–6
Smucker, Barbara, 134, 279–80
Smurfs, 94
Snape, Juliet and Charles, 234
Snow Apples, 197–8, 294
The Snow Spider, 280
Snow Treasure, 266
The Snowman, 85
The Snowy Day, 219, 233
Snyder, Zilpha Keatley, 256, 287
soap operas, 211–12
'A Song of Sherwood', 127, 166
Song of the Trees, 250
Soumchi, 101, 280
A Sound of Chariots, 294
Soup, 87, 216–17, 266
Southall, Ivan, 106, 123, 215, 220, 314
Speare, Elizabeth George, 280
Speare, Jean, 243
spending on books, 16
Spykman, E. C., 260–1
Spyri, Johanna, 99–100, 101, 259
Stahl, Ben, 264
Stamm, Claus, 239
Star Wars, 50, 207
Starry Night, 106–7, 131
Steig, William, 57–8, 209, 229, 230, 238, 241, 250, 256
Stein, Gertrude, 182, 183
Stevens, Harry, 237
Stevenson, James, 72, 74, 230
Stevenson, R. L., 28, 122, 128, 135, 281
Stig of the Dump, 64–5, 250
A Stitch in Time, 172
Stockton, Frank, 104–5, 242
The Stone Book, 266
Stone Fox, 65, 250
Storm, 120
Storr, Catherine, 79, 243, 261–2, 295
The Story About Ping, 3, 37–8, 238
The Story of Ferdinand, 238
The Story of the Amulet, 149–50, 217
The Story of the Treasure-Seekers, 266
Strachan, Ian, 291
A Stranger Came Ashore, 280
Stren, Patti, 248
Strugnell, Ann, 246
Struwelpeter, 83, 88
Summer of My German Soldier, 108, 280
The Summer of the Swans, 266
A Summer's Lease, 280–1
Sunshine, 44, 236
Sutcliff, Rosemary, 128–30, 268, 277
Swallows and Amazons series, 121–4, 266
Sweet Dreams series, 217
'Swimmy', 42
The Sword in the Stone, 173, 281

Sylvester and the Magic Pebble, 238
Szekeres, Cyndy, 251

The Tailor of Gloucester, 238
The Tale of Peter Rabbit, 94, 143, 238
A Tale of Two Cities, 27
Taylor and Braithwaite, 227
Taylor, Andrew, 194
Taylor, Mildred D., 250, 279, 290
Taylor, Sidney, 253
Teach Your Child to Read in 30 Days, 24
teenage fiction, 183–204, 284–96
television, impact of, 5, 13–16, 17, 49, 59, 145, 211–12
Tell Me a Mitzi, 94–5, 238
Tell Me a Trudy, 238
Tender is the Night, 193
Tennyson, Alfred Lord, 28
Tex, 192, 281
Thank You for the Tadpole, 238–9
That Scatterbrain Booky, 266–7
Them That Glitter and Them That Don't, 294–5
Then Again, Maybe I Won't, 186–7
Thing, 63, 251
Thirty-Six Exposures, 190–1
This Strange New Feeling, 295
Thomson, Pat, 238–9
The Three and Many Wishes of Jason Reid, 267
Three Big Hogs, 239
Three Little Pigs, 79, 239
The Three Royal Monkeys, 267
Three Strong Women, 80–1, 239
Thunder and Lightnings, 96–7, 267
Tikki Tikki Tembo, 77, 239
Tikta 'Liktak, 267
time travellers, in children's books, 167–80
The Tin-Lined Trunk, 251
To the Lighthouse, 211
Tolkien, J. R. R., 4, 144, 145, 158, 259, 291, 296
Tom Tiddler's Ground, 224, 267
The Tombs of Atuan, 159–60, 296
Tomes, Margot, 243
Tom's Midnight Garden, 178–80, 267
Torch, 281
Townsend, John Rowe, 200, 201, 224, 267, 288, 289, 302
Townsend, Sue, 293
A Traveller in Time, 170–1, 281
Travers, P. L., 148–9
Treadgold, Mary, 133, 268
Trease, Geoffrey, 127, 254
Treasure Island, 122, 128, 135, 281
The Treasure-Seekers, 79
A Tree Grows in Babylon, 193, 198
A Tree Grows in Brooklyn, 294
The Trek, 239
Trelease, Jim, 210, 301
Truss, Jan, 260
Tuck Everlasting, 111–12, 267–8
Tucker, Nicholas, 18, 99, 145, 301
Tulku, 295
Turkle, Brinton, 231
Twain, Mark, 137–9, 219, 284
The Twelve and the Genii, 268

311

INDEX

The Twenty-One Balloons, 268
The Twenty-Two Letters, 282
Twins series, 50
Two Piano Tuners, 268
Two Shoes, New Shoes, 297
Two's Company, 295

An Ulster Childhood, 24
Underground to Canada, 134
Ungerer, Tomi, 244
Up a Road Slowly, 199, 282
Up to Low, 82, 282
Ure, Jean, 194, 293
Uttley, Alison, 170–1, 281

values, need to inculcate in children, 11–13
Very Last First Time, 251
A Very Long Way from Anywhere Else, 295
Vestly, Ann-Cath., 52–3, 241
The Vigananee and the Tree Toad, 77–8, 239
The Village by the Sea, 197, 282
The Violin, 251
Viorst, Judith, 228
Voigt, Cynthia, 121, 275, 293

Waber, Bernard, 234
Wagner, Jenny, 36–7, 229
Walkabout, 282
The Walker Book of Poetry for Children, 298
Wallace, Ian, 230, 251
Walsh, Jill Paton, 21, 136–7, 182, 197, 257, 271, 273, 281, 288, 292
Walter the Lazy Mouse, 251
Warrior Scarlet, 128–30, 268
Watson, Clyde, 228
Watson, Wendy, 228
The Way to Sattin Shore, 108–9, 268
We Couldn't Leave Dinah, 133, 268
We Didn't Mean to Go to Sea, 123–4, 266
Weiss, Ellen, 239
Wells, Rosemary, 236
Welsh, Andrew, 251
Westall, Robert, 215, 216, 220, 291
We've All Got Scars: What Boys and Girls Learn in Elementary School, 221–2, 301–2
What About Tomorrow?, 314
When Marnie Was There, 175–6, 269
When the Wind Blows, 85
Where Are You Going, Little Mouse?, 240
Where the Lilies Bloom, 282
Where the Wild Things Are, 35, 239
Where's Julius?, 74, 239
Whiskers Once and Always, 251
Whistle for Willy, 233
White, Antonia, 287
White, E. B., 147, 150, 243
The White Mountains, 283
White, T. H., 173, 281

Whitlock, Pamela, 5, 299–300
Whose Mouse Are You?, 39, 40, 240
Why Am I Grown So Cold? Poems of the Unknowable, 299
Why Mosquitos Buzz in People's Ears, 219, 240
Why the Chicken Crossed the Road, 240
Wiese, Kurt, 38, 245
The Wild Washerwomen, 240
Wildcat under Glass, 132–3, 269
Wilder, Laura Ingalls, 54–5, 247
Wildsmith, Brian, 39, 230, 298
Willard, Barbara, 290
Williams, Garth, 54, 245, 247
Williams, Jay, 231
Williams, Vera B., 230
The Wind in the Willows, 145–6, 269
Wingman, 61–2, 251, 263
Winnie-the-Pooh, 4, 5
Wiseman, David, 276
Witch Week, 156, 269
The Witches, 90
A Wizard of Earthsea, 158–60, 295–6
Wojciechowska, Maria, 265
women, in children's books, 87
Wood, Audrey, 236
Wood, Don, 236
Wood, Muriel, 249
Woolf, Virginia, 211
Words by Heart, 196, 283
Words on Water, 299
Wordsworth, William, 2, 10, 16–17
working class writing, 6
Worse than Willy, 72, 74
The Worst Witch, 252
Would You Rather?, 240
Wrightson, Patricia, 158, 161–3, 192, 275–6, 289
Writers, Critics and Children, 206
Written for Children, 302
Wyeth, N. C., 269, 281
Wylie, Philip, 87
Wynne-Jones, Tim, 240

Yashinsky, Don, 11
A Year and a Day, 28, 150–1, 153
The Yearling, 256, 269
The Yellow Aeroplane, 252
Yeoman, John, 240
Yorinks, Arthur, 233, 238

Zei, Alki, 132–3, 269
Zemach, Harve, 75–6, 231, 234–5
Zemach, Margot, 75–6, 231, 234–5, 243
Zindel, Paul, 185
Zion, Gail, 104, 233
Zlateh the Goat and Other Stories, 252
Zolotow, Charlotte, 236
Zoom at Sea, 240